100 Best

ALL-INCLUSIVE

RESORTS

OF THE

WORLD

Third Edition

**Packed with Solid Advice on the
Best All-Inclusive Vacations Worldwide**

JAY PARIS AND CARMI ZONA-PARIS

REVISED AND UPDATED BY CAROL FOWLER

The
Globe
Pequot
Press

GUILFORD, CONNECTICUT

ACKNOWLEDGMENTS

We wish to acknowledge the indispensable efforts of the following researchers and writers who generously helped make this book possible: Bill Abell, Cory Atkins, Marcia Burchstead, Megan Carney, Moira Desney, Sarah Dickey, Damian Galeone, Amy Hachey, Kevin Hachey, Tina James, Sara Jerdenius, Margarite Jordan, Patsy Kelley, Martin Kolanda, Charlotte Ljungberg, Elysse Magnotto, Dave O'Conner, Angela Ottaviani, Owen Paris, Shannon Roddy, Denise Russell, Claudia Sansone, and Mary Ellen Schultz.

Text design by Nancy Freeborn
Photo layout by Sue Preneta

ISSN 1535-8216
ISBN 0-7627-2816-7

Manufactured in the United States of America
Third Edition/First Printing

100 Best
ALL-INCLUSIVE
RESORTS
OF THE
WORLD

A PHOTO ESSAY

Rancho La Puerta

Banyan Tree

Peter Island

Cal-a-Vie

Rancho La Puerta

**Canyon Ranch
in the Berkshires**

Curtain Bluff

Galley Bay

Lizard Island

Bedarra Island

Royal Plantation

Laramie River Ranch

Banyan Tree

Banyan Tree

Huka Lodge

Banyan Tree

Divi Aruba

Lost Creek Ranch

The Cloister

LaSource

Hilton Head Health Institute

Banyan Tree

CONTENTS

CARIBBEAN ISLANDS AND THE BAHAMAS

AFRICA

ASIA

THE PACIFIC

The prices and rates listed in this guidebook were confirmed at press time but under no circumstances are they guaranteed. We recommend that you call establishments before traveling to obtain current information.

INTRODUCTION

Five decades ago, a savvy Olympic water polo champion, Gerard Blitz, realized that single vacationers in Europe were at a disadvantage when traveling. They often paid premium rates for rooms that had been created and priced for double occupancy. When they dined in restaurants, they sat alone and were less likely to take advantage of evening entertainment. In response, he decided to create a resort village for singles and couples in Alcudia, Majorca, overlooking the clear azure waters of the Mediterranean at a per person, per week cost for everything including rooms, meals, activities—even alcoholic drinks at meals. Seasoned hoteliers predicted he would go broke within months, but history, of course, proved them wrong. Blitz discovered that the casual, beach-based resort he called "Club Med" appealed to the younger, hipper crowds of the rock 'n' roll era. Eventually the Club Med team created variations of the same theme in Tahiti, in Mexico, and in the Caribbean, where Blitz's model was immediately copied and coined as "all-inclusive." By definition, one price bought all services, gratuities, food, and board for a week's stay. As the success of these resorts became known in the hotel industry, all-inclusives began to pop up throughout the tropical Atlantic region.

Club Med grew to own 140 resorts that are no longer swinging singles' clubs but open to couples, singles, and even families. Other companies followed Club Med's example, and brand names such as Sandals, Allegro, Couples, and SuperClubs became known to vacationers seeking one-price-for-all getaways in the Caribbean and Mexico. Today there are more than 500 resorts from Africa to Hawaii that collectively claim more than 50,000 rooms, netting several billion dollars per year at prices that start at $800 per person, per week (double occupancy).

All-Inclusive Criteria

Amid the many hotel and resort packages available throughout the world are many promotions that fall short of being "all-inclusive." Our criteria in selecting contenders for this book were hotels or resorts where at least 50 percent of the guests choose an all-inclusive package, which includes room, board, entertainment, and a majority of on-site activities. In most cases these all-inclusive packages include alcohol and surprising extras such as unlimited golf, scuba lessons, and massages. None, however, includes airfare, except through occasional special promotions. Because of the sheer volume of passengers visiting their resorts each week, Club Med offers airfare discounts to its visitors on selected airlines. Butch Stewart, the owner and adroit marketer of the popular Sandals chain, also has the controlling interest of Air Jamaica, which is fighting American Airlines for market share to the Caribbean. As a result, visitors to any of the ten Sandals resorts often gain a transportation savings.

Some resorts sell an "American Plan," which includes breakfast and dinner but nothing else. This approach was created for Europeans who wanted to control their budgets item by item. Now there is even an expanded American Plan that includes lunch and a glass of wine at dinner, but it is far from all-inclusive.

But as more hotels and resorts have converted from the traditional approach to a true all-inclusive mode, the niche has become more defined and stratified. Some all-inclusives emphasize fitness, water sports, or golf; others offer ample romance, a spa environment, or the pursuit of culture, such as the Native American programs offered by Red Mountain Spa in Utah, which takes guests on hikes to petroglyphs and offers Native American card readings. There is an all-inclusive resort in a remote corner of British Columbia devoted to people who have a passion for hiking (Mountain Trek). Cancun and Puerto Vallarta have all-inclusives, as do Bali, Thailand, and South Africa. There are places where you can ride a personally assigned elephant through high grasses (Tiger Tops Jungle Lodge in Nepal) or eat caviar while sipping an aged Rothschild on a deserted, private beach (Necker Island in the Caribbean), fully naked if you want. But as varied as their opportunities are, all adhere to the principle of creating special environments where the petty details of vacationing, such as organizing and paying for activities, drinks, and, in most cases, gratuities, are eliminated in safe and secure environments created for relaxation, pleasure, and even enlightenment.

Virtually every all-inclusive operates its own restaurants for guests, and many serve meals from dawn to midnight. Pubs and clubs serving an endless array of libations are also plentiful at many all-inclusives. Swimming pools, beaches, elaborate water sports, and strikingly landscaped grounds with romantic garden hideaways are also common. The all-inclusive philosophy espouses no surprises (unless surprise is part of the program), especially unexpected costs. It promises consistency and quality— good beverages and fare, safe and comfortable accommodations, caring staff, and plenty of accessible activities. As the number and variety of all-inclusive resorts increase worldwide, finding and choosing the one best suited to your tastes and needs becomes more of a challenge.

The 100 Best

The purpose of *100 Best All-Inclusive Resorts of the World* is to become the first and most comprehensive resource about one of the fastest-growing vacation opportunities. To help you make the most of your efforts to plan the best all-inclusive vacation, we have organized the top 100 entries into five geographic sections.

- North America
- Caribbean Islands and the Bahamas
- Africa
- Asia
- The Pacific

We chose not to include Europe when selecting our 100 best all-inclusive resorts, even though there are a notable number of Club Meds and health spas across the Continent. Our decision was based on the fact that most Americans tour Europe to enjoy its heritage and culture. Although the trend may change, those relatively few Americans who do settle into a European locale for an extended stay tend to seek travel experiences off the beaten track. With the convenience and superb beach offerings of the Caribbean all-inclusives, Americans prefer to stay closer to home for these kinds of vacations. The same is true for spa seekers: There are now many highly rated spas in the United States; Americans don't need to cross the Atlantic for bodywork and pampering. However, for those of you who are contemplating visiting an all-inclusive in Europe, review our comprehensive listing of resorts for possibilities and contact numbers (see Appendix 2).

When researching this book, we discovered that some resorts actively target couples, families, or singles. You will find this information listed under the Group/Getaway heading that follows each resort's address. Although some resorts encourage all of these groups to visit at the same time, we have largely limited our choice to one per resort, to emphasize the resort's main target group. Because some resorts specialize in specific *types* of getaways, we've also included a Spa & Wellness, Sports & Fitness, or Adventure designation for those resorts.

By reviewing the activities list in each resort profile, or by taking a look at the chart in Appendix 1, you can quickly and easily surmise how well each resort suits your needs. Each profile also includes key attributes such as costs, distinctive features that set it apart from other resorts, most frequently asked questions, and other useful tips that will allow you to use this guidebook as a reference.

Entry Requirement Considerations

Entry requirements to countries vary somewhat around the world. Although there are a few countries that accept a U.S. driver's license or birth certificate for entry, the best way to travel outside of the country is with a passport. Kudos to our State Department for making it easier and faster than ever to obtain one. If you're in a rush, a passport can be obtained in a few days and rarely takes much longer than two weeks. All Caribbean and Bahamian countries accept American passports without visas. When traveling to Latin America (except some countries in Central America), Africa, the Pacific, and Asia, however, visas are often required and can be arranged at local consulates, or even arranged when entering a country while at the airport. In the fast-paced world of international travel, entry requirements do change. To assure being prepared, either ask the resort you are visiting or the airline you are using when booking.

A Word about Rates and Special Packages

As you begin your all-inclusive adventure, you'll find that rates vary by season, type of accommodation, circumstance, and package.

Seasons. Seasons can affect pricing by as much as 20 percent. In the Caribbean, rates are at their peak in the winter—you'll find your best deals in the late spring and early summer. The rates then rise slightly when children are out of school for the summer, and drop again in the fall. In Central America and Mexico, the hotter summer months also constitute the low season. March and April are the wettest months in many parts of Africa, pushing the prices down in countries such as Tanzania and Kenya during

those months. In Asia, the high season tends to be governed by humidity: May through October are the steamiest months of the year and, consequently, make up the less-expensive low season.

Accommodations. A good rule of thumb is that room prices rise in relationship to the quality of the view: The higher the room sits in the building and the more visible the sea or mountain range is from its windows, the greater the cost. "Ocean View," for example, will always be more expensive than "Garden View." Also keep in mind that Suites are larger and more expensive than Superior Rooms, which in turn are larger than Deluxe Rooms. In the pages that follow, you'll find average room rates that will serve as a starting point. To find out specifics about price variations due to season, specials, and accommodation, it's always best to call a resort's toll-free reservation service or visit its Web site.

Circumstances. It is also important to note that while rates fluctuate according to season and accommodation, they can also vary by circumstance. For example, in the Caribbean, hurricanes often create entire months of fire-sale rates. (Even islands that were untouched by these ferocious storms were affected, due to public misperceptions about their geographic locations.) And parts of Hawaii, Fiji, Indonesia, Australia, and Thailand have suffered dramatic business losses because of Asia's economic woes. In fact some resorts have even offered specials in the middle of the high season in order to attract more business. Since 2001, the slumping American economy and the threat of terrorist attacks have cut back both business and leisure travel. While this is difficult for the travel industry, it does benefit the consumer. Researching this third edition of the book, we found that rates for the all-inclusive resorts had dropped in many cases.

Packages. It is also common for all-inclusive resorts to reduce costs by offering special packages. For example, prices for children under sixteen years of age are often less than for adults, and honeymooners and couples celebrating anniversaries regularly receive extras such as complimentary room upgrades. Families, if large enough, can often obtain a free extra room when holding a reunion or special event.

It will be well worth your effort to take the extra few minutes necessary to contact a resort's reservationist, Web site, or front desk to ask about seasonal rates and other ways to reduce your costs. We found that almost a third of the time, you will find a better price than has been published.

■ Which all-inclusive resort is right for you?

It is important to mention that one person's pleasure can become another person's dismay. What one couple finds romantic and rapturous, another couple might find boring. We tried to be objective in selecting the top 100 all-inclusive resorts, but between contenders, the line sometimes grows thin. Such fine differences speak to the challenges of selecting the right resort not only for this book but also for your vacation. To assist in this process, consider the following questions when planning your getaway.

■ Should I use a travel agent or go direct?

There is no question in our minds that booking through a travel agent has many advantages if you do some preliminary research first, using this book and the Internet (we list Web sites with each selection). Once you have narrowed down your search to a certain kind of all-inclusive in a preferred region of the world, ask the resort whether it can recommend a travel agent who specializes in booking all-inclusives or whether it prefers that you book direct.

We have found that travel agents are able to get the same good pricing as going direct and can often secure free upgrades and/or packages that include airfare. Additionally, they are often a good source of information for other travel details, such as

regional attractions, local customs, entry requirements, and packing tips. But you have to ask. Since travel agents are paid by resorts and other travel suppliers, it may cost you nothing extra, though some travel agents have begun to charge a small fee as commissions have been cut.

We have found that some resorts have reservations desks that are not open on weekends or are closed at night. If you are not able to reach a reservations desk, call the hotel directly. Or, again, seek the help of a travel agent who may be able to book your trip on a closed reservation system. Finally, some of the all-inclusive resorts do not put their all-inclusive rates on the property's Web sites, nor do they advertise them. You may have to ask for the plan on the telephone.

■ What about kids (my own or others)?

This is an important question for many people considering an all-inclusive vacation. Of the 500 all-inclusives in the world, about a third are megaresorts that provide romance for honeymooners while at the same time operating kids' programs for children and varied adult activities for parents. If you're a honeymooner who doesn't like the idea of having children around, ask the hotel reservationist or your travel agent to find out how many families will be present during the week you wish to visit. They will be able to give you good estimates based on yearly patterns tracked by every resort. If you are traveling with family and don't want to be surrounded by starry-eyed couples, inquire about the number of honeymooners present.

If you plan to travel with children, the good news is that child care at all-inclusives has become very sophisticated, with many resorts offering programs with educational and adventure components for various categories of kids. The staff at the resorts we included in this book impressed us as being very loving and well trained, making for happy times for and many return visits by families who've discovered the low-effort aspects of all-inclusive vacationing.

Another important component of bringing children to an all-inclusive is that food and beverages are readily available, ridding parents of the added expense of shelling out yet another five-dollar bill for an extra snack or refreshment. For families with children of varied ages, all-inclusives are able to give each child special attention in the company of other children his or her own age—often from different parts of the United States, if not the world. Baby-sitting at a nominal price is also common at family-oriented resorts, allowing parents who wish to spend days with their kids and evenings alone a chance to enjoy on-site dining and entertainment at night, only paces from where their kids are sleeping.

■ What's my budget?

From consumer studies and our own research, we found that most couples and families save up to 25 percent of the cost of a vacation by booking at an all-inclusive. But even more important, an all-inclusive allows you to stay within a realistic budget. Travelers can estimate what they are likely to spend, eliminating the mysterious "X" factor of travel that can add hundreds and even thousands of dollars to a trip. Rates begin as low as $800 per week, per adult, and often children are discounted. On average a couple pays about $2,500 per week vacation at an all-inclusive, but there are many resorts that charge twice or even three times that amount. Resorts in Mexico and the Dominican Republic are less expensive than most other destinations in the Caribbean. Asia, India, the Pacific, and even Africa may be relatively inexpensive, but airfare to these far-flung places can be much higher.

There is a growing number of all-inclusives on mainland United States, including a Club Med in Florida and another in Colorado. It is also the chief locale of special-interest all-inclusives such as spas, dude ranches, and sport resorts. Because transportation can add as much as 50 percent to the cost of a weeklong all-inclusive vacation, deciding where and when you go is paramount. Many couples and families are choosing all-inclusives they can drive to, spending a week touring the country and then a week at a resort. Others have discovered that it is much less expensive to fly to the Caribbean in summer, and often not much hotter. With the devaluation of Asian currencies, there are often outstanding airline deals to Thailand and even Fiji and Australia during North America's spring and fall.

■ What's included?

Most all-inclusives offer excellent and varied menus and after-dinner shows and dancing. Many people love the idea of free alcoholic drinks, sometimes even premium liquor, as well as water and land activities. On the other hand, some people question the logic of paying for everything if they don't drink, or dance, or want to do much other than read on the beach. Our experience, after visiting many all-inclusive resorts, is that guests are apt to try new activities if they don't have to pay for them. Many visitors to these places have developed new passions and learned new hobbies, especially activities that require skill and sometimes expensive training such as scuba diving, windsurfing, waterskiing, golf, and tennis. Instructors at all-inclusives are in abundance and often very well trained.

We advise making a priority list of activities you enjoy and activities you would like to try. Spend a few extra minutes talking to the toll-free reservation desks of the resorts about precisely what they offer and whether there are any additional costs. Among the important items to discuss are taxes, service charges, airport transfers, and tours and transportation away from the resorts.

It is also very important to note a resort's requirement for minimum stays, which vary greatly. If you intend to stay for a week and the minimum is a few days or less, ask if upgrades are available for longer stays. There are also many creative ways that resorts include children. Many times kids two and under are free. At other resorts, children are only allowed during a specific time of the year.

In the fast pace of American life, it is not surprising that all-inclusive resorts have grown so popular among individuals, couples, and families who want to make every vacation day special. Since the terrorist attacks in September 2001, vacationing Americans eye all destinations with understandable wariness, asking if where they are going is truly safe. All-inclusives, by their very nature, are controlled environments that provide layers of security that are reassuring in these changing travel times. And they should be. To many of you, a week represents a substantial block of time—a block that should bring you much enjoyment and value. We have organized this book to help you maximize your vacation time while staying within budget, and to choose a destination that gives you the opportunity to have joyous fun in a safe and appealing environment. We hope that this book expands your vacation possibilities and brings each of you many lasting, wonderful memories.

NORTH AMERICA

CANYON RANCH IN THE BERKSHIRES HEALTH RESORT

Lenox, Massachusetts

Canyon Ranch's historic Bellefontaine Mansion overlooks a magnificent 120-acre woodland estate in the Berkshire Mountains of western Massachusetts. The property serves as the base for all the resort's many programs and activities. In contrast to the Southwest, where Canyon Ranch and many other spas also have resorts, this location offers a fascinating array of experiences governed by the seasons. Guests can enjoy the brilliant foliage of a New England fall, the musical and theatrical offerings of Tanglewood and environs in summer, or the skiing and snowshoeing adventures of winter.

Canyon Ranch also operates very extensive spa, gym, and health facilities, connected by long, glass-encased walkways that extend to the hotel, classrooms, and dining facilities in the Bellefontaine Mansion. Because of this convenient layout, guests can go from massage table to dining room to bedroom without even touching snow in the winter or breathing dog-day humidity in August.

The stated mission of Canyon Ranch is to create a retreat for busy people who want to establish new directions in their lives. As a step toward reducing the stresses of hectic lives, the resort prohibits cell phones in certain areas. Guests begin their stay with a health assessment by a registered nurse, followed by a meeting with a program coordinator who helps them choose classes and treatments from a fifty-six-page activity book. Choices are made in three areas: medical, which ranges from cardiac risk and cholesterol assessment to testing for sleep apnea; behavioral, which ranges from lifestyle consultation to a course on lifecrafting; and physiological, which includes an advanced training program for triathletes and customized exercise programs for any age or physique.

Canyon Ranch's nutritious gourmet cuisine is renowned in spa circles for its freshness and creativity, and is designed to be a learning experience for guests as well. Entrees are listed with calorie, fat, and fiber content rather than by price. On most days, the resort chef provides "Lunch and Learn" classes where guests can discover how to make nutritious meals that they have sampled at Canyon Ranch.

One of the key features that makes this resort one of the world's best is its dedication to helping couples and families enjoy the spa together. Although each person designs an individual program to match his or her own interests, couples and families can participate in activities together. Singles also find the resort comfortable.

Canyon Ranch in the Berkshires Health Resort

165 Kemble Street
Lenox, Massachusetts 02140
Phone: 800–742–9000 or 413–637–4100
   (direct)
Web site: www.canyonranch.com

Group/Getaway: Singles, Couples, Spa & Wellness

Accommodations: Deluxe Rooms accommodate one or two people and have two double beds or one king-size bed and a sitting area; Luxury Rooms for up to four people have king-size beds or two twin beds, a washer and dryer, and a sitting room with a sleeper sofa.

Points of Distinction: The staff-to-guest ratio is one to three, to assure that each guest receives highly individualized attention. The outdoor program (including hiking, cross-country skiing, and kayaking) is outstanding.

Open: Year-round.

Minimum Stay: Three nights.

Rate: Based on a three-night stay, per person rates range from $1,460 to $2,090.

Frequently Asked Question: *What types of programs does Canyon Ranch offer guests who want to focus on specific wellness issues?* Special health packages focus on certain themes, such as Optimal Living, Ultra-Prevention, Arthritis/Pain Management, Weight Loss, Smoking Cessation, Stress Management, Ayurvedic Health, Pregnancy Health, and Brain Wellness. Packages include selection of services based on length of stay.

Don't Forget to Bring: Appropriate clothes for seasonal outdoor activities.

Favorite Side Trips: Tanglewood, summer home of the Boston Symphony Orchestra; the Norman Rockwell Museum in Stockbridge.

Nearest Airports: Bradley International in Hartford, Connecticut (73 miles, or one hour and twenty minutes), and Albany International, in New York (60 miles, or one hour and ten minutes).

ALL-INCLUSIVE SERVICES AND ACTIVITIES

Food and Beverages: Three gourmet meals daily, low-cal fruits and beverages.

Outdoor Activities: In summer, hiking, tennis, and river kayaking are part of Canyon Ranch's famed outdoor program. In autumn faster river waters and incredible displays of foliage enhance these same activities. In winter there are snowshoeing and cross-country skiing in the Berkshire valleys, and in spring there are jogging, hiking, and biking.

Water Sports: Swimming and aqua aerobics.

Facilities: Spa, gym, classrooms, indoor and outdoor pools, lending library.

Other: Use of all spa facilities, including fifty-minute massage; herbal wrap or aroma wrap; thalassotherapy aqua massage; Sisley essential oil facial; shampoo and hairstyling; makeup consultation; personal training/spiritual awareness session; private sports lessons (racquetball, squash, and tennis); health and fitness assessment; cooking instruction; workshops and educational lectures. Also included: round-trip airport transfers from Hartford or Albany Airport or Albany-Rensselaer train station; unlimited local calls and incoming fax transmissions; access to long-distance carriers and toll-free numbers without surcharge.

Available for a Fee: Various services and activities offered by the resort are available on an a la carte basis.

THE KRIPALU CENTER FOR YOGA AND HEALTH

Lenox, Massachusetts

For someone wishing to enrich his or her own "self," whether mentally, spiritually, or physically, a trip to this extraordinarily serene, 350-acre consciousness-raising resort in Lenox, Massachusetts, will surely do the trick. Nestled in the rolling Berkshires of western Massachusetts, The Kripalu Center is the largest yoga and holistic health center in North America. The center is the inspiration of eminent yoga master Swami Kripalvananda, whose life was dedicated to the goal of providing people with the tools to attune their inner, spiritual selves to be more creative, balanced, and loving. He taught his students how to access inner wisdom and the importance of creating support for the ongoing process of growth and spiritual development necessary to having a fulfilling life. The Kripalu Center has become a place where these core principles are successfully taught and practiced through a specially designed curriculum that is separated into four broad categories: Yoga, Self-Discovery, Spiritual Attunement, and Wellness and Body Work.

Courses or programs—such as Rebalancing Body, Mind, and Spirit; Deepening Conscious Connection; Metta Mediation and Yoga Retreat; and Energy Balancing—can be applied to life outside the center.

The facilities at Kripalu are modest by design. Originally used as a Jesuit seminary, the Kripalu Center building is a large, 300-room dorm-style structure with a layout and design that clearly reflects the simplicity of a spiritual and educational mission. There are 176 guest rooms with total space to accommodate up to 574 people. Guests at Kripalu have access to 350 acres of forests, meadows, meditation gardens, and woodland walking trails. There is also a private beach on Lake Mahkeenac that can be used for swimming and sunning. The setting is very beautiful and peaceful and is maintained to be a supportive environment to help each visitor achieve his or her goals.

Guests and staff at The Kripalu Center are asked to dress modestly, refrain from wearing perfume, adhere to nonsmoking and no-alcohol policies, and respect each other's needs. There are no radios or televisions on the premises. And in spite of the instruction and very supportive and kind staff, the purpose of the center is to allow each person to become more effective at nurturing his or her own spirituality. Guests must eat at scheduled times but otherwise may rise or retire whenever they desire, choose their courses, and pursue the activities on their schedule.

Kripalu programs are open to guests age eighteen and older; Kripalu youth programs are offered during the summer for ages nine to nineteen. These programs include age-appropriate activities, providing a unique opportunity for young people to explore their place in the world and to experience the power of healthy self-esteem. At all other times, ages thirteen to seventeen may visit Kripalu only if accompanied by an adult. Children age twelve and younger are welcome if they are supervised at all times by a parent or guardian.

Although Kripalu is a nonprofit organization whose staff is made up of many volunteers, it is an outstanding group committed to making your time at the center a meaningful one, so that you can take your experiences with you to help guide you through life.

The Kripalu Center for Yoga and Health

P.O. Box 793
West Street, Route 183
Lenox, Massachusetts 01240-0793
Phone: 800–741–7353 or 413–448–3152
(direct)
Web site: www.kripalu.org

Group/Getaway: Singles, Spa & Wellness

Accommodations: The rooms are modest and include the following options: Semi-Private Rooms are shared with another guest. You can request a room with two low twin beds, a double, or a queen-size bed, but doubles and queens are not guaranteed. In a Standard Room-for-Two there is no maid service. A Standard Plus Room-for-Two is more spacious, but also without maid service; some have nearby hall baths and some have private baths. If you snore, they have special accommodations for you: a Standard Room-for-Two, shared with another snorer. Please request this room when you make your reservations.

Points of Distinction: The Kripalu Center has invented a unique exercise program called DansKinetics. It is a combination of yoga and low-impact aerobic dance that is very popular with guests.

Open: Year-round, except for three days after Labor Day.

Minimum Stay: Two nights.

Rates: $116 to $265 per person per night. Children younger than thirteen sharing a room with one adult are $30 per night; those sharing with two adults and those younger than five stay free. Call for summer rates after Memorial Day weekend, when additional activities for enhanced renewal are offered.

Frequently Asked Question: *What does yoga mean?* The word *yoga* means "oneness," or unity. Yoga teaches that beneath all of life's apparent conflict, distress, and separation, there exists an innate wholeness.

Don't Forget to Bring: An open mind and heart.

Favorite Side Trip: In summer, the Tanglewood Center for the Performing Arts.

Nearest Airports: Albany, New York, one hour and fifteen minutes away; Bradley International Airport in Hartford, Connecticut, less than one hour and thirty minutes away.

ALL-INCLUSIVE SERVICES AND ACTIVITIES

Food and Beverages: Three delicious, well-balanced vegetarian meals per day; tea, water, and milk.

Outdoor Activities: Walking on private trails.

Water Sports: Swimming on private lake.

Facilities: Meditation room, separate saunas and whirlpools for women and men, weight room, video lounge.

Other: More than 30 classes and healing arts in yoga, massage, shiatsu, reflexology, acupuncture, and ayurvedic consultations and treatments.

Not Included: Airport transfers.

Available for a Fee: Various health products; other beverages; evening health service classes and lectures.

THE BALSAMS GRAND RESORT HOTEL

Dixville Notch, New Hampshire

In 400 years, little has changed in the part of New Hampshire's "Great North Woods," where The Balsams is situated. Back then, forests grew from steep, craggy mountainsides. Rainfall and snow melts swelled the brooks that form the Connecticut River. The scent of fir and spruce was ever present. All that still exists today. The difference between then and now, however, is that a modest road runs through these mountains to a town that holds a post office and a few shops. There is also a majestic 15,000-acre resort, itself unchanged since it was built more than a century ago.

On the banks of Lake Gloriette, in the year 1866, the pioneers of Appalachia's northernmost reaches built The Dix House, The Balsams's former name. The inn's first owner, the Whittemore family, named the hostelry for Colonel Timothy Dix, a Revolutionary War hero and the area's first landowner. The Whittemores took in travelers on the old Coos Trail through Dixville Notch. Guests paid for their rooms but were also given meals, seasonal activities, and other services at no extra cost. This was typical of New England frontier inns and gradually became known as the "American plan," a term in use today often synonymous with "all-inclusive."

Gradually The Dix House evolved into the sophisticated resort destination housed in the graceful building between the forested slopes and shimmering Lake Gloriette. In 1895 a wealthy Philadelphia inventor and industrialist named Henry S. Hale purchased the inn and renamed it The Balsams. In 1918 he added a wing called Hampshire House, still called the "new wing."

Today, meals are exquisitely presented throughout the day by Phil Learned, who has been the inn's chef for thirty-seven years. Throughout his tenure, he and his culinary staff have prepared plates with French and Spanish names we couldn't always pronounce but had no trouble consuming in the mountain air. Indeed, The Balsams menu is lengthy, descriptive, and continental. But delicacies imported from almost anywhere in the world comfortably share the same plate as items expertly grown in local gardens.

The Balsams is exceptional for families who wish to be together far from the distractions that separate them throughout the rest of the year. It is also an opportunity for those who love nature to truly connect with the pristine environment, which is as unspoiled today as it was centuries ago. It is a chance to experience a change of season or to view a herd of deer drinking from a clear pond. With the traffic jams of Montreal and Boston hundreds of miles away, the odds of traffic piling up in the Dixville Notch area are limited to a few mountain bikes waiting for a meandering moose to cross a dirt road, at its own leisurely pace, of course. Otherwise, the stresses of daily life have long since left you.

The Balsams Grand Resort Hotel

Route 26
Dixville Notch, New Hampshire 03576-9710
Phone: 800–255–0600, 800–255–0800 (in
   New Hampshire), or 603–255–3400 (direct)
E-mail: info@thebalsams.com
Web site: www.thebalsams.com

Group/Getaway: Families, Sports & Fitness

Accommodations: The resort offers accommodations for about 400 guests. There are Family Suites, Parlor Suites, and Deluxe Suites, each with views of the magnificent mountain walls of Dixville Notch. All of the rooms are designed along a gracious New England traditional theme.

Points of Distinction: The wide variety of activities available, the level of elegance, and the serenity and peace of the surrounding woods.

Open: Late May to mid-October and late December to the end of March.

Minimum Stay: Four nights over summer weekends; some packages dictate the length of one's stay. Otherwise there is no minimum.

Rates: Based on double occupancy, rates are $135 to $259 per person, per night, depending on the season.

Frequently Asked Questions: *Are the winters too harsh?* In the middle of a blizzard or ice storm, New England winters can be brutal. However, most days are comfortable with the proper clothing and, of course, The Balsams keeps its rooms and its entire inn nice and toasty. *Who is the resort best suited for?* Families, couples, groups, and anyone who loves the seasons, tennis, golf, hiking, cross-country skiing, painting and photography, and exploring pure natural surroundings.

Seasonal Activities: Packages are designed for every season. The winter package, called the Wilderness Package, begins in late December and is the perfect time for skis, skates, and sleds. The Balsams property is large enough to hold both downhill slopes and cross-country trails. Lake Gloriette allows a skater thirty-two acres of smooth ice. In summer, golf and tennis are big, as are hiking and mountain biking. Summer lasts from late May until mid-October with a break for the inn's "Social Season." The Social Season runs from early July through the first week of September and is a time reserved for individual and family guest parties.

Don't Forget to Bring: Dress for the season. Winters and summers are predictable, but spring and autumn weather, though beautiful, can change in a matter of minutes. Attire is informal during the day and semiformal at night.

Favorite Side Trip: The "Old Man of the Mountains," an outcropping of rocks at the peak of a mountain that used to resemble the profile of a man. (The rocks tumbled in 2003, though people still go to the area.)

Nearest Airports: Portland Jet Port International Airport, Portland, Maine (a two-and-a-half-hour drive). Also, airports in Manchester, New Hampshire, Montreal, and Boston.

ALL-INCLUSIVE SERVICES AND ACTIVITIES

Food and Beverages: All meals are included in the summer season, breakfast and dinner during the winter season; tea, coffee, milk, and soda.

Outdoor Activities: Golf, tennis, hiking, mountain biking, badminton, bocce, horseshoes, volleyball, and cross-country skiing, snowboarding, snowshoeing, ice skating.

Water Sports: Swimming, rowing, paddleboating.

Facilities: Tennis courts, heated outdoor pool.

Entertainment: Nightly.

Other: Natural history programs, wine tasting.

Children's Services: Two children's camps, Camp Wind Whistle, geared for children five to thirteen, runs during the summer Social Season; Camp Wee Whistle is offered for a limited number of weeks for even younger children. Both are offered from 9:00 A.M. to 4:00 P.M. daily. A nursery service is complimentary to registered guests in the winter.

Children's Activities: Outdoor activities, arts and crafts.

Not Included: Taxes, gratuities, service charges.

Available for a Fee: Other nonalcoholic beverages, alcoholic beverages, equipment rental, lessons.

THE POINT

Saranac Lake, New York

There are no road signs to The Point. Even the detailed map of Upper Saranac Lake provided by the brochure from this exclusive resort does not reveal its exact location. You'll get that privileged information only after you've received confirmed reservations. It's not that Christie and David Garrett, owners of The Point, are unfriendly—far from it! They just want to be able to maintain the privacy and natural serenity that The Point is famous for. Once you've arrived at this former Great Camp built by William Rockefeller on the edge of the pristine Adirondack wilderness in upstate New York, you'll be treated like family in an atmosphere of rustic elegance and homey comfort.

The four carefully maintained log buildings holding the huge Great Hall, the Pub, and eleven unique guest quarters maintain the aura of a rich man's fishing and hunting lodge, which, of course, it was. The primitive edges have been softened with an absolute classiness, but original bathroom fixtures, views of Saranac Lake from every room, the many stone fireplaces, polished pine paneling, vast, inviting couches, and local antique furniture are wonderfully preserved. Add gourmet food and attentive but in no way overbearing service, and you will bear up like a Rockefeller, a Roosevelt, or Hemingway, who stayed here at one time or another.

Because there are accommodations for only eleven couples, guests soon get to know one another. A high point of each day is dinner, served "en famille" in the Great Hall. The Garretts are proud of the many lasting friendships that have begun at The Point, though we emphasize that guests in search of solitude have also come to the right place. The point is, what you do to fill your days here is entirely up to you—consuming novels, fly-fishing, wandering through the woods, canoeing, antiquing, admiring fall foliage, or simply allowing the Garretts to exercise their considerable creativity to help you make it a special day are part of the experience. The landscape is breathtaking. We photographed moose and eagles in the morning (we kept cameras with us at all times), then fished successfully for trout, and finally played nine holes of golf—all on the second day. Eventually we calmed down, enjoying the quietude and the character of this great place.

What places this resort among the top in its class is its restorative powers. It very quickly relaxes the body, mind, and soul without requiring a trip to the massage table. Do a lot, or do little. It still heals, and the resort's caring and fine staff seems to only enhance these qualities.

The Point
HCR #1 Box 65
Saranac Lake, New York 12983
Phone: 800–255–3530 or 518–891–5674
    (direct)
E-mail: info@thepointresort.com
Web site: www.thepointresort.com

Group/Getaway: Couples

Accommodations: The Point has eleven cottage-style guest quarters, all with lake views and fireplaces. Each room has a private bath and shower. The Main Lodge has two wings with two guest rooms in each. The Boathouse's one guest room is directly above the water and features a king-size white-canopied bed in the center of the room, a pair of twin beds in an alcove to the side, and a pair of swinging twin beds suspended from the ceiling on the wraparound deck outside. The room has a panoramic view, large bathroom with a double soaking tub, an oversize shower, and two separate sitting areas.

Points of Distinction: The cuisine at The Point is exceptional. The executive chef, Kevin McCarthy, and his entire staff have been trained by the world-renowned Albert Roux, a culinary genius and a three-star Michelin chef based in London. Many up-and-coming chefs spend time cooking at Le Gavroche in London for six- to eighteen-month periods. Because of this practice, the menu is always fresh with new ideas and talent.

Open: Year-round, except for the first three weeks in April.

Minimum Stay: Seven days.

Rates: Based on double occupancy, $1,200 to $2,200 per night for two people and $250 per night for each additional person; singles deduct $250 from the rate.

Frequently Asked Questions: *Is there a dress code?* Jackets and ties are appropriate for evening; black tie is required Wednesday and Sunday evenings. Casual dress is primarily worn during the day. *Are children allowed?* Children under eighteen are not allowed. Exceptions can be made when one group books the entire facility for a private party.

Seasonal Activities: The Adirondacks have four distinct seasons, and every outdoor activity is by definition seasonal, from volleyball games and picnics in summer to cross-country skiing, "snow barbecues," and dogsledding in winter.

Don't Forget to Bring: Appropriate outdoor clothing and footwear, and a camera; the surroundings are some of the most beautiful you'll ever see, especially during foliage season.

Favorite Side Trips: Lake Placid, New York, is only a short drive away. Famous for hosting the Winter Olympics, Lake Placid makes a wonderful day trip away from The Point. You'll find a public bobsled and luge run, tobogganing, dogsledding, speed skating, ski jumping, alpine ski competitions, figure skating, downhill skiing, and snowmobile rides. There's also the Adirondack Museum at Blue Mountain Lake and skiing at Whiteface Mountain.

Nearest Airport: Saranac Airport, a twenty-minute drive from the resort.

ALL-INCLUSIVE SERVICES AND ACTIVITIES

Food and Beverages: Three meals, non-alcoholic beverages, afternoon tea; wine and liquor, including twenty-four-hour "help-yourself" bars throughout the property. Food is flown in from as far away as Switzerland.

Outdoor Activities: Tennis, volleyball, hiking, bicycling in warmer months; cross-country skiing, ice skating, snowshoeing in winter.

Water Sports: Boating, waterskiing, swimming, fishing in warmer months; ice fishing in winter.

Facilities: Boathouse with canoes, sailboats, and motorboats for waterskiing.

Other: Sunset cruises, snow barbecues, gratuities, airport transfers.

Not Included: Taxes.

Available for a Fee: In-room massages, golf, guided hunting and fishing, horseback riding, dogsledding, downhill skiing, activities at Olympic facilities in nearby Lake Placid.

TOPNOTCH

Stowe, Vermont

Topnotch at Stowe Resort and Spa sits on a 120-acre country estate with spectacular panoramic views that fan across Vermont's Mount Mansfield. Because of its northern Vermont location, we had heard that Topnotch was a great place to enjoy and then retreat from snow in winter. But we also heard it offered unparalleled joys in the height of Vermont's spectacular autumn. Then another friend told us of Topnotch in the glorious month of May. So we made visits in summer and winter to this special escape just 5 miles from the village of Stowe. We discovered that each season adds its own unusual signature; you can choose from an array of services that take advantage of each time of year, while still highlighting the resort's main focus of enhancing your body, mind, and spirit.

Topnotch has succeeded in utilizing its location to incorporate the natural beauty of the surroundings in various indoor and outdoor sports and fitness classes. And the spa offers more than 100 treatments to select from, many of which make use of local plants and herbs. The resort's many hiking, bicycling, and jogging trails wind through the countryside and to the center of Stowe Village. Topnotch also offers one of the country's top-rated tennis academies; guests can participate in various clinics and round-robins. Of equally high regard is the Equestrian Center, which offers group and private riding lessons as well as guided Western and English trail rides.

Despite the number of choices offered, we liked the fact that Topnotch maintains a quiet, intimate atmosphere. The lodge's interiors are beautifully detailed with wood and stone. Walls of glass were designed to bring the outdoors into its interior spaces. Antiques are abundant in its variety of well-appointed spacious rooms, many of which feature mountain views. Because it is a combined spa and resort, guests are invited to choose their own individual pace and regimen with the help of a staff that very much impressed us.

We were fascinated by the many body therapies that Topnotch features. We tried the whirlpool with the cascading hydromassage waterfall and the unique Vermont wildflower herbal wrap, using indigenous herbs from the Vermont countryside. They were spectacular. This world-class spa offers packages that let you add the treatment of your choice to a stay of as many days as you wish. All packages include accommodations and use of all facilities, including workout rooms with state-of-the-art equipment and fitness classes. Most programs include three gourmet spa cuisine meals daily, meals that are as tasty as they are healthy. Maxwell's, the dining room at Topnotch, offers American cuisine with classical, regional, and seasonal influences; it includes a creative spa menu and an award-winning wine list. During summer months, guests may enjoy lunch or dinner outside on the Patio Terrace or at the Poolside Gazebo. The Buttertub Bistro offers a lighter menu.

For those who think no getaway is complete without a little shopping, there are four comprehensive retail outlets: the Nordic Barn, featuring a full line of active apparel and equipment; the Tennis Pro Shop with footwear, tennis apparel, and rackets; the Spa Source, which has cosmetics, hair care, and yoga wear; and L'Armoire, which features Vermont foods, specialty gifts, and resort clothing.

After two visits, we decided that it is the depth and quality of Topnotch's offerings in any season that make it among the 100 best. With so many programs available, you can absolutely customize your own package to create a spa experience unlike any other.

Topnotch
4000 Mountain Road
Stowe, Vermont 05672
Phone: 800–451–8686 or 802–253–8585
  (direct)
E-mail: info@topnotch-resort.com
Web site: www.topnotch-resort.com

Group/Getaway: Singles, Spa & Wellness

Accommodations: The resort comprises a total of ninety-two spacious rooms, four junior suites, three deluxe suites, and forty-eight town houses, including thirty town houses offering pool, garden, or mountain views.

Points of Distinction: Skiing at Stowe Mountain Resort, Stowe Village, country bazaars, auctions, antiquing, art festivals, craft shows, designer boutiques, concerts, and theater.

Open: Year-round.

Minimum Stay: No requirements except on weekends (two nights) and holidays (varies).

Packages: Various honeymoon, spa, fitness, ski, and tennis packages are available.

Rates: Based on double occupancy, guest rooms and suites range from $85 to $360 per person, and town houses from $280 to $900 per unit. Children under twelve stay free, but there's a daily charge of $70 for Mud City Adventures.

Frequently Asked Questions: *Are pets accepted at Topnotch?* A definite yes; well-behaved pets are welcome and cookies for your dog are provided. Dog walkers and sitters are also available. There's even a canine menu! *Do I need an appointment for spa treatments?* Yes, you should schedule your treatments two weeks before your arrival date.

Don't Forget to Bring: Proper footwear for activities such as tennis and aerobics, and a bathing suit for the coed whirlpool, sauna, and indoor pool.

Favorite Side Trip: Stowe Village; Ben and Jerry's ice-cream factory tours; cider mill, where Vermont maple syrup is made; Cabot Cheese tour; outlet malls.

Nearest Airport: Burlington International Airport, forty-five minutes from the resort; car rental or shuttle bus available.

ALL-INCLUSIVE SERVICES AND ACTIVITIES

Food and Beverages: Inquire about meal plans that are available at any time during your stay.

Outdoor Activities: Swimming, tennis, horseback riding, in-line skating, hiking, mountain biking.

Water Sports: Canoeing, fly-fishing, swimming.

Facilities: Tennis courts, indoor and outdoor pools, equestrian center, mountain bike shop, tennis academy, spa.

Entertainment: Live entertainment on most weekends in the Buttertub Bar.

Children's Services: Mud City Adventures for ages six to fifteen; Top Notch Junior Tennis Academy.

Children's Activities: Sailing, canoeing, kayaking, hiking, rock climbing, mountain biking, backpacking, overnight camping.

Available for a Fee: Hayrides, horse-drawn carriage and sleigh rides, skiing at Stowe Mountain Resort, eighteen-hole championship golf nearby, personal laundry service, airport transfers. If not already included in your package you can use the athletic facilities on a daily basis ($18 per day) as needed.

THE TYLER PLACE

Highgate Springs, Vermont

This family resort on the northern edge of Vermont has grown from its humble start in the 1930s as a getaway for a large clan and their friends into one of America's most acclaimed family resorts. Located on a bucolic shore of Lake Champlain near the Canadian border, it is composed of 165 acres of recreational splendor that features thirty cottages with fireplaces, as well as a modern country inn. There are playing fields, woods and hiking trails, heated indoor and outdoor swimming pools, an elaborate waterfront boating area, tennis courts, and much more. Each week from early June until late September, the Tyler family—now in their second and third generations—hosts sixty-three families who come to the resort from all over the world. The strength of the Tyler Place is its uncanny ability to enthrall kids of all ages, from babies to teenagers, while parents are given time to relax, have a great deal of fun, and spend private time together. The staff is simply superb, the activities diverse, and the food is the best we've experienced at family resorts of any kind.

There is a certain magic about this place. Many other resorts have imitated the Tyler Place, but none has managed to reproduce its overall effect on the families who spend a week in its midst. Children beam about their experiences and are often the driving force that brings so many back for repeat visits. Parents rejoice in the renewed spark in their relationships. Lifelong friendships seem to be a natural by-product of the experience. In the still-small arena of all-inclusive resorts for families, the Tyler Place holds a high place in this special niche.

The Tyler Place

P.O. Box 1, Old Dock Road
Highgate Springs, Vermont 05460
Phone: 802–868–4000 (direct)
E-mail: tyler@tylerplace.com
Web site: www.tylerplace.com

Group/Getaway: Families

Accommodations: The Tyler Place offers cottages, studios, and suites to accommodate families of all sizes. Each is uniquely designed and offers such amenities as screened-in porches, fireplaces, bunk beds for children, kitchenettes, and full baths.

Points of Distinction: The food is often of gourmet quality, served in a dining room at informal but attractive, candlelit tables, well suited for couples who want to be alone or wish to sit with newfound friends. The wait staff is excellent and efficient. Next to the dining room is a bar where guests can buy reasonably priced alcoholic beverages.

Open: Late May to early September.

Minimum Stay: Seven nights (Saturday to Saturday).

Rates: Based on double occupancy, $78 to $277 per person, per night for seven nights. Rates for children are $23 to $94, depending on age. Discounts available first and last two weeks of season. Private three- or five-night family retreats offered in May.

Frequently Asked Question: *Will I still be able to relax, even though I have a newborn and a toddler?* The Tyler Place welcomes and nurtures infants as young as newborns. For newborns to two-and-a-half-year-olds, options include Infant Program/Playroom, Toddler Program, and Parents' Helpers. In addition, cribs, high chairs, and child seats and helmets for bicycling are available at no charge. The child-to-staff ratio is one caregiver to two or three children. Caregivers are warm and experienced, and most parents want to take them home!

Don't Forget to Bring: Sweaters for cool nights and rain gear for the occasional rainy day.

Favorite Side Trip: Montreal, which is only an hour and a half away, for good music, history, major-league sports, shopping, and gaming.

Nearest Airports: Burlington Airport, an hour away, and Montreal International Airport, an hour and a half away.

ALL-INCLUSIVE SERVICES AND ACTIVITIES

Food and Beverages: Three meals, first drink on first evening at staff-sponsored gathering, romantic candlelight dinner nightly (alone or with other adult guests), tea, snacks. Nonalcoholic beverages and snacks are included only when children are in the group; additional cost at other times.

Outdoor Activities: Tennis, volleyball, hiking, bike touring, archery.

Water Sports: Canoeing, kayaking, fishing, swimming.

Facilities: Heated indoor and outdoor pools, tennis courts, exercise room, Jacuzzi.

Other: Guided canoe and nature trips, yoga, pottery and bread-making classes, daily housekeeping, gratuities.

Children's Services: Children are divided into nine age-appropriate programs. The children's groups meet at breakfast and break up after lunch, then regroup for supper. Afternoons are reserved for families to spend together.

Children's Activities: Outdoor activities, water sports, hayrides, bonfires, parties and socials, petting farm.

Not Included: Service charges and meal tax.

Available for a Fee: Parents' Helpers/sitters, waterskiing, evening champagne cruise, massage, laundry service, alcoholic and nonalcoholic beverages (nonalchoholic beverages are free if children are in the group).

CLUB MED SANDPIPER

Port St. Lucie, Florida

Club Med Sandpiper is off the beach but on the St. Lucie River, a location that maintains its proximity to the open Atlantic waters while providing guests a seclusion not found elsewhere on the Florida coast.

Sandpiper's charm is in its effort to please family members of all ages. Children from the age of four months and up have access to kids' clubs designed for four different age groups: Baby, Petit, Mini, and Junior. For young adults, parents, and grandparents, Sandpiper excels at creating activities that match the interests of its guests.

Parents who have a passion for golf will love Sandpiper's eighteen-hole golf course. The course is a leisurely par seventy-two and is perfectly manicured for each day's rounds. As it is wise to practice your swing, a 330-yard driving range is available, as well as a driving net and a three-par, nine-hole warm-up course. There are also practice putting greens, chipping greens, and sand traps. The on-site Golf Academy provides two and a half hours of professional instruction, course play, and video analysis.

The Team Scandinavia Tennis Academy is no less rigorous in its ability to help resort guests improve their games. Professional instructors give a total of eight hours of lesson time at intermediate and advanced skill levels that prepare you for play on one of Sandpiper's nineteen Plexipave courts, nine of them lighted for night play, and to compete in ongoing tournaments. This course is designed for ages twelve and older and is not recommended for professionals. Because only six participants are permitted, you must remember to prebook.

But tennis and golf are only at the top of a very impressive list of sports, including basketball, volleyball, and soccer, with pickup games forming daily. There are plenty of smooth surfaces for in-line skating. Water exercise classes meet every day at one of the four swimming pools. There is a fully equipped fitness center. Also, kids (and adults who wish they were) enjoy The Circus, where they can swing on the flying trapeze, bounce and flip on the trampoline, or walk the high wire—all with professional instruction. They also learn to juggle.

Sandpiper's grounds are thick with palm trees and tropical plants. Sun worshippers can meet at any number of poolside decks, or they can find a hidden nook between shrubs. There are two restaurants, a central bar, and a nightclub. Throughout the day, the sounds of Mozart, Strauss, and the like provide a mood of serenity and ease. After dark, the atmosphere gets a bit funkier, with entertainment nightly.

Club Med Sandpiper offers athletic families more opportunities to enjoy sports than any all-inclusive we've seen. But even more impressive, this resort has created an environment in which families can spend quality time together, enjoying the sun, water, and each other's company.

Club Med Sandpiper

3500 SE Morningside Boulevard
Port St. Lucie, Florida 34952
Phone: 800–CLUB–MED or 772–398–5100
   (direct)
Web site: www.clubmed.com

Group/Getaway: Families, Sports & Fitness

Accommodations: Surrounded by fountains and gardens are 337 air-conditioned double-occupancy rooms in three-story lodges. Rooms include private terrace, walk-in closet and dressing area, television, phone, refrigerator, and private bath. Conference facilities are available.

Points of Distinction: Club Med Sandpiper is a virtual "country club" getaway, with nineteen Plexipave tennis courts, a tennis academy with instruction from pros, access to an eighteen-hole championship golf course designed by Mark Mahanna, and a golf academy.

Open: Year-round.

Minimum Stay: Seven nights and some three-night options.

Rates: Based on double occupancy, $840 to $1,120 per person for seven nights; children ages four to fifteen, $252 to $560; children ages two and three, $252 to $266. Membership is $55 per adult and $25 per child.

Frequently Asked Question: *Is there a beach at Sandpiper?* Sandpiper is actually on the St. Lucie River, where waterskiing and sailing are available. The resort is within driving distance of the coast.

Don't Forget to Bring: Golf clubs, your favorite tennis racket, and salve for blisters.

Favorite Side Trips: Orlando, South Beach, and Miami Beach.

Nearest Airports: West Palm Beach Airport, an hour away, and Orlando Airport, an hour and a half away.

ALL-INCLUSIVE SERVICES AND ACTIVITIES

Food and Beverages: Three meals available throughout the day, all non-alcoholic beverages. Unlimited beer and wine during meals and alcoholic beverages, including premium brands, throughout the day—a new Club Med policy.

Outdoor Activities: Tennis, volleyball, bocce, soccer, basketball, in-line skating.

Water Sports: Swimming, waterskiing, sailing.

Facilities: Four swimming pools, fitness center, nineteen Plexipave tennis courts, eighteen-hole golf course.

Entertainment: Nightly.

Other: Taxes and gratuities. Airport transfers included if you make your airline reservations through Club Med.

Children's Services: Baby, Petit, Mini, and Junior groups for children ages four months and up.

Children's Activities: Outdoor activities, water sports, picnics, circus program (including lessons on trapeze, trampoline, and juggling).

Available for a Fee: Golf, Tennis Academy and Golf Academy, deep-sea fishing, Excursion Programs, which include trips to Disney World, Kennedy Space Center, Seaworld, Epcot Center, Universal Studios, Key West, Palm Beach, Miami.

THE CLOISTER HOTEL

Sea Island, Georgia

The Cloister Hotel first opened its doors in 1928. Since then, the hotel's underlying Southern charm and ability to put its loyal guests at ease have remained unchanged. President Bush chose the hotel for the 2004 G–8 summit, so stellar is its reputation.

The Spanish Colonial–style hotel is located on Sea Island, the outer of three islands found off the rural coast of Georgia. A fifteen-minute drive from the mainland, the Cloister is east of St. Simons Island and north of Jekyll Island.

Although a beautiful stretch of beach runs the length of the resort, much of what happens here revolves around the fairways. With three eighteen-hole courses spanning two islands, the tees and greens remain crowd-free. St. Simons Island, a ten-minute drive, is where you'll also find the Golf Learning Center, where nationally known golfers head the instruction team.

But the Cloister isn't just for golf enthusiasts. In fact the resort features a wide range of outdoor activities that will appeal to sports buffs of all stripes. Tennis lovers can spend their time playing on any of the resort's eight fast-dry clay courts. Those who enjoy boating can cruise the open ocean or wind their way through the mid-isle sea grass. There's also horseback riding, which provides a keen opportunity to explore Sea Island. In the "change of pace" category, the resort's shooting school offers archery ranges and skeet shooting. Families always find time for playing croquet, shuffleboard, chip and putt, and traditional and blacklight volleyball.

Cloister guests can follow a full regimen of health and exercise activities on their own or with a personal trainer. The sun is barely above the horizon before a morning session of t'ai chi begins on the beach, and walks of varying distances and speeds are conducted throughout the day. A room full of strength and cardiovascular equipment is available, as well as many exercise and wellness classes. Soothe both body and mind at the spa, where you can treat yourself to a massage, various treatments, or a one-hour reflexology session.

Dining is always a highlight of the Cloister experience, and guests have choices of both location and formality. For an elegant evening of fine dining, the Main Dining Room provides an atmosphere of ease and indulgence. A more casual mood presides at the Beach Club, the Terrace, or Davis Love Grill. On nearby Rainbow Island, a buffet of low-country delicacies is served. Complimentary shuttle service is available every thirty minutes to St. Simons Island, which is less than fifteen minutes away. Changes are afoot at the property. A two-year renovation, starting in late 2003, will polish and enhance this already prime facility.

The Cloister Hotel
100 Hudson Place
Sea Island, Georgia 31561
Phone: 800–732–4752 or 912–638–3611
Web site: www.seaisland.com

Group/Getaway: Couples, families

Accommodations: There are 212 rooms distributed among eight categories of rooms.

Rooms in the Guest, Terrace, Beach, and Ocean Houses sleep a family of four or five. All rooms include hair dryers, private bath, and king-, queen-, or double-sized beds. Many rooms have sleeper sofa beds.

Points of Distinction: The Cloister has been named one of "America's Best 100 Golf Courses" and one of "America's 75 Best Resort Courses," by *Golf Digest* magazine.

Travel and Leisure magazine named the Cloister the "Number 1 Spa in North America," while *Condé Nast Traveler* designated the hotel as both one of the "Top 20 Mainland Resorts" and one of the "Top 100 Worldwide Travel Experiences."

Open: Year-round.

Minimum Stay: Weekend and holiday minimum requirements vary. Call for details.

Packages: An array of all-inclusive packages is available (including golf, tennis, shooting, spa, and romance packages). Call for details.

Rates: Based on double occupancy, room rates begin at $220 September through February and $300 March through August. A $35 daily service fee is additional. Meal plans are $80 per adult per day and $45 per child age six through fifteen per day. No meal charge for children age five and under.

Frequently Asked Questions: *Are there special children's programs available?* Playtime is a fee-based program available year-round, six days a week during the summer and spring break and five days a week the remainder of the year. Children's dinners are offered on the same schedule and on weekends year-round. There is a complimentary children's dance party and petting zoo at the stables. Unusual offerings are a CD-recording workshop and a wildlife encounters certificate program. *Does the resort have family nature programs?* Activities include bird-watching, stargazing, and ocean seining with nets. A Sea Turtle EcoAdventure program takes place during summer months with nightly excursions in search of turtle tracks, nesting mothers, and hatchlings.

Don't Forget to Bring: Golf clubs and tennis racket, and a coat and tie for dining after 6:00 P.M. in the Main Dining Room (required for men and young men over the age of twelve). Formal attire is preferred, but optional, on Wednesday and Saturday.

Favorite Side Trip: St. Simons Island, to visit The Christ Church and Fort Frederica.

Nearest Airport: Jacksonville International Airport, one hour and fifteen minutes (70 miles) away.

ALL-INCLUSIVE SERVICES AND ACTIVITIES

Food and Beverages: Three meals a day are included at any of five restaurants: Cloister Main Dining Room, the Terrace, Colt & Alisons, the Beach Club, and Davis Love Grill.

Outdoor Activities: Lawn sports, including shuffleboard; a chip and putt course and putting green; croquet; volleyball; and blacklight volleyball.

Entertainment: Ballroom dancing in the Club Room, which features an orchestra and includes a lounge and bar area. Live entertainment during meals.

Children's Services: A special dinner program is available for children from June through Labor Day and during spring break (March through April). Parents can have a relaxing dinner while their children enjoy dining with other kids. Parents must reserve space for their children one day in advance.

Children's Activities: Nightly entertainment (from 6:00 to 9:00 P.M.) includes jugglers, clowns, and movies. From June through Labor Day, there are supervised children's programs (including lunch and beverages) for kids ages three to twelve, and unsupervised activities (including outdoor activities, arts and crafts, board games) for kids ages thirteen to eighteen.

Other: Dance instruction Monday through Saturday; tours and talks focusing on Sea Island art, architecture, and history; and weekly wine cellar and kitchen tours, an old Sea Island tradition.

Not Included: Taxes, gratuities, airport transfers.

Available for a Fee: Alcoholic and non-alcoholic beverages; golf; charter boats; horseback riding; bicycles. Baby-sitting is available for a fee and should be reserved one week before arrival.

HILTON HEAD HEALTH INSTITUTE

Hilton Head Island, South Carolina

Off the coast of South Carolina, on Hilton Head Island, is a health spa that offers a unique twist on the all-inclusive theme. While many health spas feel like medical clinics or even military boot camps, the atmosphere at Hilton Head Health Institute is one of a luxury resort combined with a college campus. The institute maintains a professional and educational affiliation with the University of South Carolina. In this capacity the resort has the ability to combine recreation with new awareness that makes each stay a "learning vacation." Rather than dictating the activities of their program, lifestyle counselors prefer to educate guests about motivating and disciplining themselves. In the course of their stay, guests acquire the skills needed to achieve lifelong wellness.

Because vacations are often chosen to be elixirs for stress, a growing number of resorts have created spa and wellness programs for their clients. The Health Institute recognizes that stress is an enormous factor in American life, and so it created The Healthy Lifestyle Program to make the purpose of a wellness vacation primary instead of secondary to visiting a beach or playing golf.

While at the institute, take advantage of the island's amenities, which include boating, golfing, and sea kayaking. A wide beach is only minutes away, and golf courses abound. You can also enjoy the tranquillity of the resort's wooded, bucolic setting to hike or bike when not using the extensive fitness facilities.

The institute maintains a rigorous schedule of lectures, demonstrations, fitness options, and classes that teach meditation, stretching, breathing techniques, and even cooking. A variety of massages and spa treatments are available for an additional charge.

In addition to The Healthy Lifestyle program, the institute offers a variety of specialty programs that focus on important wellness issues: The Healthy Table cooking school, Mindful Eating, Making Peace with Mind, Body, and Food (for women only), Making Order Out of Chaos: Coping and Thriving with Change, and Living Consciously and Creating a Balanced Life.

Hilton Head Health Institute
14 Valencia Road
Hilton Head Island, South Carolina 29928
Phone: 800–292–2440 or 843–785–7292
Web site: www.hhhealth.com

Group/Getaway: Singles, Spa & Wellness

Accommodations: Guests stay in one-, two-, or three-bedroom private or semi-private cottages. Those in semi-private cottages have a private bedroom and bath and share living and laundry areas. Studio accommodations do not include living, kitchen, or laundry areas. All accommodations are close to the institute. All buildings are smoke-free.

Points of Distinction: Hilton Head Health Institute offers a serene environment in which to pursue personal insight, healthy cuisine, physical challenge, and mindful nourishment, all of which will help you initiate the steps for making lasting lifestyle changes.

Open: Year-round.

Minimum Stay: One week; however the institute does offer a four-day Health Retreat program. Many guests remain for several weeks, or even months.

Packages: An array of packages on lifestyle management, including weight reduction, smoking cessation, and stress management, is available based on the individual guest's needs and abilities.

Rates: $2,795 per person for seven nights; $3,095 per person for specialty programs; $1,850 per person for the Health Retreat.

Frequently Asked Questions: *Is this a resort or clinic?* It is both. Guests are given all the pampering they would get at any resort, while also receiving the proper, expert attention they would expect at the nation's best health institutions. *What is the temperature like?* Summer months can be humid with temperatures in the nineties. However, cooling breezes of the Atlantic are constant. In winter, nighttime temperatures can dip into the thirties, while daytime temps are generally in the fifties and sixties.

Don't Forget to Bring: Beach gear. You'll have plenty of time to wander along the island's uncrowded shore.

Favorite Side Trips: Charleston and Savannah. Both are modern, elegant cities with intriguing history and well-preserved architecture. Shopping is abundant.

Nearest Airport: Savannah Airport, thirty to forty-five minutes from the resort.

ALL-INCLUSIVE SERVICES AND ACTIVITIES

Food and Beverages: All meals and snacks, tea, coffee, and juices.

Outdoor Activities: Hiking.

Water Sports: Swimming.

Facilities: Guest lounge with entertainment center, reading library, and games; fitness center; pool; demonstration kitchen; indoor and outdoor sports; classes and activities, including Pilates and yoga.

Other: Taxes and gratuities; all lectures, demonstrations, and classes; individual lifestyle assessment, including nutrition, blood screening, fitness, and behavior components. Bring your own alcoholic beverages.

Available for a Fee: Additional nonalcoholic beverages, shopping, horseback riding, golf and tennis, sea kayaking, fishing, sailing, cultural events, movies, bike rentals, spa services.

BLACKBERRY FARM

Walland, Tennessee

Blackberry Farm is a gentle place to indulge the senses. Once you've driven the 20 miles out of Knoxville into the valleys of the southern Great Smoky Mountains, a stately Virginian fence announces your approach to the entrance of this elegant farm, where rows of towering trees lead you to the front door. Your first impression is that a few days will not be enough of this, and it will remain true until you leave.

This Smoky Mountain getaway is posh and expensive but offers such high value that those who can afford it seem thrilled to have made the effort. Rated one of the finest mountain estate hotels in the United States, Blackberry Farm is a member of the exclusive Relais & Chateaux organization and ranked by the Zagat survey as America's No. 1 small hotel, No. 1 hotel for service, and No. 2 hotel for dining. There are forty-four rooms in five buildings whose names describe their layout: the Guest House, the Main House, the Gate House, and the Holly Glade and Cove Cottages. There are several meeting rooms that are complimentary with a block of ten or more rooms.

There are three things that bring people to this 2,500-acre retreat. First is its reputation for some of the finest cooking in heartland America. Of no less repute is its fly-fishing opportunities along carefully managed and stocked Hesse Creek, where Orvis, a maker of fly-fishing gear, became so impressed that the company named the farm an Orvis-endorsed lodge. Finally, Blackberry Farm is noted for its most popular activity of simply stepping onto the veranda, selecting a rocking chair, and letting the spirit of the Smokies lull you into a "Blackberry" state of mind.

Although the farm can accommodate almost 100 guests at a time, its owners, Kreis and Sandy Beall, treat their guests as though they are visitors to their home. Obviously, their standards are high. The executive chef, John Fleer, has created a Tennessee gastronomy he calls "foothills cuisine," which is a combination of haute cuisine and Southern comfort food. He also started a cooking school at Blackberry Farm called "Cooking for Friends" that operates ten times a year. Each class consists of two-day sessions that are entertaining as well as educational.

More about fly-fishing. Blackberry Farm's Orvis program is diverse and can accommodate beginners and experienced anglers. Private and group lessons are available as well as guided trips on and off the property. Blackberry Farm provides all flies and rods for your use at no additional charge.

When not fishing and dining, you can also enjoy secluded mountain trails and explore rolling meadows for wildflower and ornithological opportunities. Activities include tennis, swimming, horseback riding, mountain biking, spa pampering, wine tasting, and the cooking school. There are many ways to have a wonderful time here, including choosing to do very little of anything.

Blackberry Farm
1471 West Millers Cove Road
Walland, Tennessee 37886
Phone: 800–273–6004 or 865–380–2260
(direct)
E-mail: info@blackberryfarm.com
Web site: www.blackberryfarm.com

Group/Getaway: Couples

Accommodations: There are forty-four elegant guest rooms furnished with English antiques, fine art, feather beds, and private baths. Twenty-three Main House and Guest House Estate Rooms have access to living room with two fireplaces, pantry, veranda with rocking chairs, and mountain views. Eight Holly Glade Cottages have sixteen suites with walk-in closet, fireplace, whirlpool bath, pantry, sitting area, and private porch with rocking chairs. Cove Cottage is a three-bedroom home with a full kitchen, sitting room, fireplace, living room with seating for eight, and a porch with swing and rocking chairs. Gate House is a two-bedroom cottage with living room, pantry, and private porch with rocking chairs.

Points of Distinction: The breathtaking beauty of Tennessee's Smoky Mountains and the fly-fishing opportunities are part of the appeal of Blackberry Farm.

Open: Year-round.

Minimum Stay: Two nights; three nights on weekends in October and during holidays.

Rates: Based on double occupancy, guest rooms are $545 to $745 per night per couple, and cottages from $945 to $1,995 (depending on cottage and season).

Frequently Asked Questions: *My husband likes to fly-fish, but I never have. Are lessons available?* Private instructions can be provided at an additional cost. Guided fly-fishing trips can also be arranged with at least two weeks' advance notice. *Is golf available?* There are four golf courses, all within a fifteen- to forty-five-minute drive.

Don't Forget to Bring: Dining attire, which includes jackets for gentlemen and casual elegance for ladies. Sturdy hiking boots and comfortable casual clothing for day activities.

Favorite Side Trips: Cades Cove, an 11-mile loop in the Great Smoky Mountains National Park; Tuckeleechee underground caverns; a one-hour hike to Clingman's Dome, the highest mountaintop in the Great Smoky Mountains National Park; Pigeon Forge antiques stores and outlet malls.

Nearest Airport: McGee Tyson Airport in Knoxville, Tennessee, just one-half hour from the resort. Taxi fare is approximately $25 one-way.

ALL-INCLUSIVE SERVICES AND ACTIVITIES

Food and Beverages: Breakfast, brunch, and candlelight dinners are served in the dining room, while the midday meal is always a gourmet picnic lunch. Soda and juice included. Tennessee Tea in the afternoon.

Outdoor Activities: Fly-fishing, tennis, mountain biking, hiking.

Water Sports: Swimming.

Facilities: Outdoor pool, fitness room.

Other: Fly-fishing instruction, use of golf carts.

Children's Services: Children under age ten are not suitable guests and are allowed only on certain holidays and during July.

Not Included: Airport transfers, service charges, taxes.

Available for a Fee: Alcoholic beverages, guided fly-fishing trips, horseback riding, golf, guided hikes, cooking school, spa services.

THE GRAND HOTEL

Mackinac Island, Michigan

In 1887, when the Grand Hotel opened, guests arrived by horse and carriage from the ferry dock. Today they ride up to the red-carpeted front steps exactly the same way. The Grand Hotel makes its home on Mackinac (say "Mackinaw") Island, where automobile traffic is banned.

The motorized vehicle–free setting sets a mood for a Grand Hotel vacation. Guests are likely to gravitate to the 660-foot porch—the longest in the world, according to the hotel—and sit in a rocking chair taking in the geranium-fringed view over the vast lawns and Mackinac Straits. When they bestir themselves from the rocking chair or the afternoon tea table in the parlor, they might indulge in some lawn games, croquet perhaps, or bocce. Those with more activity in mind may head for the serpentine-shaped Esther Williams swimming pool, named for the star who filmed the 1949 *This Time for Keeps* here. Clay courts beckon those who want to play tennis or take some lessons from the resident pro.

Golfers will find a course with a view, over the straits. It's named The Jewel, and offers the Grand nine holes, created in 1901 and redesigned in 1987, and the Woods nine, added in 1994. Jerry Matthews designed the latter, which features extensive ponds and woodlands.

All of this activity takes place against the backdrop of the Grand Hotel, which sits in cupola-topped, white clapboard grandeur on its lawns that rise above Mackinac Straits, which connect Lake Michigan and Lake Huron and divide Michigan's Upper and Lower Peninsulas. Mackinac Island is an 8-mile sliver of land in the blue water that has been attracting wealthy Midwesterners and just plain folks for generations. The National Trust for Historic Preservation named it to its Historic Hotels of America list.

A popular way to explore the island is on a bike—single or tandem. The hotel will pack a fine picnic lunch—well, perhaps not so fine as the Grand Luncheon Buffet served in the Main Dining Room—for island outings. You may also book an island carriage tour, or even more fun, rent a horse and carriage and do the driving yourself. For those who prefer to remain in the saddle, a nearby stable rents horses, and the island offers 40 miles of bridle paths.

American Indians were the island's first inhabitants, followed by French and British fur traders in the early eighteenth century. The French brought lilacs, which bloom all over the island in late May and early June and make it a beautiful time to visit. The Grand Hotel offers a package during the island's Lilac Festival. The Astor Fur Post and Biddle House are other historic sites from this early period that may be toured.

In the evening everyone returns to the hotel and puts on his or her finest to meet the hotel's dress code—jackets and neckties for men and dresses or dressy pants for women. It applies to all public rooms in the hotel, not just the dining room. The evening might start with cocktails in the Cupola Bar at the top of the hotel, which looks out over the panorama of the straits and the Mackinac Bridge, which connects Mackinaw City on the Lower Peninsula to St. Ignace on the Upper Peninsula, but soars over the island.

A five-course dinner is served in the vast Main Dining Room. Guests covet window tables, but you probably won't get one in midsummer unless you've been coming for decades. The day ends with demitasse in the parlor and perhaps dancing the night away in the Terrace Room to the Big Band sounds of the Grand Hotel Orchestra.

Grand Hotel

286 Grand Avenue
Mackinac Island, Michigan 49757
Phone: 800–334–7263 or 906–847–3331
Web site: www.grandhotel.com

Group/Getaway: Family, honeymoons

Accommodations: Each one of the 385 rooms and suites is decorated in a unique style. New York interior designer Carleton Varney created lordly fittings for the suites. Six named suites pay tribute to former first ladies, including Jacqueline Kennedy and Nancy Reagan. Some rooms have balconies and many have lake views.

Points of Distinction: The longest front porch in the world stretches to 660 feet across the front of the hotel and is lined with thousands of geranium plants. Mackinac Island, the hotel's home, bans automobile traffic, which gives guests the chance to fantasize about living in another era.

Open: Early May through late October.

Minimum Stay: None.

Packages: Packages are tied to special events at the hotel or holidays and include activities to match the theme. A Tea for Two package offers afternoon tea, but also one 18-hole round of golf on the Jewel course ($199 per person, double occupancy). A Murder Mystery Weekend has mystery activities and entertainment, a cocktail reception, and a 50 percent discount on greens fees at the Jewel course ($859 per couple for the weekend).

Rates: Based on double occupancy, peak season (mid-June to late August) rates are $199 (for an interior room) to $314 per person per night. Shoulder season (May through early June and late August through October) rates are $179 to $294 per person per night. When sharing a room with a parent, children through age eleven are free. Children ages twelve through seventeen are $49 per day and those eighteen and older are $99.

Frequently Asked Questions: *Is the ferry the only way to get to Mackinac Island?* No, it's possible to take an air taxi from the Pellston, Michigan, Airport, located 12 miles south of Mackinaw City on the Lower Peninsula or from the St. Ignace Airport on the Upper Peninsula. *What event brought the hotel the most notoriety?* Filming *Somewhere in Time* in 1980 with Christopher

Reeve, Jane Seymour, and Christopher Plummer. It is the centerpiece of a weekend at the hotel each October when the film is screened several times and other activities related to it take place.

Don't Forget to Bring: Sunscreen, sweater for chilly evenings, and a willingness to pretend it's another era.

Favorite Side Trips: Explore Fort Mackinac, built by the British and then occupied by the Americans, where interpretive guides take on the role of U.S. soldiers from the War of 1812 in fourteen original buildings; renting a horse and carriage from one of the local liveries is another favorite way to spend the day.

Nearest Airport: Mackinac Island Airport.

ALL-INCLUSIVE SERVICES AND ACTIVITIES

Food and Beverages: Breakfast and dinner for modified American plan, or breakfast, lunch, and dinner for full American plan; nonalcoholic beverages with meals.

Outdoor Activities: Tennis, hiking, strolling, bocce.

Water Sports: Swimming in the pool.

Children's Activities: A children's program takes place during the day and in the evening. Youngsters have pool time and go for bike rides and picnics or have outings on the island, including a trip to the butterfly house. It's all included in the room rate.

Facilities: Esther Williams swimming pool, sauna, whirlpools, tennis courts, gardens, Vita Course, fitness facility, golf course.

Not Included: Transportation and baggage transport from the airport or ferry dock.

Available for a Fee: Golf on the eighteen-hole Jewel and Woods courses, horseback riding, carriage and garden tours. Room rates do not include carriage taxi or baggage transport from the ferry dock or airport, although most of the packages cover these costs.

RED MOUNTAIN RESORT AND SPA

Ivins, Utah

Guests arriving at Red Mountain Resort and Spa are likely to be pale from spending too many hours in work cubicles. When they leave they're likely to have picked up a wonderful glow. It's not just from the sun or even a reflection from the extraordinary red-rock canyon country of southwestern Utah, but rather the sense of well-being that comes from the holistic, adventurous approach at this desert resort and spa.

What makes Red Mountain somewhat unique is its emphasis on challenging outdoor activities. Its subtitle is "The Adventure Spa," a name it earns from the menu of fitness programs offered. An array of daily hikes starts at the Discovery Level for beginners or those traveling from lower elevations. (The resort is about 3,000 feet above sea level on the high desert.) Guided biking outings with similar levels are also offered daily through the bike school.

Red Mountain, however, does not take the "no pain, no gain" approach. The staff encourages guests to get a METAbeat Cardio-Metabolic Assessment, which determines the metabolic profile, fitness level, and caloric needs of each guest. Often people exercise at heart rates needlessly higher than their fat-burning zones.

Some of the newer programs are orienteering done with Global Positioning System (GPS) devices. One of the most challenging activities is geo-caching, in which guests use the GPS to figure out where "treasure" is buried around the fifty-five-acre property. Those who find it get to keep the prize, which may be a logbook or a trinket.

Fitness classes run to various aerobics and cardio classes, including a New York City Ballet workout and spinning, and to those emphasizing stretching and flexibility.

Since you can't exercise without fuel, great emphasis is placed on wonderful, nutritious food from chef Jim Gallivan. Red Mountain has divided the cuisine into three levels to meet the needs of different guests. "PowerFuel" is designed for sports enthusiasts who need extra calories and for those looking to build muscle mass. Lean meats and whole grains are the basis, which appear on the plate as beef tenderloin with sweet potato pancake and sautéed spinach, or lamb brochette with collard greens and chickpea griddle cake.

"Call of the Wild" focuses on natural local ingredients — vegetables and herbs harvested from the resort's organic garden, as well as indigenous game and greens. It's lower in calories than "PowerFuel" and has 20 percent or fewer calories from fats. Expect seared mahimahi with rice croquette or char-grilled bison with spinach risotto. "Green Cuisine" features the lowest-calorie dishes, and it's vegan, including choices such as roasted Japanese eggplant filled with squash and chickpeas in mushroom broth and grilled vegetable and herbed tofu lasagna with roasted red bell pepper sauce.

Lest guests worry that the weight they may have lost in a week will be quickly regained when they return home, the resort has nutrition and healthy living classes.

The spirit isn't forgotten in this holistic approach. T'ai chi, yoga, and ai chi are offered, as well as spirit hikes, moonlight walks, and Native American card readings. What most nourishes the spirit, though, is the spectacular red-rock canyon country of southwestern Utah. The resort is near the entrance to Snow Canyon State Park, where nature has sculpted the rocks into twisted, folded graceful shapes. Watch the light change on these rocks at sunset. There's not a more intense red-orange-lavender spectrum on a painter's palette.

Red Mountain Resort and Spa

P.O. Box 2149
St. George, Utah 84771 (mailing address)
1275 East Red Mountain Circle
Ivins, Utah 84738
Phone: 800–407–3002 or 435–673–4905
Web site: www.redmountainspa.com

Group/Getaway: Adults only

Accommodations: There are 116 guest rooms in terra cotta–colored buildings holding up to 202 guests. Some of the buildings are two-bedroom villas with king beds or two queens.

Points of Distinction: The spectacular setting in red-rock canyon country of southwestern Utah is the backdrop for many outdoor activities. The learning thrust of the programs is designed to send guests home smarter about lifestyle choices than when they arrived.

Open: Year-round, except for a few days around Christmas.

Minimum Stay: None.

Packages: Some packages focus on cuisine, others are for groups of three to five people staying in a single two-bedroom suite, and others are for mothers and daughters. Call for details.

Rates: Based on double occupancy, rates per person per night during the winter (January and February) and summer (June through August) for villas are $345 to $445. Standard rooms are $305, and $205 per person for three people sharing a room. Spring and fall seasons, the villa rates based on double occupancy are $385 to $485. Standard rooms are $345 per person for two and $245 per person for three in a room.

Frequently Asked Questions: *Can I eat all I want?* Yes. Breakfast and lunch in the Canyon Breeze dining room are buffets. Table service is offered at dinner. *Can I bring my own alcohol?* Although alcohol is not served at Red Mountain, you may bring your own to consume in your quarters. However, once you taste chef Jim Gallivan's Red Mountain Shandy, you might lose interest in anything alcoholic.

Don't Forget to Bring: Hiking boots, biking shorts, comfortable fitness clothing, sunscreen.

Favorite Side Trips: The West's great canyon trio: Zion, Bryce, and Grand.

Nearest Airport: St. George (Utah) Airport, served by commuter flights, is the nearest. Most guests arrive at Las Vegas–McCarran International Airport, about a two-hour drive.

ALL-INCLUSIVE SERVICES AND ACTIVITIES

Food and Beverages: Breakfast, lunch, and dinner; an early morning juice and fruit bar; nonalcoholic beverages with meals.

Outdoor Activities: Guided hiking, guided cycling and bike school, survival skills classes, spirit and moonlight walks, orienteering, archaeology walks, stargazing.

Water Sports: Aqua classes, swimming.

Facilities: Two swimming pools (one indoor), fitness center, spa, salon.

Other: Taking a holistic approach to well-being, the resort offers classes in nutrition, healthy living, creative expression, and "The Inner Game" Wellness series. Fitness activities cover aerobics, spinning, yoga, t'ai chi and ai chi, aqua aerobics, stretch and flexibility classes, and a New York City Ballet workout. Activities nurturing the spirit are moonlight walks, Native American card reading, and breath meditation.

Not Included: Transportation from the airport.

Available for a Fee: Massage and salon services, excursions outside of the property, personal trainer, golf at nearby Entrada Golf Course and Snow Canyon Country Club, kayaking, horseback riding.

LARAMIE RIVER RANCH

Glendevey, Colorado

The cookie jars are always full at Laramie River Ranch, which we found to be symbolic of the way this operation works. Bill and Krista Burleigh bought their ranch several years ago and lovingly invested capital and creativity to give families the opportunity to experience what Big Sky Country and the Wild West are about. The Laramie River Ranch is in one of the most striking landscapes in the United States, where two rivers and open foothills break away from the wild Rawah Mountains. You can see for miles in any direction, and that is what most first-time visitors spend hours doing—looking down the face of nature to simply absorb the raw beauty that this dude ranch presents.

Nestled around a curve in the trout-rich Laramie River, the ranch is composed of a lodge, small cabins, and an elaborate barn area that houses forty horses. The riding program here is geared to meet any rider's whims, from the beginner to the seasoned equestrian. Organized trail rides occur daily, fanning out into the sage or climbing the wooded mountains.

Although horseback riding at Laramie River is the most exciting and diverse we experienced, there is no pressure to do so. The staff of Laramie is particularly sensitive to children's needs, providing a range of activities for families, adults, and kids that lets them decide how to spend each day. If you prefer to stake out a spot on the porch to read a book or to spend an afternoon roping a mechanical steer, no one will object.

But for those wishing to log hours in the saddle, a cookout ride is scheduled weekly and cattle drives are scheduled for experienced riders. Overnight pack trips are also available, giving families a chance to sleep under stars so bright they seem to have no earthly obstructions. Although children under six cannot be taken out on the trail, pony rides at the corral are available daily.

Great dude ranching happens with flexibility. Time and again, we observed the staff of Laramie River Ranch offering activities for both young and old, giving kids plenty of opportunities to leave their parents behind and parents an opportunity to have a few hours to themselves. As kids went on impromptu tubing adventures, adults went wading up the Laramie River with fly rods or scouted out the beaver ponds of LaGarde River with the ranch's naturalist. Volleyball, horseshoes, square dancing, western entertainment, and hiking were also on the agenda most days.

The Burleighs' activities go from early June through September. What impresses us is that visitors share the owners' passion for horses, fresh mountain air, and open spaces. They are moved by it all and leave better for it.

Laramie River Ranch

Mailing Address:
25777 County Road 103
Jelm, Wyoming 82063
Phone: 800–551–5731 or 970–435–5716
E-mail: Vacation@LRRanch.com
Web site: www.LRRanch.com

Group/Getaway: Families, Adventure

Accommodations: Twenty-five lodge and log cabin accommodations have private baths, daily maid service, daily fresh flowers, and your own filled cookie jar. The lodge accommodates guests with handicaps.

Points of Distinction: Laramie River is in Colorado, but has a Wyoming address. It operated as the UT Bar Guest Ranch for more than forty years, and 1890s structures still stand. Renovated in 1996, the lodge still maintains its cowboy charm with all the modern comforts.

Open: Early June through September.

Minimum Stay: Three nights.

Rates: Begin at $890 per adult for three nights; $680 for children ages six to twelve, $500 for ages four and five, and $135 for under four. Ask about 20 percent early-season discounts and 15 percent Rodeo Special discounts (seven-night requirement; July 4 to 11), and Laramie Jubilee Days (also July 4 to 11).

Frequently Asked Questions: *Does the ranch provide overnight camp-out trips?* Yes, but there is an extra charge of $65 per person per day. If you want to schedule a night under the stars, it's important to let them know ahead of your arrival date. *Does the ranch serve alcohol?* No, but you are welcome to bring your own.

Don't Forget to Bring: Sunscreen, riding boots, and a hat.

Favorite Side Trips: Laramie Jubilee Days celebration and rodeo in early July and Cheyenne Frontier Days rodeo at the end of July.

Nearest Airports: Laramie Airport, in Wyoming, is fifty minutes from the ranch and Denver International Airport, in Colorado, is a three-hour drive.

ALL-INCLUSIVE SERVICES AND ACTIVITIES

Food and Beverages: All meals (family-style dinners), snacks, picnics, nonalcoholic beverages.

Outdoor Activities: Morning and afternoon rides, cattle drives, volleyball, hiking, horseshoes, river tubing.

Water Sports: Fishing, swimming.

Facilities: General store, laundry facilities.

Other: Riding lessons, fly-fishing instruction once a week, evening square dancing once a week, gratuities, airport transfer.

Children's Services: Baby-sitting available for children three and younger.

Children's Activities: Outdoor activities, arts and crafts, riding lessons, learning the two-step, naturalist programs.

Not Included: Taxes.

Available for a Fee: White-water rafting, overnight pack trips.

THE LODGE AND SPA AT CORDILLERA

Edwards, Colorado

Situated in Vail, Colorado, The Lodge and Spa at Cordillera stands four floors high and has a width that should be measured in hectares rather than square feet. The hillfront before it is layered with mountain grasses and deep-purple wildflowers, and Cordillera is nestled so snug between the high, rocky peaks, that the views are majestic from anywhere at the resort. Thick hardwood forests are mere steps away.

This spa getaway was founded in 1985 and has grown into one of the most enticing resort properties in America, if not the world. Although its official name is The Lodge and Spa at Cordillera, a more accurate name might be The Lodge, the Spa, and Most Things Pleasurable. Cordillera's philosophy is to treat its guests' physical senses and emotional states by offering a long and fantastic list of options. Nutritionists, physiologists, and other bodywork experts help guests choose from five different styles of massage and thirteen different body treatments.

Among a few of the more esoteric that impressed us are the apricot exfoliation treatment, the oxygen facial, and the seaweed body wrap. Also at the spa are personal trainers and the high-end machines and facilities you'd expect at a good fitness center, including Trotter Cybex equipment and Concept II biking/rowing machines, as well as different types of weightlifting machines. Also available are a heated 25-meter indoor pool, an outdoor pool heated throughout the year, and indoor and outdoor Jacuzzis. Although these elements are de rigeur in upscale spas, what distinguishes The Lodge and Spa at Cordillera is its ability to create an unparalleled environment of renewal and rejuvenation.

Reminiscent of a Belgian country estate, the resort overlooks Vail Valley and the Sawatch Range and consists of a main lodge, several outlying villages, a challenging eighteen-hole golf course, and a scenic short course. Most of the fifty-six rooms and suites offer luxury accommodations such as in-room fireplaces and terraces. Cordillera also offers well-appointed four- and five-bedroom private homes for rent. The owners of Cordillera have created an award-winning eatery called Restaurant Picasso, featuring fresh local produce and estate-grown herbs.

Activities abound year-round: whitewater rafting and hiking in the warmer months; cross-country skiing, and dogsledding in winter. There are four golf courses: the Hale Irwin–designed Mountain Course, the Tom Fazio–designed Valley Course (both eighteen-hole championship courses), the Dave Peiz–designed Short Course, and the Summit Course, a Jack Nicklaus–designed eighteen-hole loop course.

Cordillera has won numerous awards for its excellence in lodging, dining, and spa work, including accolades from *Condé Nast Traveler* and *Travel and Leisure* as one of the top ten spas in the world. Spa, lodge, golf resort, or hideaway for relaxation, this resort is a good bet to please all comers.

The Lodge and Spa at Cordillera
P.O. Box 1110
Edwards, Colorado 81632
Phone: 800–877–3529 or 970–926–2200
E-mail: TheLodgeandSpa@cordillera-vail.com
Web site: www.cordillera-vail.com

Group/Getaway: Singles, Spa & Wellness, Golf

Accommodations: There are fifty-six spacious and elegantly appointed guest room accommodations and suites with terraces and panoramic views of Vail Valley, the Sawatch Range, and New York Mountain. Four- and five-bedroom private homes are available to rent.

Points of Distinction: *Travel and Leisure* magazine gave Cordillera a place on its list of "Best Hotel Spas" and *Condé Nast Traveler* gave it first place in its annual listing of the "Top Fifty Ski Resorts."

Open: Year-round.

Minimum Stay: Two nights.

Rates: From $150 per night for a Double Queen Room to $950 for the Segovia Suite; children twelve and under stay free. Packages that include breakfasts and some dinners and golf, spa treatments, or ski-lift tickets range from $400 to $2,249 for two to three nights.

Frequently Asked Questions: *What is the dining like*? Dining is a culinary experience. There are four restaurants to choose from, including the award-winning Restaurant Picasso. *What type of spa program is provided?* Designed for personal wellness, the spa offers programs that ensure that guests relax and attain a renewed enthusiasm for life. Personal trainers stress the importance of a balanced fitness program, healthy nutritional habits, and holistic healing.

Don't Forget to Bring: Sandals or thongs for spa, and, in season, golf equipment and ski equipment.

Favorite Side Trips: Vail Valley, Beaver Creek, Aspen, and Steamboat Springs.

Nearest Airports: Eagle County Airport is 25 miles from the lodge and Denver Airport is 120 miles away (two and a half hours).

ALL-INCLUSIVE SERVICES AND ACTIVITIES

Food and Beverages: Fruit and mineral water replenished daily in guest's room. Hors d'oeuvres served from 4:30 to 5:30 P.M. daily. Breakfasts and some dinners with packages.

Outdoor Activities: Horseback riding, mountain biking, tennis, golf, and hiking in warm weather; downhill and cross-country skiing, dogsledding, and snowshoeing in winter.

Water Sports: Swimming.

Facilities: Spa, sauna, steam room, indoor heated pool, indoor and outdoor hot tubs, fitness center, business center.

Other: Baby-sitting (by arrangement), shuttle to both Vail and Beaver Creek, airport transfers.

Not Included: Taxes.

Available for a Fee: Snacks, soda, liquor, hot-air ballooning, white-water rafting, fly-fishing.

OLD GLENDEVEY RANCH

Glendevey, Colorado

This dude ranch rests in Colorado at the headwaters of the Upper Laramie River. Old Glendevey sits at an altitude of 8,500 feet and is located at the base of the spectacular snowcapped peaks of the Medicine Bow Range. Old Glendevey Ranch is so close to the Wyoming border that it actually has a Wyoming address. The ranch belongs to two generations of the Peterson family, who live and work the land amid some of the most breathtaking scenery and wildlife in the West.

Glendevey Lodge was built in the early 1920s and was known as a "haven in the glen" to trappers. The lodge had been sitting idle for some years when the Petersons decided to make it a base for elk, deer, and moose hunters, as well as for anglers who were willing to take mules into the high elevations for wilderness fishing. The ranch that has evolved is warm and comfortable, but it still retains the feeling of a wilderness camp. Guest rooms are simple but attractive and are served by two college-style bathrooms—one for women and one for men. Since there are only sixteen to eighteen guests, dining is family-style. Guests are as likely to sit with wranglers and the extended Peterson family as not. To call this spread a "dude" ranch would be incorrect: It is more homey than fancy, and its beauty lies in the surrounding wilderness, rather than the simple barns and grounds.

As a gateway to the Rawah Mountains, Old Glendevey offers the best opportunities for riding, fishing, and wildlife watching and photographing that we have seen. To enhance this experience, the Petersons built a wilderness base camp at 10,000 feet in the Rawah Wilderness Area, a two-hour ride from the main lodge. It is the only camp of its kind licensed in Colorado and must be operated without the use of any motorized equipment or machinery. The staff cuts all logs for the stoves by hand; all water and food is hauled in by mule and horse.

We thought the wilderness camp might be too rough and primitive for resort seekers, but we were amazed by how wonderful the barbecued steaks tasted, not to mention homemade soups, breads, and even fresh fruit pies. And hot showers are available! The camp is so uniquely tied to this pristine, protected wilderness area that a moose or elk wandering through the camp is almost as common as a bird flying overhead. With the timberline only a few minutes above the camp on horseback, you will experience mountain meadows filled with wildflowers and majestic vistas that are absolutely breathtaking.

As on most western ranches, the heart of the experience is horseback riding. Whether you ride from the main ranch or the wilderness camp, throughout the week you can take half-day or full-day rides of any type on a Glendevey horse, chosen to match your riding ability. Riding instruction is available at no extra cost. Children are welcome, although those under eight are not permitted to ride alone.

We rate the fly-fishing program as one of the best in the West. Available at no extra charge are fishing opportunities on the Upper McIntyre Creek and the streams, beaver ponds, and high lakes of the Rawah Wilderness. In addition to these bodies of water, for an additional charge, the Petersons can guide you to 11 miles of quality private streams that have the best supply of wild brown trout in the state.

Old Glendevey Ranch

Glendevey Colorado Route
3219 County Road 190
Jelm, Wyoming 82063
Phone 800–807–1444 or 970–435–5701
E-mail: OGRanch@aol.com
Web site: www.glendevey.com

Group/Getaway: Couples, Adventure

Accommodations: There are seven guest rooms in the historic log lodge. All have been remodeled, are carpeted, and are very comfortable. There is a large bathroom facility for men and another for women. At the Rawah Wilderness base camp, where guests spend four days and three nights, the comfortable guest tents include cots with pads and woodstoves. You'll also find a large cook tent, staff tents, tack tents, a "potty" tent, and a shower tent.

Points of Distinction: Glendevey's wilderness camp is the only one of its kind in the country.

Open: Year-round.

Minimum Stay: Three nights during July and August.

Packages: Combination ranch-wilderness package is $1,600 per adult and $1,350 for children ages nine through fifteen for one week.

Rates: For ranch-only stays, summer rates (July to September) are $1,400 per adult, per week, based on double occupancy. Rates for children under ten are $900 per week. Call for special winter rates and private-stream fly-fishing rates.

Frequently Asked Question: *Are there special children's activities?* A Kids Korral program is available during the summer. Kids enjoy fishing, crafts, archery, pony rides, and learning how to swing a lariat. They also help the wranglers feed the horses.

Seasonal Activities: Ranch and wilderness camp experiences from June through August including fully guided stream, beaver pond, and high-lake fishing for brook, cutthroat, and brown trout. In winter, cross-country skiing on groomed trails, snowshoeing, snowmobiling. Nearby (one and a half hours away): downhill skiing.

Don't Forget to Bring: Warm jackets for cool evenings, rain gear, riding boots.

Favorite Side Trip: Any of the trails that take you to the top of the Rawah Mountains.

Nearest Airports: Laramie Airport, in Wyoming, one hour away, or Denver International Airport, a three-and-a-half-hour shuttle ride to the ranch.

ALL-INCLUSIVE SERVICES AND ACTIVITIES

Food and Beverages: Three home-style, hearty meals a day; nonalcoholic beverages. Bring your own wine and liquor.

Outdoor Activities: Fishing (unguided), winter sports (see "seasonal activities"), horseback riding.

Facilities: Pool table, hot tub.

Other: Maid service, service charges, taxes.

Available for a Fee: Private guided fishing, fishing gear, and flies.

RAWAH RANCH

Laramie River Valley, Colorado

Located just south of the Colorado-Wyoming border, Rawah Ranch sits on the edge of the striking Laramie River Valley. To Native Americans, *Rawah* meant "abundance," which is still true of the ranch today, especially regarding wildlife. This ranch, with sweeping views of snowcapped peaks, is 8,400 feet high in the Rockies, adjacent to a 76,000-acre national wilderness area where no motorized vehicles or tools of any kind are allowed. Beyond the wilderness area is the huge Roosevelt National Forest. With restricted hunting, moose, deer, and elk meander along the Laramie River in terrific numbers, often greeting guests emerging from their cabins to have breakfast in the main lodge.

By their nature, dude ranches become extensions of their owners, and Pete and Libby Kunz have demonstrated a remarkable ability to create a place where guests can ride and hike with limitless possibilities—through forests; along sage-covered hills; past tumbling streams, beaver dams, and ponds; and next to granite outcrops and rainbow-ribboned sandstone cliffs.

The Kunzes realize that in wilderness settings, rituals become important. Among our favorites at Rawah is that mornings begin with coffee and cocoa delivered to your room, followed by a full ranch breakfast served beside a crackling fire in one of the lodge's stone fireplaces. Perhaps it's the altitude, or perhaps the exercise in the high and clear Colorado air, but food is of paramount importance to guests, and the ranch provides it in gourmet style and with abundance.

Part of the ranch's uniqueness is its flexibility and the many activities offered. Each day, guests are asked what they would like to do and at what pace, whether it's riding on trails that range from the steep and narrow to the more level open areas with top-of-the-world views, or trout fishing, hiking, or river rafting. Family members (including children six years and older) can participate in the fun together or separately.

The premier activity at Rawah, though, is riding, and the ranch prides itself on owning horses to match all riders. The staff will match you with a horse for the length of your stay, based on your level of experience. With plenty of wranglers, there is plenty of attention, and groups are small. Rides are typically half-day, morning and afternoon, or all day, in any weather. High, low, fast, slow, short, long . . . it's your choice.

Rawah's incredible location brings wildlife to your door, and the magnificent scenery refreshes both mind and body. Whether you cast a dry fly, backpack into the wilderness, or ride across open range, it is quite awesome. Equally appealing is the ambience of this remote ranch, with its easygoing wranglers, fabulous meals, and humorous after-dinner tales of owner Pete Kunz.

Rawah Ranch

Summer address: Glendevey Colorado Route
11447 North County Road 103
Jelm, Wyoming 82063
Winter address: 1612 Adriel Circle
Fort Collins, Colorado 80524
Phone: 800–820–3152, 970–435–5715
  (summer), or
970–484–8288 (winter)
E-mail: ride@rawah.com
Web site: www.rawah.com

Group/Getaway: Families, Couples, Adventure

Accommodations: Six single or duplex cozy log cabins warmed by fireplaces, all with electricity, wood floors, and a full bath; or rooms in the log cabin lodge, all with private bath.

Points of Distinction: Unparalleled scenery and riding possibilities and hearty meals with the freshest vegetables and prime cut meats.

Open: Mid-June to late September.

Minimum Stay: One-week minimum (Sunday to Sunday) from July 2 to August 20. Three- or four-night stays are available June 11 to July 2 and August 20 to September 24.

Rates: Based on double occupancy, $1,310 to $1,925 per person for seven nights from June 29 to August 10. Single person rate is $2,400; children ages six to nine $1,550. Ask about special discounts. September is "Adults only" month. Rates are discounted at certain times of the year.

Frequently Asked Questions: *Do I need to buy cowboy boots if I don't own a pair?* The ranch has used boots you can borrow. *Do you have to be an experienced rider?* Rawah offers individual or group instruction at no extra charge. There are horses to match all levels of riders, even beginners. *What is the weather like during the summer?* Temperatures are highest in July, when they may be in the eighties during the day and then drop to the forties at night. Brief afternoon showers are not uncommon.

Don't Forget to Bring: A warm jacket for cool mornings and evenings, rain gear (just in case), riding boots, and several pairs of jeans.

Favorite Side Trip: Hiking in the Rawah Wilderness on the Roosevelt National Forest trails.

Nearest Airports: Denver International Airport is three hours from the ranch and Laramie Airport in Wyoming is a one-hour drive.

ALL-INCLUSIVE SERVICES AND ACTIVITIES

Food and Beverages: All meals (cowboy family-style), snacks, coffee, and tea.

Outdoor Activities: Horseback riding, hiking, fishing, rafting.

Indoor Activities: Ping-Pong, pool, and shuffleboard.

Facilities: Hot tub.

Entertainment: Western dancing.

Other: Fishing instruction, educational talks led by geologist, daily maid service, tips, service charge.

Children's Activities: Outdoor activities, water sports.

Not Included: Taxes.

Available for a Fee: Transfer from Laramie Airport; soda, wine, and liquor. (Feel free to bring your own, or the kind owners at Rawah will order it and have it ready for you. Their cost is your cost.)

VISTA VERDE

Steamboat Springs, Colorado

Nearly 8,000 feet high in the Colorado outback, Vista Verde is more of a hideout than a mountain getaway. Occupying a "tiny" nook, 500 acres of the state's northwest corner, it is surrounded by sky-scratching peaks and thick evergreen forests that serve to protect the mountain silence. In winter, deep snows refresh a path-filled landscape, affording skiers and snowshoers the opportunity to lay fresh tracks to the fields and slopes of untouched powder.

In summer those same fields and slopes become waist-deep grasslands dotted by wildflowers. Given the resort's remote location, one might assume the list of activities to be limited. Despite its isolation—in fact, because of it—there is much more to do here than anyone can manage in a single day. Backwoods trails and open fields are excellent for horseback excursions, mountain biking, and hiking. Lakes and streams are stocked for fly-fishing, while many prefer the excitement of white-water rafting through snow-fed rivers. Sites for rock climbing and rappelling are plentiful as well, but the best view of the valley is from a hot-air balloon, which might, at times, zoom to dizzying heights and other times sail so low as to nearly touch the treetops.

Vista Verde is a working ranch where no one goes without a horse. For thirty-five to forty guests, there are seventy horses. Everyone is invited to participate in daily chores, such as herding cattle by horseback or preparing the steers for rodeo. Kids love riding the ponies and burros, as well as feeding rabbits and collecting chicken eggs in the morning. Dining is family style, a social time embellished with loads of hearty, down-home cooking. No one counts calories in this rugged environment.

Guest cabins are isolated, not in groups, and despite the image one might have of sleeping in a mountain cabin, no one has to rough it. The cabins are carpeted, decorated with antiques, and equipped with woodstoves and full baths. Beds are warmed by thick down comforters that are snug and cozy.

We found that at Vista Verde guests are allowed to be as energetic and adventurous as they wish. Families seem to grow closer together. In fact, no activity at the resort excludes any member of the family, regardless of age. We suspect it's the horses. An adage one of the wranglers likes to recite rings true: "In the mountains, the outside of a horse is good for the inside of a person."

Vista Verde

P.O. Box 770465
Steamboat Springs, Colorado 80477
Phone: 800–526–7433 or 970–879–3858
Web site: www.vistaverde.com

Group/Getaway: Families, Adventure

Accommodations: Guests have the option of staying in quiet mountain log cabins or deluxe rooms in the lodge. Cabins offer one, two, or three bedrooms, a living room, full bath, snack bar, and woodstove.

Points of Distinction: Vista Verde is a working horse and cattle ranch covering 500 acres of forest, meadow, and pasture. The ranch limits the number of guests to forty.

Open: June through October, depending on seasonal activities, and December through March.

Minimum Stay: Three nights.

Rates: Based on double occupancy, $250 to $360 per person per night in winter; for children under twelve, deduct $150 to $260 per night. Summer rates range from $1,850 to $2,600 per person for a week; for children under twelve, $1,350 to $2,100.

Frequently Asked Question: *Where is Vista Verde located?* Vista Verde is 7,800 feet up in Rocky Mountain high country, about 25 miles north of Steamboat Springs, in northwestern Colorado.

Seasonal Activities: For more serious riders, a good time of year to visit is during cattle drives or elk-hunting season. The first drive of the year is held in early June, and the second is held in September. Elk hunting can be done from October 24 to 28, on the back of a well-trained horse. Winters at Vista Verde are as active as summer, with dogsledding, downhill and cross-country skiing, and snowmobiling. The resort even has a luge course and ice climbing outings.

Don't Forget to Bring: Appropriate warm clothing for winter, bathing suit and appropriate sturdy boots/shoes for summer. For cool summer nights, bring a few sweaters or a light jacket.

Favorite Side Trip: The rodeo and shopping in Steamboat Springs—a cowboy town.

Nearest Airports: Yampa Valley Regional Airport in Hayden, about an hour from the resort, or Denver Airport, a four-hour drive.

ALL-INCLUSIVE SERVICES AND ACTIVITIES

Food and Beverages: Three meals, snacks, juices, wine, beer, Sunday evening cocktail party; stocked refrigerator upon arrival.

Outdoor Activities: Snowshoeing, dogsledding, sleigh rides, horseback riding, mountain biking, hiking.

Water Sports: White-water rafting, fly-fishing, swimming.

Facilities: Hot tubs, exercise equipment, sauna.

Children's Services: There is a program for youngsters six to eleven and another for teens twelve to seventeen.

Children's Activities: Outdoor activities, water sports, sleep outs.

Available for a Fee: Take-out beverages, hot-air ballooning, downhill skiing, massages.

WILDERNESS TRAILS RANCH

Bayfield, Colorado

Wilderness Trails Ranch, situated in the southwest corner of Colorado, is the epitome of all the stereotypes of classic ranch settings that Hollywood has ever put on celluloid. The images pile up in our minds: rocking softly on wide front porches in the early morning light; looking down miles of river valley that give way to mesas and distant mountains; a trout breaking the silence as it jumps at a dragonfly; a horse whinnying as the sun shines on its coat in an adjacent pasture.

It might be your horse. Here, everyone is assigned a horse to ride, groom, and love during a weeklong stay. The choice is shared by you and a wonderful group of wranglers who must pass rigorous riding and teaching tests before working with guests. Every effort is made to match your riding ability (or even lack of ability), your personality, and the kind of riding you wish to do—gentle trail, wilderness rides, mountain packing—to a particular mare or gelding. Many of the horses have been raised with care by owners Gene and Jan Roberts and their children. At Wilderness, the Roberts family believes that good riding comes from good relationships between horse and rider. You'll find the bond grows very strong at this special place.

Like most of the 100 best resorts in this book, Wilderness Trails is more than just the sum of its parts. Not that there is anything wrong with its parts. The cabins are well designed and comfortable for singles, families, and even grandparents. The food is sumptuous and exceptional, and there is plenty of it, from thick fillets of fish and steak to fresh soups, vegetables, and desserts. The 72-foot heated pool and hot tub are also a pretty nice way to end a day of hiking, fishing, waterskiing, rock climbing, or white-water rafting. And lots of riding.

Gene and Jan Roberts have a unique way of making every guest feel very special. The ranch is the product of more than thirty years of constant devotion by these two very kind people who have figured out how to give visitors a magical dose of the West. The place has heart. You can sense that the Robertses and their staff love what they do and, sooner or later, it seems to touch all who stay. It is why so many guests return year after year.

Each fall the ranch invites guests who excel on horseback to a weeklong cattle roundup. For six days the "team" brings the cattle down from the high pastures to winter in Durango. Even the thought of such an opportunity in these remarkable mountains inspired us to ride as much as we could.

Wilderness Trails Ranch

23486 County Road 501
Bayfield, Colorado 81122
Phone: 800–527–2624 or 970–247–0722
E-mail: wtr@wildernesstrails.com
Web site: www.wildernesstrails.com

Group/Getaway: Families, Adventure

Accommodations: Comfortable two- and three-bedroom cabins have private baths, hair dryers, and coffeemakers.

Points of Distinction: In 1997, Wilderness Trails was chosen by both *Good Morning, America* and the PBS special *Going Places* with Al Roker as an outstanding representative of guest ranches in the United States.

Open: Late May through October.

Minimum Stay: One week (Sunday to Saturday).

Rates: Based on double occupancy, $1,525 to $1,750 per person; singles, $2,450; children, $1,050 to $1,510, depending on age.

Frequently Asked Questions: *Is horseback riding safe?* If done with guidance, riding is very safe. *Can I bring my pet?* Sorry, no, but there is a kennel about an hour away in Durango. *Will I see eagles?* Yes, eagles populate the area. *Do I have to ride?* Absolutely not. There is much to do every day on foot or by car.

Don't Forget to Bring: Clothes that will let you stay cool during the day and warm during the cool nights. Boots and cowboy hats can be rented at the ranch, but you can also bring your own.

Favorite Side Trip: The famous cliff dwelling site at Mesa Verde.

Nearest Airport: Durango, one hour away.

ALL-INCLUSIVE SERVICES AND ACTIVITIES

Food and Beverages: Breakfast, lunch, snacks, and dinner. The ranch does not have a liquor license, but guests are welcome to bring their own.

Outdoor Activities: Riding, hiking, fishing.

Water Sports: Swimming, rafting, waterskiing.

Facilities: Pool, hot tub, lake.

Entertainment: Evening hoedowns, square dances, singers, campfires, barbecues.

Children's Activities: Pony Express for ages three to five, the Saddle Tramps for ages six to ten, the Bandits for ages eleven and twelve, and the Posse for teens. The riding instruction is geared toward each child's abilities and children can learn at their own pace. In addition, the programs offer outdoor education about the woods, the area, and Native American traditions.

Available for a Fee: Special trout fishing outings to world-class Gold Medal waters of the Rio Grande in New Mexico with outstanding fishing guide Glen Roberts.

TRIPLE CREEK RANCH

Darby, Montana

At the base of Trapper Peak, the highest peak in the Bitterroot Range of the Rocky Mountains, clear streams and evergreen forests surround the log cabins of Triple Creek Ranch. This is not a dude ranch; it is a sophisticated Relais & Chateaux property in what remains of the untamed American West. Two centuries ago a young Native American woman named Sacagawea led Lewis and Clark through this region, which was her homeland. The Lewis and Clark expedition was captured in essays written by Washington Irving, and anyone reading his account will see that these mountains are the same mountains visited by Lewis and Clark.

Moose, wild turkey, deer, elk, and bighorn sheep still roam wild as they did back then. The same pristine forests cover the mountainsides. Anglers and amblers alike enjoy the same sparkling rivers. Triple Creek Ranch is situated on 450 wooded acres in this unspoiled western landscape, surrounded by a national forest in three directions. At the center of the ranch sits an impressive log and cedar lodge beside a creek. Enormous picture windows and tiers of balconies look out to the forest. Inside the soaring structure shelters a rooftop lounge, library, and intimate dining room.

In winter guests ride horseback through fresh powder, snowshoe along a ridgeline, or snowmobile the high country. Excellent skiing, both cross-country and downhill, is just thirty minutes away. At the end of a bracing outdoor day there are in-cabin massages, soothing hot tubs in the forest, and crackling fires.

Popular summer activities include hiking, biking, fly-fishing, horseback riding, cattle drives, swimming, tennis, and all-terrain vehicle rides, or simply stretching out on a hammock and listening to the ponderosa pines. White-water rafting on the nearby Salmon River is also available. Golfers practice on the ranch putting green, then play in nearby Hamilton. History buffs can trace the Lewis and Clark trail on a guided tour. Wildlife enthusiasts may catch sight of a mountain lion cub, bald eagles, or an elusive golden eagle.

In the evening guests sample hors d'oeuvres and fine wine in the rooftop lounge. By candlelight, they dine on world-class cuisine, such as herb-crusted rack of lamb coated with rosemary, Dijon mustard, and panko, served alongside black truffle potato puree and merlot-thyme *jus*, or sesame-seared salmon wrapped in wakame seaweed.

Triple Creek Ranch is a place where time slows down and one's appreciation for all things large and small grows stronger. Guests enjoy being alone with their own thoughts or forging new friendships in this pristine place.

Triple Creek Ranch
5551 West Fork Road
Darby, Montana 59829
Phone: 406–821–4600
E-mail: tcr@bitterroot.net
Web site: www.triplecreekranch.com

Group/Getaway: Couples, Adventure

Accomodations: Each of the nineteen cabins has a wood-burning fireplace, direct dial phones with separate dataports, voice mail, satellite television, VCR, and a fully stocked bar. Some cabins feature a separate living room and bedroom, steam shower, and hot tub on the deck. Fresh baked cookies are delivered daily to cabins.

Points of Distinction: Triple Creek Ranch offers luxury in the deep mountain wilderness. On the same day, guests can climb the side of a mountain, ride white-water rapids, relax in a hot tub, enjoy a massage beside a fire, and dine by candlelight.

Open: Year-round.

Minimum Stay: None.

Rates: Based on double occupancy, from $510 to $995 per couple per night. Add $200 per person for more than two people. Children over age sixteen are welcome if accompanied by an adult.

Frequently Asked Question: *How primitive are the cabins?* Cabins at Triple Creek Ranch are luxury accommodations. Each is nestled amid pines and situated around one of Triple Creek Ranch's three streams.

Seasonal Activities: Seasons are very distinct in the Bitterroot Mountains. Winter activities include snowmobiling, skiing, snowshoeing, winter horseback riding, and sleigh rides. In summer guests enjoy hiking, horseback riding, cattle drives, all-terrain vehicle rides, fly-fishing, and white-water rafting.

Don't Forget to Bring: Two weeks prior to your arrival, Triple Creek Ranch sends a suggested packing list.

Favorite Side Trip: The towns of Wisdom or Darby, where the Old West and newer West come together. There are art galleries, many small shops, wildlife viewing, and a historic national battlefield along the way.

Nearest Airport: Missoula International Airport in Montana, a 75-mile (one-hour-and-forty-five-minute) drive from the resort. Ravalli County Airport in nearby Hamilton, Montana, for small private aircraft, including jets.

ALL-INCLUSIVE SERVICES AND ACTIVITIES

Food and Beverages: All meals, beverages including alcoholic beverages, snacks.

Outdoor Activities: Tennis, hiking, horseback riding, fishing, fly-casting, snowshoeing, downhill and cross-country skiing.

Water Sports: Fishing, swimming.

Facilities: Swimming pool, hot tub, putting green, tennis court, fitness center.

Other: Fly-fishing clinic.

Not Included: Airport transfers, taxes, gratuities.

Available for a Fee: Guided fishing trips, scenic floats, cattle drives, snowmobile/all-terrain vehicle excursions, white-water rafting, flight seeing, massages.

THE LOST CREEK RANCH

Moose, Wyoming

Just outside Jackson Hole, Wyoming's Grand Tetons are the awe-inspiring backdrop for the rustic and luxurious Lost Creek Ranch, once a private family retreat. Today the Halpin family welcomes between forty and fifty guests each week, who make it their own "home on the range."

At the heart of this secluded mountain resort is a grand lodge built around the original homestead, which remains much as it did when built in the 1920s, echoing the mythic American West from its vaulted ceilings and roaring fireplace to the original western artwork on the walls. The panoramic mountain views have transformed many a city slicker into a wrangler at Lost Creek. But there's more to this rugged-appearing cowboy haven than raw cowboy icons. This is a resort of very high standards with a down-home personality. Ranch staff—nearly one for every guest—mask painstaking attention to detail with an air of effortless informality.

Guests stay in private log cabins with full kitchens and fireplaces but gather at the rambling main lodge for conversation, games of poker, chess, or billiards, and gourmet meals served family-style. Large portions of beautifully prepared entrees are followed by delicacies such as homemade huckleberry ice cream.

In the early evening, entertainment is customary and optional, with an emphasis on music and musings on the romance of cowboy culture. Spit-shine those cowboy boots if you want to look good doing some late night two-stepping. At The Lost Creek Ranch, the sun has a special way of retreating behind the Tetons that lingers in the mind long after you have left the resort.

Lost Creek Ranch offers a large array of outdoor activities, from swimming and tennis to scenic float trips on the Snake River and mountain hikes in Grand Teton and the breathtaking Yellowstone National Park. The on-site spa offers a full range of treatments and therapies tailored to each guest's needs and preferences, including massage and treatments, mineral baths, aerobics, and workouts with personal trainers. While the choices are diverse, horseback riding remains the main event at Lost Creek Ranch. Guests are paired each Monday morning with just the right horse, a matchmaking that often brings tearful good-byes at week's end.

Lost Creek Ranch has managed to mix many opposing elements—ruggedness, wilderness, spa treatments, gourmet desserts, hard riding, and soft beds. If it seems overdone, don't be fooled. The Lost Creek Ranch has managed to tame some part of the Wild West, while leaving the best parts accessible, giving the all-inclusive experience a unique dimension.

The Lost Creek Ranch

P.O. Box 95KRW
Moose, Wyoming 83012-0095
Phone: 307–733–3435
E-mail: ranch@lostcreek.com
Web site: www.ranchweb.com

Group/Getaway: Families, Adventure

Accommodations: There are ten log cabins with cowboy-inspired decor. Living Room Cabins, which can accommodate up to eight people, include two bedrooms, two baths, and a living room with a fireplace. One-half Duplex Cabins have one bedroom and a bath.

Points of Distinction: What makes Lost Creek Ranch stand out is its stellar location in one of the most pristine wilderness areas of the continental United States; yet it is only a short drive to two world-class golf courses. Its cuisine and service rate four stars by Mobil.

Open: May 28 through October 15.

Minimum Stay: Seven nights (Sunday to Sunday) in summer, three nights in fall.

Rates: Begin at $5,560 for two people staying in a one-bedroom for seven nights, and $13,050 for four people staying in a two-bedroom; additional person, $860. Three-night spa rates begin at $900 to $1,050 for two people, double occupancy.

Frequently Asked Questions: *Do you offer specific spa all-inclusive packages?* The spa offers three- to seven-day all-inclusive packages in the fall that include meals, lodging, unlimited use of the spa facilities, three treatments or training sessions per day, use of the weight room, yoga, stretch-and-tone classes, and personal training. *Do you provide baby-sitting services?* Baby-sitting for children up to five years of age is provided from 7:00 until 8:30 P.M. during the adult-only dinner.

Don't Forget to Bring: Casual attire that can accommodate a temperature drop of forty degrees from day to night; cameras; film; and fishing equipment. Most fishing guides include bait in their fees and provide for the purchase of flies or lures.

Favorite Side Trip: Jackson Hole for sightseeing and shopping.

Nearest Airport: Jackson Hole Airport, twenty minutes from the resort.

ALL-INCLUSIVE SERVICES AND ACTIVITIES

Food and Beverages: All meals, snacks, nonalcoholic beverages.

Outdoor Activities: Tennis, horseback riding, hiking in Grand Teton National Park.

Water Sports: Swimming.

Facilities: Tennis court, heated swimming pool, hot tub.

Other: Float trip on Snake River, riding instruction, ticket to Jackson Hole Rodeo in season, Yellowstone National Park van tour, gratuities.

Entertainment: Nightly.

Children's Services: Group youth activities for children ages six to thirteen are available from 4:00 to 8:30 P.M. on Monday, Tuesday, Thursday, and Friday during the summer.

Children's Activities: Outdoor activities, arts and crafts, cookouts.

Not Included: Taxes.

Available for a Fee: Fishing trips, whitewater rafting trips, wine or beer purchased in the dining room, baby-sitting, skeet range, a la carte spa facilities and services, faxes and photocopies.

MIRAVAL LIFE IN BALANCE SPA AND RESORT

Catalina, Arizona

Situated amid the Santa Catalina Mountains just north of Tucson, Miraval Life in Balance Spa and Resort extends over more than 135 acres of secluded desert. The facility is impressive: three swimming pools, horseback riding stables, two full-service restaurants, elaborate spa facilities, and unique outdoor adventure areas.

But a physical description falls short. Think about floating at night past a cascading waterfall in the Arizona desert with the secluded and serene Santa Catalina Mountains hovering on the horizon. You can do this in one of Miraval's swimming pools. As the sky fills with a trillion stars, saunter down an acupressure stonewalk into a whirlpool, then finish off the night with a hot stone massage, fresh fruit, and relaxation music. So it goes at Miraval, considered by many to be the best spa in the Southwest.

Miraval favors labels for its programs that are reminiscent of 1970s-vintage psychotherapy (thinking in the present rather than worrying about tomorrow). Activities are grouped in clusters, such as Body Mindfulness, Creative Expression, and Meditation and Mindfulness. Although they sound a little clichéd, we have to admit that they work.

Miraval's approach to balancing mind, body, and spirit is certainly all-inclusive in every way, from price to philosophy. At this casita-style resort spa, guests are encouraged to work with Miraval specialists to design their own fitness and recreational programs while learning effective techniques for balancing life's demands. Among the choices are stress management, nutrition, and self-discovery courses, integrated with recreational and spa activities.

Courses range from t'ai chi, yoga, and meditation to the Equine Experience, which involves grooming, leading, and interacting with horses as a way to understand unspoken messages and body language, a lesson that can be applied to human interactions. The Challenge Course is designed to help team-building and problem-solving skills. Guests can rock climb or stand atop a 25-foot pole in the Quantum Leap activity, or spend the afternoon playing outside-the-lines tennis. For meditative moments clients can have a private interlude with nature in the Zen rock garden, or they can hike or mountain bike the high desert trails.

Anyone who is spa-bound knows that good gastronomy is essential. At Miraval it's called Conscious Cuisine (of course) and includes California-sounding delicacies such as toasted barley-whipped potatoes with braised turnip greens and pan-seared pheasant breast. Alcohol isn't free but can be purchased for those too tired to face any more fears or challenge courses by suppertime. On the other hand, for purists, even the drinking water at Miraval is special—naturally pure, drawn from a subterranean aquifer. And so it goes at Miraval: In spite of its trendy, trademark titles, everything is done precisely and well.

Miraval Life in Balance Spa and Resort

5000 East Via Estancia Miraval
Catalina, Arizona 85739
Phone: 800–232–3969 or 520–825–4000
E-mail: reservations@miravalresort.com
Web site: www.miravalresort.com

Group/Getaway: Singles, Spa & Wellness

Accommodations: There are five casita-style villages surrounding a courtyard. Standard deluxe rooms come with a king- or queen-size bed or two double beds; Catalina Suite offers a larger bath with a king-size or two double beds; and the Miraval Suite has a king-size bed, sitting room, and a fireplace.

Points of Distinction: As their minds and spirits integrate, Miraval's guests are expected to rediscover the natural pace and rhythms of their lives, assisted by the rugged tranquillity of the desert.

Open: Year-round.

Minimum Stay: None; however, three nights are recommended.

Packages: Miraval Ultimate Package.

Rates: For Miraval Ultimate Package, rates per person, per day range from $365 to $945 for double occupancy and $400 to $1,145 for single occupancy. Ask about special summer rates.

Frequently Asked Questions: *What spa service is most recommended?* Hot Stone Massage. *What class or activity is the most popular?* The Equine Experience.

Don't Forget to Bring: Sunscreen, good walking shoes, and a hat.

Favorite Side Trip: Biosphere II, just 15 miles away.

Nearest Airports: Tucson International Airport, forty-five minutes away; Phoenix, an hour and a half away.

ALL-INCLUSIVE SERVICES AND ACTIVITIES

(The following are included in Miraval's Ultimate Package.)

Food and Beverages: Three gourmet meals daily and all nonalcoholic beverages.

Outdoor Activities: Horseback riding, volleyball, croquet, hiking, mountain biking, rock climbing. Nearby: A round of golf at the Golf Club at Vistoso (an eighteen-hole, par seventy-two course designed by Tom Weiskopf).

Water Sports: Swimming.

Facilities: Three swimming pools open twenty-four hours, including a trilevel pool with waterfalls; acupressure stonewalk; whirlpool; saunas; fitness center with state-of-the-art equipment, including Cybex machines, treadmills, LifeCycles, StairMasters, and free weights; washer and dryer facilities.

Other: One spa service at the Personal Services Center, where twenty-eight rooms are devoted to hot stone massage, body wraps, hydrotherapy, facials, meditation, stress relief, and more. Airport transfers, taxes, and gratuities.

Available for a Fee: Alcoholic beverages; additional spa and salon services; phone and fax; use of Miraval's Catalina Center, a state-of-the-art facility for business meetings.

RANCHO DE LOS CABALLEROS

Wickenburg, Arizona

Fifty-four miles northwest of Phoenix, the land is red with high, rocky ridgelines and hillsides full of cactus. It is a land rich in history, from the cattle drives of the Spanish caballeros to the American cowboys who built their towns, worked hard to survive, and established a roughshod brand of justice still famous today. It is on this land that the Rancho de los Caballeros was built.

Rancho de los Caballeros was constructed in 1948 in an Old West style that has changed little since. Thirty-four of its original forty guest rooms are still in use, and the pool built that first year still cools ranch visitors as it did so long ago. Hard-booted heels step hollow against stone patios where cushioned wooden chairs allow for the viewing of brilliant sunsets of red, orange, and pink. Lodges are of sturdy construction with solid brick walls and thick wooden beams. At night patios are lit by the glow of Mexican lanterns.

The day starts with a dramatic roundup of the ranch's ninety horses, an event producing a whole lot of hootin' and hollerin' while the thunderous hooves kick up a massive cloud of dust. For a better look, kids, who delight in this spectacle, climb the wooden rails of the hand-built fence.

Throughout Caballeros' 20,000 acres, hiking and riding trails wander this portion of the upper Sonoran Desert, where the sun is reputed to shine an average of 345 days out of every year. Horseback rides depart the corrals twice daily, with all-day sandwich rides and cookouts scheduled regularly. Within riding distance are mountain peaks and spectacular displays of desert flora and wildlife. The Jail Tree is nearby as well, where for half a century townfolk chained their outlaws before finally building a jail in 1909.

The ranch is owned by the same family that built the place more than fifty years ago, which explains the homey atmosphere that permeates the entire ranch. The spacious yet cozy living room of the main lodge is redolent with the scent of mesquite burning in a copper-hooded fireplace. Families are called to dinner by the ringing of a triangle dinner bell. They join together for hayrides and cookouts, and sing rodeo songs around the high flame of a bonfire. Home-cooked meals are prepared with fresh local ingredients, and pies, cookies, and pastries are served for dessert.

The Sonoran Desert is a sprawling museum of American history. The trails are short between Rancho de los Caballeros and dozens of ghost towns and old mines. The red mountains and rugged terrain remind visitors of the days when residents were native peoples who felt a spiritual connection with the land rather than a pride of ownership. Families who wish to experience this historic piece of America can do no better than a stay at this special resort.

Rancho de los Caballeros

1551 South Vulture Mine Road
Wickenburg, Arizona 85390
Phone: 800–684–5030 or 520–684–5484
E-mail: home@sunc.com
Web site: www.sunc.com

Group/Getaway: Families, Adventure

Accommodations: Guest rooms and suites reflect the region's Spanish and Native American cultures. Interior furnishings and artwork are brought in from Mexico and from the Art Colony of Santa Fe. Most rooms have complete kitchenettes, fireplaces, walk-in closets, and private patios and baths.

Points of Distinction: Not a bit of luxury was sacrificed while providing the ambience of the rugged West. Visitors get an honest feel of the way things used to be, yet surrender none of the comfort expected of a top-rated resort.

Open: Mid-October until mid-May.

Minimum Stay: Three nights.

Rates: Based on double occupancy, $172 to $259 per person, per night.

Frequently Asked Questions: *What if I don't know how to ride a horse?* In the ninety-horse stable, there is a horse suited for you, and great effort is made to fit a horse to your comfort level. Experienced ranch cowboys accompany most rides. *Does the temperature tend to be excessively hot?* Arizona heat is well known, but temperatures in this area tend not to reach the high levels common to desert regions farther south.

Don't Forget to Bring: Boots, jeans, and gloves for comfort while riding horseback.

Favorite Side Trips: The Desert Caballeros Western Museum has a permanent collection of Native American and nineteenth-century decorative arts, nineteenth- and twentieth-century paintings and sculpture, authentic period rooms, and a replica of a nineteenth-century street. The Del E. Webb Center for the Performing Arts adds another dimension to the stay.

Nearest Airport: Phoenix Sky Harbor International Airport, about an hour and fifteen minutes from the ranch.

ALL-INCLUSIVE SERVICES AND ACTIVITIES

Food and Beverages: All meals, afternoon tea, lemonade, iced tea.

Outdoor Activities: Two rides per day, tennis, trap and skeet shooting, Jeep tours, Native American program.

Water Sports: Swimming.

Children's Services: Caballeros Kids Program for children ages five to twelve.

Children's Activities: Outdoor activities, talent shows, games.

Not Included: Taxes and gratuities.

Available for a Fee: Children's trail rides, baby-sitters, soda, alcoholic beverages.

THE GREENHOUSE

Arlington, Texas

Attention ladies! If you're in need of some self-indulgence and luxurious pampering, have we got the answer for you. The moment you step off of the plane at Dallas–Fort Worth Airport, the experience begins. Your personal chauffeur will greet you at the airport and take you on a short hop down the interstate into Arlington, where The Greenhouse spa is located. As you enter what looks like a beautiful, suburban Texas mansion you soon realize that your only responsibility is to make your flight home on time. From all reports, it won't be easy.

At the center of The Greenhouse is a large swimming pool enclosed in a striking, white-latticed atrium. Surrounding the atrium are two floors of thirty-six guest rooms, one of which is yours for the week. The rooms are particularly elegant and come with such amenities as a personal maid whose responsibilities are to accommodate every whim—from doing your laundry to scrubbing your Nikes. Service at The Greenhouse is a prime concern, and nothing is left to chance. Consultants—professionals of health and beauty, including a resident nurse, nutritionist, and exercise physiologist—create individual programs to fit all needs.

With its heightened service, The Greenhouse differs from most spas and resorts, but all of this attention is geared toward world-class activity. Each day is carefully planned to meet a guest's needs. A typical day begins with breakfast in bed precisely at 7:00 A.M. and moves on a scheduled beat through an evening program that commences at 8:00 P.M. In between are a morning power walk, stretch classes, yoga, and countless ways to exercise on mats and in water. Along the way is a potassium broth break at 9:45 A.M., followed by body therapies and salon treatments. The resort's instructors are among the best in the business, and they use facilities that are state-of-the-art.

Peppered throughout a stay at The Greenhouse are special events, including informative lectures, fashion shows, cooking classes, and discussions on contemporary issues of concern to today's woman. All events are presented by experts who have achieved excellence in their particular fields.

The Greenhouse has become one of the world's finest resorts for women who wish to enrich their minds and bodies. It is a full week of purification through exercise, fine and healthy cuisine, thought-provoking events, and interaction with others who are there for the same reasons.

The Greenhouse
P.O. Box 1144
Arlington, Texas 76004
Phone: 817–640–4000
Web site: www.thegreenhousespa.net

Group/Getaway: Women only, Singles, Spa & Wellness

Accommodations: Each luxurious room is tastefully decorated and includes a queen-size bed and hand-embroidered linens.

Points of Distinction: The spa is filled with experts: A resident physiologist evaluates all fitness regimens; expert beauticians and color technicians are available to cater to all hair and skin needs; massage therapists provide the ultimate in stress relief; and a helpful staff will give you personalized care with a soothing smile.

Open: Year-round.

Minimum Stay: Seven nights (Sunday to Sunday) or a four-day program (Wednesday through Sunday).

Rates: Begin at $5,775 per person for seven nights.

Frequently Asked Questions: *Who is the resort best suited for?* The spa is reserved exclusively for women who seek a self-indulgent, pampered stay in the serenity of a beautiful estate. *Are there any outdoor activities?* Yes, though this is the kind of vacation that takes place primarily indoors. *How should I dress?* The Greenhouse provides an atmosphere suitable for casual elegance.

Don't Forget to Bring: Rather, don't forget to leave behind the travails of everyday life. Prepare to indulge in the luxurious personalized pampering The Greenhouse can offer. Bring only casual clothing.

Favorite Side Trip: Thursday shopping excursions in Dallas.

Nearest Airport: Dallas–Fort Worth, a ten-minute drive from the resort.

ALL-INCLUSIVE SERVICES AND ACTIVITIES

Food and Beverages: All meals, breakfast in bed, room service, nonalcoholic beverages, afternoon tea, snacks, hors d'oeuvres, dinner by candlelight.

Water Sports: Swimming, water fitness.

Facilities: Indoor Olympic-size pool for all water classes, outdoor pool.

Other: Body ballet, yogarobics, t'ai chi, Pilates, body sculpting, meditation class, yoga therapy, creative dance class, aromatherapy, cellulite treatment, reflexology, acupuncture, four-layer facial, glycologic acid treatment.

Available for a Fee: Services of expert beauticians and color technicians, many specialized spa and beauty treatments.

YES BAY LODGE

Ketchikan, Alaska

Yes Bay Lodge is the best in its class for sportfishing and wilderness adventures. Located 50 air miles north of Ketchikan, the lodge is accessible only by floatplane or boat. We liked the cozy atmosphere created by the twenty-four-guest limit. Two guests and a guide can comfortably troll for salmon or jig for halibut aboard one of the twelve 20-foot Olympic convertible soft-top boats. All boats are equipped with Furuno graphs as well as downriggers. The lodge also provides graphite rods with Penn reels for both salmon and bottom fishing.

At Yes Bay weather can change quickly, but almost nothing fazes its extraordinarily savvy staff, who are always prepared with foul-weather gear, peanut-butter sandwiches, infinite fishing knowledge, and just about anything else you might need. The lodge is run by a staff of thirty, which gives each guest individual attention. All guides are Coast Guard–licensed and are trained in CPR and first aid.

Unlike most lodges and resorts in the state, Yes Bay Lodge offers a choice of freshwater and saltwater fishing on the bay or in the many lakes, streams, and rivers within a short distance of the resort. As a guest, you prepare your own itinerary, choosing either venue during your stay. Although fly-in fishing—not to be confused with fly-fishing—is not part of the package, it is available upon request. Steelhead and Dolly Varden trout await spin-casting and fly-fishing enthusiasts; the salmon fishing is world class.

Yes Bay is a nature paradise where sea otters, porpoise, and killer and gray whales inhabit the clear, frigid waters while bald eagles fly overhead. Brown and black bear and Sitka black-tail deer are commonly seen by hikers walking through the muskegs (bogs). We came across many as we discovered waterfalls and hot springs, then enjoyed the solitude of kayaking along the moody inlets.

Southern Alaska is inextricably bound to weather that changes as fast as mercury runs off glass. Fog and rain are divided by bursts of sun, and temperatures grow cool at night but are comfortable by day. Most days we fished and hiked through calms, soft rains, and breathtaking sunsets, glad to come home to large Alaskan feasts of local salmon, halibut, Dungeness crab, and shrimp.

Yes Bay Lodge specializes in great fishing, good service, and understated but excellent accommodations, mainly thanks to the Hack family, who have reigned over the lodge since they bought it in 1977. With thirty well-trained staff members attending to the needs of just twenty-four guests, it's no wonder that this is one of Alaska's finest fishing and resort experiences.

Yes Bay Lodge

P.O. Box 8660
Ketchikan, Alaska 99901
Phone: 800–999–0784 or 907–225–7906
E-mail: info@yesbay.com
Web site: www.yesbay.com

Group/Getaway: Singles, Adventure

Accommodations: Double rooms with two twin beds or one queen and a private bath accommodate twenty-four guests.

Points of Distinction: Yes Bay guests can design their own daily itineraries with the help of their experienced guides.

Open: June 1 through September.

Minimum Stay: Four nights.

Rates: Based on double occupancy, four nights are $2,740 per person, five nights $3,320, and six nights $3,900. Additional nights are $580.

Frequently Asked Questions: *What is the weather like during the season?* Guests can expect temperatures to range between mid-fifties to about eighty degrees. During May through June temperatures average about sixty degrees, while in July and August they average sixty-five degrees. *What type of fishing does Yes Bay offer?* Yes Bay Lodge offers saltwater fishing for salmon, halibut, and rock-fish; freshwater fishing for trout, salmon (July, August, and September), and steelhead (May and June). *Are children allowed?* Yes Bay accepts children eight years and older.

Don't Forget to Bring: Warm clothing that you can layer; warm (and waterproof) jacket and gloves; fly rod, tippets, and line; and insect repellent.

Favorite Side Trips: A tour on the floatplane through the Misty Fjords National Monument to view sheer cliff walls, rugged mountain terrain, deep waterfalls, and possibly land on a pristine mountain lake. Boat trips can be arranged to view the hot springs located near Bally Bay or the Tongass National Forest for a hike.

Nearest Airport: Ketchikan Airport, 50 miles from the resort, accessible only by boat or seaplane.

ALL-INCLUSIVE SERVICES AND ACTIVITIES

Food and Beverages: Three hearty meals a day, nonalcoholic beverages.

Outdoor Activities: Guided hiking.

Water Sports: Fully guided saltwater fishing and freshwater fishing, guided kayaking.

Facilities: Exercise and game rooms.

Other: Round-trip scenic floatplane flight between lodge and Ketchikan; use of all-weather gear, wetlock fish boxes, and fly-fishing equipment, including waders; daily maid service.

Not Included: Taxes and gratuities.

Available for a Fee: Alcoholic beverages, fishing licenses, king salmon stamp, fly-outs, trip and cancellation insurance policy, fishing flies (available in the gift shop).

CAL-A-VIE

Vista, California

For those seeking a seven-day experience entirely devoted to their personal well-being, Cal-a-Vie offers an extraordinary program. Forty miles north of San Diego, this estate of terracotta-roofed cottages is nestled on 150 secluded acres that form a valley oasis.

Cal-a-Vie's mission is to give its guests the feeling that the world has stopped turning, that within the gated walls of this intimate and luxurious retreat, nothing matters more than your relaxation and well-being. In keeping with its objectives, the resort limits its number of guests to twenty-four each week to assure that its staff knows each and every one of them by name, habits, and preferences.

Although Cal-a-Vie has been adopted by the rich and famous (actress Kathleen Turner has said in her throaty, velvety tones that Cal-a-Vie is one of the best gifts she's ever given herself), every person who spends a week here receives highly individualized and personal attention. And while the emphasis is on wellness, what thrusts this resort into the top 100 all-inclusive resorts is its dedication to meeting the every whim and care of its clients with a nineteenth-century European elegance and passion. If you think such lavishness is over the top and unnecessary, don't bother coming to Cal-a-Vie. But if you think every person deserves a week in splendor, traipsing through elegant courtyards to receive treatments that have been created to see how special they can make you feel, Cal-a-Vie deserves your interest and time.

International health experts developed Cal-a-Vie's exclusive beauty and skin care treatments. Sophisticated Asian and European beautifying techniques have been developed and modified for Cal-a-Vie, including Ayurvedic Body Glo, a skin treatment using herbs and clays from India to cleanse and prepare skin for thalassotherapy, a seawater and seaweed wrap that helps rebalance body chemistry, stimulate body functions, and assist in the elimination of toxins within the skin system; and hydrotherapy, a therapeutic underwater massage in multijet tubs that uses various seaweed and essential oils. These treatments are administered to help guests regain their natural balance. Each guest's fitness program is designed to achieve personal goals of weight control, stress reduction, relaxation, and toning. Equipment, trainers, and progressive coaching are all state-of-the-art.

Dieting at this spa is luxurious. Vegetables and herbs that help slim, balance, and revitalize are grown in Cal-a-Vie's own gardens. Personal nutritional needs are considered in all meal preparations by chefs who can make a carrot taste like cheesecake and look even better.

One of the features we admire about Cal-a-Vie is its European Plan, which includes meals, accommodations, all therapeutic treatments, and all fitness classes. This all-inclusive approach was among the first of its kind in the industry and avoids the kind of a la carte spa experience that always seems to be extra expensive.

Cal-a-Vie

29402 Spa Havens Way
Vista, California 92084
Phone: 760–945–2055 or 866–772–4283
E-mail: info@cal-a-vie.com
Web site: www.cal-a-vie.com

Group/Getaway: Singles, Spa & Wellness

Accommodations: There are twenty-four private cottages with lovely views of the valley. Each can accommodate one person or a couple. All cottages are individually decorated to achieve an atmosphere of peace and tranquility. Each has hand-carved furniture with pastel floral chintz upholstery, a private terrace, and a view of rolling, wooded hills.

Points of Distinction: Cal-a-Vie's dedicated staff, which outnumbers guests by four to one, is dedicated to assisting guests change lifelong habits and adopt a whole new outlook for their bodies and minds. This approach accounts for its being rated the top spa in the *Condé Nast Traveler* "Readers' Choice Awards."

Open: Year-round.

Minimum Stay: Three nights.

Rates: From $4,695 to $5,395 per person for seven nights, depending on plan. Petite week is $2,495 for three nights and $3,495 for four nights.

Frequently Asked Questions: *Should I bring my jewelry?* Safety deposit boxes are available, but jewelry and valuables are best left at home. A*re laundry services available?* Yes, and they are complimentary.

Don't Forget to Bring: Several sets of leotards and tights, a couple of bathing suits, gym shoes and socks, and lightweight hiking boots.

Favorite Side Trips: La Jolla for shopping, Balboa Park, and the San Diego Zoo.

Nearest Airport: San Diego International, forty-five minutes away from the resort.

ALL-INCLUSIVE SERVICES AND ACTIVITIES

Food and Beverages: All meals and non-alcoholic beverages.

Outdoor Activities: Hiking, walking, tennis.

Water Sports: Swimming.

Facilities: Walking trails throughout the hills; fitness center with state-of-the-art equipment, tennis courts on-site, golf course at adjacent private country club.

Other: Aerobics, stretching, meditation, yoga, Qi Gong, cooking class, abdominal plus (focusing on stomach muscles), facials, massage, hand and foot treatments, Ayurvedic Body Glo, thalassotherapy, hydrotherapy, aromatherapy massage, reflexology. Tips not required.

Not Included: Taxes.

Available for a Fee: Golf, private tennis instruction, additional spa treatments.

THE GOLDEN DOOR

Escondido, California

One of the first things you can do upon arriving at the Golden Door is to embark on a 5-mile hike to the top of Devil Mountain, led by an assortment of guides and staff members. This excursion takes you through rich avocado groves and a large thicket of oak trees lining a stream, then proceeds up easy slopes to the peak of Devil's Mountain, reminding all that life on Earth can be very special. Welcome to the coastal valleys of northern San Diego County, where year-round the days are rarely too warm or too cold. If you can afford this experience, it is a special journey.

The Golden Door spa was created to help its clients achieve inner peace and health by enjoying its natural surroundings while benefiting from the superlative treatments of its highly trained staff. Every week a maximum of forty guests arrive to explore the spa's 377 acres of lush gardens, groves, orchards, and hiking trails, exclusively reserved for their use. The property is graced with Japanese-style cottages, ponds, and gardens, which also enhance the sense of serenity that the resort evokes.

With many times more staff than guests, the Golden Door offers a cornucopia of activities that exceed even the most ambi-tious visitor's desire to do them all. But the variety is motivational: Advisers guide you through each day, helping to select classes, hikes, and treatments that most suit your goals. Meditation, yoga, and t'ai chi are interwoven with multiple sessions of sooth-ing treatments for body, skin, hands, and feet. The days are carefully planned, blend-ing an assortment of fitness and meditative sessions to fortify all parts of the body, mind, and spirit. But just as the surround-ings and treatments have a harmonious effect on one's psyche, the Golden Door has created a cuisine that is completely healthy and original, made from freshly picked fruits and vegetables from the estate's own gardens.

The idea behind The Golden Door is not revolutionary. But, like so many of the top resorts in the world, it is the subtle combi-nation of its activities and high standards that make a guest's visit a world-class expe-rience.

In the end, your time at The Golden Door is meant to be a purification of sorts, and it works in intangible ways that prompt the majority of its guests to return. Forty-six weeks are women only; coed and men's weeks are available several times a year.

The Golden Door

P.O. Box 463077
Escondido, California 92046-3077
Phone: 800–424–0777 or 760–744–5777
Web site: www.goldendoor.com

Group/Getaway: Singles, Spa & Wellness

Accommodations: Simple but elegant rooms in Japanese-style buildings. Each room includes a queen-size bed, private bath, and a wood deck with view of Japanese gardens.

Points of Distinction: The Golden Door has what it calls a "classical labyrinth," which is a mind/body experience that will quiet the mind and restore inner peace. The grounds at The Door are breathtaking: four hushed courtyards; waterfalls; a koi (ornamental carp) pond; jewel-encrusted entrance gate flanked by camellias, fuchsias, or other seasonal blossoms; meditative sand gardens; and hundreds of specimen trees and shrubs.

Open: Year-round, except for two weeks in December.

Minimum Stay: Seven nights (Sunday to Sunday).

Rates: Begin at $6,025 to $6,275 per person for seven nights.

Frequently Asked Question: *What will I not have to bring?* The Golden Door provides almost everything you will need, including warm-up suits, T-shirts and shorts, a bathrobe, and a Japanese yukata.

Don't Forget to Bring: You need only bring comfortable hiking shoes or boots, aerobics shoes, socks, undergarments, bathing suit, toothbrush, and toiletries.

Favorite Side Trips: The San Diego Zoo and the boardwalk at the Seaport Village.

Nearest Airport: San Diego International, forty minutes from the resort.

ALL-INCLUSIVE SERVICES AND ACTIVITIES

Food and Beverages: All meals, snacks, afternoon tea, one glass of wine served at Saturday night dinner (additional cost for all other liquor), room service for breakfast only (unless requested in advance).

Outdoor Activities: Hiking, tennis.

Water Sports: Swimming.

Facilities: Two swimming pools, therapy pool, beauty court.

Other: Fitness classes, daily massage, body scrub, herbal wraps, transportation to San Diego.

Not Included: Taxes and gratuities.

Available for a Fee: Hairstyling, private tennis lessons, additional evening massages, private yoga lessons.

HOTEL HANA-MAUI AT HANA RANCH

Hana, Maui, Hawaii

You have to work a bit to get to Hotel Hana-Maui. It lies on the southeast corner of Maui, 55 miles from the flat center of the island near the airport at Kahului. It will take you about two-and-a-half hours, even without stops, to make the drive. The road hugs the coast, twisting and turning around one headland and gulch after the other. The 55 miles traverse 600 curves and fifty-four one-lane bridges, so drivers pull aside and wait for traffic in the other direction about fifty-four times.

The Road to Hana is legendary, and it gets voted one of the most beautiful drives in the country in various polls. Some eager people drive straight through, but it's worth it to stop at the many waysides and parks along the way, where waterfalls tumble down off the flanks of Haleakala and offer a cooling shower to those who duck under them.

The reward at the end of this journey is the luxurious Hotel Hana-Maui. The moment we stepped out of the car an "auntie" wearing a muumuu greeted us by name—and slipped a cool tropical punch in our hands.

Chatting all the way, a bellman drove us to our Sea Ranch cottage in a little golf cart. The green board cottages with tin roofs are patterned after houses for sugar plantation workers. But don't be fooled by their exterior simplicity. Step inside onto the cool bleached wood floors and take in the soothing colors, real Hawaiian quilts and numerous orchids scattered around the room and spacious bathroom. Many of these units have whirlpool baths on the decks. The Sea Ranch cottages had a total renovation completed in August 2002.

Much of the property's luxury comes from the spacious grounds. Fragrant plumeria punctuates rolling lawns that overlook the intensely blue ocean. The hotel's Wellness Pool, set outside of the fitness area and spa, is a horizon pool. From water level, the blue of the pool merges with the infinite expanse of the sea. At dusk, torches are lighted around this pool. Anyone who has ever been in Hana in the evening will have the peaceful image of that torch-lit pool to carry into stressful times.

This is, however, not part of a manicured megaresort development. The hotel sits at the edge of the town of Hana. The people who work at the hotel live in town. When there's Hawaiian music and hula in the evening, the people performing may have tidied up your room during the day or helped with the coconut cake you're just polished off.

Hotel guests use Hamoa Beach, called the "most beautiful in the Pacific" by James Michener, just a short distance away. Palms back up its gorgeous crescent of sand. The hotel runs a beach shack where you'll find boogie boards and beach towels.

San Franciscan Paul Fagan bought the property in 1946 and converted it to a ranch. He also owned the San Francisco Seals baseball team, so he built a ballpark and a small hotel to accommodate the players for spring training. That was the beginning of the Hotel Hana-Maui.

Fagan no longer owns the hotel, but the ballpark is still there. It's fun to wander down and watch the local kids play or go into town and visit the old Court House, now a museum, to catch something of the flavor of days gone by.

People who visit the islands frequently have an almost holy quest to find the "real Hawaii." If you're in Hana, you're there.

Hotel Hana-Maui at Hana Ranch

P.O. Box 9
Hana, Hawaii 96713
Phone: 800–321–HANA or 808–248–8211
E-mail: res@hotelhanamaui.com
Web site: www.hotelhanamaui.com

Group/Getaway: Couples, families

Accommodations: Sixty-six units are spread over sixty-seven acres. Garden Suites overlook rolling lawns. The remaining forty-six units are Sea Ranch cottages, patterned after plantation workers' houses and scattered over a hillside with ocean views or oceanfront locations. Many of them have private whirlpool tubs on the deck.

Points of Distinction: Location in the small town of Hana, a trip back to the old Hawaii, and access to Hamoa Beach, one of the most beautiful in the Pacific.

Open: Year-round.

Minimum Stay: Five nights for the all-inclusive plan; otherwise no minimum.

Packages: Romance/honeymoon packages range from $2,412 to $3,132 for two people for four nights and include a candlelit dinner and two sixty-minute Tropical Blend Massage treatments.

Rates: The all-inclusive plan is $2,875 to $4,525 for two people for five nights. Based on double occupancy, room rates are $295 to $725 per night and $340 to $917 for the holiday season, December 20 through January 5. If you stay for five nights, the sixth night is free. Children age eighteen and under are free when staying with their parents.

Frequently Asked Question: *Do I have to drive the narrow road to Hana?* No, you can take a fifteen-minute commuter flight on Pacific Wings from Kahului International Airport or a flight from Honolulu International Airport, Maui's main air terminal, to Hana. The hotel's 1932 Packard "jitney" will meet you at the airport.

Don't Forget to Bring: Swimsuit, hat, and suntan lotion for daytime. You might want to bring a church-going outfit for Sunday services with locals at Wananalua Congregational Church or St. Mary's Catholic Church, both on the hotel grounds.

Favorite Side Trips: Oheo Gulch in Haleakala National Park and Kipahulu, where Charles Lindbergh is buried in the tiny churchyard.

Nearest Airport: Hana Airport, althou[gh] people drive from Kahului Internationa[l] [air]port, Maui's main air terminal.

ALL-INCLUSIVE SERVICES AND ACTIVITIES

Food and Beverages: Breakfast, lunch, and dinner in the main dining room or Hana Ranch Restaurant or the Paniolo Bar; chilled bottle of champagne and snack basket in cottages.

Outdoor Activities: Tennis, jogging, yoga, aqua aerobics classes.

Water Sports: Snorkeling, boogie boarding.

Facilities: Two swimming pools and whirlpool, three-hole practice golf course, tennis courts, jogging trails, croquet course, fitness center.

Entertainment: Local Hawaiian dancers Sunday and Thursday nights in the main dining room; musicians in the Paniolo Bar Sunday and Thursday nights.

Other: Activities designed to involve guests in the cultural and historical richness of "Old Hawaii," including hula and ukulele lessons, lei making, medicinal plant walk, nature walks, Historical Hana tour.

Not Included: Taxes and gratuities.

Available for a Fee: Alcoholic beverages, meals for those not on the all-inclusive plan, spa treatments and skin care, personal trainer, salon services, Jeep excursions to Oheo Gulch and Kipahulu or to Ulaino, a remote shore with large beach rocks and a spring-fed pool.

KONA VILLAGE RESORT

Kailua-Kona, Hawaii

Kona Village hugs Kahuwai Bay, an oasis in the midst of a vast lava field from Mount Hualalai's last eruption in 1801. But on the resort grounds, lush landscaping surrounds fishponds that once belonged to *ali'i,* or Hawaiian royalty. The resorts consists of 125 *hales,* or bungalows, built in the traditional architecture. Spreading over an eighty-two-acre sanctuary, the units have thatched roofs, so you might pretend it's your little grass shack in Hawaii. But step inside, and you've left modest pretension behind. The interiors, often divided into rooms or separate areas, are tastefully decorated in muted colors, silvery woods, and pillows with traditional Hawaiian kapa cloth prints. The coconut may be used as a doorstop, or, placed outside at your door, it means "do not disturb."

The setting and level of luxury are nothing short of spectacular. Kona Village Resort appeared on *Travel & Leisure* magazine's 2002 "Top 50 Romantic Getaways" list and *Condé Nast Traveler*'s 2001 Gold List. *Gourmet* magazine rated it among the top five hideaway resorts worldwide in 1998. It received the 1999 and 2000 Kahili Award for Preserving and Perpetuating Hawaiian Culture.

Given the seclusion of the *hales,* passing an entire day in a hammock is a good option. While laziness is tempting, the resort offers an exceptionally long list of things to do, especially for children. Complimentary supervised activities and tours in the "Na Keiki in Paradise" program offer parents time for themselves while providing children with a chance to experience Hawaii's unique culture and environment. Designed for kids from ages six to twelve, the program begins with activities such as hula classes, lei making, and coconut painting, as well as a full schedule of water sports and pool activities. Younger children are invited to participate when accompanied by a parent or adult guardian. Teens have their own program.

Kona Village has two oceanfront restaurants that serve Pacific Rim cuisine. The Hale Samoa offers an intimate adults-only dining experience; the Hale Moana is more informal. The resort has hosted a legendary luau on Fridays for more than twenty-six years. *Hawaii* magazine named it the "Best in the Islands."

A unique aspect of the resort is, of course, its fantastic location on Hawaii's Big Island. A short drive into the upcountry in Volcanoes National Park, Kilauea spews steam and oozes red lava from open vents. Kona Village guests may sail by catamaran to one of the most exciting snorkel and dive sites in the world. Reef formations and deep-water ecosystems combine to challenge divers, who make shark sightings on most days. These waters are also rich in world-class marlin and yellowfin tuna. Humpback whales migrate to these waters in December, and green sea turtles stay close to shore.

The ancient Hawaiians left petroglyphs among the rocks on a fifteen-acre site on the property. The resort owners have built a boardwalk over the site so it can be visited without damaging the delicate rock images.

The resort site was also the site of an old fishing village. You will find some of the lava rock house foundations still on the grounds.

Ohana is the Hawaiian word for "family," and this feeling gives another special reason to visit here. In the lobby, there are pictures of the Kona Village *ohana,* whose members are the staff. When you stay there you are also treated as family. That's the reason so many people come back year after year.

Kona Village Resort

P.O. Box 1299
Kailua-Kona, Hawaii 96745
Phone: 800–367–5290 or 808–352–5555
E-mail: kvr@aloha.net
Web site: www.konavillage.com

Group/Getaway: Families

Accommodations: There are 125 individual *hales* in nine different styles that are scattered over eighty-two acres. Guests can choose between garden, lagoon, or ocean views, and between bedding options. All rooms include private lanai, mini refrigerator (stocked with complimentary beverages and mixers), coffeemaker, and safe. Private whirlpool spas are available in most oceanfront *hales*.

Points of Distinction: Fridays at Kona Village are full of Hawaiian traditions for families to share. On Friday nights there is an authentic Polynesian luau and a show.

Open: Year-round, except for one week in early December.

Minimum Stay: None, except seven nights for dates from December 19 to January 3.

Rates: Based on double occupancy for two adults, rates begin at $505 per night for Standard Rooms and $895 for a Royal Ocean Front Suite; additional adult over age thirteen, $193 per night. For single occupancy, deduct $113. Children ages six to twelve, $143; ages three to five, $38; two and under stay free.

Frequently Asked Question: *Should I rent a car?* Most guests prefer to relax the first few days, then rent. The concierge can assist with transportation needs.

Don't Forget to Bring: Sandals or thongs are popular with the locals and good for casual walking around the resort. Dinner requires collared shirts and slacks for men and slacks or dresses for women.

Favorite Side Trips: Volcanoes National Park for views of the crater and the active vents on the side of Kilauea, an active shield volcano. Puuhonua o Honaunau National Historic Park, where ancient Hawaiians were given refuge when they had broken *kapu* (taboo).

Nearest Airport: Kona International Airport, a fifteen-minute drive from the resort.

ALL-INCLUSIVE SERVICES AND ACTIVITIES

Food and Beverages: Three meals a day, welcome rum punch upon check-in, daily in-room coffee, afternoon tea.

Outdoor Activities: Tennis, shuffleboard, volleyball, croquet, jogging.

Water Sports: Kayaking, sailing, snorkeling, swimming.

Facilities: Fitness center, tennis courts, two swimming pools, whirlpool spas.

Other: Historical and petroglyph tours, washer (and laundry soap) and dryer use, welcome lei greeting, weekly cocktail party, glass-bottom boat tours, special guest lecturers, demonstrations (cooking, arts and crafts, cultural).

Children's Services: Na Keiki in Paradise program for children ages six to twelve (day and evening; times vary). Note: No children are allowed May 1 through 31 or September 4 through 30.

Children's Activities: Sports, arts and crafts, cultural activities.

Not Included: Taxes and gratuities, airport transfers.

Available for a Fee: Wine and liquor; juice and soda; deep-sea fishing; catamaran snorkel cruises; scuba lessons; dive excursions; horseback riding; whale watching (December through April); helicopter tours; massage and spa treatments; baby-sitting.

MOUNTAIN TREK

Ainsworth Hot Springs, British Columbia

For vacationers who refuse to be sedentary, Mountain Trek offers a different choice. Located in the British Columbian Rockies, halfway between Vancouver and Calgary and directly north of Spokane, Washington, is the world's only self-proclaimed hiking resort.

Mountain Trek was started in 1988 with the notion that the body, mind, and spirit can be greatly affected in a week if guests spend time in an incredibly beautiful and remote setting hiking and eating carefully planned menus. The founders wanted to keep crowds to a minimum and limit the number of guests, who are accommodated in twelve rooms in a lodge on a fantastic escarpment that faces a deep blue lake and high mountain peaks.

Just a five-minute walk from naturally heated hot springs, the lodge provides each guest with a private bath and use of all spa and fitness center facilities. An expert staff offers fine cuisine. In this pristine environment, each outdoor adventure is meant to expand into a deeply enriching experience.

The first thing guests learn at Mountain Trek is that hiking is a multidimensional endeavor that covers fitness levels from gentle forest hikes to alpine hikes. Indeed, one of the most impressive aspects of the resort is the number of programs it offers. Among the options are a gentle hiking/walking program to "kick-start" a fitness program on relatively easy trails. More ambitious hikers can mountain climb on steeper trails with experienced guides. Expert hikers walk six to eight hours per day, covering 13 miles or more with elevation gains of 4,000 feet. Their program includes off-trail hiking, ridge walking, and scrambling.

We were also impressed with Mountain Trek's Hiking, Biking, and Kayaking Adventure. This program includes selected day hikes, day cycle rides, and day kayaking trips. All instruction necessary for first-time kayakers is included.

Two important elements of Mountain Trek's offerings are its FitPlan Weight Loss Spa program and its Fasting and Health Vacations. These are based on the belief that an annual fast is a good addition to your lifelong health plan. These vacations involve supervised water and juice fasting, body cleansing, and natural hygiene programs with a naturopathic physician. The focus of this approach is prevention and education, but it has proven to be an excellent means of detoxification and weight loss.

If fasting sounds a bit radical for climbers who find they can eat most of a grocery store when at altitude, don't rule out Mountain Trek. Many visitors do not choose to fast; however, as the staff explains, many religious groups fast to attain spiritual awareness, and Native tribes, from the Iroquois in the Northeast to the Hopi in the Southwest, fasted to the point of hallucination, hoping to call forth the spirits that govern the land, sky, and water. Although Mountain Trek is not affiliated with a specific religion or philosophical doctrine, the resort's philosophy is that the benefits of fasting are worth pursuing in this very supportive environment. We noticed that when we fasted and exercised, our sense of time changed, as did our sensibilities. Watching people go through this experience, it is clear that Mountain Trek is a life-enriching experience. No one leaves this place the same way he or she came.

Mountain Trek

P.O. Box 1352
Ainsworth Hot Springs, British Columbia V0G
    1A0 Canada
Phone: 800–661–5161 or 250–229–5636
E-mail: webinquiry@hiking.com
Web site: www.hiking.com

Group/Getaway: Singles, Sports & Fitness

Accommodations: The mountain lodge has twelve guest rooms with private baths and a lounge with a fireplace.

Points of Distinction: Mountain Trek specializes in vacations for the mind, body, and spirit, under the supervision of a naturopathic physician.

Open: Late December through mid-November.

Minimum Stay: Three nights.

Packages: All packages include yoga, stretch classes, therapeutic massages, and private accommodations. Most programs offer a three-, four-, or seven-night plan. Packages include Mountain Hiking for beginners to experienced hikers (rates from $1,115 for a three-night package to $2,375 for seven nights), Gentle Hiking and Walking ($1,055 to $2,235), and the Challenge Boot Camp Week, which includes difficult trails for expert-level hikers (from $2,585), plus Hiking, Biking, and Kayaking Adventures ($1,725 to $2,710). The resort also offers Yoga Retreat, FitPlan Weight Loss Spa Retreat, Snowshoe, Supervised Fasting, and Weight Loss programs.

Rates: Based on single occupancy, three-night stays range from $675 to $790 and seven-night stays range from $1,465 to $2,585 for the hiking packages.

Frequently Asked Questions: *Are the fasting programs safe?* Fasting and Health Vacations are run by a trained and government-licensed naturopathic physician. Weekly tests are given to ensure a safe and healthy experience for all participants. *Are guides provided for hikers?* The resort employs three guides each week to hike with each group of fourteen guests.

Seasonal Activities: Fasting programs are March and April. Hiking and related activities take place May through October. Snowshoe-ing during Christmas through New Year's week.

Don't Forget to Bring: Swim suit, appropriate athletic footwear, and active wear.

Favorite Side Trips: Buchanan Lookout, at an elevation of 12,000 feet, offers panoramic views of the region's mountains. The late planner and architect David Brown fulfilled his vision of finding a practical use for empty embalming fluid bottles by building the Glass House out of 500,000 of them. Sandon Historical Site and Museum, a once bustling silver mining city, now offers insight into the past with photographs, artifacts, and ghost-town buildings.

Nearest Airport: Castlegar Airport in Castlegar, one hour and fifteen minutes from the resort.

ALL-INCLUSIVE SERVICES AND ACTIVITIES

Food and Beverages: All meals and snacks, nonalcoholic beverages, afternoon tea. Wine and liquor are prohibited.

Outdoor Activities: Hiking, biking, kayaking.

Water Sports: Kayaking, canoeing, lake swimming.

Facilities: Outdoor Jacuzzi, natural mineral hot spring pool, sauna, weight room, thermal baths.

Other: Personal laundry service; use of sweatshirts, T-shirts, robes, backpacks, water bottles; transfers from airport.

Not Included: Taxes and gratuities.

Available for a Fee: Spa treatments such as shiatsu and reflexology, private one-hour consultation with naturopathic physician.

RANCHO LA PUERTA

Tecate, Baja California, Mexico

More than sixty years ago, a young couple named Edmond and Deborah Szekely opened a retreat in Baja California. Visitors to this summer camp paid $17.50 a week to study the finer principles that lead to a sound, simple, healthy way of life. They called their camp Rancho La Puerta. Today this breathtaking ranch hosts guests from all over the world. They come to participate in the ranch's "Inner Journey" program designed to treat the mind, body, and spirit with trademark techniques that evolved from the Szekelys' early experiments. Many are now commonplace in spas all over the world. Body wraps, for example, date back to 1940, when Edmond Szekely used them at Rancho La Puerta as a way to relieve the aches and muscle spasms that afflicted guests unaccustomed to any form of exercise. He also began to experiment with herbal wraps, observing that they eased the mind into a very deep form of relaxation.

The Szekelys also experimented with the effects of massage on toning muscles and releasing endorphins. These practices eventually evolved into the classic massage with aromatic oils and hot stone massage, which employs smooth, glassy stones heated in water and essential oils. The massage therapists use the stones as an extension of their hands, allowing them to work at deeper levels with the added benefit of lingering heat. Another huge favorite with a delectable result comes from the Szekelys—brisk massage with a salt, oil, honey, almond, and oatmeal paste applied to the entire body (but not the face), to thoroughly cleanse the pores.

As you might expect today, all of these therapies are supplemented by a long and strong list of activities, including yoga, mountain hiking, Pilates, labyrinth, men's aerobic circuit training, morning stretch, self-defense, sculpt and strengthen, African dance workout, t'ai chi, and dumbbell training. Guests follow well-structured, customized programs to help them establish and achieve their health goals.

Located on more than 3,000 acres of pristine, rolling countryside just 40 miles south of San Diego, the ranch is graced with many gardens and threaded with hiking trails. With only 150 guests, the staff of 250 is adept at making your stay pleasurable and informative. Guests stay in smartly designed Spanish Colonial–style cottages with fireplaces and gardens.

Rancho food is known for its quality and its quantity. The plentiful high-fiber, low-fat cuisine is heavy on sprouts, beans, tubers, leaves, fruits, cheese, yogurt, and tofu, with a South of the Border influence. The recipes have become so popular that chef Bill Wavrin's *Rancho La Puerta Cookbook* can now be found in bookstores or ordered from the resort's Web site.

Rancho La Puerta

P.O. Box 463057
Escondido, California 92046-3507
Phone 800–443–7565 or 760–744–4222
E-mail: reservations@rancholapuerta.com
Web site: www.rancholapuerta.com

Group/Getaway: Singles, Spa & Wellness

Accommodations: Rancheras and haciendas are cottages decorated with Mexican arts and crafts. They have private patios and gardens. All of the thirty-three rancheras have a studio bedroom with bath; nine are set aside for the exclusive use of single women. Haciendas have a bedroom with sitting area, kitchenette, and bath. Villa Suites and Villa Studios are cottages in a parklike setting adjacent to a swimming pool and whirlpool hot tub. Studios have living room, kitchenette, bedroom in alcove, and bath; suites have a living room, kitchen and dining area, two bedrooms, and two baths. No two are alike.

Point of Distinction: The ranch has more than six acres of gardens, which provide much of the organic produce.

Open: Year-round.

Minimum Stay: Seven days (Saturday to Saturday).

Rates: From $1,970 to $3,360 per person for seven nights, double occupancy.

Frequently Asked Question: *How old are the facilities at Rancho La Puerta?* The facilities were built in 1939. Prior to the resort's fiftieth anniversary, Rancho La Puerta spent more than $10 million over a ten-year period updating and rebuilding the facility.

Don't Forget to Bring: A comfortable pair of hiking shoes.

Favorite Side Trip: The Ranch is located adjacent to Mount Kuchumaa, a place of spiritual importance for local Native Americans.

Nearest Airport: San Diego International Airport, an hour and a half drive from the resort.

ALL-INCLUSIVE SERVICES AND ACTIVITIES

Food and Beverages: All meals, nonalcoholic beverages, and wine and beer served at Friday dinner.

Outdoor Activities: Hiking, tennis, volleyball.

Water Sports: Swimming, aqua aerobics.

Facilities: Hot tubs, saunas, weight room.

Other: Yoga, aerobics, circuit training, educational classes (on topics such as women's health and menopause), complimentary airport transfers on Saturdays, taxes.

Not Included: Gratuities.

Available for a Fee: Shopping at the Mercardo, massages, herbal wraps, scalp treatments, hairstyling, art studio. Alcoholic beverages are not available, but you can bring your own to drink in the privacy of your room.

OCCIDENTAL ALLEGRO COZUMEL

Cozumel, Mexico

Occidental Allegro Cozumel is about families and about water. Whether they like to play above it, beneath it, or at its edge, water sports enthusiasts of all ages seek Occidental Allegro Cozumel for its beaches, its boating, and its proximity to some of the world's best reefs.

Occidental Allegro Cozumel is a gathering of thatched-roof huts set flush against Isla Cozumel's San Francisco Beach. The resort faces southward toward an 8-mile-long community of coral known as the Palancar Reef. The Palancar sits a five-minute drift away from the resort and is world-renowned for the plant and animal species it holds, for its vibrancy of color, and for its 150-foot visibility. Occidental Allegro Cozumel has daily dives to the Palancar and a litany of other water activities organized through the resort's beachfront Water Sports Center.

Families are Occidental Allegro's primary customers. For this reason, the resort makes a strong effort to design its activities to include the entire family—or to entertain the kids while the adults have their own playtime. On-site there is a kid-oriented game room and a colorful beach-sand playground with slides, swings, and jungle gyms. The Little Village Club conducts a Children's Activity Program under adult supervision from 9:00 A.M. to 9:00 P.M.

For families who have spent the day together, baby-sitting by the resort's corps of super sitters, for a fee, allows parents to enjoy the resort's restaurants and disco. At night, the disco often fills to capacity, but not for hard partying as much as a place to kick back and talk about the day's dive or to rest for the next day's dive. In Cozumel, and particularly at Occidental Allegro, there is much friendliness between locals and tourists without the competition that sometimes plagues other tourist destinations. This laid-back approach to life is full of good cheer that does much to help families relax and enjoy each other. Occidental Allegro Cozumel has put together a total package that works as well for adults as children, separately and together. This combination is a rarity in the all-inclusive world. Few do it so well.

Occidental Allegro Cozumel

Kilometro 16.5
Carretera Sur Cozumel, El Cedral
San Francisco Palancar
Cozumel, Quintana Roo, Mexico 77666
Phone: 800–858–2258 or
   011–52–987–872–9770
Web site: www.occidentalhotels.com

Group/Getaway: Families

Accommodations: Rooms and suites have two double or one king-size bed and can accommodate two adults and two children. All rooms and suites include air-conditioning, ceiling fan, telephones, private balcony or terrace, shower and full bath, and satellite television.

Points of Distinction: Occidental Allegro Cozumel is distinguished by world-class diving and snorkeling and a family ambience that keeps all ages smiling.

Open: Year-round.

Minimum Stay: None.

Rates: Based on double occupancy, Standard Rooms are $131 to $177 per person, per day for adults; $54 per child two to twelve years old; children under two stay free.

Frequently Asked Question: *Is there anything to do inland on the island?* Not much. Cozumel is strictly a water paradise. However, the ferry ride to the Yucatan Peninsula is only twenty minutes long. Once there, guests can tour many well-preserved Mayan ruins.

Don't Forget to Bring: Waterproof sunscreen and history books about Mayans. Remnants of Mayan and early Spanish cultures exist throughout the region, including some on the island itself.

Favorite Side Trip: Coba, a once stately city that prospered between 1100 B.C. and A.D. 400. Large temple pyramids still stand above the jungle setting.

Nearest Airport: Cancun International Airport, one hour away from the resort.

ALL-INCLUSIVE SERVICES AND ACTIVITIES

Food and Beverages: All food and beverages, including wine and liquor; room service (between 9:00 and 10:00 A.M. only).

Outdoor Activities: Bicycling, beach soccer and volleyball, tennis, golf, archery.

Water Sports: Kayaking, sailing, windsurfing, paddleboating, boogie boarding, snorkeling, aqua aerobics, banana boat rides, water polo.

Facilities: Putting greens, four lighted, hard-surface tennis courts, two pools, Jacuzzi.

Entertainment: Nightly, with local talent and staff shows; disco.

Special Events: Weekly manager's cocktail party.

Other: Aerobics and exercise classes, billiards, darts, taxes and gratuities.

Children's Services: Lunch provided. The Little Village Club, operating from 9:00 A.M. to 9:00 P.M.

Children's Activities: Outdoor activities, water sports, arts and crafts, playground area with adult supervision.

Not Included: Airport transfers.

Available for a Fee: Use of the dive shop, motor scooter rentals, services of tour desk, baby-sitting, exchange bank, fax, laundry service, scuba diving.

HOTEL SIERRA NUEVO VALLARTA

Nuevo Vallarta, Mexico

Nuevo ("New") Vallarta, located in the state of Nayarit on Mexico's Pacific Coast, is just 6 miles from Puerto Vallarta, the setting for the 1964 film *The Night of the Iguana*. Although Puerto Vallarta is already a well-known resort community, its sister town is slowly becoming one of Mexico's best tourist destinations. Blessed with gorgeous weather, crystal-clear waters, and golden sand, the region has attracted many new hotels. A standout among them is the Sierra Nuevo Vallarta. This activity-oriented all-inclusive features 361 spacious rooms that face the ocean or the surrounding mountains, offering equal opportunity for all to admire the daily dawn and sunset sky shows. From November through mid-April, humpback whales gather in the vicinity, and you just might spot one spouting off in the distance.

Available recreational activities run the gamut here from swimming or lounging in the resort's two pools to giant lawn chess, miniature golf to scuba lessons, canal boat rides to bicycling, sweating on the tennis court to sailing on 18-foot Hobie Cats.

Two restaurants and a snack bar serve up gourmet Mexican specialties, international cuisine, grilled fresh fish, and seafood, guaranteeing the proper ratio of protein and carbohydrates needed to maintain an even energy keel. There are two nightclubs at the resort. A different nighttime activity that impressed us is the outdoor Sierras Beach-Disco, an enjoyable alternative to the smoky, light-flashing indoor club at Sierra Nuevo Vallarta.

The Kid's Club for ages five to twelve provides parents and children with the occasionally welcome break from too much togetherness, or just adds some variety to the day. It is well run and offers children a good array of beach and pool activities.

We were very impressed with Nuevo Vallarta's public services along the country's largest (and the world's second largest) natural bay. Nearby Puerto Vallarta is a lively, cosmopolitan city with cobblestone streets and stucco houses; it's fun for shopping, and easy to reach down Highway 200. The resort can arrange shuttles along the 6 miles of beach, where marinas and hotels occasionally intersect the sand.

Another excursion we recommend is a boat trip to the Marieta Islands off the coast of Nuevo Vallarta. Here humpback whales give birth to their calves during the winter months, and from the boat you can see baby whales floating on the surface of the very clear and warm water as their mothers swim in circles around them, orienting them to the vast Pacific Ocean.

Hotel Sierra Nuevo Vallarta
Paseo de los Cocoteros
Nuevo Vallarta, Nayarit, Mexico 63732
Phone: 800–448–5028 or
    011–52–322–297–1300
E-mail: sierranv@pvnet.com.mx
Web site: www.vallartaonline.com/
    accommodations/hotels/hotelsierra/

Group/Getaway: Families

Accommodations: There are 350 air-conditioned rooms on six floors with two double beds or one king, bath with hair dryer, minibar, in-room safe, and balcony.

Points of Distinction: Sierra Nuevo Vallarta, an activity-oriented resort, is nestled against the Sierra Madre Mountains on the longest and most spectacular beach on Banderas Bay.

Open: Year-round.

Minimum Stay: Five nights.

Rates: Based on double occupancy, from $130 to $220 per room per night. Children under age twelve are free.

Frequently Asked Question: *Are the food and water safe?* Because the hotel is relatively new, it has its own charcoal water-filtering system, making the water relatively safe. However, we recommend drinking only bottled water as a precaution.

Favorite Side Trips: The charming colonial Old Vallarta for shopping and dining with the locals; the Southern Area, with its peaceful secluded beaches backed by palms and cliffs; Marina Vallarta for championship golf, tennis, shopping, and a world-class marina.

Nearest Airport: Puerto Vallarta Airport is just twenty minutes from the resort.

ALL-INCLUSIVE SERVICES AND ACTIVITIES

Food and Beverages: All food, nonalcoholic beverages, wine and liquor, and room service.

Outdoor Activities: Biking, moped riding, tennis, lawn chess, miniature golf.

Water Sports: Swimming, snorkeling, kayaking, windsurfing, sailing, aqua aerobics, canal boat rides in Nuevo Vallarta.

Facilities: Health club, steam room, whirlpool, two lighted tennis courts, two swimming pools for adults, game room.

Entertainment: Theme parties, karaoke, Sierras Beach-Disco.

Other: Yoga classes, tennis clinics, scuba lessons, taxes, gratuities, airport transfers.

Children's Services: Kid's Club for ages five to twelve (open 10:00 A.M. to 5:00 P.M.).

Children's Activities: Outdoor activities, water sports, arts and crafts, games, game room with television.

Available for a Fee: Motorized water sports (such as waterskiing, Jet Skiing, and parasailing), golf, horseback riding, baby-sitting.

MELIÁ COZUMEL

Cozumel, Mexico

Another country, another lush, green island with swaying palms and sugar-white beaches caressed by the Caribbean's sapphire waters? Yes, but before you "ho hum," there is more to this resort than meets the eye.

Managed by the renowned Sol Meliá group of Spain and formerly known as Paradisus Cozumel, this resort is situated on one of the loveliest beaches in Cozumel. Two miles long and plenty wide, the beach is a backdrop for fun and adventure and a certain amount of serenity.

The property is a splendid replica of a Mayan temple rising from the sands, reflecting the magnificence of authentic Mexican architecture. There are 147 deluxe rooms with balconies or terraces.

Europeans have been working on their tans here in increasing numbers over the last few years, and Americans have begun coming here for a change from the sometimes contrived holiday atmosphere of Cancun. Mexico's largest island and one of the world's renowned dive destinations, Cozumel lies in crystal waters just 12 miles off the Yucatan peninsula. Visibility of up to 200 feet along 20 miles of the second-longest reef in the world allows divers to explore limestone caves and tunnels and view rare black coral. It's an enchanting undersea kingdom that is tough to leave, even briefly, to come up for air.

Nowhere near as built up as Cancun, Cozumel is for those who desire more privacy and whose love of beach and water are paramount. But there are activities available beyond water sports, such as horseback riding on the beach, at dawn or into the sunset, plus basketball and tennis. Meliá also has an outstanding staff whose members pride themselves on making their guests feel more like Mayan royalty than city-slick Americans and Europeans. Considering that their charges range from nearly oblivious honeymooners looking into each other's eyes to giggling kids looking for the Children's Club, it is a notable feat.

Dining at the resort is diverse: Four restaurants range from casual-at-poolside to evening-only, with no bathing suits allowed. The fare is international, but we guarantee there will be excellent Mexican entrees and plenty of hot sauce. The resort's five bars make it easy for you to quench your thirst.

Meliá Cozumel has attracted guests from all segments of the vacationing population. Many of them are repeat escapees from urban jungles.

Meliá Cozumel

Carretera Costera Norte 5.8
Cozumel, Quintana Roo, Mexico 77600
Phone: 888–95–MELIA or
    011–52–98–720411
E-mail: melia.cozumel@solmelia.com
Web site: www.solmelia.com

Group/Getaway: Families

Accommodations: A three-story structure has 147 rooms with double beds, a sitting area, private bath, and a balcony or terrace with views of the gardens or the ocean.

Point of Distinction: Located at Playa Maya in the middle of the dive corridor, the resort is a quick boat ride to Cozumel's best reefs, including the legendary Palancar Reef.

Open: Year-round.

Minimum Stay: None.

Packages: The Meliá has a cornucopia of packages, including wedding, honeymoon, and dive packages.

Rates: Based on double occupancy, rates begin at $147 per person, per night for garden-view rooms and $220 for an ocean view; single supplement $80 additional per person, per night. Up to two children under twelve are free.

Frequently Asked Question: *Is it safe to drink the water and mixed drinks with ice?* Yes; the resort was built in 1989 and has its own water-purification system.

Don't Forget to Bring: Casual clothing for dining; divers should bring regulator and any equipment they choose not to rent.

Favorite Side Trips: Cancun for nightlife and shopping; Tulum, the only Mayan city built on the coast and one of the last Mayan outposts left standing during the Mayan revolt against Mexican rule in the War of the Castes during the 1840s.

Nearest Airport: Cozumel Airport, which is ten minutes from the resort.

ALL-INCLUSIVE SERVICES AND ACTIVITIES

Food and Beverages: Unlimited meals; drinks are on the house.

Outdoor Activities: Volleyball, basketball, shuffleboard, tennis, horseback riding.

Water sports: Windsurfing, sailing, kayaking, snorkeling, swimming.

Facilities: A gym, two pools, steam baths.

Entertainment: Nightly.

Other: Taxes and gratuities.

Children's Services: The Children's Club, for children age four to twelve, is supervised by certified teachers. It runs from 10:00 A.M. to 5:00 P.M. each day.

Children's Activities: Arts and crafts.

Not Included: Transfers from airport.

Available for a Fee: Scuba diving, moped rental, motorized sports (such as waterskiing).

REEF CLUB COZUMEL

Cozumel, Mexico

Inaugurated in 1997, the Reef Club has all the best attributes of Mexico's Caribbean island of Cozumel. The combination of nature's colors—turquoise sea, white sand, multiple shades of green, Day-Glo flowers—the pleasantly isolated sensation that comes from being on an island, plus the casually elegant Mexican-Caribbean architecture of the resort all conspire to inspire relaxation. Only twenty minutes from the airport and fifteen minutes from downtown, this resort sits on the island's largest beach. Guests arriving really do enter a getaway zone where the biggest decisions of the day fast become what to eat and what to do with the luxury of free time.

The Reef Club attracts a cosmopolitan clientele, mostly Canadians and Europeans, who tend to have more vacation time and take longer stays. The result adds to the casual and almost homey atmosphere made interesting by conversations in Italian, Spanish, French, and English that occur poolside. Having fun is the common thread at the resort that breaks down cultural and language barriers. Year-round temperatures hover at the eighty-degree mark, so the decision to hang out by the pool (slathered in sunscreen) or kayak, sail, windsurf, play beach volleyball, ride a horse, or take snorkeling or scuba lessons in sight of one of the world's most famous reef dive sites involves some pleasantly difficult decision making.

A definite plus for this resort is the on-site dive shop, not found in many of the establishments here. Naturally, many of the visitors to the Reef Club have an interest in diving, which the staff of the resort is quick to satisfy. For non-divers, the resort offers a free introductory demonstration lesson that is hailed along Cozumel's beach as one of the better ways in the Caribbean to start a life of scuba diving.

The midsize resort's 261 light-filled rooms and suites feature ocean, pool, or garden views and authentic Mexican furniture made from Guadalajara wood. Adjoining the hotel are three restaurants—one a more casual eatery and one that is more formal and romantic, although "formal" here means no bathing suits. The third offers international cuisine in the new suites area.

The wedding and honeymoon packages combine attention to detail with romantic touches. We saw a spangle-bedecked mariachi band serenading the happy couple cutting the cake. And, according to several hand-holding guests, the dive package offered at the resort encourages lots of waterlogged flirting. Like many of Mexico's resorts, the Reef Club has a fully staffed Kids' Club.

The staff knows the subtle difference between being obsequious and graciously accommodating, from the dive shop to the front desk, to the cook grilling your fish to order, to the housekeeping staff placing your book neatly on the night table. The Reef Club is an appealing addition to the all-inclusive niche in Mexico.

Reef Club Cozumel

Carretera Costera Sur 12.9
Zona Hotelera Sur
Cozumel, Quintana Roo, Mexico 77600
Phone: 888–773–4349 or
    011–52–987–872–9300
E-mail: reefclubcozumel@prodigy.net.mx
Web site: www.reefclubcozumel.com

Group/Getaway: Families

Accommodations: The 240 standard rooms in a sprawling, three-story building are reserved as "run of the house," which means you can request a garden or ocean view. Studios and junior suites are in a new three-story building with its own swimming pool.

Points of Distinction: The reef off Cozumel is one of the best in the world, attracting divers in large numbers. Scuba diving at the resort is outstanding.

Open: Year-round.

Minimum Stay: None, except seven days during the December/January holidays.

Packages: Dive, wedding, and honeymoon packages are available.

Rates: Based on double occupancy, $79 to $144 per person per night; single rooms $129 to $194. Children six and under can stay with parents for free; children ages six to twelve add $30 per night for standard rooms, free in studios and junior suites; infants and children up to age one, free.

Frequently Asked Question: *Can I bring my kids, even though only I want to dive?* Kids are welcome and will be entertained daily at the children's Kids' Club, with a host of activities that include swimming and other water sports, crafts, Spanish songfests, and movies. The club is offered at no additional cost.

Don't Forget to Bring: Sunscreen, scuba fins and regulator, tennis rackets.

Favorite Side Trips: Ferry ride to Cancun for shopping or to Playa Del Carmen to enjoy turtle watching, snorkeling, and dining.

Nearest Airports: Cozumel International Airport, or fly to Cancun International Airport and take the forty-five-minute ferry ride to Cozumel.

ALL-INCLUSIVE SERVICES AND ACTIVITIES

Food and Beverages: All food, nonalcoholic beverages, wine and liquor.

Outdoor Activities: Tennis, beach volleyball, horseback riding.

Water Sports: Snorkeling, paddleboats, windsurfing, sailing.

Facilities: Two tennis courts.

Special Events: Theme parties.

Other: Scuba diving demonstration, tax, gratuities.

Children's Services: Kids' Club includes supervised activities between 8:00 A.M. and 6:00 P.M.

Children's Activities: Outdoor activities, water sports, arts and crafts.

Not Included: Airport transfers.

Available for a Fee: Scuba equipment and tours, baby-sitting, room service, bungee jumping.

OCCIDENTAL ROYAL HIDEAWAY PLAYACAR

Playa del Carmen, Mexico

Only decades ago, native families raised coconut palms for copra (dried coconut meat) on this once-deserted Caribbean beach. A government-funded, carefully orchestrated beautification plan has transformed Playa del Carmen into the preferred destination for vacationers seeking easy access to fine beaches and nearby archaeological wonders.

Sitting near a turquoise sea, with beaches so dazzlingly white that sunglasses are more than just a fashion accessory, and only 40 miles from Cancun on Mexico's mystical Yucatan peninsula, Occidental Royal Hideaway Playacar in Playa del Carmen is the first all-inclusive to be included among AAA's elite Preferred Hotels and Resorts Worldwide. Opened in late 1998, this newest five-star addition to the Occidental Allegro Resorts' group is designed for discriminating sybarites with the luxury of time on their minds.

The multibuilding complex with 200 luxury rooms and suites, five swimming pools (one with a sand bottom) and private beach club, full-service spa, and fitness center blend privacy with luxury. Activities range from aqua aerobics, beach soccer, and volleyball to outdoor chess, kayaking, boogie boarding, and even bocce.

Five restaurants please eye and palate with various cuisines. Personable and professional, the staff members appear to have been chosen for their uncanny ability to anticipate guests' whims. Because the Hideaway is located in a fast-developing tourist mecca, it's not for everyone. The area has been discovered by Europeans who stay for weeks at a time, giving it a much more international ambience than Cancun, including a disproportionate number of topless sunbathers.

While children age thirteen and older are welcome, this is an intriguing place to consider for a long weekend (three-night stays are encouraged) of serious romancing. Then, who knows? Within a year or so, the courting couple might well be thinking of returning, this time with an eye to making use of the children's program.

Occidental Royal Hideaway Playacar

Lote Hotelero #6, Desarollo Playacar
Playa del Carmen, Quintana Roo,
Mexico 77710
Phone: 800–999–9182 or
    011–52–984–873–4500
Web site: www.occidentalhotels.com

Group/Getaway: Couples

Accommodations: Occidental Royal Hideaway offers Luxury Single Rooms and Hideaway Duplex and Royal Hideaway Duplex Suites, totalling 200 rooms all air-conditioned, with either sea or garden views and either a terrace or balcony, an in-room safe, minibar, satellite cable television, VCR, CD player, and full bath with hydromassage tub.

Points of Distinction: Pampering, twenty-four-hour room service, and five gourmet restaurants.

Open: Year-round.

Minimum Stay: Christmas and New Year's require a minimum four-night stay.

Packages: This resort offers a variety of packages, including dive and fishing excursions, wedding celebrations, and golf specials.

Rates: Based on double occupancy, rates range from $275 to $950 per person, per night.

Frequently Asked Questions: *Are all the meals served buffet style?* In addition to the main buffet restaurant, guests enjoy world-class Italian, Caribbean, and Californian cuisine in the other restaurants. Service is gracious, and the staff friendly and efficient. *Are children allowed at the resort?* While singles and families with children are welcome, Occidental Royal Hideaway attracts well-heeled, overworked adults seeking maximum spoiling in a gorgeous tropical setting without having to travel long hours to get there.

Favorite Side Trips: Visits to the archaeological sites of Tulum, Coba, and Chichen Itza make fascinating, even haunting, excursions.

Also within easy driving is the Sian Ka'an Biosphere Reserve, which includes the 1.3-million-acre Boca Paila Peninsula, a 22-mile strip of land named a UNESCO World Heritage Site in 1986.

Nearest Airport: Cancun International Airport, a one-hour drive from the resort.

ALL-INCLUSIVE SERVICES AND ACTIVITIES

Food and Beverages: All food, nonalcoholic beverages, wine and liquor, room service.

Outdoor Activities: Shuffleboard, basketball, horseshoes, beach soccer, beach volleyball, bocce, tennis, outdoor chess, bicycling.

Water Sports: Swimming, kayaking, paddleboating, sailing, windsurfing, pool volleyball, pool polo, aqua aerobics, boogie boarding.

Facilities: Lighted hard tennis courts, three swimming pools, three relaxation fitness centers, scuba dive center, game room, the 220-seat Royal Theater for dinner shows and entertainment (open Wednesdays and Saturdays).

Entertainment: Nightly live entertainment, theme nights.

Other: Taxes and gratuities, transportation to and from the airport, scuba and snorkeling lessons, billiards.

Available for a Fee: Golf at nearby championship course, deep-sea fishing, spa treatment package at on-site spa, Royal Diver excursions on deluxe vessel, horseback riding, beauty salon services, laundry services.

PRESIDENTE INTER-CONTINENTAL IXTAPA

Zihuatanejo, Mexico

Largely undeveloped and pristine, Ixtapa is blessed with secluded beaches hugged by the gentle Pacific. The few resorts that are here are luxurious, in contrast to the simplicity of the small towns that intersect them. In the nearby fisherman's village of Zihuatanejo are many restaurants and shops linked by cobblestone streets, where visitors can buy silver, hammocks, and local crafts. Both towns also have informal, cozy restaurants serving seafood and local fare where the dollar goes very far. Mariachi bands beckon from the street corners.

A large resort with an even larger beach, the Presidente prides itself on offering every water sport available on the Pacific Ocean. These include snorkeling, scuba diving, waterskiing, sailing, windsurfing, and fishing. The resort also claims a marina where boat charters are easily arranged, as well as Jet Ski rentals for wave hopping over the big rollers that meet the shore. Launches regularly explore the turtles, fish, and pelican sanctuaries at El Morro de los Pericos or tour Ixtapa Island, which served as the location for the film *Robinson Crusoe.*

Considering its size, the Presidente Inter-Continental has notable service. Few countries have friendlier or kinder people than Mexico, and these qualities are most apparent in the resort's helpful staff. Rooms come equipped with satellite television and plenty of bottled water, which is crucial in Mexico.

What impressed us about this resort is the diverse number of activities that are all-inclusive. There are beach barbecues, theme parties, all-day bar service, and regular tennis clinics. On the grounds is one incredibly large pool: One side is for quiet reflection, while the other is for activities and games. There is also a Chiqui Club, which operates daily for children ages four to eleven. We also noted that children under six stay for free and children under twelve cost only an additional $30 per day—a bargain considering all of the activities on hand.

In trying to decide who is best suited for this resort, the Presidente Inter-Continental surprised us. Most all-inclusives are geared toward a particular niche, but this property is successfully accommodating romantic couples, families, and even small groups. The Presidente Ixtapa is large enough to allow a couple to disappear from view and a family to bond and/or split up in order to enjoy the many activities available. The common denominator is that the happiest guests at the resort were those with the highest energy level, busily taking part in the myriad activities on and off the water.

Presidente Inter-Continental Ixtapa
Boulevard Ixtapa S/N
Zihuatanejo, Mexico 40880
Phone: 800–327–0200 or
    011–52–755–30018
E-mail: ixtapa@interconti.com
Web site: www.ixtapa.intercontinental.com

Group/Getaway: Families

Accommodations: The 420 rooms include twelve Junior Suites with sitting areas, 143 Ocean-View Tower Rooms, and 265 Private Garden View Lanais. All accommodations include air-conditioning, satellite color television, and an indoor private sitting area.

Points of Distinction: Ixtapa borders a wide bay dotted with small rocky islands inhabited solely by seabirds. The beach in the nearby town of Playa del Mar is a 2-mile stretch of white sand that gives Ixtapa its Nahuatl Indian name, which means "the white place."

Open: Year-round.

Minimum Stay: None.

Packages: Promotional packages are occasionally offered, including the Leisure Option and the Business Option, which offers you a choice between a free room upgrade or bonus frequent-flyer miles. Inquire at time of booking.

Rates: Based on double occupancy, rates begin at $225 to $260 for an Ocean View room per person, per night. Children under six years of age stay free with their parents; ages six to twelve are an additional $30 per night. Ask for the all-inclusive rate on the telephone.

Frequently Asked Question: *Is there a shopping area close by?* Next to the hotel is a main shopping area.

Don't Forget to Bring: Cash for shopping bargains (some shops will not take credit cards).

Favorite Side Trips: Zihuatanejo, an old fishing village, is approximately 5 miles from the resort. The ocean waters of Zihuatanejo are famed for their abundance of game fish, including sailfish, marlin, and rooster fish.

Nearest Airport: Ixtapa International Airport, a twenty-minute taxi ride.

ALL-INCLUSIVE SERVICES AND ACTIVITIES

Food and Beverages: All food and beverages, wine and liquor, twenty-four-hour room service.

Outdoor Activities: Tennis, beach volleyball.

Water sports: Swimming, snorkeling, scuba diving, sailing, water polo, windsurfing, aqua aerobics.

Facilities: Pool, sauna and steam room, fitness center.

Entertainment: Nightly; weekly theme parties.

Other: Language and cooking classes, drink-mixing demonstrations, taxes and tips.

Children's Services: Chiqui Club (ages four to eleven) operates daily from 9:00 A.M. to 5:00 P.M.

Children's Activities: Arts and crafts.

Not Included: Airport transfers.

Available for a Fee: Water-sports equipment rentals, motorized sports (i.e., waterskiing), land and boat tours, car parking, deep-sea fishing.

PRESIDENTE INTER-CONTINENTAL LOS CABOS

San Jose del Cabo, Mexico

The lower Baja is essentially a desert of mountains that plunge into one of the most fertile fishing grounds in the world. The incredible beaches and clear waters of Los Cabos were not lost upon visiting fishermen or hoteliers. The popularity of Los Cabos has resulted in a vacation wonderland of hotels and resorts that offer championship golf, tennis, and diving. With a climate that is always dry and sunny, and plentiful connections to American airports, the area has met with great success. Among the all-inclusives in the Baja region, the Presidente Inter-Continental is topflight.

The hotel is a complex of tasteful, earth-colored adobe buildings overlooking the snowy white beaches and cobalt waters of the Sea of Cortez. Because the resort is located near the charming coastal town of San Jose del Cabo and a thirty-minute drive from the glitzy, cruise port/playground of Cabo San Lucas, the Presidente's guests can venture into either world and retreat to the peace and quiet of this secluded property when they choose.

Of the resort's 395 rooms and suites, many have spectacular ocean views, most with patios or balconies. The rest have vistas of a quiet, protected wildlife preserve in the middle of a richly vegetated lagoon and estuary. Large waves roll in along the beach, creating a rhythmic sound that resonates through the open-air corridors of the resort, which are attractively planted with myriad species of local cacti. Tropical birds sing aloud. With the hotel's orientation toward nature, we weren't surprised that the property's beach is groomed on horseback rather than with motorized equipment.

What we found particularly interesting at the Presidente are the dual modes of life that happen here. It is a peaceful place that seems very married to the natural elements of the Baja. For couples seeking a private place to retreat or a chance to appreciate nature, the resort offers serenity and seclusion. And in winter months there are all those whales just offshore, attracting attention. But the resort is also committed to providing many high-octane opportunities for guests who want to play hard. These dynamic beach and sports activities include scuba diving and tennis clinics, volleyball, snorkel lessons, water polo, jogging, swimming, bicycle tours, world-class golf, and sportfishing. We were also impressed with the fully equipped twenty-four-hour fitness center.

Because the undertow and surf can make swimming at the beach dangerous, the large pools are the center of activity at the resort, complete with a swim-up bar and elegantly shaded grounds for sunbathers. The pool areas spill onto the beach and are close to the fitness center, making it a natural base to pursue all offerings of the resort. The activity areas also are near the clubhouse of the resort's well-run program for children. Called Chiqui Club, it is operated by professional child-care workers for kids five to twelve years old from 10:00 A.M. to 5:00 P.M. daily.

The people of Mexico love to celebrate life through food, and their cuisine is exotic and spicy, incorporating a variety of chilies, from the mild poblano to the fiery habanero. There are six restaurants on the grounds, including a gourmet dining spot that prepares elegant world-class cuisine, and two more casual restaurants offering everything from seafood to traditional Mexican fare and light snacks. Those who want to experience more of the Baja culture can take the Spanish lessons offered each morning at the pool. A car-rental desk on the premises arranges for private vehicles, so guests can also explore the surrounding area.

Presidente Inter-Continental Los Cabos
Boulevard Mijares S/N
Zona Hotelera
San Jose del Cabo
Baja California Sur, Mexico 23400
Phone: 800–327–0200 or
    011–52–114–20211
E-mail: loscabos@interconti.com
Web site: www.los-cabos.intercontinental.com

Group/Getaway: Families

Accommodations: There are 395 spacious,
air-conditioned rooms. Choices include Standard, Superior, and Deluxe Rooms and Junior,
two-level Master, and Presidential Suites. All
rooms have either mountain or ocean views,
satellite television, continental breakfast, and
twenty-four-hour room service. Many rooms
have private terraces.

Points of Distinction: This is one of only a
few places in the world where a resort area is
situated where two bodies of water meet: the
Pacific Ocean and the Sea of Cortez.

Open: Year-round.

Minimum Stay: None.

Rates: Based on double occupancy, rates
begin at $202 per person, per night. Children
under six years of age stay free with their parents; ages six to twelve, $30 per night; thir-
teen and older pay adult rates. Ask for the
all-inclusive rate on the telephone.

Frequently Asked Question: *Are there golf
courses in the vicinity of the resort?* The
Palmilla Hotel Golf Course is available to
guests who choose a golf package.

Don't Forget to Bring: Golf clubs; binoculars
for whale watching.

Favorite Side Trip: Take a water taxi to the
hidden cove of Lover's Beach, also known as
Playa de Dona Chepa—very scenic and just
around the corner from Divorce Beach.

Nearest Airport: Los Cabos International Airport, a fifteen-minute drive from the resort.

ALL-INCLUSIVE SERVICES AND ACTIVITIES

Food and Beverages: All food, nonalcoholic beverages, wine and liquor included.

Outdoor Activities: Tennis, beach volleyball, bicycle touring.

Water Sports: Water polo, swimming,
snorkelling lessons, aqua aerobics.

Facilities: Fitness center, pool with swim-
up bar, estuary pool, massage center.

Entertainment: Theme nights, including
a Mexican fiesta, casino, and beach party,
keep guests entertained after dark.

Children's Services: Chiqui Club for children ages five to twelve (10:00 A.M. to
5:00 P.M.).

Children's Activities: Outdoor activities,
water sports, arts and crafts, cultural
activities, beach and pool parties.

Available for a Fee: Laundry and baby-
sitting services, deep-sea fishing, golf and
transportation to courses, horseback riding, room service.

PRESIDENTE INTER-CONTINENTAL PUERTO VALLARTA

Puerto Vallarta, Mexico

One of Mexico's most popular Pacific Coast vacation spots, Puerto Vallarta once attracted Spanish and British pirates who rested from their pillaging and plundering on this geographically perfect location on the *Bahia de Banderas*, or "Bay of Flags." It is the second-largest natural bay in the world. As recently as thirty years ago, this sleepy farming and fishing community on the edge of the Sierra Madre mountain range was a tropical hideaway for those in the know. The movie director John Huston was bewitched by this earthly paradise and filmed *The Night of the Iguana* here. Lead actor Richard Burton and paramour Liz Taylor worked on their "relationship" here, and the rest is another chapter in tourism history.

Guests sometimes complain good-naturedly while lounging poolside at this luxurious five-star resort about being so comfortably ensconced that they simply don't want to be bothered taking the fifteen-minute cab ride to Puerto Vallarta's whitewashed, red-tiled, colonial downtown. "Maybe tomorrow," is the standard response.

A mere twenty-five-minute drive from the international airport, the Presidente Inter-Continental Puerto Vallarta is set on a hillside, smack in the middle of lush, barely controlled vegetation. Hibiscus bushes add splashes of red, yellow, and hot pink against the property's white walls. Small wonder that guests are sometimes indeci-sive about leaving one of the 120 airy, light-filled suites and heading for the hotel's meandering pool (complete with swim-up bar), steps away from a secluded cove and golden beach on the Bahia de Banderas. Tennis courts, a fitness center facing the ocean, and the jungle paths of the southern Sierra Madre mountains across the street have been known to lure vacationers down from their balconies.

The Presidente Inter-Continental doesn't try to be all things to all people, positioning itself as a high-end, value-for-price tropical boutique. It appeals to sweethearts of all ages, working couples needing a break, retired couples chasing the sun, families, even singles who are made to feel like visiting friends. Women guests occasionally send letters to the management commending the staff on how welcome and safe they felt during their stay.

The facilities are family-friendly too. Kids six and under stay free in an adult's room, and children up to age twelve can participate in the Chiqui Club, a supervised on- and off-property daytime program offering a range of activities. Baby-sitting services can be arranged for those nights when Mom and Dad want to go out on the town.

Staff and service are *simpatico*, the food in the two restaurants and snack bar is deliciously prepared, and, yes, you can arrange a visit to the set of the movie that put Puerto Vallarta on the map.

Presidente Inter-Continental Puerto Vallarta

KM 8.5 Carretera a Barra de Navidad
P.O. Box 448
Puerto Vallarta, Jalisco, Mexico 48300
Phone: 800–327–0200 or
    011–52–322–80191
E-mail: puertovallarta@interconti.com
Web site: www.puerto-vallarta.
    intercontinental.com

Group/Getaway: Families

Accommodations: The 120 luxuriously appointed guest rooms and suites feature large marble baths with balconies overlooking the ocean, air-conditioning, remote-control satellite color televisions, in-room movies, telephones, radios, hair dryers, minibars, and purified water.

Points of Distinction: Unlike the other rocky beaches of this area, this small all-inclusive boutique resort is situated on a lovely white-sand beach on Banderas Bay.

Open: Year-round.

Minimum Stay: None.

Rates: Begin at $252 for two people, per night. Children ages six and under stay free, ages seven to twelve $25 additional per night, thirteen and older $50 additional. Ask for the all-inclusive plan on the telephone.

Frequently Asked Question: *Where is the closest golf course?* Marina Vallarta, a Joe Finger–designed course, is just nine minutes from the resort.

Don't Forget to Bring: Snorkeling equipment, tennis racket, and hiking boots.

Favorite Side Trips: Hiking and nature walks through the lush hiking trails of Puerto Vallarta; deep-sea fishing for marlin.

Nearby Airport: Puerto Vallarta Airport, just thirty minutes from the resort.

ALL-INCLUSIVE SERVICES AND ACTIVITIES

Food and Beverages: All food and beverages (alcoholic and nonalcoholic), twenty-four-hour room service.

Outdoor Activities: Tennis on lighted court.

Water Sports: Snorkeling, swimming, sailing, windsurfing, kayaking, boogie boards.

Facilities: Swimming pool, fitness center, steam room, on-site travel agent, tennis court, billiards, Ping-Pong.

Entertainment: Live bands, dancing.

Other: Scuba clinics in pool.

Children's Services: Chiqui Club for children to age twelve, open 10:00 A.M. to 5:00 P.M.

Children's Activities: Outdoor activities, water sports, arts and crafts, cultural activities, movies.

Not Included: Taxes.

Available for a Fee: Motorized water sports (such as waterskiing and deep-sea fishing), baby-sitting.

CARIBBEAN ISLANDS
AND THE BAHAMAS

OCCIDENTAL GRAND PINEAPPLE BEACH

St. John's, Antigua

Pineapple Beach is laid-back, kicked back, unpressured, and unpretentious. Anyone who wants to spend a full week on a beach chair or a bar stool is certainly free to do so. An extensive schedule of activities runs day and night, yet no one is pressured to do any of it. If you don't feel like dancing and singing, don't do it. If you don't feel like mingling with the neighbors, don't do it. If all you want to do is soak in the sun, mellow out, and do nothing, then that's what you should do. That's why they call it a vacation. Many resorts hire people to prod guests through every activity offered. At Pineapple Beach, however, employees spend much of their time urging people to relax and enjoy the day.

That isn't to say there's nothing to do. In fact the list of activities is as lengthy as that of any resort. With a stretch of reef directly off its own shore, some awesome snorkeling can be done right from the beach. The cove is excellent for sailing, windsurfing, kayaking, and any number of water sports.

Live music is played nightly, including Caribbean steel band, jazz, and island pop. For those willing to risk their chips, there's The Pirate's Den electronic casino.

Pineapple Beach has put $5 million into renovations, improving upon the already luxurious facility. There are now two restaurants and a snack bar. For those who like to sweat, the fitness center has a full complement of cardiovascular machines, free weights, and exercise machines. For sports fans and soap opera fans alike, the resort pipes in U.S. television on its satellite TVs. There is also a daily 7:30 A.M. walk to Devil's Bridge, a stone arch carved by the pounding of the sea.

A stay at Pineapple Beach is truly refreshing. Most people spend fifty weeks out of a year running themselves ragged, and all they need is some time away. Here they have that time away to do anything they want, and that includes doing everything possible or nothing at all.

Occidental Grand Pineapple Beach

P.O. Box 2000
Long Bay
St. John's, Antigua, West Indies
Phone: 800–858–2258 or 268–463–2006
E-mail: cfresco@antigua.allegroresorts.com
Web site: www.occidentalhotels.com

Group/Getaway: Couples

Accommodations: The resort comprises 180 air-conditioned rooms in a half dozen low-rise wooden buildings, several of them directly on the beach. Standard Beachfront rooms are located directly on the beach; waterside rooms are less than a minute's walk from the beach.

Points of Distinction: The management at Pineapple Beach wants guests to enjoy their time at the resort itself but at the same time would hate to see anyone leave without fully experiencing Antigua. During a stay at the resort, most guests will have seen the capital city of St. John's at least once, they will have seen many of the island's historical and natural sites, and they will have come to know the island's people.

Open: Year-round.

Minimum Stay: Five nights.

Rates: Based on double occupancy, rates range from $175 to $311 per person, per night. Daily rate for children ages six to fifteen ranges from $87 to $155. Children age five and under stay free.

Frequently Asked Question: *What are the chances of being hit by a hurricane?* The Caribbean sees at least a dozen hurricanes every year from June to October. Antigua, however, only receives a small portion of that activity.

Don't Forget to Bring: For dinner, slacks and shirts with sleeves for men, and proper attire for women.

Favorite Side Trips: English Harbor, where many of Antigua's historical and cultural sites are located, including Nelson's Dockyard, now a mooring place for luxury yachts and a center for upscale shops and eateries. Nearby Shirley Heights has eighteenth-century ruins and exceptional views.

Nearest Airport: V. C. Bird International Airport, on Antigua, a forty-minute drive from the resort.

ALL-INCLUSIVE SERVICES AND ACTIVITIES

Food and Beverages: All meals, nonalcoholic beverages, afternoon tea, hors d'oeuvres, wine and liquor, weekly beach barbecue.

Outdoor Activities: Daily guided walk to Devil's Bridge.

Water Sports: Swimming, windsurfing, sailing, snorkeling, reef fishing, kayaking. All water sports include instruction.

Facilities: Open-air fitness center, four tennis courts, swimming pool, electronic casino.

Entertainment: Nightly.

Other: Hair braiding; service charges, taxes, gratuities; shopping excursions to St. John's.

Not Included: Airport transfers.

Available for a Fee: A 62-foot Seabreeze catamaran cruise, St. John's shopping spree, historical trips to Shirley Heights and English Harbor, massage and aromatherapy, trips to Kings Casino in downtown St. John's, golf, baby-sitting, massage, Sunday morning church trips, rental cars.

CURTAIN BLUFF RESORT

St. John's, Antigua

We were told that Curtain Bluff is a truly unique all-inclusive resort with a following so strong that it resembles a religion. After a visit, we understood the truth of the statement. Almost forty years in the making by owners who have poured their perfectionist hearts and souls into this property, Curtain Bluff is a very special, elegant getaway that breeds loyalty. The owners, Howard and Michelle Hulford, live on the premises, so there is an attention to detail that is not typical of many island properties in the region. Rooms that do not face the ocean enjoy the leeward side of the hotel, where dozens of varieties of palms and exotic tropical flowers flourish. The owners love wine as well, and Curtain Bluff maintains the best wine cellar in the Caribbean—a rarity that is highly prized by its discriminating guests.

Set on a dramatic seaside bluff on Antigua's southern shore, the resort is surrounded by a natural paradise that gives Curtain Bluff its romantic atmosphere. The turquoise waters surrounding the resort are crystal clear, with a reef that protects its two snow white beaches. Relaxing with a drink on the beach is considered a primary activity here, but if it's not your thing, you can also enjoy an array of sports on land or sea. On water this adds up to snorkeling, diving, waterskiing, sailing, and deep-sea fishing.

We were impressed with this selection of water sports, but of even greater distinction are the resort's five-star tennis facilities, including four lighted championship courts, a pro shop, and a full-time tennis pro. If that isn't enough to lure the tennis fan,

Curtain Bluff also hosts Antigua's annual Tennis Week in May. Tennis Week began in 1975 and has evolved into a pro-am event, featuring international-caliber talent. During the seven-day gala, guests enjoy activities ranging from hitting for prizes to instructional clinics. Curtain Bluff regularly sponsors local children with talent so that they can receive tennis lessons and instruction, resulting in a top island junior tennis team. Beyond tennis, the resort also features an excellent seaside fitness center, putting greens, and outstanding squash courts.

The rooms at Curtain Bluff are among the nicest we have seen. Spacious and elegant, many are situated to give fantastic views of the Caribbean and receive its cool trade winds. Of equal caliber are the resort's dining rooms, featuring the creations of chef Christophe Blatz. His international presentations are very creative and change nightly. Owner Howard Mulford is so insistent on fresh ingredients in his kitchen that he started his own import company to collect the best ingredients from around the world. Most dine in the garden pavilion surrounded by lawns, a gazebo, and a dance floor under the tamarind tree. For a more intimate and romantic approach, you may also have dinner brought to your private balcony or patio.

You can enjoy a steel band at Curtain Bluff's weekly beach party, which is held in the afternoon so it won't interfere with your quiet evening plans. Every evening, live music fills the starry sky and dancing commences around the tamarind tree.

Curtain Bluff Resort
P.O. Box 288
St. John's, Antigua, West Indies
Phone: 888–289–9898 or 268–462–8400
E-mail: curtainbluff@curtainbluff.com
Web site: www.curtainbluff.com

Group/Getaway: Families, Sports & Fitness

Accommodations: Deluxe Rooms and forty Junior Suites, including twenty-one interconnecting units for families. The remainder are individually decorated Executive Deluxe suites and the new, luxury Grace and Morris Suites on the third level. The resort has built 42 suites in the last two years.

Points of Distinction: Curtain Bluff's terrific wine cellar has 30,000 bottles, and foods are imported from around the world for the resort's fine cuisine.

Open: Mid-October to late July.

Minimum Stay: Three nights.

Rates: Based on double occupancy, from $495 to $1,995 per night for two. Children ages two to four stay in parents' room for $65 per night; ages five and up are charged a singles surcharge of $140 to $180 per night.

Frequently Asked Question: *Are children welcome?* Yes, but there are restrictions. Children under twelve are not allowed during February. Children under six are not permitted in the bar or dining room after 7:00 P.M. and youngsters six to twelve must be accompanied by an adult.

Don't Forget to Bring: Casual clothes for daytime and beach cover-ups; jacket for dinner is suggested for men. No jeans allowed at dinner.

Favorite Side Trips: Shopping in St. John's and the historical Nelson's Dockyard; there are also convenient day trips to four islands within sight of Curtain Bluff.

Nearest Airport: V. C. Bird International Airport, half an hour away.

ALL-INCLUSIVE SERVICES AND ACTIVITIES

Food and Beverages: All meals, nonalcoholic beverages, bar drinks, afternoon tea, hors d'oeuvres at cocktail time.

Outdoor Activities: Tennis, squash, putting green, croquet, yoga.

Water Sports: Swimming, sailing, snorkeling, windsurfing, waterskiing, scuba diving, deep-sea fishing, sea kayaking.

Facilities: Four lighted tennis courts, pro shop, seaside fitness center.

Entertainment: Live music and dancing nightly, weekly beach party.

Other: There is a no-tipping policy.

Not Included: Government taxes, service charges, airport transfers. (A one-way taxi ride for up to four people costs $22 to $25.)

Available for a Fee: Laundry service, tennis lessons, sailing on the hotel yacht.

GALLEY BAY

Five Islands, Antigua

In Antigua they say there are 365 beaches, one for each day of the year. The Galley Bay resort sits quietly among one of the island's finest, adjoined by acres of bird sanctuary.

The rich cultural nightlife and a multitude of outdoor activities that are enjoyed on the island contrast nicely with the quiet seclusion of Galley Bay. The essence of this very beautiful resort on one of the Caribbean's most attractive isles is romance. If embers are burning but need some still moments to jump-start them into flames, Galley Bay does its part with wonderful effectiveness. The resort and beachfront hideaway were renovated in 2000, making the facility new again. Amid the jungle foliage, palm-thatched huts distance themselves from one another just steps from the beach. Gauguin Cottages lie on the edge of a bird sanctuary lagoon, or guests may opt for one of a variety of beachfront accommodations, including one-bedroom beachfront suites. The rooms and suites are spacious and elegant, yet unpretentious.

Antigua is the largest of the British Leeward Islands, but is still only 14 miles long and 11 miles wide. The island averages 20 to 30 inches of rain a year, with temperatures ranging from the mid-seventies in winter to the mid-eighties in summer. A coral island, Antigua has so many beaches that not even residents visit them all. But that seems to be fine with visitors. The Galley Bay people claim they haven't met a tourist yet who couldn't find one relatively empty and attractive stretch of sand to call his or her own. But with just seventy rooms, fifty-five of which are right on the resort's mile-long crescent of brilliant white-sand beach, most visitors never have to wander farther than outside their front door.

We did take a day trip, organized by Galley Bay, to visit two very long beaches called Fort James and Deep Bay, both on the northeast side of the island, where surfers gather in the winter months. For the more adventurous, there are less developed beaches on the lee side of the island, such as Rendezvous Bay and Doigs Beach, prized stretches of sand with flat waters that are worth the rough travel needed to reach them. Long Bay, on the east coast, and Half Moon Bay, now a national park, are very popular with families.

The clear waters that meet Antigua's grand beaches are ideal for kayaking, windsurfing, and sailing, all offered by Galley Bay. Snorkeling over the rich array of coral reefs is also tremendously rewarding and easy to do.

An authentic taste of Antiguan cuisine is very creatively prepared at Galley Bay by resident chefs who, by tradition, are graduates of the French Culinary Institute in New York City. Meals are served in two restaurants on the grounds, both of which require men to wear long pants. The food is so good, it is worth the extra effort to maintain a bit of casual elegance. Although nightlife is limited to music combos, for fun seekers there is a midnight club scene off the resort (try the Zone, the Lime, or the Web), which is easily accessible by taxi.

At Galley Bay the emphasis is on creating private moments—a peaceful walk or the time to be intimate without intrusion. No children under sixteen are allowed, except during the holiday season. The bottom line, so to speak, is that you don't need to pack much to maximize a stay here: A passport, a few articles of cotton clothing, sunscreen, and a significant other will do just fine.

Galley Bay

P.O. Box 305
Five Islands, Antigua, West Indies
Phone: 800–345–0356 or 268–462–0302
Web site: www.antigua-resorts.com

Group/Getaway: Couples

Accommodations: Gauguin Cottages, situated on the edge of a bird sanctuary lagoon, consist of two separate thatched Polynesian-style "rondovals" connected by a breezeway. Superior Beachfront Rooms have a private patio that steps directly onto the beach; Deluxe Beachfront Rooms are larger. One-bedroom Beachfront Suites are the resort's largest and most luxurious beachfront accommodations of the resort's 70 units.

Points of Distinction: With forty acres of tropical gardens, the resort is set between an incredible lagoon and a bird sanctuary along a secluded mile-long beach.

Open: Year-round.

Minimum Stay: Three nights April 22 to December 20, five nights January 3 to April 21, except seven nights February 8 to 24 and December 21 and January 31.

Rates: Based on double occupancy, from $550 to $1,000 per night for two. Deduct $150 per room per night for single occupancy. Third person in room add $150 per night (available only in Deluxe Beachfront and Premium Beachfront suites).

Frequently Asked Questions: *What types of credit cards are accepted in Antigua?* The big three—Visa, American Express, and MasterCard—are commonly used. Personal checks drawn on U.S. banks are accepted. *Are children permitted?* Only during the December/January holiday season. Children under age sixteen are not allowed the rest of the year.

Don't Forget to Bring: Proof of citizenship (passport, birth certificate, or photo I.D.).

Favorite Side Trips: Nelson's Dockyard and Shirley Heights.

Nearest Airport: V. C. Bird International Airport, fifteen minutes from the resort.

ALL-INCLUSIVE SERVICES AND ACTIVITIES

Food and Beverages: All meals and beverages (including wine and liquor), hors d'oeuvres, early morning coffee, afternoon tea.

Outdoor Activities: Tennis, croquet, walking, horseshoes.

Water Sports: Windsurfing, sailing, kayaking, snorkeling.

Facilities: Championship tennis court, swimming pool.

Entertainment: A few nights a week.

Other: Water sports instruction, tips, taxes, and service charges.

Available for a Fee: Motorized watercraft at nearby marinas, golf, optional excursions.

JUMBY BAY

Jumby Bay Island, Antigua

When we arrived at Jumby Bay, we recognized that it had gained more accolades than most resorts in the world—voted the third-best luxury resort on the planet by a distinguished group of travel editors, a sought-after refuge of royals and celebrities, the favorite Caribbean site of Robin Leach (who ended up building his own rich and famous house next door)—so we weren't in a mood to be easy on this place.

But it took only minutes to beat down our resistance. Jumby Bay takes up about sixty-five acres of a 300-acre private island off Antigua in the West Indies. After taking a twenty-minute taxi ride from Antigua's V. C. Bird International Airport, we boarded the resort's private motor launch for a five-minute ride across a reef that guards this hidden place. The ride is a kind of buffer that separates the pedestrian press of everyday life from what Jumby Bay offers as well as any resort in the world: a carefree, luxurious existence where problems disappear as quickly as clouds melt in the skies above. Service, ambience, and the pleasure of recreation are what Jumby Bay is all about.

With only fifty-one guest chambers, your privacy is held sacred by staff. Guests feel like the island belongs to them; three long, crescent-shaped beaches are mostly empty. You can explore the miles of trails, then play a game of night tennis, followed by drinks in one of three spectacular bars, each featuring singers and bands at night.

Jumby Bay is a place to recline with a book or a favorite friend, with toes in tropical waters and passion fruit drinks lined up at your elbow. There are no phones or televisions or even air conditioners to compete with the gentle sounds of small waves lapping on the sand. The trade winds take care of you as effectively as the outstanding staff that is never far away.

If you do shake off the inclination to luxuriate under the sun, you can visit the fitness center or take part in kayaking, snorkeling, sailing, or windsurfing. Sooner or later you'll find the resort's two eateries, the open-air Verandah Terrace for breakfast, lunch, and dinner, and The Estate House, a 230-year-old English plantation, open six days a week for elegant dining that specializes in European, American, and Caribbean cuisine and offers an exceptional wine cellar. Both serve more wonderful food than you'll want to decline. Cocktails are served upstairs in the Estate House's library next to the outdoor veranda and at Jumby Bay's other two bars.

One of the endearing features of Jumby Bay that also speaks to its privacy is the fact that its main beach, Pasture Bay Beach, is home to an endangered species of turtles and many rare birds. About every other year, hundreds of female hawksbill turtles trek up the beach and lay their eggs deep in the sand. If you are lucky enough to experience this remarkable event, you will witness one of nature's great phenomena that is as unforgettable as days spent on this pristine island.

Jumby Bay

Mailing address: P.O. Box 243
St. John's, Antigua, West Indies
Phone: 800–421–9016 or 268–462–6000
E-mail: jumbybay@jumbybayresort.com
Web site: www.jumbybayresort.com

Group/Getaway: Couples

Accommodations: Jumby Bay offers six spacious Junior Suites, each with Queen Anne–like furniture, a four-poster bed, and a terrace overlooking the ocean; eleven luxurious Superior Junior Suites with oversized bathrooms, large closets, and a private patio or balcony with ocean views; twelve expansive Deluxe Junior Suites, and eight Deluxe Suites. There are also ten two-bedroom Villas and one three-bedroom Villa that offers the finest furniture and art, and breathtaking views of the Caribbean Sea from a private terrace.

Points of Distinction: Jumby Bay takes pride in its individually decorated suites, which blend the tradition and tranquillity of Jumby Bay with modern conveniences. The resort recently received the World Travel Award as the world's leading private island and has been listed in *Condé Nast Traveler*'s Reader's Choice Awards, placing fifth in the Caribbean small hotel category.

Open: Year-round.

Minimum Stay: None, except during holidays.

Rates: Suites are $700 to $1,500 per couple, per night; Villas are $1,500 to $2,800 per night.

Frequently Asked Questions: *What is the dress code?* "Bare elegance," which means no jackets or ties are required. Casual dress for breakfast and lunch and long trousers and shirts (with collars) at dinnertime are appropriate for men. Bathing suits are discouraged during mealtimes. Shorts are acceptable on Barbecue Night. *How far away is the beach?* The beach can be reached via a two- to three-minute leisurely walk or a brief bicycle ride.

Don't Forget to Bring: Binoculars. A short boat trip will take you to tiny, uninhabited Great Bird Island, where you can see the nesting grounds of the red-billed tropic bird. From April to September, laughing gulls, purple martins, terns, and brown noodles populate the island.

Favorite Side Trips: Shopping and Casino Night in St. John's; the Bat Cave, located on the north side of English Harbor, home to hundreds of bats hanging upside down from the ceiling. Legend has it that the cavern actually travels under the sea all the way to Guadeloupe.

Nearest Airport: The V. C. Bird International Airport is a five-minute drive from the resort's private ferry. The cruise to Jumby Bay takes seven minutes.

ALL-INCLUSIVE SERVICES AND ACTIVITIES

Food and Beverages: Sunrise coffee service, three gourmet meals daily, afternoon tea service, hors d'oeuvres at cocktail time, unlimited cocktails and bar drinks, imported house wine with all meals.

Outdoor Activities: Tennis, hiking, croquet, biking.

Water Sports: Swimming, snorkeling, waterskiing, windsurfing, sailing, fishing, sea cycling.

Facilities: Fully equipped fitness center, freshwater pool, 80-foot lap pool, three tennis courts (two with lights), putting green.

Other: In-room welcome amenity, Antigua Rum departure gift, boat launch service, airport taxi service, weekly sunset cruise, postage and mail service.

Children's Services: Jungle gym, mini basketball court, play area, nursery; children's menu for lunch and dinner.

Available for a Fee: Spa options, including both Eastern and Western techniques of massage and reflexology, acupuncture, in-house masseuse; babysitting; chartered day sailing, deep-sea fishing, reef diving.

ST. JAMES'S CLUB
Mamora Bay, Antigua

The St. James's Club is almost an island within an island—a resort that has been created on a private, isolated peninsula that follows the curve of a spectacularly broad beach. The underpinning of St. James's Club's success is its ability to create a self-contained world for couples and families who wish to experience an upscale, elegant vacation on one of the Caribbean's most attractive islands.

Because there are 178 rooms, suites, and villas, guests at this resort can settle into private accommodations that allow them to be as social or private as they wish. All of the rooms and villas have either balconies or patios, many with spectacular views of the rolling hills that rise from the aquamarine waters across the bay. It was along these shores that Columbus discovered Antigua in 1493, thinking he was edging into Eden. Although the island has become a popular vacation destination, it is still underdeveloped by Caribbean standards, retaining a serenity that has great appeal.

After a $3 million renovation in 1997, the resort instituted an all-inclusive Platinum Plan that makes almost everything at the resort free. For families with children, the Platinum Plan includes a Club Kidz program that divides children into age groups. Activities include studying island ecology and culture, arts and crafts, beach picnics, crab racing, kite flying competitions, and lots of water activities.

The general consensus seems to be that the St. James's Club is exceptional—American Express card holders voted it one of the best hotels in the world, and other hospitality organizations have honored its success. We think that it is a resort whose sum is truly greater than its parts, even though its parts are exceptional. Great resorts have intangible attributes of ambience, quality, and service that fall together so seamlessly that they are hard to recognize as separate components. The food at St. James's Club, as an example, is of European caliber, beautifully prepared and presented in the resort's five main restaurants and five bars, each with a distinguished wine list. The casino is small but attractive and is part of an entertainment package that allows guests to enjoy music, dancing, and live performances without leaving the property. Also on the property are a beauty salon and spa with full massage and body treatment services.

Guests have access to four large pools and two fine beaches. The well-protected coral reefs and historic shipwrecks have created a rich venue for divers and snorkelers. Near the main lodge is a private marina that always has a handful of power yachts tied to its docks. For guests wishing to go deep-sea fishing or take overnight boat charters, all can be easily arranged.

You won't find glitzy statues or mock, neo-Greek porticos at St. James's Club. Instead there are hundreds of coconut palms surrounding patios and bougainvillea in bright colors lining intimate pathways. This is an understated resort that relies on its elegance, beauty, and sure-handed service to carry the day. For most of its guests, it does so very nicely.

St. James's Club

P.O. Box 63
Mamora Bay, Antigua, West Indies
Phone: 800–345–0356 or 268–460–5000
E-mail: reservations@antigua-resorts.com
Web site: www.eliteislandresorts.com

Group/Getaway: Families

Accommodations: Rooms in the main building are rated in Club, Premium, and Suite categories. The remaining units are private villas overlooking Mamora Bay. All rooms include air-conditioning, either two double or one king-size bed, ceiling fans, hair dryer, private bath with shower and tub, safety deposit box, direct-dial telephone, color cable television, alarm clock, radio, bathrobes, and private balconies or patios. Suites have one bedroom with king-size beds, a separate living room, full bath, and patios or balconies. Two-bedroom villas have two baths, full kitchen, and dining and living areas with balcony and patio overlooking Mamora Bay. The magnificent Hillside Homes overlook the entire property and feature private swimming pools and luxurious furnishings.

Points of Distinction: Situated on its own private peninsula, St. James's Club has two beaches to choose from: Mamora Bay Beach, a quiet, tranquil bay where you can enjoy the water sports; and Coco Beach, the "windy beach," where guests enjoy the breezes while relaxing on a hammock or chaise longue.

Open: Year-round.

Minimum Stay: Three nights; seven nights February 8 to 24 and December 21 to 31.

Packages: The all-inclusive Platinum Plan.

Rates: Based on double occupancy, rates range from $450 to $860 per room, per night. Rates for children under thirteen staying with parents are $50 per night.

Frequently Asked Question: *Is scuba diving offered?* St. James's Club has its own dive master and diving school for anyone interested in becoming certified in coral reef and deep-sea diving. There is an additional charge for this service.

Don't Forget to Bring: Casual clothes, sunscreen, and a great novel.

Favorite Side Trips: Nelson's Dockyard at English Harbor; Shirley Heights Lookout, which offers a spectacular view of the harbor and is the island's hottest spot for live steel and reggae music on Sunday nights.

Nearest Airport: V. C. Bird Airport, thirty-five minutes from the resort.

ALL-INCLUSIVE SERVICES AND ACTIVITIES

(The following are included under the Platinum Plan.)

Food and Beverages: All meals, champagne upon arrival, unlimited liquor and beverages by the glass, afternoon tea.

Outdoor Activities: Croquet, tennis, volleyball.

Water Sports: Swimming, nonmotorized sports such as snorkeling, kayaking, windsurfing, sailing, pedal boats.

Facilities: Six all-weather tennis courts, four swimming pools, Jacuzzi, fitness center, karaoke, Foosball, table tennis.

Children's Services: Club Kidz and Teenz Club.

Children's Activities: Outdoor activities, water sports (for Teenz Club only), arts and crafts, cultural activities, excursions, beach picnics.

Available for a Fee: Tennis lessons, scuba diving, deep-sea fishing, yacht charters, full-service eighteen-slip marina, catamaran trips, golf, laundry, babysitting, currency exchange, use of full-service casino, massage and salon services. Rainforest, hiking, and museum tours can all be arranged at the guest services desk.

DIVI ARUBA MEGA BEACH RESORT
Oranjestad, Aruba

Unique to its Caribbean cousins, Aruba is a desert that is 20 miles long and 6 miles wide. Iguanas lounge in divi trees. Cacti dot the rocky hillsides and the low, sandy dunes.

In stark contrast to its arid interior, the island's white sandy beaches are plush with palm trees and tickled by the blue waters of the sea. This is an island like no other. This is the island the Divi Aruba Mega Beach Resort calls home.

As unique as Aruba itself, the Divi is unusual because guests have full use of two resorts, the Divi Aruba and its sister property next door, the Tamarijn Aruba. Guests sleep—eventually. But if they're awake, they're using the waters of the Caribbean as a toy, snorkeling, waterskiing, or canoeing. They're toning in the fitness center or tanning on the beach. They might romp into the capital city of Oranjestad or around the island's "outback" on bicycle. They might play tennis or volleyball, and it's never a bad time to ask for that first slushy drink of the day.

At night, most locals are stomping their feet and clapping their hands to the brash Caribbean music. Many risk their chips in the casino. At any time, during any day or night, guests of the resort have something to do and plenty of people around to help them do it. It is an exceptionally social atmosphere.

Between the bars, the beaches, the casino, and all the on-site activities, there is never a slow moment—unless a slow moment is what is needed.

There are food festivals and music festivals, including **Bon Bini** ("Bon Bini" means "welcome"). Arawak holidays are celebrated simultaneously with European holidays. Marathons, biathlons, and triathlons are held throughout the year, as well as other competitions, such as windsurfing, bowling, soccer, sailing, golf, and deep-sea fishing. There is even an annual contest among bartenders to see who is the best drink mixer on the island.

Today's Arubans are descendants of Arawaks, whose history on the island goes back 2,000 years, and of Europeans, who arrived as pirates and buccaneers. The language spoken here is a Creole called Papiamento, which is a blend of Dutch, Spanish, English, French, Portuguese, several African languages, and Arawak. Don't panic! Although Dutch is the official language of Aruba, both English and Spanish are commonly spoken everywhere on the island.

Divi Aruba Mega Beach Resort

J.E. Irausquin Boulevard #45
Oranjestad, Aruba
Phone: 800–554–2008 or 011–29–78–23300
E-mail: info@diviaruba.com
Web site: www.diviaruba.com

Group/Getaway: Families

Accommodations: The Divi Aruba Beach Resort is a low-rise resort offering 203 rooms with ocean views. Each room includes air-conditioning, telephone, private bath, and satellite color television.

Points of Distinction: The ocean can be seen not only from all of the rooms but also from the bar, lounge, and dining areas, which also overlook the beautiful blue Caribbean Sea.

Open: Year-round.

Minimum Stay: Five nights from Christmas Eve to New Year's and during the month of February, three nights in January, March, and April 1 to 14. No minimum the rest of the year.

Rates: Based on double occupancy, rates begin at $145 to $225 per person, per night; children under eighteen stay free.

Frequently Asked Question: *If Aruba is a desert, won't I be too hot?* The nights are cool, and during the day you are never too far from the beach or a freshwater pool.

Don't Forget to Bring: Sun protection for hot, sunny days, warm clothes for cool, breezy nights.

Favorite Side Trips: The capital city of Oranjestad (a fifteen-minute bike ride away) is filled with open-air markets, boutiques, and unlimited cuisine. Also, don't miss Aruba's rugged north shore, where the waves have formed giant, odd-shaped monoliths of hardened sand.

Nearest Airport: Queen Beatrix International Airport, a ten-minute drive from the resort.

ALL-INCLUSIVE SERVICES AND ACTIVITIES

Food and Beverages: All meals and beverages, snacks, wine and liquor.

Outdoor Activities: Tennis, bicycling, volleyball, shuffleboard.

Water Sports: Sunfish sailing, canoeing, windsurfing, snorkeling.

Facilities: Small fitness area located next door at Tamarijn Resort, swimming pools.

Entertainment: Nightly, including theme nights.

Other: Taxes and gratuities, lessons in snorkeling and windsurfing, match-play casino chip (with a coupon, Divi will match one bet) for adjacent Alhambra Casino, tickets to the Bon Bini Festival, full use of facilities at the adjacent Divi Beach.

Children's Services: Children's camp at the adjacent Tamarijn Aruba Beach Resort.

Children's Activities: Outdoor activities, arts and crafts, movies, cooking, storytelling, dancing, carnival fiesta.

Available for a Fee: Car rentals, laundry and dry cleaning, baby-sitting, golf.

BREEZES BAHAMAS

Nassau, Bahamas

Breezes Bahamas is located on the intriguing, small island of New Providence. The resort's front porch, so to speak, is Cable Beach, and its neighbors are the high-rise and low-rise casinos that run the length of the shoreline. Nassau's historic district is also nearby, with its many pubs, restaurants, and cafes, which make for a varied and exciting night out on the town. However, before planning a trip to take advantage of shopping and island nightlife, note there are many reasons not to leave this well-designed and smoothly run operation.

Breezes has three pools, each with its own purpose. One is for play, one is a misting pool, and the other hosts a swim-up bar for "sipping and dipping." There are lawn chairs by the pool, and there are lawn chairs in the pool. The beach spreads endlessly left and right and runs at least 50 yards in width. From the beach, snorkeling is as easy as stepping into calm, blue waters protected by a coral reef. Windsurfing, water-skiing, and sailing can fill an entire afternoon until sunset. Kayaks are available as well, so you can explore the open waters.

Breezes is famous for its countless couples "games" that are organized throughout the week. Our favorite was dressing in giant, padded sumo-style wrestling outfits (not as scanty as the real ones) and wobbling on the beach, trying to knock each other out of a sandy ring. There is also "Bouncy Boxing," which lets two fighters pummel each other with immensely oversized gloves. The "Off With Your Head" competition puts you in medieval dress with an extra head mounted on top of your own. You look through eye holes in the chest of the uniform while you try to knock your opponent's head off with lances in a good-natured jousting match.

The most unusual pursuit at Breezes is ice skating. The resort has the Caribbean's first all-weather, synthetic ice surface, located at the East Terrace lobby level. Skates are provided, as well as hockey sticks and pucks. Never been on the silver blades before? Not to worry. Clinics are offered on a regular schedule. The 1,600-square-foot rink is one of the newer additions to Breezes, along with a rock-climbing wall.

For those energetic enough to make a night of it, guests dance and sing until the wee hours, enjoying karaoke or the on-site disco. There are four bars at Breezes that have no official closing time. The sounds of reggae, rock, disco, and country can be heard, along with the softer sounds of the piano bar. They are there for your pleasure, open until you are ready to quit.

This attitude of supreme accommodation is the dominant theme at Breezes. The resort's staff members seem outlandishly committed to pleasing guests and satisfying their interests.

As you might expect in this environment, dining is a pleasure, with delicious and varied food served in three restaurants. Equally comfortable are the 400 rooms and suites that look down on the quiet, deep blue bay or the gardens adjoining it. Easy to reach, Breezes Nassau is enormously convenient, earning it many accolades as an all-round, topflight couples getaway.

Breezes Bahamas
P.O. Box CB-13049
Cable Beach
Nassau, Bahamas
Phone: 800–GO–SUPER or 242–327–5356
Web site: www.superclubs.com

Group/Getaway: Couples

Accommodations: There are 400 rooms and suites that look out on gardens or the ocean. All rooms are air-conditioned and include a king-size or two twin beds.

Points of Distinction: Although all-inclusive in the extreme, Breezes Bahamas Cable Beach also adjoins one of the internationally famous shopping areas in the Americas, with an exceptional nightlife and casinos.

Open: Year-round.

Minimum Stay: Two nights.

Rates: Based on double occupancy, from $140 per person, per night for a Garden View Room, to $507 for an Ocean Front Suite; single rates begin at $295.

Frequently Asked Questions: *Is golf available?* Golf is available at the Cable Beach Golf Course, which is near the resort. Greens fees are approximately $55, and $50 for a golf cart. *Can you get married at the resort?* With a three-week notice, the resort will plan a complimentary wedding that includes a wedding cake, champagne, a marriage license, a non-denominational marriage officer, flowers, and even witnesses. The bride and groom "to be" are required to be in Nassau forty-eight hours prior to their wedding day. Contact the resort for more information.

Don't Forget to Bring: Bathing suit, sunglasses, and appropriate athletic clothing and shoes.

Favorite Side Trip: Duty-free shopping in Nassau on Bat Street, just 5 miles from the resort.

Nearest Airport: Nassau International Airport, about fifteen minutes from the resort.

ALL-INCLUSIVE SERVICES AND ACTIVITIES

Food and Beverages: All meals, unlimited premium bar drinks and wine, afternoon tea, champagne oasis.

Outdoor Activities: Tennis, basketball, biking, jogging, beach volleyball.

Water Sports: Swimming, windsurfing, sailing, kayaking, waterskiing, pool volleyball, pool basketball.

Facilities: Fitness center, four freshwater pools, Jacuzzis, jogging trail, three lighted tennis courts, game room.

Entertainment: Nightly live music, theme parties, karaoke, disco, piano bar, pajama party, guest/staff talent show.

Other: Scuba diving lessons in swimming pool, tennis instruction, body-painting contests, ice-skating, ice hockey clinic, reggae and merengue dance classes, mixology classes, airport transfers, hotel taxes, gratuities.

Available for a Fee: Golf, snorkeling, scuba diving, motorized water sports (such as parasailing and Jet Skis), and cruises.

CLUB MED PARADISE ISLAND

Nassau, Bahamas

To appreciate this resort, you have to toss out aging stereotypes of the way Nassau used to be—glitz pitted against poverty, overdevelopment, and price gouging. After millions of dollars of investment, Nassau is a much rehabilitated city with less crime and more good restaurants and nightclubs adjoining its casinos than ever before. Across the bay from the town's brisk action is Paradise Island, a barrier landmass that has indisputably great beaches lined by resort hotels. One of the standouts is an impressive all-inclusive belonging to Club Med that now has one of the best niche sports programs in the field. For tennis players who want all the benefits of an active resort vacation while polishing the finer points of their game, there may be no better.

From the shores of Club Med, the sparkling, docked cruise ships and Goombay nightlife appear quite beautiful across the bay. They glow with energy in full contrast to the relative stillness of the colonial-style village of the resort, where stately garden areas with more than 100 species of exotic flora envelop the three grand mansions that anchor the Club Med village. The silvery half-moon beach provides an excellent setting for a host of water sports, plus an intensive tennis program with nineteen Har-Tru courts and a full tennis center.

For the ambitious racket player, the heart of the Club Med experience on Paradise Island is a two-and-a-half-hour clinic that begins each morning under the guidance of tennis professionals, who use ball machines, backboards, video analysis, and playing time to improve each guest's game. Following a lunch break and an afternoon of snorkeling or beach lounging, the Tennis Center organizes round-robins, full-set competitions, and even more individual lessons for those who wish to continue.

Unlike traditional tennis clubs, Club Med Paradise Island adds the benefit of on-site bars, a nightclub, and restaurants only yards away from the tennis action, so on the fourth or fifth day, when your feet are blistered and aching, a day off is completely enjoyable.

It is also worth remembering that Paradise Island is linked to New Providence (the name of the island that holds Nassau and two-thirds of the Bahamas' population) by a short bridge, making access to the city with its shopping and entertainment venues very easy. Along with Club Med on Paradise Island is the sensational Atlantis Resort, a championship golf course, and a famous casino. Whether you answer the call of "Tennis, anyone?" in the affirmative or negative, at this Club Med you won't go wrong.

Club Med Paradise Island

P.O. Box 7137
Nassau, New Providence, Bahamas
Phone: 800–CLUB–MED or 242–363–2640
Web site: www.clubmed.com

Group/Getaway: Singles, Sports & Fitness

Accommodations: There are 306 air-conditioned bungalows enclosed by exotic gardens and featuring two twin or one queen-size bed, television, phone, and hair dryer. Two-story Bahamian Villas feature a living room, fully equipped and stocked kitchenette, bedroom with queen-size bed, and wrap-around porches on each level.

Points of Distinction: Paradise Island, a renovated plantation, is known as a tennis resort. It has a saltwater swimming pool and access to two beaches that overlook Nassau Harbor.

Open: Year-round.

Minimum Stay: Seven nights; some three- and four-night options.

Rates: Based on double occupancy, rates begin at $1,120 per adult and $336 per child age two to fifteen for seven nights. Children under two stay free. The Club Med annual membership fee is $55 per family member; children eleven and under, $25.

Frequently Asked Questions: *Do I need to bring my own tennis equipment?* Rackets are provided, but you can bring your own equipment. Tennis balls are provided and are also available at the resort's boutique. *What lessons are offered?* Snorkeling, gymnastics, tennis for all levels, windsurfing, sailing, golf for beginners.

Don't Forget to Bring: Sandals and appropriate athletic clothes and shoes for sports.

Favorite Side Trips: Shopping, visiting historical sites and Exuma Islands, and playing at the casinos in Nassau.

Nearest Airport: Nassau International Airport is 20 miles from the resort.

ALL-INCLUSIVE SERVICES AND ACTIVITIES

Food and Beverages: All meals, served throughout the day, and alcoholic beverages, including premium brands.

Outdoor Activities: Tennis, volleyball, basketball, bocce.

Water Sports: Sailing, kayaking, snorkeling, swimming.

Facilities: Nineteen Har-Tru tennis courts, seven of them lighted; clubhouse; swimming pool.

Entertainment: Nightly live shows feature the resort's "gracious hosts" (staff) and guests as part of the entertainment. Two bars, karaoke.

Other: Boat trips, table tennis, billiards, taxes. Airport transfers included only if you book air reservations through Club Med. No tipping allowed.

Available for a Fee: Golf at a nearby eighteen-hole course; scuba diving; excursion program activities, which include deep-sea fishing, Coral World, sailing trips, swimming with dolphins, parasailing, and helicopter rides.

RADISSON CABLE BEACH AND GOLF RESORT

Nassau, Bahamas

West of Nassau is historic Cable Beach, which is sometimes called "the Bahamian Riviera." Among the world's choice oceanfront real estate strips dotted with all-inclusive resorts, Cable Beach is second only to Negril in Jamaica. If vacationing on easy-to-reach Nassau appeals, with its hopping ambience of Waikiki, the French Riviera, and Florida's super-trendy South Beach all rolled into one, the Radisson Cable Beach and Golf Resort is bound to please.

After Nassau, "the Strip," as the Cable Beach area is known locally, has the best infrastructure in the Caribbean Sea, which means access from most American cities is easy. There is never a lack of excitement: Next to the hotel is the Caribbean's largest casino, replete with live entertainment and all of the temptations that come with one-armed bandits, roulette wheels, and card games.

Adjacent to the hotel is its eighteen-hole championship golf course for unlimited use by Radisson Cable Beach guests. There are complimentary introductory scuba courses and nonmotorized water sports, a fitness center featuring tennis courts, squash, and racquetball, and six restaurants. Food and unlimited beverages are available around the clock. It's big, it's diverse, and it manages to serve the guests in its 700 rooms with amazingly good care.

The motto at Radisson Cable Beach is that it offers a complete vacation experience. This isn't a place to slip off the grounds and find exotic culture or undisturbed beaches where you will be alone. This resort is a social experience where you will meet a rich diversity of vacationers from all parts of the globe with similar goals—to have a high-energy vacation with plenty to do and plenty to eat. Radisson is expert at managing and caring for large numbers of people who take part in dozens of activities day and night.

To recommend this resort without mentioning its revamped campus would not do it justice. The landscaping around its seven acres of waterscape pools with cascading waterfalls and Jacuzzis nestled among rock formations is beautiful and inviting. This horseshoe-shaped, nine-story complex embraces a wide beach that is so expansive, it is never crowded. The smooth, clear waters are ideal for all swimming abilities.

Radisson Cable Beach and Golf Resort

P.O. Box N 4914
West Bay Street
Nassau, Bahamas
Phone: 800–333–3333 or 242–327–6000
E-mail: info@radissonbahamas.com
Web site: www.radisson-cablebeach.com

Group/Getaway: Families, Sports & Fitness

Accommodations: The 700 spacious rooms and suites have private balconies overlooking the ocean, waterscape, or the garden areas. Accommodations include Junior Suites, with a king-size bed, separate sitting area, and views of the ocean; and International Suites, with one or two bedrooms and separate dining and living rooms. Some rooms are handicapped accessible; non-smoking rooms are available.

Points of Distinction: The resort is set upon a stretch of white, sandy beach and adjacent to one of the Caribbean's largest casinos. Its Camp Junkanoo is becoming the best children's program on Cable Beach, making the resort an appealing destination for families.

Open: Year-round.

Minimum Stay: None.

Rates: Based on double occupancy, rates begin at $165 to $265 per person, per night, $352 at the holiday season. Children under twelve eat and stay free when sharing a room with adults. Maximum two children free per room. Teens age thirteen to sixteen are $30 or $65 per person, per night depending on the plan.

Frequently Asked Question: *Do you need to eat all your meals at the same restaurant?* There are six restaurants that you can choose from each day and night; cuisine ranges from local Bahamian and Caribbean specialties to Mexican, Italian, steakhouse, seafood, and continental meals.

Don't Forget to Bring: Golf clubs, sunscreen, and sunglasses.

Favorite Side Trips: Atlantis; Paradise Island; the Nassau Marriott Crystal Palace and Casino, next door to the Radisson Cable property.

Nearest Airport: Nassau International Airport, a ten-minute drive from the hotel.

ALL-INCLUSIVE SERVICES AND ACTIVITIES

Food and Beverages: All meals and beverages, including wine and liquor.

Outdoor Activities: Golf, tennis, squash, racquetball, beach volleyball.

Water Sports: Sailing, snorkeling, kayaking, scuba diving.

Facilities: Eighteen-hole golf course, fitness center. Nearby: casino.

Other: Scuba-diving lessons, weddings, taxes, gratuities, airport transfers.

Children's Services: Fully supervised Camp Junkanoo.

Children's Activities: Sports, nature walks, treasure hunts, movies, arts and crafts.

Available for a Fee: Golf carts, babysitting, laundry service, business center, motorized water sports such as parasailing.

SANDALS ROYAL BAHAMIAN RESORT AND SPA

Nassau, Bahamas

The Royal Bahamian Resort and Spa can only be described as the crown jewel in Sandals' string of Caribbean resorts—perhaps the best-known group of all-inclusive properties. The Sandals brand name has become synonymous with the entirely all-inclusive way of life that creates a full vacation experience within the resort's walls, so that you need never leave. In true form, The Royal Bahamian has restaurants, shops, pools, beaches, entertainment, sports facilities, and a state-of-the-art spa. All Sandals guests are met at the airport and brought to the facility as part of the package. Tips are refused, and everything is included except what is for sale in the shops.

The emphasis at the Royal Bahamian is service and luxury, which are not as easy to find in the Caribbean as in many other places in the world. In fact, the Bahamas has had one of the more checkered service records of any tourist-oriented destination in the world, but this Sandals resort is proving that all that is changing. The staff is first-rate and seems genuinely excited to have its guests on hand.

Located on Nassau's world-famous Cable Beach, which has become the Bahamian Riviera, the shine of this relatively new property still glistens. Once inside, an ambience of elegant European spa traditions is maintained amid facilities that are thoroughly modern. The management of the facility talks about the "magic wand treatment" that transforms stressed guests who arrive from the mainland in need of recuperation. It is facilitated by an attitude that no wish of a guest is too large or small to tackle. Even if they can't comply, the staff's intent is impressive. And there's something about those Greek statues in the gardens and Roman columns by the pool that made us think they mean it.

A day at the Royal Bahamian starts and ends in an ocean- or garden-view room, but the options in between are many. Will it be canoe or kayak today? Do you feel like Caribbean or Italian tonight? Or what about sailing over to Sandals Cay (the resort's private offshore island) this evening for a moonlight swim and supper? For many who come here, the ever-present opportunities only segue into the vast array of a la carte spa packages that are at the core of this resort experience. Herbal body massages, facials, and eucalyptus steam baths complement candlelight dining, free alcohol, and live bands that play near a very broad and soft beach during daily dramatic sunsets. Sandals has been accused of ordering all of this up from central casting and of institutionalizing romance, but we think the way they are doing it at the Royal Bahamian is pretty alluring.

As you might expect in this environment so accessible and close to Florida, many honeymooners visit, making for a very cheery and affectionate crowd. It is also worth noting that the Sandals Royal Bahamian has combined weddings and honeymoons into a package called the WeddingMoon to simplify the planning and budgets of couples wishing to marry. If it sounds a bit hokey, Sandals assured us that hundreds of couples take WeddingMoons each year. As a result, the resort knows how to do it well and is willing to customize to suit each couple's desires.

Sandals Royal Bahamian Resort and Spa

P.O. Box 39-CB-13005
Bay Street
Cable Beach
Nassau, Bahamas
Phone: 800–SANDALS or 242–327–6400
E-mail: info@sandals.com
Web site: www.sandals.com

Group/Getaway: Couples, Spa & Wellness

Accommodations: Royal Bahamian offers 405 rooms in twelve categories, including Suite Concierge service. Each room includes air-conditioning, a king-size bed, hair dryer, telephone, private bath and shower, safe, clock radio, satellite television, and spectacular views of the ocean or lush gardens. Luxurious oceanfront suites as large as private villas are also available.

Points of Distinction: The resort offers a guarantee that in the unlikely event a hurricane should interrupt your stay, a complimentary replacement vacation with round-trip airfare will be awarded.

Open: Year-round.

Minimum Stay: Three nights.

Rates: Based on double occupancy, $325 to $690 per person, per night.

Frequently Asked Question: *What makes this resort different from other Sandals resorts?* Voted one of *Condé Nast Traveler*'s "Top 10 in the World" spas, the Sandals Royal Bahamian Resort is renowned for its Old World European elegance. There are formal gardens inspired by Versailles, stately Doric columns, Florentine statuary, and Roman-inspired pools. The opulence of the European-style spa is magnificent. Even the restaurants have a Mediterranean/Caribbean flair.

Don't Forget to Bring: Exercise clothes if you plan to use the fitness center; diver certification; sunscreen.

Favorite Side Trip: Nassau—a ten-minute drive—is replete with shopping, clubs, and casinos.

Nearest Airport: Nassau's International Airport, ten minutes from the resort.

ALL-INCLUSIVE SERVICES AND ACTIVITIES

Food and Beverages: All meals, nonalcoholic beverages, snacks, afternoon tea, wine and liquor.

Outdoor Activities: Tennis, volleyball, horseshoes, lawn chess, shuffleboard.

Water Sports: Kayaking, windsurfing, sailing, snorkeling, scuba diving, swimming, waterskiing, paddleboating.

Facilities: Fitness center, hot and cold plunge pools, saunas, three pools, five whirlpools, steam baths.

Entertainment: Live music at sunset, piano bar and lounge, karaoke.

Other: Billiards, gratuities, taxes, airport transfers, transportation from the airport.

Not Included: Departure taxes.

Available for a Fee: Casino gambling, golf, off-property excursions, laundry service, valet, secretarial facilities, car rental, spa and salon services, including massage, hydrotherapy, facials, body treatments.

CLUB MED COLUMBUS ISLE

San Salvador, Bahamas

Columbus Isle is located 200 miles southeast of Nassau and an hour by plane from Miami on the remote Bahamian island of San Salvador. It is one of Club Med's most alluring properties—if superb diving, snorkeling, beachcombing, and water sports are your aim. Columbus Isle is not for everyone, however. It is a flat, simple island whose main excitement is its connection to crowds of turtles, exotic fish, dolphins, and stingrays darting among the coral reefs. Locals are mostly fishermen who operate with kindness and appreciation for the money Club Med patrons bring. Nighttime entertainment is imported to Club Med, whose population swells to about 500 when it's full.

Club Med Columbus Isle is made up of brightly painted Bahamian cottages, trimmed in white gingerbread, which form a self-contained village. Each cottage has a private balcony or patio and is within easy walking distance from an equally attractive spa, where massage and beauty treatments are offered throughout the day and evening.

Also in the village complex are three good restaurants that offer large selections of fresh fruits, breads, fish, and vegetables, mostly from the island. The clientele is largely European, which many Americans enjoy. Club Med prides itself on the friendships that develop between guests, often lasting a lifetime.

With the island's 3 miles of dazzling white-sand beaches, the focus is on doing activities in and out of the outstandingly clear waters. The dive center, called the Sea Center, is staffed by top professionals who can speak many languages and inspire novices as well as experts. Divers should ask for rooms close to the Sea Center, which also houses a gym, a rollicking disco, two restaurants, and a delightful bar where you can watch the molten sun set.

Club Med Columbus Isle

Columbus Isle
San Salvador Island, Bahamas
Phone: 800–258–2633 or 242–331–2000
Web site: www.clubmed.com

Group/Getaway: Couples, Sports & Fitness

Accommodations: Spacious, colorful bungalows with air-conditioning; double-occupancy rooms are decorated with international handicrafts. The resort offers both Ocean View and Ocean Front Rooms with private balcony or porch. All rooms include a phone, television, hair dryer, large bathrooms, mini refrigerator, and a queen-size or two double beds.

Points of Distinction: Club Med's newest property has a world-class dive center.

Open: Year-round.

Minimum Stay: Three nights.

Rates: Based on double occupancy, beginning at $1,190 to $1,610. Higher rates during winter months. Children's rates start at $336 per week. Club membership is $55 per adult and $25 per child. Rates do not include airfare, often part of a Club Med package.

Frequently Asked Questions: *Do I need to be a member of Club Med?* Yes, membership fees are $55 per adult and $25 per child. *Who is this resort best suited for?* Scuba divers and couples and honeymooners who want remoteness and love the sea.

Don't Forget to Bring: Medical certificate and diplomas, which are required for scuba diving.

Favorite Side Trips: Renting a motor scooter and exploring the shore.

Nearest Airport: San Salvador Airport, approximately five minutes from the village center.

ALL-INCLUSIVE SERVICES AND FACILITIES

Food and Beverages: All meals served throughout the day, nonalcoholic and alcoholic beverages.

Outdoor Activities: Basketball, volleyball, tennis, bocce.

Water Sports: Sailing, windsurfing, snorkeling, kayaking, water exercises.

Facilities: Fitness center, ten Har-Tru tennis courts.

Entertainment: Nightly live entertainment featuring karaoke and your "gracious hosts," or "GH" (staff).

Other: Boat trips. Airport transfers included only if you book air reservations through Club Med.

Available for a Fee: Massage; beauty treatments, including facials, body scrubs, manicures; laundry service; scuba diving (beginners and experienced) and wet-suit rental; deep-sea fishing; sailing; gymnastics; tennis; archery for beginners.

ALMOND BEACH CLUB AND SPA

St. James, Barbados

Almond Beach Resorts are the premier all-inclusives on Barbados. Once a land of sugar plantations, the island's economy is sound and its infrastructure up to date. Barbados is a coral island, and its beaches are made from finely ground coral forming a clean, fine grain that is alluring at all times of the day. Along its western shore, light trade winds cool sunbathers, and the flat waters are ideal for boating and swimming. Bajans have a 98 percent literacy rate and a confidence about their island that is palpable in most activities one pursues. Barbados is sensuous and friendly, which tends to make locals working at resorts open and helpful.

Almond Beach Resorts has two separate properties about 6 miles apart on the island's western Gold Coast. Almond Beach Club and Spa is a formidable player in the couples' getaway niche of all-inclusives. While its sister property, Almond Beach Village (6 miles away; it's described in the following entry), caters to the family market with style, the Club and Spa is an innovative resort for couples seeking romance.

Almond Beach Club and Spa is situated on four splendid beachfront acres. Small and intimate, the resort holds great appeal for honeymooners. It was constructed to allow its guests to develop an affectionate relationship with the sea and its many wonders on the Gold Coast of Barbados. On this island, the turquoise waters are calm and alluring, becoming the focus of activities at the resort. The waterfront area is particularly well run by helpful men and women who will take you waterskiing or snorkeling, or set up windsurfing, sailing, or banana boating whenever you are inclined. Or go reef fishing, or to the fitness center, or simply lounge around one of the resort's three pools. But it is the beach, with sand so fine that it resembles sugar, that may be the club's greatest prize.

The mythology of the Almond Beach Club and Spa beach experience is that the sands on its spectacular beach have certain aphrodisiac qualities. Lie on it or walk on it—its sensuousness reaches the hearts of all who visit, inflaming passions.

Barbados has this quality anyway. Add the fineness of the Club's beach with the subtle know-how of its staff and it is not surprising that couples return often to this unusual all-inclusive.

No less complementary to romance is the "Dine-Around" Program that allows visitors to frequent either of the resort's on-site restaurants or the Almond Beach Village's many restaurants.

Almond Beach Club and Spa

St. James
Barbados
Phone: 800–425–6663 or 246–432–7840
E-mail: info@almondresorts.com
Web site: www.almondresorts.com

Group/Getaway: Couples

Accommodations: Almond Beach Club has 161 air-conditioned rooms with two twin beds or one king, a bath, hair dryer, satellite television, and coffee-tea maker.

Points of Distinction: The mythical qualities of the resort's beach sand are said to stoke passion.

Open: Year-round.

Minimum Stay: Three nights.

Rates: Based on double occupancy, rates for two people for seven nights range from $2,275 to $6,928.

Frequently Asked Question: *What is the best way to tour the island?* You can tour the island by rental car, taxi, motor scooter, or even by horseback.

Don't Forget to Bring: A driver's license if you plan to rent a car or scooter.

Favorite Side Trip: A trip to Andromeda Gardens in St. Joseph Parish to enjoy its winding paths, ponds, and abundant varieties of orchids, trees, and other plants is a perfect way to spend an afternoon in Bridgetown.

Nearest Airport: Grantley Adams International Airport, about twenty minutes from the resort.

ALL-INCLUSIVE SERVICES AND ACTIVITIES

Food and Beverages: All meals and snacks, alcoholic and nonalcoholic beverages, room service for lunch and dinner.

Outdoor Activities: Golf, tennis, squash.

Water Sports: Swimming, snorkeling, waterskiing, windsurfing, aqua biking, sailing, kayaking, catamaran sailing, reef fishing, banana boating.

Facilities: Three swimming pools, fitness center, nine-hole golf course.

Entertainment: Nightly; late-night disco.

Special Events: Weekly picnics, Barbados jazz festival in February, manager's weekly cocktail party.

Other: Transportation to Bridgetown, taxes, gratuities, service charges.

Available for a Fee: Guests are asked to bring their own golf balls and tees, or they can purchase them at the golf course. Salon and spa treatments are additional.

ALMOND BEACH VILLAGE

St. Peter, Barbados

Barbados is a sensual island that has evolved from sugar plantations, which once belonged to British royalty. Although the Brits no longer rule, they left behind a terrific educational system that has produced a 98 percent literacy rate on the island, and a confident, sophisticated citizenry claiming many accomplishments. Successfully running hotels and resorts is one of them.

Almond Beach Village is situated on thirty-two acres of prime beach with 330 rooms, four main dining areas, and five bars. The village is located 6 miles from its sister property, Almond Beach Club and Spa, described in the previous entry. In spite of the nightly live entertainment and a great array of adult activities, such as West Indian dance classes and Caribbean mixology, this resort has distinguished itself as a premier family destination.

There are a number of all-inclusives that are dedicated to vacationing families, but few that have perfected its program for children as well as Almond Beach Village. Called the Kid's Club, the program accommodates all ages with remarkable ease, even infants who stay in a separate nursery,

with one staff member for every three babies. For infants and children up to four years old, Kid's Club is open from 9:00 A.M. to 5:00 P.M.

For ages five and older, the Kid's Club program operates from morning until 10:00 P.M., which gives many parents a chance to be with their kids during the day but take time off at night. Parents and children have the option of enrolling in the program for all or part of a day, or even for a single activity. The young and enthusiastic staff supervise all activities in a clubhouse fitted with all of the latest gadgetry needed to excite Generation Y kids—Nintendo, large-screen televisions, pool tables, board games, jukeboxes, and books. But the focus for kids and adults at the Village is not on being inside clubhouses and bars, and you can be assured that your children will stay amused and excited with countless water sports and games, arts and crafts, treasure hunts, and pool games.

The stated goal of Almond Beach is to make children so happy that they will want to return, just as adults do. Many families come repeatedly, especially from North America, because of the resort's ability to make good on its mission.

Almond Beach Village

Heywoods
St. Peter, Barbados
Phone: 800–425–6663 or 246–422–4900
E-mail: info@almondresorts.com
Web site: www.almondresorts.com

Group/Getaway: Families

Accommodations: With the large number of rooms available, if a specific view is important to you, it's best to ask for it. Deluxe Rooms have a private balcony; Superior Deluxe Rooms include a large bedroom with seating area and private patio. One-Bedroom Suites have a spacious bedroom and adjoining living area. Presidential Suites have two separate bedrooms, two baths, large living and dining areas, and a private balcony with a magnificent view of gardens, the pool, and the Caribbean Sea. All rooms include hair dryer, in-room safe, direct-dial phone, coffeemaker, radio, and satellite television.

Points of Distinction: Almond Beach Village has a nine-hole, par twenty-seven, executive golf course. Greens fees, club rental, and pull carts are included in the all-inclusive package.

Open: Year-round.

Minimum Stay: Three nights.

Rates: Based on double occupancy, Standard Rooms begin at $162.50 to $513 per person, per night; a single supplement begins at $385. Children under age sixteen stay for $65 per night, $95 during the holidays.

Frequently Asked Question: *Does the resort provide day care for infants?* There is a separate nursery for infants and toddlers up to age four, with one child-care worker for every three infants. Please bring adequate supplies of diapers and formula and a change of clothing.

Don't Forget to Bring: Golf clubs, tennis rackets, and a big appetite.

Favorite Side Trips: The famous Drax Hall, one of three Jacobean homes remaining. The heart and soul of shopping in Barbados is Broad Street in the capital city of Bridgetown.

Nearest Airport: Grantley Adams International Airport, about twenty minutes from the resort.

ALL-INCLUSIVE SE[...] AND ACTIVITI[...]

Food and Beverages: Three m[...] a day, snacks, afternoon tea, alcoholic and non-alcoholic beverages, room service for lunch and dinner.

Outdoor Activities: Golf, squash, tennis.

Water Sports: Waterskiing, kayaking, sailing catamarans or Sunfish, windsurfing, snorkeling, aqua biking, reef fishing, banana boating.

Facilities: Fitness center, nine-hole, par twenty-seven executive golf course, tennis courts, ten swimming pools, four bars, four restaurants.

Entertainment: Island bands, talent night, piano bar, disco.

Special Events: Weekly beach picnic, manager's weekly cocktail party.

Other: Aerobics, taxes, service charges, gratuities.

Children's Activities: Outdoor activities, water sports, arts and crafts, cultural activities, movies and CD jukebox, computer and video games, story time, instruction in calypso and reggae dance.

Children's Services: Special menu, a pizzeria, and ice-cream parlor. Kid's Club for children of all ages, including nursery for infants. Kids' coordinators for ages two and a half to four, five to nine, and ten to twelve; teen center for ages thirteen and older.

Available for a Fee: Golf balls and tees, baby-sitters after 5:00 P.M. for children under age five ($7.50 per hour for a maximum of three children per family).

CLUB ROCKLEY

Christe Church, Barbados

Located on the popular southern coast of Barbados, Club Rockley spans an impressive seventy acres. It is so well designed that its guests have all the privacy they desire. We like the fact that while at this beautifully landscaped retreat, you feel as if you were miles from all civilization. In fact the resort is situated about 4 miles from Bridgetown, convenient to supermarkets, banking facilities, the post office, and Rockley Beach. The resort has seven Mediterranean-style buildings intersected by tropical gardens and seven pools that are only minutes from the broad beach on the Caribbean.

Club Rockley is geared for all family members. The resort is home to a nine-hole, par thirty-six golf course as well as five tennis and squash courts. There are also a good disco, a mini-mall with diverse shopping, and a fitness club to satisfy all comers. Water sports are very popular at Club Rockley, with a superb windsurfing program, snorkeling, and Sunfish sailing. But sooner or later, most visitors to all-inclusive resorts want to lounge, and at Rockley there are many options. At poolside, drinks from the bar are only a hand wave away. Massages are also available here or on the beach, where the Barbadian sand is as warm as the locals, who enjoy a good chat. For parents with young children who want solitude, Club Rockley offers a baby-sitting service and a great kids' program.

The resort is home to the Club House Restaurant, which offers a la carte dining, while a full buffet is available at the Cloud Nine Restaurant. Guests can also enjoy the Sugar Reef Restaurant at nearby Rockley Beach.

Another asset of Club Rockley is its location on Barbados, an island with a high degree of art and culture. The creative vibrancy of the community offers guests at the resort many opportunities to experience the culture of the region. The influence of African heritage is noticeable in the art, crafts, and literary works produced on the island. You will also find the Bajans a fun, quick-witted, calypso-loving people who are as quick to smile as to help a stranger. If you visit Barbados in February, you'll be there in time to attend the Barbados Jazz Festival. Each year the Caribbean's premier musical event presents internationally renowned artists such as Kenny G, Earth, Wind and Fire, and B.B. King. If you are a student of architecture, you will enjoy the Jacobean-style houses that were built in Barbados in the late 1600s: Barbados is home to two of the three remaining examples of the house style in the Western Hemisphere.

Whether it's relaxation at the pool or beach, Club Rockley offers an impressive opportunity to enjoy the fine natural wonders of the sea and sand, while also learning about a historic island and its people. It stands out as one of the few all-inclusives that offer a genuine cultural experience.

Club Rockley

Golf Club Road, P.O. Box 35W
Worthing
Christ Church, Barbados
Phone: 800–777–1250 or 246–435–7880
E-mail: clubrockley@sunbeach.net
Web site: www.clubrockley.com

Group/Getaway: Families

Accommodations: A total of 145 units includes Hillside Suites with their own pool and bar area; each has a private balcony with view of the golf course. Studio A Suites have one bedroom overlooking the first fairway only, and Studio B Suites have one or two bedrooms overlooking the golf course. Studio B Suites are in clusters with their own pool.

Points of Distinction: The resort is built around a nine-hole golf course, which is a five-minute shuttle drive to the beach. The course opens at 6:00 A.M. daily, and guests are invited to play as many rounds as they like. Special tournaments are also set up for guests.

Open: Year-round.

Minimum Stay: None.

Rates: Based on double occupancy, Hillside Suites begin at $125 per person, per night for a standard studio, and $151 for a one-bedroom; children under fourteen, $31.25 additional per night. Winter rates are $187 to $206 per person, per night.

Frequently Asked Question: *What is the temperature like in Barbados?* With trade winds blowing gently over the sea, temperatures stay steady at about eighty degrees. Humidity rises a bit in the summer, when intermittent showers fall late in the day or during the night.

Don't Forget to Bring: Golf clubs, casual clothing, sweater for chilly evenings.

Favorite Side Trips: The Plantation, St. Lawrence Gap for entertainment; Bridgetown for duty-free shopping.

Nearest Airport: Grantley Adams International Airport, a twenty-minute drive from the resort.

ALL-INCLUSIVE SERVICES AND ACTIVITIES

Food and Beverages: All meals, non-alcoholic drinks, afternoon tea.

Outdoor Activities: Tennis, basketball, golf, beach volleyball, beach cricket, early morning walks.

Water Sports: Swimming, windsurfing, Sunfish sailing, snorkeling.

Facilities: Seven pools, nine-hole golf course, two squash courts, three lighted tennis courts, fitness club, laundry room.

Entertainment: Live bands for dancing nightly, fashion show, floor show, theme nights.

Other: Hobie Cat group cruises; squash, tennis, and scuba clinics with professionals; laundry rooms; transportation from airport; taxes and gratuities.

Children's Services: Supervised children's room.

Available for a Fee: Golf clubs and carts, baby-sitting service, personal golf lessons, tennis lessons, scuba diving, parasailing, waterskiing.

HARMONY CLUB
Paget, Bermuda

Harmony Club is one of Bermuda's few all-inclusive resorts, built originally as a private home in the 1930s and now preserved with historic elegance. The edifice is an example of the quaint, traditional Bermudian cottage-style architecture so common to the island, enhanced by exquisite gardens established more than half a century ago. Even though this classic resort hotel sits on a sunny, landlocked hillside, it is close to Bermuda's famed beaches and Hamilton's shops and nightspots. Harmony Club is the only hotel in Bermuda that requires double occupancy, but a "couple" can be two aunts or two friends as well as spouses—as long as both guests are over eighteen years of age.

Upon arriving, guests find complimentary champagne in rooms tastefully decorated with Queen Anne furnishings. It is telling of a quaintness that pervades all of Bermuda. Don't expect this to be a temperate version of the Caribbean: Bermuda is extremely well managed, with no obvious poverty, no unemployment, and none of the casual culture one normally associates with the islands to the south. Every home is perfectly painted. Gardens are raked clean and the owners of rusty cars are heavily fined by scrutinizing policemen. Taxi drivers must pass a history test, and littering is a felony. And no beach attire is tolerated off the beach. Riding a cycle or appearing in public without a shirt or in a bathing-suit top is considered offensive. Even the weather here is very different, with winter days that rarely go above seventy degrees, and high rainfall. As a result, vegetation and foliage are always green and attractive.

Still, Bermuda is not for everyone. If you like the wide-open energy and casualness of Jamaica, for example, the more formal and manicured environs of Bermuda and Harmony Club will not be your place of choice. But if you seek a locale where everything has its place and managed beauty reigns supreme, this historic all-inclusive captures the island's essence. It is a resort to depart from and return to after enjoying the south shore's pink-and-white sands, as well as a genuinely wonderful locale to simply relax. Of the resort's sixty-eight rooms, all but twelve have private balconies or patios. And we cannot describe how endearing the gardens are at Harmony Club.

Visitors leaving Harmony's grounds must travel by taxi, bus, or motorbike (tourists cannot drive cars). Harmony provides each guest with a scooter, but driving is British style—on the left, with confusing roundabouts that cause the inexperienced to perspire.

No visit to Bermuda is complete without discussing the island's crowning sport. Bermuda has the highest concentration of golf courses in the world—eight in just 21 square miles, all built along the ocean. Because Bermuda is a coral island with undulating hills and valleys, each course has a different character, with fairway views that draw golfers from around the world. Visitors to Harmony Club who choose the golf package have complimentary use of three golf courses—at Port Royal, Riddell's Bay, and Southhampton Princess country club.

On the grounds there are two tennis courts with a tennis pro available, and the backyard of the hotel has two putting greens. Besides saunas and Jacuzzis and a large and attractive pool, Harmony Club has another asset: It is the only all-inclusive we know in the world that offers a traditional English high tea, with cakes, finger sandwiches, and cookies. Life is civilized at Harmony Club, even charming, as it is in Bermuda. The resort offers its guests a unique opportunity to experience both.

Harmony Club

P.O. Box PG 299
Paget, Bermuda PG BX
Phone: 800–869–5824 or 441–236–3500
E-mail: reservations@harmonyclub.com
Web site: www.harmonyclub.com

Group/Getaway: Couples, Sports & Fitness

Accommodations: Sixty-eight deluxe rooms furnished in classic Queen Anne style. All feature king-size or twin beds, bathrobes, coffeemaker, in-room safe, hair dryer, and satellite television; most have a patio or balcony.

Points of Distinction: Harmony Club is the only 100 percent all-inclusive resort on the island of Bermuda.

Open: Year-round.

Minimum Stay: Six nights.

Rates: Based on double occupancy, rates begin at $556 per couple, per night; golf packages begin at $796.

Frequently Asked Question: *Is Harmony Club strictly for couples?* The adult-oriented hotel does have a couples-only policy, but a couple can be two adults over age eighteen.

Don't Forget to Bring: Bermuda shorts, golf clubs, sunscreen, and a camera.

Favorite Side Trip: Stonington Beach, with its pink coral crystals.

Nearest Airport: Bermuda International Airport, about fifteen minutes away from Harmony Club.

ALL-INCLUSIVE SERVICES AND ACTIVITIES

Food and Beverages: All meals; unlimited open bar for beverages, cocktails, and wine 11:00 A.M. to midnight; traditional English afternoon tea; welcome sparkling wine in room.

Outdoor Activities: Tennis, golf.

Water Sports: Swimming.

Facilities: Freshwater pool, hot tub, sauna, putting green, two tennis courts, gym/exercise room.

Entertainment: Nightly.

Other: Taxes, gratuities, and service charges; one round of golf per person, per day (cart not included) at one of three area golf courses with golf package; transportation to and from golf course is included.

Available for a Fee: Deep-sea and reef fishing aboard the 65-foot *Eureka;* diving and snorkeling; glass-bottom safari; transportation to and from airport.

PETER ISLAND RESORT

Road Town, Tortola

Hundreds of years ago, Christopher Columbus and Sir Francis Drake sailed along the shores of what are now the British Virgin Islands, and the buccaneers Blackbeard and Henry Morgan walked its beaches (and may have left buried gold, it's rumored). Now the treasure to be found there is Peter Island Resort, a 1,800-acre private island 4 miles south of the island of Tortola and 25 miles north of St. Thomas (in the U.S. Virgin Islands). The promise of this almost royal resort is personal attention: You'll never be just another room number to any of the dozens of staff members who wait on you hand and foot. Wander the island's six breathtaking bays or twenty secluded coves that form a shimmering necklace of aquamarine around the island's pure white-sand beaches and towering palms. Try a piña colada at midnight. Ask your maid for herb tea and cookies at 3:00 P.M. on your veranda. Everyone will know your name. Everyone has been well trained to pamper you.

With only fifty-two rooms and two villas in this remarkable retreat, the staff treats each guest as a celebrity. From the moment you arrive, a staff member with a Caribbean smile and lilting island accent greets you by name at the tiny Beef Island Airport (your name and where you are staying is memorized). This level of service continues until you step off Peter Island's shores a week or two later. This staff is not just good—they are extraordinary.

In an era of busy resorts that all boast bright sun, brilliant blue water, and powdery white beaches, Peter Island Resort only has one guest per ten acres. You won't find parking lots, cars, or even streets. Yes, it's laid-back, but it also has a simple elegance—a blend of serenity and beauty that is not easy to find in the ever-popular Caribbean.

In 1997, when the resort was closed for a six-month makeover, Caribbean-watchers were holding their collective breath to await the results. No one has been disappointed by the renewed classic style of Peter Island's guest rooms, beachfront junior suites, and exclusive villas. The food selection and preparation are no less grand than the accommodations. And few could complain about a lack of activities, which range from diving to dozing, from sunset serenades by local musicians to private meals overlooking Drake's Passage. Of the many romantic getaways we have visited, Peter Island ranks among the top in the world and is the finest the Caribbean has to offer. It is a luxurious escape that is incredibly well managed by a staff that puts a premium on serving visiting vacationers.

Peter Island Resort

P.O. Box 211
Road Town, Tortola
Phone: 800–346–4451 or 770–476–9988
Web site: www.peterisland.com

Group/Getaway: Couples

Accommodations: There are fifty-two rooms, including Ocean View guest rooms, Beachfront Junior Suites, and two private villas, including The Crow's Nest, an elegant, four-bedroom villa on a hill high above the resort. All have air-conditioning, a minibar, ceiling fans, a coffeemaker, hair dryer, and private patio. Ocean View guest rooms overlook St. Francis Drake Channel and Sprat Bay Harbor and feature a king-size bed, sitting area, ceiling fan, bar, CD player, and cathedral ceilings. Beachfront Junior Suites overlook Deadman's Bay Beach and feature French doors to a private deck with an atrium area that separates the bedrooms from the living room.

Points of Distinction: Named one of the "Best Places to Stay in the World" in 1998 and one of the "Top 20 Islands" in 1997 by *Condé Nast Traveler,* and listed among the "World's Best Small Hotels" (under 100 rooms) by *Travel and Leisure.* The harbor attracts spectacular boats from around the world.

Open: Year-round, except for a few weeks in fall.

Minimum Stay: Rooms none, suites seven nights, except during the holidays, when all minimums are seven to ten days.

Rates: Based on double occupancy, rates begin at $415 per night for one guest and $530 for two guests.

Frequently Asked Questions: *Is there a dress code?* During the day guests wear primarily sports attire. At lunch, cover-ups are worn over swimsuits. After 6:00 P.M. shorts are not appropriate in the Tradewinds dining and lounge areas, and most guests dress in elegant casual clothing, though some dress up. Sport coats and ties and cocktail dresses are not required. *Can we get married at Peter Island?* With breathtaking spots like Deadman's Bay Beach and the romantic Honeymoon Beach, it's not surprising that Peter Island is popular for weddings most of the year. A full-time coordinator handles all aspects of the occasion, be it an intimate affair or extravagant event. *Who is the resort best suited for?* Couples and honeymooners seeking adventure in romantic seclusion in the natural landscape of a world-class resort. Children are permitted, but Peter Island discourages children under the age of eight.

Don't Forget to Bring: Your camera to capture the spectacular gardens that feature bird-of-paradise, golden shower, oleander, bougainvillea, and red hibiscus.

Favorite Side Trip: To Virgin Gorda for snorkeling at "Fallen Jerusalem."

Nearest Airport: Beef Island Airport in Tortola. Peter Island is a twenty-five-minute ride by private yacht. Helicopter service is available from St. Thomas or San Juan with access to Peter Island's own heliport.

ALL-INCLUSIVE SERVICES AND ACTIVITIES

Food and Beverages: All meals, nonalcoholic beverages, afternoon tea.

Outdoor Activities: Volleyball, tennis, hiking, and biking on resort's trails, half-court basketball.

Water Sports: Sea kayaking, windsurfing, snorkeling, swimming in pool or ocean, sailing.

Facilities: Library, fitness center.

Entertainment: Nightly movies, weekly manager's cocktail party.

Other: Gratuities.

Not Included: Taxes.

Available for a Fee: Alcoholic beverages; deep-sea fishing, scuba diving with Dive B.V.I., chartered yacht, tennis lessons, spa, massage, golf, or shopping on St. Thomas. Island tours, Jeep rentals on Tortola, helicopter tours, day trips to Virgin Gorda and baths, catered theme parties, beach picnics or parties, wedding arrangements, use of conference facilities.

BIRAS CREEK
North Sound, Virgin Gorda

There are some resorts that we are glad to have visited (100, anyway), that we have been thrilled to experience. Among those are a few we wished we owned. Biras Creek is one of them. The owner had been vacationing at this resort on Virgin Gorda for fourteen years, when he fulfilled our fantasy. He bought the property and set about making it fit his vision of luxury. The result is a resort that offers unusual privacy in a spectacular setting. Located on a small, secluded peninsula that can't be reached by road, it reopened in 1996 with loving touches.

Biras Creek offers a unique combination of setting, service, and facilities, but it is the attention to detail that vaults this splendid resort into one of the world's best. Although the resort occupies 140 acres of a peninsula that is cut off from the rest of civilization by undeveloped, hilly land (guests reach the resort by private launch), there is nothing uncivilized about vacationing here.

Arriving at the dock, you are quickly made to feel at home by one of the two young British couples on hand who serve as guest assistants, or GAs, as they're affectionately known. They'll get you settled into your waterside or garden suite, and, throughout your stay, do whatever they can to make it a happy one. If you brought kids along, they'll even take charge of entertaining them for a while to give you time to yourselves. Biras Creek can work for families, but we consider it a romantic getaway because of the seductive ambience that tends to make couples want to luxuriate on

the beach, float on the aquamarine waters, or retire to very becoming bedrooms. Indeed, privacy is enhanced by the uncrowded, elegant layout of the cottages that face open water and lagoons, which give so much of the resort a remote, Gilligan's Island feeling. With never more than sixty guests on the grounds, socializing is voluntary and casual.

Another nice touch: Two bicycles are parked right outside your door, ready at any time for a ride around the property, most of it a preserve. There are also plenty of organized water activities here, but doing only what you feel like is encouraged. Still, if you get ambitious, the resort will meet your demands. We loved exploring the North Sound at the helm of a Boston Whaler, watching flying fish lead us toward billowy clouds that lazed on the horizon. When you do return to the resort after any activity, a cornucopia of wonderful food and creative libations is available around the clock. And no tipping, please.

Because it is a self-contained community, Biras Creek is so safe that even hardened city dwellers soon relax about such matters. The staff is very friendly and genuinely helpful, which is one of the reasons many of Biras Creek's guests keep returning to enjoy the high standards of accommodation, food, and service in such a beautiful natural setting. Even the owner admits he was once one of them, returning so often that it made more sense to purchase the property than pay to vacation. We predict that anyone who visits will be glad he or she did.

Biras Creek

P.O. Box 492477
Los Angeles, California 90049
Phone: 800–223–1108 or 310–440–4225
E-mail: caribisles@aol.com
Web site: www.biras.com

Group/Getaway: Couples

Accommodations: There are thirty-three suites along Berchers Bay on the Atlantic shore, plus nine suites in landscaped gardens. Each is positioned for privacy and contains a sitting room, separate bedroom, open-air garden showers, ceiling fans, refrigerator, and a veranda. Pelican Point, a private villa high on a hillside, has two bedrooms, each with its own bath, a kitchen, and a wraparound balcony offering views over North Sound.

Points of Distinction: Gourmet cuisine is served in the hilltop "Castle" dining area overlooking three different bodies of water. Motorized boats are docked away from other guest facilities to maintain the resort's tranquillity.

Open: November through August.

Minimum Stay: None, except during Christmas and New Year's, when there is a minimum stay of ten days.

Packages: Wedding packages are available. The Biras Creek's wedding coordinator will help arrange wedding parties, marriage license, registrar's fee, floral arrangements, wedding cake, champagne toast, and photographer (couples receive the undeveloped film). The basic wedding package is available for $1,100.

Rates: Based on double occupancy, rates for two range from $525 to $1,150 per night, or $1,350 for four people in a two-bedroom suite.

Frequently Asked Questions: *Are children permitted at the resort?* The resort is mainly for couples, but children eight years and older are welcome. *Are there guides for snorkeling?* Every morning, except Tuesday and Thursday, guides will take you on complimentary excursions through the magnificent reefs of Virgin Gorda.

Don't Forget to Bring: Bathing suit cover-up for breakfast and lunch, sundresses or comfortable pant suits for dining; men should bring casual slacks and collared shirts. No shorts are allowed in the dining room after 6:00 P.M.

Favorite Side Trips: Nature walks on the island or visits to any of the neighboring islands.

Nearest Airport: Beef Island Airport in Tortola, with a thirty-minute ferry service to the resort.

ALL-INCLUSIVE SERVICES AND ACTIVITIES

Food and Beverages: All meals, afternoon tea.

Outdoor Activities: Tennis, bicycling.

Water Sports: Snorkeling, windsurfing, sailing, motorboating, swimming, kayaking.

Facilities: Two lighted tennis courts, swimming pool.

Other: Garden tour, water-sports instructor available, Boston Whaler available for visiting other islands, airport transfers.

Not Included: Taxes and gratuities.

Available for a Fee: Alcoholic and non-alcoholic beverages, sight-seeing and shopping tours, private crewed sailing and motorboat charters to surrounding islands, day and sunset sails aboard a 44-foot yacht, glass-bottom boat tours, Jet Skiing, deep-sea fishing, scuba diving, and waterskiing.

BITTER END YACHT CLUB

North Sound, Virgin Gorda

If you love the water—gazing at it sparkling in the sun, sailing on it in a sleek yacht, or diving under it to explore a sunken wreck—this is an island resort of outstanding opportunities. The choice of water-based activities is almost as diverse as the kinds of tropical fish you'll find darting about the nearby coral reefs. We signed on for the eight-day Admiral's Package to make the most of what the Bitter End has to offer. But there are smaller and shorter packages that work very well. In eight days, we were able to allow plenty of time for reef snorkeling, wreck diving, and lots of boating in anything from an ocean kayak to a Freedom-30 yacht. More than 100 sailboats and powerboats are on hand for your free and unlimited use, as well as a variety of charter and excursion vessels.

The British Virgin Islands are considered to be in the best yachting waters in the world for safe water, variety of ports, raw beauty, and diverse itineraries. We cruised to Horseshoe Reef, kayaked to the Baths, and motored to remote Anegada Island for snorkeling. On another day, we dove the wreck of the 250-foot *Chikuzen,* and, before leaving, entered a weekend regatta to test our sailing skills. We watched others beachcombing on nearby Prickly Pear Island and still other guests trying their hands at deep-sea fishing. You get the idea—the possibilities are almost endless.

For those not seasoned in sailing, the Bitter End offers a free course. If you really want to get some sailing experience, certified instructors are available to give beginner to advanced lessons in the classroom, dockside, and on the water. Those less interested in yachting can try the free instruction in snorkeling, windsurfing, and scuba diving. More advanced scuba diving instruction is also available from a local school.

Spending some time on land will be necessary from time to time, of course (though accommodations in yachts are actually available), and the Bitter End meets the challenge on this front as well. The English Pub on the grounds specializes in offering sixteen-ounce Sounder drinks that loosen the tongues of yachtsmen and -women from around the world, encouraging them to share nautical yarns. In the evening, there are local seafood delicacies served in the Clubhouse Grill, followed by dancing under the stars or a video in the open-air Sand Palace Theater.

The accommodations are also outstanding at the Bitter End. Verandas offer sweeping views of the gathered yachts, as well as fantastic sunrises and sunsets. For indulging in the marine life, the Bitter End is unbeatable.

Bitter End Yacht Club
P.O. Box 46
North Sound, Virgin Gorda, British Virgin
  Islands
Phone: 800–872–2392 or 284–494–2746
E-mail: binfo@beyc.com
Web site: www.beyc.com

Group/Getaway: Families, Couples, Sports & Fitness

Accommodations: There are eighty-six accommodations that range from beachfront or hillside villas with ceiling fans to air-conditioned suites to a spacious estate house. There also are accommodations aboard four Freedom sailboats. The twenty secluded natural timber beachfront villas are designed to catch the balmy trade winds and feature wraparound verandas with hammocks large enough for two, twin beds or a king-size bed, a large dressing area, and a shower with sea views. The North Sound Suites are bungalows spread across a flowered hillside rising high above a white-sand beach and palm-shaded pool. With views of the Bitter End anchorage and North Sound, each suite includes a telephone, air-conditioning, coffeemaker, and a marble outdoor shower big enough for two. Suites have chauffeured transportation service on call. The large Estate House, a spacious two-bedroom, two-and-a-half-bath private house, is suitable for six guests. With spectacular views of the anchorage of North Sound and the Caribbean, amenities include a wet bar, refrigerator, air-conditioning, and a wide veranda with a screened-in porch.

Points of Distinction: The resort offers a unique open-air dining experience in any of its three restaurants: the Clubhouse Steak and Seafood Grille, the English Carvery, and the English Pub. Enticing foods such as homemade pumpkin soup, honey-citrus chicken, and fresh Anegada Reef lobster are served.

Open: Year-round.

Minimum Stay: Five nights for Admiral's Package.

Packages: The Admiral's Special Inclusive Vacations. Call for details on the many packages available, including the Yacht and Villa Combination Vacation, a combination of nights ashore and afloat aboard a Freedom-30 keelboat; the Honeymoon Vacation, a seven-night or longer package that includes a sunset cocktail cruise and a starlight dinner cruise; and the Pro-Am Regatta, held the first week of November, that gives resort guests the opportunity to sail with winning America's Cup and Olympic skippers.

Rates: Based on double occupancy, prices range from $430 to $850 per couple, per night.

Frequently Asked Question: *Are there any special events?* The Pro-Am Annual Regatta takes place the first week of November; Women's Sailing Week is the first week of November; and during Thanksgiving Family Week, children ages six to sixteen are invited to stay for half price.

Favorite Side Trip: A Blue-Water Excursion, which involves hopping aboard one of the many excursion boats for a guided snorkeling trip to such destinations as Anegada, the Baths, the Dog Islands, and Savannah Bay.

Nearest Airport: Beef Island Airport, with connections from San Juan, Puerto Rico, St. Thomas, United States Virgin Islands, or Antigua, is a thirty-minute ferry ride from the resort.

ALL-INCLUSIVE SERVICES AND ACTIVITIES

Food and Beverages: All meals, nonalcoholic beverages and rum drinks at lunch and dinner.

Outdoor Activities: Hiking, beachcombing.

Water sports: Snorkeling, scuba diving, windsurfing, swimming, rowing, kayaking, sailing, motorboating.

Facilities: Sand Palace Theater (for movies), swimming pool.

Entertainment: Dancing under stars to music of local bands, weekly manager's cocktail party.

Other: Regattas, private charters, use of resort's fleet.

Children's Activities: Although there is no special children's program, the following activities are arranged for different age groups: junior sailing instruction and water sports, arts and crafts, movies, outdoors activities.

Not Included: Taxes and gratuities, airport transfers.

Available for a Fee: Guided deep-sea and bonefishing day charters in the *Freedom-30* Yacht or *Bradley-22* powerboat; underwater dive tours; instruction for sailing, windsurfing, and high-performance windsurfing; snorkel and masks for snorkeling.

NECKER ISLAND

The Valley, Virgin Gorda

In the early 1980s an interesting piece of real estate was up for sale at the most northeastern point of the British Virgin Islands. It was a small island comprising seventy-four acres of beautiful, sandy beaches, panoramic hillsides, and stretches of rocky landmass, almost completely encircled by coral reefs and clear, pristine waters. Amazingly, this island had remained relatively untouched by humans until billionaire Richard Branson, owner of Virgin Airlines, purchased what is now known as Necker Island.

Originally, Necker was to be used as a vacation spot for Branson's family and friends, but when he realized it was being occupied only a few weeks a year, he decided to rent it. The guest accommodations include the Great House, which is a ten-bedroom villa, and two authentic one-bedroom Balinese guest houses. The maximum guest capacity is twenty-four people—not many for an entire island.

Your time on Necker can be spent exactly as you wish. You can take advantage of myriad activities, from waterskiing or snorkeling to fishing. As for cuisine, you can eat what you want, when you want, and arrange to eat it anywhere on the property you desire by merely consulting the island's chef and his staff. Menus can be tailored to each party's tastes and desires.

While there are many man-made amenities on Necker, the wonderful natural surroundings are impossible to overlook. Wild horses and pigs run free, and there is a wonderful assortment of birds and freshwater fish. Celebrities migrate here too, attracted by the seclusion. You may, for example, see Oprah Winfrey on your arrival or departure. One trip to Necker, and you'll understand why it is worth the high price.

Necker Island
P.O. Box 1091
The Valley, Virgin Gorda
British Virgin Islands
Phone: 800–557–4255 or 284–494–2757
    (fax)
Web site: www.neckerisland.com

Group/Getaway: Families

Accommodations: Guests can stay in either the Great House or one of two private houses—Bali Hi and Bali Lo. The Great House includes one master bedroom with bath and Jacuzzi, four double bedrooms with adjoining baths (available as two suites), and five more double bedrooms with adjoining baths. All have terraces with beautiful views. The two guest houses each have double bedrooms, private baths with ocean views, a futon-lined relaxation area, a furnished outdoor living area, a fully equipped kitchen, pagoda dining area, and private swimming pool.

Points of Distinction: Few places in the Caribbean are more beautiful or private. The largest marlin in the world was caught only a few hundred yards from the island.

Open: Year-round.

Minimum Stay: None.

Rates: Daily rates include the ten-bedroom Great House and the two Balinese houses, and are dependent on the number of guests on the island. The cost ranges from $22,500 to $40,000 per day.

Frequently Asked Question: *Are there any dangerous animals or poisonous plant life on the island?* The island is inhabited only by some deer, horses, pigs, and small reptiles, such as lizards and geckos. There are no poisonous plants anywhere on the island.

Don't Forget to Bring: A camera for this island of beauty.

Favorite Side Trip: The famous baths off Virgin Gorda are a collection of giant granite boulders that enclose beautiful pools of water. They were formed by volcanic activity.

Nearest Airport: Beef Island Airport, a thirty-minute ferry ride from Virgin Gorda.

ALL-INCLUSIVE SERVICES AND ACTIVITIES

Food and Beverages: All meals and drinks, including wine and liquor.

Outdoor Activities: Tennis (equipment provided).

Water Sports: Swimming, windsurfing, sailing, waterskiing, snorkeling, sea kayaking, fishing (light tackle equipment provided).

Facilities: Fully equipped gym, two tennis courts, two freshwater pools, freshwater Jacuzzi, full-size snooker table, laundry.

Other: Use of boats for visiting other islands.

Children's Activities: Books and board games available.

Not Included: Taxes and gratuities.

Available for a Fee: Helicopter sightseeing, beauty treatments, scuba diving, yacht charters, deep-sea fishing.

SPANISH BAY REEF RESORT

West Bay, Grand Cayman

Spanish Bay Reef sits amid a group of dive sites that are among the best in the world. Locations like Tarpon Alley, Ghost Mountain, Hopp's Wall, Orange Canyon, and Stingray City are short drifts from a shoreline of Grand Cayman that experienced divers know well. At Spanish Bay Reef Resort, taking advantage of these famed natural resources is the objective—straight and simple. The resort is located directly offshore from Spanish Bay Reef, where coral walls are high and miles wide. Visibility is a constant, reliable 150 feet and the waters remain warm throughout the year. Common and uncommon species are found here in large number, including stingrays, various sharks, and school after school of angelfish and other rainbow-hued fish.

Although the resort sits alone on the island's farthest northwest point, it is only ten minutes away from the resort-lined center of Seven-Mile Beach, where the nightlife beckons if anyone has enough energy after a day of diving to seek it out. The Spanish Bay sits high on a rocky ledge. Brick patios give guests a chance to enjoy food and drinks and look over the same waters where they passed daylight hours exploring the Caribbean's underworld. The restaurant, outdoor bar, and outdoor spa pool are all centrally located on the resort's property, making it easy to observe another highlight of the resort—watching the sun's vibrant and dramatic dip over the horizon.

Divers share a certain camaraderie.

Guests, therefore, become friends quickly and, inevitably, talk revolves around everyone's most recent dive. The mood remains lighthearted. Boasting is common and expected. At Morgan's Bar, the main event of the night is viewing the dive caught that day on videotape.

In the afternoon and into evening, lots of good food can be found at various spots around the resort. Meals at Governor's Terrace are served buffet style and are casual. Those who prefer a bit of pampering visit the Spanish Main restaurant, where a wait staff provides very nicely prepared, locally caught seafood such as fresh yellowtail and lobster.

Morgan's Bar remains open through most of the night; divers seem to have an impressive capacity to imbibe. It is friendly fun and a good place to pick up good pointers for future dives.

There is no mistaking Spanish Bay's appeal. It is a dive mecca of the first order. Even restaurant staff are expected to be certified divers, as well as enthusiastic and knowledgeable about the region's reef formations. Most visitors to this resort leave already planning their next visit, for it would take more days of consecutive diving than most visitors can spare to see all of the reefs in this spectacular formation. But whether a guest spends a few days or several weeks, no one seems to leave Spanish Bay without a larger appreciation of the many wonders of the Caribbean.

Spanish Bay Reef Resort

P.O. Box 903, George Town
West Bay
Grand Cayman, British West Indies
Phone: 800–482–3483 or 345–949–3765

Group/Getaway: Couples

Accommodations: There are sixty-seven guest rooms, including Superior Rooms with a water view; spacious Junior Suites with living area, sofa, bar, and double bed; Ocean View and Ocean Front Rooms with patios; and one- and two-bedroom Ocean Front Villas.

Points of Distinction: The resort is set on the northwest side of the island, located on Seven-Mile Beach. The resort offers guests access to Jeeps that they can use for up to three hours a day.

Open: Year-round.

Minimum Stay: None.

Rates: Based on double occupancy, rates begin at $160 to $280 per person, per night; one-bedroom oceanfront suites begin at $325 per couple, per night. No charge for children six and under staying with parents; for children ages seven to twelve, it's $50 per day; for ages thirteen to seventeen, $75 per day.

Frequently Asked Question: *Do you need to bring your own diving gear?* Guests are offered snorkeling gear, tanks, and weight belts for unlimited snorkeling and offshore diving. For guests who are taking scuba lessons for their diver's certification, the dive shop can provide you with all gear except wet suits.

Don't Forget to Bring: Bathing suit, sandals, light sweater for cooler evenings.

Favorite Side Trips: George Town; snorkeling at Stingray City.

Nearest Airport: Owen Roberts Airport, about fifteen minutes from the resort.

ALL-INCLUSIVE SERVICES AND ACTIVITIES

Food and Beverages: All banquet-style meals, nonalcoholic beverages, wine and liquor (not premium).

Outdoor Activities: Bicycling.

Water Sports: Sailing, snorkeling, scuba diving.

Facilities: Freshwater pool, private beach.

Entertainment: Entertainment twice weekly, disco, weekly barbecue on the beach.

Other: Taxes, gratuities, and airport transfers; access to resort Jeeps.

Children's Services: Camp Scallywags Children's Center for ages three to twelve (8:00 A.M. to 3:00 P.M. daily).

Available for a Fee: Deep-sea diving and fishing, regulators, wet suits, golf (5 miles away), baby-sitting in evening.

OCCIDENTAL CLUB
ON THE GREEN

Puerto Plata, Dominican Republic

Occidental Club on the Green is located in the heart of the Playa Dorado complex on the northern coast of the Dominican Republic, known for calm, clear waters. It's also less than a half mile from the island's famed golden beaches. Guests may simply stroll or sun on the beach, or they may enjoy it more actively with kayaks, snorkeling equipment, sailing, boogie boards, banana boat rides, and windsurfing, all part of the inclusive price.

Spreading over sixteen tropical acres, Occidental Club on the Green borders a championship golf course designed by Robert Trent Jones. The resort's 336 rooms are clustered in forty-five pastel pink and/or green villa-style buildings with blue roofs. All units look out over the garden or the golf course. Decor runs to Mediterranean style, with rooms having two queen-size beds or a king-size bed. Suites have one queen-size bed with a living room with a sofa bed, ideal for families. Youngsters will be kept busy morning through the evening with supervised activities at the Kid's Club.

Cigar lovers might well be attracted to this resort. Although it no longer offers a Cigar Apassionado program, Occidental Club on the Green is in the Dominican Republic, the world's leading producer and exporter of cigars. Guests can visit cigar makers to watch master *tocedors* bind and hand-roll fine cigars and to learn about the special production techniques that give each brand its unique flavor. We were impressed with the resort's congenial staff and their good efforts to make special arrangements for guests who sought cigar events. Opportunities to visit plantations, curing sheds, and cigar stores never stopped.

Occidental Club on the Green

P.O. Box 653
Playa Dorada
Puerto Plata, Dominican Republic
Phone: 800–858–2258 or 809–320–1111
Web site: www.occidentalhotels.com

Group/Getaway: Couples

Accommodations: The resort's 336 rooms are contained in forty-five pastel pink and/or green villa-style buildings. Each is beautifully appointed in Mediterranean decor with one king-size or two double beds, private bath with tub and shower, air-conditioning, color cable television, telephone, and a private balcony or patio overlooking the golf course or gardens. Junior Suites have one queen-size bed, a separate living area with a sofa bed, a ceiling fan, air-conditioning, and a private balcony or patio.

Points of Distinction: Guests dine around the world at the resort. El Pilon, the main restaurant, offers a buffet of various international dishes for dinner. Firenze has a la carte Italian choices for dinner each night, and Miranda's offers typical Brazilian dishes.

Open: Year-round.

Minimum Stay: None.

Rates: Based on double occupancy, rates per person are $92 to $108 per night.

Frequently Asked Question: *Who is this resort best suited for?* Although puffing on cigars and playing a hard round of tennis or some water sports may seem contradictory, the resort offers a huge variety of sporting facilities. A small stadium offers six clay tennis courts, two lighted for night play. Diving, sailing, and waterskiing are also offered, making this resort a favorite among not only those who love cigars but also those who seek adventure and relaxation.

Don't Forget to Bring: A good appetite and questions about your favorite cigars.

Favorite Side Trips: Visit the city that Columbus named "Silver Port," Puerto Plata. See the fort, which is now a museum, the Central Park, the amber museum, and the wooden houses with their Victorian style. Drive along the Malecon and visit the residential area of Costambar. Take a ride on the cable car to the top of the mountain called Isabel del Torres, which has a beautiful botanical garden. Try your luck at the nearby casino (within walking distance).

Nearest Airport: Puerto Plata International Airport, located about twenty minutes from the resort.

ALL-INCLUSIVE SERVICES AND ACTIVITIES

Food and Beverages: All meals, alcoholic and nonalcoholic beverages, snacks, afternoon tea.

Outdoor Activities: Volleyball, tennis, bicycling, horseback riding, archery, beach, tennis, table tennis.

Water Sports: Water polo, windsurfing, snorkeling, sailing, kayaking, aqua aerobics, boogie boarding, banana boat rides.

Facilities: Eighteen-hole championship golf course, clay tennis courts with night lighting, swimming pool, fitness club with sauna and whirlpool, games room.

Entertainment: Nightly, featuring local talent and staff shows.

Other: Aerobics, scuba diving lesson in pool, Spanish lessons, darts, billiards, playing cards, taxes and gratuities.

Children's Services: Supervised Kids' Club activities for ages four to twelve.

Available for a Fee: Golf, laundry services, baby-sitting, Jeep safaris through the many plantations of the Dominican Republic.

HAMACA CORAL BY HILTON BEACH HOTEL AND CASINO

Boca Chica, Dominican Republic

The majority of Hamaca Coral's business comes from repeat visits from its loyal customers—a fact that it is understandably proud of. There is much to like about this resort, recently brought under the Hilton Caribbean umbrella, but all of it is prefaced by the notion of convenience. There are many flights from the United States to the Dominican Republic, and most stop at its historic capital, Santo Domingo. In ten minutes, you can travel from the airport sidewalk to one of the widest beaches in the Caribbean at the Hamaca Coral by Hilton Beach Hotel and Casino. For young families, or even mature families who want a low-effort, easy-to-manage vacation, these conveniences are a plus for those who want to avoid spending a full day in transit.

Located on the southern coast of the Dominican Republic, along the shores of Juan Dolio, this 603-room hotel and casino faces the pristine waters of the Bay of Boca Chica. Not far offshore is the famed Saona Island, which has a spectacular reef formation and tropical fish population that attracts divers from around the world. Snorkeling and scuba are very popular here; the resort offers a scuba clinic that has won much praise in the diving industry for its success in introducing beginners to undersea wonders. All costs of the scuba and snorkelling clinics are included in the all-inclusive package.

Along the beach are the usual sports activities, including sailing, windsurfing, and banana boating, organized for kids and adults. Children are heartily welcome at this resort, which has a well-run Kids Club that provides children with age-appropriate activities from early morning until supper time.

Baby-sitting is also available. Because it's in a Spanish-speaking destination with a remarkable ecology, the Kids Club emphasizes learning Spanish language basics, taught through songs and games. Kids also get a chance to take field trips to some of the more beautiful and ecological spots in the area, including the famed Parque Nacional del Este, which is a botanical haven.

With children happy, parents will have little trouble finding adult things to do. Gaming is popular and legal throughout the Dominican Republic. The resort has a small but fun casino with craps, card games, and plenty of slot machines to handle the crowd. There are also six bars, a disco with entertainment, and plenty of dining. The variety of menus is impressive and includes Chinese, Mexican, Italian, Caribbean seafood, continental, and American cuisine. Local fruits and vegetables are superb, as is beef that mostly comes from local cattle ranches. To help you work up an appetite, there is a very good gym with sauna; massages are extra but reasonably priced.

When it is time to take a break from the sun and sea, we recommend visiting the restored colonial city of Santo Domingo, a sixteenth-century settlement with well-preserved fortress palaces, stately mansions, and churches. Tours are easy to arrange. For die-hard golfers, the eighteen-hole Los Marlins Championship Golf Course is next door, in Juan Dolio. A bit farther afield are cigar factories, a resource famous to this island and well worth visiting for those wanting to save large sums while stocking their humidors. Just tell the concierge what you like to smoke, and he'll make all of the arrangements.

Hamaca Coral by Hilton Beach Hotel and Casino

P.O. Box 2973
Boca Chica, Dominican Republic
Phone: 800–HILTONS; 809–526–2244 (direct)
E-mail: hamaca@coralhotels.com
Web site: www.hilton.com

Group/Getaway: Families

Accommodations: There are 212 Hamaca Garden Rooms, 171 Deluxe Garden View Rooms, 101 Deluxe Ocean View Rooms, 83 Deluxe Beach Rooms, 24 Ocean View Junior Suites, and 8 Beachfront Suites. Deluxe rooms and suites offer ocean views, while Hamaca Garden Rooms open to the lush vegetation of a tropical resort. All rooms offer king-size or full-size beds, air-conditioning, telephone, cable television, minibar, and safe deposit box.

Points of Distinction: The Hamaca Coral by Hilton Beach Hotel and Casino maintains one of the travel industry's highest occupancy rates throughout the year. It is also the only hotel in the Dominican Republic of its class within ten minutes of Santo Domingo's airport, making it a very convenient destination.

Open: Year-round.

Minimum Stay: Three nights.

Rates: Based on double occupancy, rates begin at $150 to $263 per person, per night for a Superior Garden View Room and $225 to $313 for a Superior Ocean View Room.

Frequently Asked Question: *What kinds of activities are available outside of the resort?* Santo Domingo is a sixteenth-century settlement with palaces, mansions, cathedrals, and chapels. You can go river rafting, mountain hiking, sailing, and diving to explore the living reefs.

Don't Forget to Bring: Spanish language book.

Favorite Side Trips: Santo Domingo, for its historic attractions and shopping; ecological tours to the Parque Nacional del Este; Saona Island, known for its tropical fish and transparent waters.

Nearest Airport: Las Americas International Airport is ten minutes from the resort.

ALL-INCLUSIVE SERVICES AND ACTIVITIES

Food and Beverages: All meals, nonalcoholic and alcoholic beverages, snacks, afternoon tea, room service.

Outdoor Activities: Tennis, horseshoes, volleyball, basketball, bicycling, horseback riding.

Water Sports: Sailing, kayaking, snorkeling, banana boating, canoeing, aqua aerobics, windsurfing.

Facilities: Two swimming pools, fitness center, sauna, game room, four Jacuzzis.

Entertainment: Disco and casino.

Other: Scuba clinics, Spanish lessons, aerobics, taxes, airport transfers, gratuities.

Children's Services: Kids Club for ages four to eight, and the Junior Place for children eight and older. Includes a nap room with air-conditioning.

Children's Activities: Outdoor activities, water sports, table games, kids' pool.

Available for a Fee: Baby-sitting, twenty-four-hour taxi service, massage, tennis lessons, beauty salon services, laundry, motorized water sports, golf.

PARADISUS PUNTA CANA
Higüey, Dominican Republic

The Paradisus Punta Cana resort is located on the eastern tip of the island of Hispaniola, on the Caribbean Sea in the Dominican Republic. The resort represents the very best of Caribbean living, boasting the world-famous Bavaro Beach, swaying palm trees, relaxing days, exciting nights, and lots of fun in the sun. The Paradisus Punta Cana epitomizes the "all-inclusive" resort, offering everything from meals and beverages to entertainment, sports facilities, services, and amenities, all complimentary and unlimited.

The "Coconut Coast," from Higüey and along the northeastern shore, is a more than 25-mile stretch of white-sand beaches, crystal-clear, often shallow, waters, and endless coconut groves. Along the coastline are the beaches of Macao, Cortesito, Bavaro, Punta Juanillo, and, finally, Punta Cana, which is host to this world-class resort.

The resort consists of thirty-five two-story bungalows—542 superior rooms in all—only steps from the beach. The bungalows include an elegant lower-level living area in addition to the upstairs sleeping quarters. The accommodations are quite pleasing and impressed us with their privacy. Turn-down service and room service are available twenty-four hours a day.

Although room service is a nice touch, you'll want to visit one of Punta Cana's eleven all-inclusive restaurants. Each eatery has a different serving style, from buffet to a la carte, formal to informal. The resort's two newest restaurants feature Japanese and Chinese cuisine. Pastries and light snacks are also available throughout the day.

Between meals, Punta Cana does an exceptional job of helping you burn off those calories with a wide variety of recreational activities available to guests. Scuba diving, snorkeling, tennis, shuffleboard, canoeing, and windsurfing are just a few of the many ways you can occupy your time. And don't forget about the resort's numerous bars and casinos. Spend some time in one of the Jacuzzis, go horseback riding, take an aerobics class, or take a guided ecological walk through the mangrove forest.

The resort has a decidedly romantic edge, with a Latin heart that will appeal to couples who want to play hard during the day and dance the merengue at night. We liked the resort's energy, as well as the fact that guests can plug into that energy as desired and still escape when they want privacy. The beach is exceptional and the staff is very friendly. Like most resorts on this Spanish-speaking island, the price is right.

Paradisus Punta Cana
Playa de Bavaro
P.O. Box 1783
Punta Cana
Higüey, Dominican Republic
Phone: 888–33–MELIA or 809–687–9923
E-mail: paradisus.punta.cana@solmelia.com
Web site: www.solmelia.com

Group/Getaway: Couples

Accommodations: Thirty-five two-story bungalows with 542 superior rooms in all. Each guest room consists of an upstairs sleeping area and elegant downstairs area. The rooms have a furnished terrace, air-conditioning, private bath (including hair dryer and shaving mirror), ceiling fan, king-size or double beds, remote-controlled satellite color television, refrigerator, direct-dial telephone, and safety deposit box.

Points of Distinction: The resort prides itself on its eleven restaurants and giant buffets. Reservations are required at the El Romantico. It is suggested that you make your reservations prior to your arrival.

Open: Year-round.

Minimum Stay: None.

Rates: Rates range from $150 to $335 per person, per night.

Frequently Asked Question: *Are there any kids' programs?* Yes, there is a complete staff dedicated to entertaining children through different educational programs and activities. Many couples who have honeymooned here return years later to relight the fire while their children enjoy the kids' programs.

Don't Forget to Bring: A hat, plenty of sunscreen, appropriate athletic footwear, and clothing for horseback riding.

Favorite Side Trips: Tour of Higüey, the nearest town, or a visit to the market area right outside of the resort, where you can purchase souvenirs, jewelry, and Dominican cigars (which are legal in the United States).

Nearest Airports: The Punta Cana International Airport is thirty minutes away, and the Romana Airport is approximately one and a half hours away.

ALL-INCLUSIVE SERVICES AND ACTIVITIES

Food and Beverages: All meals and snacks, alcoholic and nonalcoholic beverages.

Outdoor Activities: Horseback riding, tennis, shuffleboard, beach football, archery, table tennis, giant chess, volleyball, basketball, darts, Ping-Pong.

Water Sports: Snorkeling, scuba diving, fishing, swimming, sailing, windsurfing, waterskiing, sea biking, paddle boating, canoeing.

Facilities: Gym, aerobics room.

Entertainment: Live music and merengue dancing, dance classes, theme nights.

Other: Room service, aerobics classes.

Children's Activities and Services: Available.

Not Included: Taxes, gratuities, and transfers.

Available for a Fee: Parasailing, Jet Skis, tours.

LASOURCE

St. George's, Grenada

LaSource is located on the southwest tip of Grenada, on the secluded Pink Gin Beach. The property, which opened in 1994, is set on forty acres of lush tropical vegetation. In spite of its relative newness, it has fast claimed a place as one of the best all-inclusives in the world.

Grenada is the Isle of Spice, one of the Caribbean's last undeveloped islands that still claims a pristine rainforest that echoes with the chatter of monkeys. Beyond its lush interior and the volcanic remains of its origin, Grenada is encircled by forty-five elegant beaches that are never crowded.

The LaSource all-inclusive experience was created to appeal to the stressed executive, whether that person is part of a couple, a single woman looking for an uncomplicated place to get away, or someone traveling with good friends who seek relaxation in the extreme. Not that we found LaSource offered little to do. Even with its overall atmosphere of relaxation, the range of activities is greatly varied. Impressive facilities for tennis, scuba, sailing, volleyball, golf, fencing, and archery are in place with lots of help around to instruct and get you started. But it is LaSource's a la carte approach to filling your days that is particularly distinctive, whether you want to order piña coladas from your beach chair all day or take on the island with unbridled energy. The staff can and will accommodate any interest or demand of its guests on almost any level.

Single women in particular have discovered LaSource and attend in fair numbers. Beyond sports and hassle-free beach days, they patronize the resort's spa, Oasis, which offers a full fitness program. Walk, jog, cycle, or row your way to aerobic fitness, then try yoga, t'ai chi, stress management, and meditation classes. Add full body massage, facial or foot massage, and aromatherapy, and you get the idea. Even personal training is included in the price.

Unlike the more narrowly focused health spa resorts, LaSource is committed to helping any interested guests relax and revitalize both body and mind without shunning the benefits of a luxury, all-inclusive resort that offers exotic daiquiris, nighttime dancing, and sinful desserts. Here the philosophy is that relaxing and experiencing pleasure are key to getting back into mental and physical shape. It's hard to argue when you are lolling on your back, examining the underside of a bright Caribbean sun while getting your feet massaged and sipping a cool libation.

LaSource

Pink Gin Beach
P.O. Box 852
St. George's, Grenada, West Indies
Phone: 800–544–2883 or 473–444–2556
Web site: www.theamazingholiday.com

Group/Getaway: Singles, Spa & Wellness

Accommodations: There are 100 guest rooms and Junior Suites that feature air-conditioning, ceiling fans, balcony or terrace, private bathroom, mahogany king-size four-poster beds or two double beds, radio/alarm clock, direct-dial phone, Italian marble throughout, mini refrigerator, and balcony or terrace with ocean or garden views. All rooms on the top floor have cathedral ceilings; some Junior Suites have sofa beds.

Points of Distinction: LaSource is the only all-inclusive resort on the island of Grenada.

Open: Year-round.

Minimum Stay: None.

Rates: Based on double occupancy, from $440 to $690 per night; single supplement, $75 per night. A Christmas surcharge of $45 per person, per night applies December 19 to January 2.

Frequently Asked Questions: *Can I take scuba lessons?* The dive shop offers scuba instruction at no extra cost. *Who is the resort best suited for?* Single adults, particularly women who want a hassle-free vacation with countless options, as well as couples seeking an unregimented, active resort experience. *Can I bring my kids?* Children under age sixteen are not allowed.

Don't Forget to Bring: Bathing suits, appropriate footwear, and workout clothes for fitness activities.

Favorite Side Trip: The spice factory. The island is the world's largest producer of nutmeg, and there are spice plantations and factories islandwide.

Nearest Airport: Point Salines Airport, just minutes from the resort.

ALL-INCLUSIVE SERVICES AND ACTIVITIES

Food and Beverages: All meals, snacks, afternoon tea, nonalcoholic beverages, wine and liquor, room service (with twenty-four-hour advance notice).

Outdoor Activities: Golf, fencing, hiking, archery, volleyball, badminton, table tennis.

Water Sports: Snorkeling, scuba diving, water volleyball, waterskiing, windsurfing, swimming, Sunfish sailing, kayaking.

Facilities: Spa, nine-hole, nonregulation golf course, sauna, gym.

Entertainment: Dinner music fills the air from steel band to rhythmic calypso; manager's cocktail party once a week.

Other: Spa activities and services, including aerobics, weight training, wraps, salt and oil loofah rub, sauna, massage for two, yoga, stress management, t'ai chi, meditation, Swedish massage, aromatherapy, hair and scalp rejuvenation, facials, reflexology; service charges; hotel taxes; airport transfers; gratuities; safety deposit box.

Available for a Fee: Car hire service, trips and tours arranged with any operator, manicures, pedicures, beauty salon services, snorkelling excursions.

HALF MOON GOLF, TENNIS, AND BEACH CLUB
Montego Bay, Jamaica

For those times when you want to feel privileged in a royal way and sip champagne on a balcony, hypnotized by the glistening movement of the sea, Half Moon fits the bill. Or, if a requirement for that vacation is golfing, golfing, more golfing, and great food with sun, sea, and sand thrown in, you hit the target again. But whatever is being pursued, Half Moon's quiet elegance pervades all that happens at this luxurious hideaway.

Half Moon Golf, Tennis, and Beach Club, a member of the Elegant Resorts of Jamaica, is situated on a crescent-shaped bay, an easy 6 miles east of Montego Bay's Sangster International Airport. It sits on 400 well-manicured acres that have gained worldwide recognition as one of the Caribbean's best properties. Winner of four CHA (Caribbean Hotel Association) Green Hotel Awards, the hotel lives up to these plaudits.

Those lucky enough to have visited Half Moon prior to March 1997 will note that there have been many changes due to a devastating fire that destroyed the resort's lobby, restaurants, and kitchens. Six months later it reopened with panache, after updating its highly rated restaurants. Highlights from Half Moon's menus are West Indian specialties served alfresco at Seagrape Terrace. Il Giardino's Italian cuisine and the Sugar Mill's gourmet dishes are more formal and creative in their presentations. Beachside barbecues reign on Mondays and Fridays. To provide guests with convenience and security, a new shopping village was built on the property. Other new additions include Sakuru, an Oriental restaurant; a coffee shop; and Royal Stocks, an English pub. For a taste of Jamaican nightlife, there are calypso shows, limbo dancing, and, in honor of Jamaica's own Bob Marley, there is the Bob Marley Museum, which has a one-hour movie feature on the life of the reggae music legend.

One of the most distinguished elements of Half Moon is the way its 419 quaint rooms, cottages, and villas are furnished in Georgian Colonial elegance with Queen Anne–inspired mahogany furnishings, chintz fabrics, and Jamaican paintings. They mostly face a ravishing sea. Among the many blessings of the resort's accommodations are fifty-one semiprivate swimming pools—enough to please the most discriminating clientele. Recently, Half Moon built thirty-two Royal Villas with five to seven bedrooms each, along with a pool and a private staff consisting of a chef, maid, and butler.

Half Moon Golf, Tennis, and Beach Club claims this moniker for good reason. First, the on-site eighteen-hole Robert Trent Jones–designed championship golf course is one of Jamaica's oldest and finest courses, with a driving range, putting green, and, of course, award-winning drinks at the nineteenth hole. There are thirteen tennis courts, of which seven are lit and four are Omni courts. And, finally, there is the beach, where the grand half moon is defined, alluring as it ever was.

Half Moon Golf, Tennis, and Beach Club

Half Moon Post Office, Rose Hall
Montego Bay, Jamaica, West Indies
Phone: 866–648–6951 or 876–953–2211
E-mail: reservations@halfmoonclub.com
Web site: www.halfmoon-resort.com

Group/Getaway: Couples, Sports & Fitness

Accommodations: There are 176 suites, thirty-two villas, and forty-seven rooms. Each features Queen Anne–inspired mahogany furniture and four-poster beds. Junior Suites include twin beds and a living area, most with views of the bay, others with views of the patio and garden. Superior Suites have twin beds or a king-size, upon request, and a living room.

Points of Distinction: It's a sports lover's dream come true with a signature eighteen-hole Robert Trent Jones–designed golf course, thirteen tennis courts, fifty-one swimming pools, and unlimited water sports.

Open: Year-round.

Minimum Stay: During Christmas and New Year's there is a fourteen-night minimum stay; Presidents' week and Thanksgiving week, a seven-night minimum stay.

Packages: The resort's five packages include the Leadbetter Golf Plan and the Spa Plan. The Leadbetter Golf Plan features golf greens, carts, and caddie fees; Leadbetter-certified instructions (one hour daily); club rental; driving range and balls; club/shoe storage; and a gift of a towel and three balls. The Spa Plan features manicure/pedicure, reflexology, facials, herbal wrap, body scrub, massage, hydrotherapy tub, drench and vichy showers, and sauna. Call for more details on all packages.

Rates: Based on double occupancy, rooms begin at $240 to $490 per person, per night; suites begin at $350 to $690 per person, per night. Meal-activity plans range from $50 to $300 per day for two people, in addition to the room rate.

Frequently Asked Questions: *We have an extended family and need additional bedrooms. Can you accommodate us?* There are thirty-two five- to seven-room villas that cater to families seeking privacy and independence. Each villa has its own swimming pool and a staff that includes a chef, maid, and butler. *Is Jet Skiing allowed?* It is not allowed at Half Moon. However, the activity can be arranged for you at a nearby facility.

Don't Forget to Bring: Golf clubs and comfortable clothing for spa visits.

Favorite Side Trips: Martha Brae Rafting, Rose Hall Great House, Ocho Rios, Dunn's River Falls.

Nearest Airport: Sangster International Airport, fifteen minutes from the resort.

ALL-INCLUSIVE SERVICES AND ACTIVITIES

(All plans include the following.)

Food and Beverages: All meals, alcoholic and nonalcoholic beverages, a bottle of champagne upon arrival, lunch and dine-around program at seven different restaurants, afternoon tea.

Outdoor Activities: Tennis, basketball, volleyball, badminton, golf, horseback riding.

Water Sports: Sailing, windsurfing, snorkeling, kayaking, scuba diving, waterskiing, parasailing.

Facilities: Nautilus, gymnasium/fitness center, sauna, pool, equestrian center, squash courts.

Entertainment: Live music during dinner.

Other: Welcome gift, taxes, gratuities, and service charges. Airport transfers included for Platinum Plan packages only.

Children's Activities: Separate activities are planned for three age groups: three to six, seven to eleven, and twelve to fourteen, including outdoor activities, water sports, story time, disco, tennis clinic, and group tours for teenagers.

Available for a Fee: Deep-sea fishing, glass-bottom boat rides, squash and tennis lessons, adult and teen's golf clinic, nanny service.

SANDALS MONTEGO BAY

Montego Bay, Jamaica

Sandals Montego Bay is the birthplace of the Sandals empire. It sits on the original acres and longest private beach in Montego Bay that inspired founder Butch Stewart to chuck his other ventures and go for broke in the resort business in the early 1980s. Eleven resorts later, Stewart can afford to live anywhere in the Caribbean—or the world for that matter—but still maintains a home on this property.

The twenty-five-acre complex is five minutes by Sandals van or ten seconds by jet from Montego Bay's Sangster Airport. When we first arrived and the occasional jet flew by, we were startled to see it so low as other staff and guests simply waved at it without looking up, an old tradition that we admit quickly turned our surprise into an ongoing element of amusement. After the first few hours, if jets flew overhead, we can't remember how many or even seeing them again. So it goes for the ability of Sandals Montego Bay to put people at ease.

Although Sandals Montego Bay been recently renovated and new elegant buildings have been added that give it an attractive ambience, it is not elegance that sets it apart. It is much more about the attitude of the staff and the way guests reciprocate their love and warmth that supersede its bricks and mortar. Jamaicans are famous for their high energy and humor; the Mo Bay staff epitomizes these qualities in a way that few others do. Add to this a relatively tiny turnover of staff since the property opened in 1981 and it is understandable why more guests return to this Sandals than to any other in the chain—maybe any other resort in the West Indies. Managers say that when a staff person leaves, guests around the world who maintain friendships with the Sandals team often deluge them with e-mails, regaling them to do whatever is necessary to bring the departing person back. When you come, you feel as if a very large Jamaican family is adopting you.

If anyone is head of that family it is undoubtedly Daddy Stone, one of Jamaica's most colorful characters and among the first to be hired at the hotel. He has worked almost every job at the resort, and now, at an advanced age of somewhere between 60 and 80 (no one knows and he won't say), his job is just to show up and be helpful to the guests. He has a remarkable memory for detail that endears him to all who return. He will remember what you like in your coffee, the ages of your children, your favorite wines, and what you like to do and eat. If there is a problem or an issue, he always has a solution. Every all-inclusive would love to have a Daddy Stone, but they are rare—and none more naturally skilled and charming than he.

At many Sandals resorts, young people tend to dominate, but not at Sandals Montego Bay, where all generations mix easily in the spirit of happiness that so naturally is part of this establishment. There are older couples, singles, and honeymooners. Sandals pioneered the "weddingmoon" concept, hosting about 100 weddings a month here, which are still free if you include it with your vacation.

So what else distinguishes this resort from others? The beach, mon. It is the largest private strip of sand in Jamaica, cut off from hawkers and distractions that could interrupt your relaxation. And with it come all of the water sports that Sandals is known for: sailing, kayaking, snorkeling, windsurfing, and tubing. The pool is large and beautiful, with the requisite swim-up bar that serves drinks day and night. It boasts five restaurants—all appealing to us with lots of wonderful Jamaican fare, topped by diverse entertainment at night.

Sandals Montego Bay

P.O. Box 100, Kent Avenue
Montego Bay, Jamaica, West Indies
Phone: 800–SANDALS or 876–952–5510
E-mail: smbmail@smb.sandals.com
Web site: www.sandals.com

Group/Getaway: Couples, honeymooners

Accommodations: There are 245 rooms in ten categories, including almost a third of the rooms receiving Suite Concierge Service, a Sandals program that guarantees a personal assistant will be available to help you plan dinner reservations, make off-property excursions, and answer questions around the clock. The Concierge Suites have sitting rooms, mahogany furnishings, marble-accented bathrooms, four-poster king-size beds, views of oceans or gardens, and in-room bars that are stocked with premium-brand spirits. Standard Room features include king-size beds, satellite television, private bath, hair dryer, safety deposit boxes, and telephones. Accommodations are also available for physically challenged guests.

Points of Distinction: Sandals Montego Bay boasts the largest private white sand beach in Jamaica. There are also two special room categories for newlyweds: Honeymoon Water's Edge Concierge Room and Water's Edge Honeymoon Penthouse Concierge Room. Also exclusive to Sandals Montego Bay is an attractive church called the Frank Warren Chapel.

Open: Year-round.

Minimum Stay: Three days recommended.

Rates: $984 to $1,495 per couple for a three-day stay.

Frequently Asked Question: *What kind of nightlife do you have?* On property is the Escapades Disco, which stays open till 2:00 A.M.; there is also the Piano Bar, which stays open until 1:00 A.M. Every Monday night is a beach party, and on Friday there is international buffet night.

Don't Forget to Bring: Long pants. There are two Sandals properties in Montego Bay that offer full exchange privileges, Sandals Royal Caribbean and Sandals Inn. These include a total of eleven restaurants to choose from, some of which require more formal attire.

Favorite Side Trips: Trek across to the renowned Dunn's River Falls. Another popular tour is the Tropical Dreamer Catamaran, which stops in the Marine Park for snorkeling.

Nearest Airport: Sangster International Airport is ten minutes away.

ALL-INCLUSIVE SERVICES AND ACTIVITIES

Food and Beverages: All meals at five restaurants, all beverages—alcoholic and nonalcoholic—at four bars and five restaurants, snacks.

Outdoor Activities: Tennis, rainforest walks.

Water Sports: Motor boating, snorkeling, fishing, catamaran sailing, sailboarding, paddle boating, waterskiing.

Facilities: Four swimming pools, four whirlpools, five restaurants, wedding chapel, fitness center.

Entertainment: Escapades Disco, piano bar; every Monday night is a beach party and on Friday nights there is international buffet.

Other: Saltwater swimming pool, library, beach picnics, twenty-four-hour self-service bar, video library of recent releases and classics.

Available for a Fee: Scuba lessons and diving certification, dry cleaning, horseback riding, tours, private charters for romance and for game fishing.

WYNDHAM ROSE HALL GOLF RESORT AND COUNTRY CLUB
Montego Bay, Jamaica

After a ten-minute drive from Sangster International Airport, the gates to a lush eighteenth-century plantation appear, surrounded by deep blue water and long lines of palms. Wyndham Rose Hall Golf Resort and Country Club, once a stately manor house, received an extensive $12.6 million makeover by its parent company, Wyndham Hotels, to create an all-inclusive suited for business travelers and their families. Of the all-inclusives we have discovered around the world, this large and historic property is the only one that was designed for meetings and conferences, yet still has all of the elements to make it a world-class resort.

Rose Hall is a 400-acre beachfront resort that is connected to a 1,800-foot secluded beach. Adjacent to the beach is a 200-year-old historic Great House, still beautifully intact, that is the signature monument of this property. The Great House is surrounded by 489 lovely rooms and suites with balconies overlooking the Caribbean Sea or Jamaica's Blue Mountains. Interspersed among them are 11,000 square feet of meeting space, including ballrooms for up to 800, smaller meeting rooms, and outdoor function areas that all add up to being the largest meeting and conference facility in Jamaica. No less formidable a feature of Rose Hall is its $7.5 million Sugar Mill Falls fantasy water and pool complex, which has become the top water park in the Caribbean.

When conventioneers come to Rose Hall, they are treated to exceptional sports opportunities. The resort hosts an eighteen-hole, par seventy-two championship golf course that is as challenging as it is spectacular. For tennis players, the resort's seven-court complex is one of the island's finest, featuring galleries, a clubhouse, and lighted courts. The dive and water sport center is also lavishly outfitted to accommodate all levels of divers, from novices interested in resort courses to seasoned divers wishing to explore wrecks.

We noted "children" up to the age of eighty splashing in Sugar Mill Falls. In one of the three pools is a "lazy river" for tubing, rafting, and swimming, with a water tunnel and rapids. But most impressive is a 280-foot slide with a 30-foot drop that makes hearts race. In spite of the business air of this hotel, the beach and sports complex is complemented by a well-thought-out children's program called Kids Klub for youngsters between the ages of three and twelve. Naturally, they often visit the water park, but they also learn about the ecology and culture of Jamaica through song, arts and crafts, and boat trips.

Food is exotic in Jamaica, and Wyndham Rose Hall has embraced the locally distinctive use of fresh fruits, spices, and creative cooking of meats. The Cafe, The Terrace Restaurant, The Ambrosia Restaurant, Crusoe's, and The Pool Grill offer an array of options, including Mediterranean and Caribbean cuisine. After dinner at one of the five upscale restaurants, you can listen to the calypso and reggae music pounding in The Cricket Club until the final sounds fade and the lights go out in the wee hours, when only crickets can be heard echoing across the property, just as they have for almost 200 years, making Wyndham Rose Hall seem historic again.

Wyndham Rose Hall Golf Resort and Country Club

P.O. Box 999
Montego Bay, Jamaica, West Indies
Phone: 800–996–3426 or 876–953–2650
Web site: www.wyndham.com

Group/Getaway: Families, Sports & Fitness

Accommodations: The 489 elegantly appointed rooms, each with a balcony, include Standard Rooms with partial ocean or mountain view, Superior Rooms with partial ocean and swimming pool view, Deluxe Rooms with full ocean view, and Ultra Deluxe rooms with beach and ocean views. Suites have a sleeper sofa and separate living area with beach and ocean views.

Point of Distinction: A big draw is Wyndham Rose Hall's water park, Sugar Mill Falls, with water slides and a lazy river for tubing.

Open: Year-round.

Minimum Stay: None.

Rates: Based on double occupancy, Standard Rooms begin at $300 to $375 per night to $500 for Deluxe Rooms; children ages three to seven, $75 additional per day, and children eight to eighteen, $95. You must ask for the all-inclusive plan when you telephone for a reservation. You will be quoted room rates only if you don't ask. Packages that include golf start at $380 per night for single occupancy, $505 for double.

Frequently Asked Questions: *How challenging is the golf course?* Wyndham Rose Hall Golf Course, cradled in Jamaica's Blue Mountains, is a challenging, eighteen-hole championship golf course. *What other activities could be arranged nearby?* Parasailing, waterskiing, scuba diving, and horseback riding are within five minutes, shopping within ten minutes.

Don't Forget to Bring: Tennis rackets, golf clubs, and golf shoes.

Favorite Side Trips: Straw market, just 1 mile from property; Martha Brae river rafting excursions; shopping in Ocho Rios.

Nearest Airports: Sangster International Airport, ten minutes away.

ALL-INCLUSIVE SERVICES AND ACTIVITIES

Food and Beverages: All meals, nonalcoholic beverages, wine and house-brand liquor, room service.

Outdoor Activities: Golf, tennis, basketball.

Water Sports: Swimming, windsurfing, sailing, kayaking, snorkeling.

Facilities: Championship eighteen-hole, par seventy-two golf course; three freshwater swimming pools; canoes and paddleboats; fitness center, lazy river; lagoons; swim-up bar; lighted tennis courts; five restaurants.

Entertainment: Casino, live band music.

Other: Dance lesson, gratuities, taxes.

Children's Services: Kids Club, for children ages three to twelve, open 10:00 A.M. to 4:00 P.M.

Children's Activities: Outdoor activities, arts and crafts. Children can participate in all supervised activities.

Available for a Fee: Boat rental for snorkeling, golf cart and caddie.

BEACHES NEGRIL

Negril, Jamaica

Beaches may be new to the "island of wood and water" but, as a member of the Sandals family, the resort is no rookie at providing luxury to its worldly visitors. On Jamaica's western shores, the appropriately named Beaches resort occupies a wide stretch of oceanfront property. Two-storied villas peek from a forest of palm trees toward the blue waters of the Caribbean. Wooden promenades meander through plush gardens, which boast nearly 200 species of plants. An asymmetrical pool of mineral water runs the length of the estate, while swim-up bars and marble-decked Jacuzzis tickle many a midriff.

With its tropical beauty and architecture of stone and local wood, Beaches Negril matches the extravagance of its sibling resorts. The difference is that this newest point of paradise was built primarily for families, not the hordes of couples that Sandals resorts have spoiled over the years.

Full-family activities occupy the entire clan, yet at the same time, Beaches Negril affords Mom and Dad every opportunity to sneak away for some time alone.

An endless agenda of kids' activities keeps the young minds busy. With a distinction made between teens, preteens, and toddlers, kids of all ages mingle with others of their own approximate age, thereby eliminating the risk of "Mom, we're bored. We don't have anything to do."

And it is on the family front that Beaches Negril has earned its top ranking. Not only are the children's programs entertaining and original, the staff has gained a reputation for keeping even the most challenging kids in the vacation loop. When kids are happy, parents are happy. We applaud Beaches Negril for keeping the highest ratio of smiles to faces of any resort we have seen below the Tropic of Cancer. It's a huge accomplishment.

Beaches Negril

Norman Manley Boulevard
P.O. Box 12
Negril, Jamaica, West Indies
Phone: 888–BEACHES or 876–957–9270
E-mail: info@beaches.com
Web site: www.beaches.com

Group/Getaway: Families

Accommodations: There are 215 rooms in nine categories. Suite Concierge service is available for guests staying in a concierge room or a suite.

Points of Distinction: No matter where guests stay, in the most expensive or least expensive rooms, everyone is treated royally. Children's activities are superb, including the Sega Center, with twenty-four games that Sega made especially for Beaches. There's also a big-top amphitheater and live entertainment every night.

Open: Year-round.

Minimum Stay: Three nights.

Rates: Based on double occupancy, deluxe rooms start at $250 per person per night; beachfront two-bedroom suites start at $765.

Frequently Asked Questions: *What is the maximum number of people who can stay in one room?* A two-bedroom suite can comfortably sleep seven people, with a maximum of five adults. *Is there a nanny service for infants?* For infants to age two, there is a nursery open for ten and a half hours a day, with one staff member for each three children. After hours, a private nanny service costs $5.00 per hour for up to two children.

Don't Forget to Bring: Casual wear, plenty of sunscreen, and your dancing shoes.

Favorite Side Trips: Dunn's River Falls, Rick's Cafe to watch the local divers.

Nearest Airport: Sangster International Airport, Montego Bay, a one-and-a-half-hour drive from the resort. Air Jamaica Express will get you to the resort in twenty minutes for approximately $95 per person.

ALL-INCLUSIVE SERVICES AND ACTIVITIES

Food and Beverages: All meals and snacks, alcoholic and nonalcoholic beverages.

Outdoor Activities: Tennis, beach volleyball, board games, shuffleboard, croquet, lawn chess, miniature golf.

Water Sports: Scuba, snorkeling, wind surfing, kayaking, sailing, aqua cycling, water skiing.

Facilities: Lighted tennis courts, exercise and weight room, three Jacuzzis, amphitheater, saunas, steam rooms, two pools, a kiddie pool, fitness center with Cybex equipment.

Entertainment: Theater bar, piano bar, disco, beach bandstand, Safari bar, theme parties, beach parties, swim-up pool bar.

Other: Weddings, tips, gratuities, service charges, round-trip airport transfers.

Children's Services: Rainbow Nursery (newborn to age three), open 9:00 A.M. to 5:00 P.M.; Kids Camp (ages four to twelve), open 9:00 A.M. to 5:00 P.M. and 7:00 to 9:00 P.M.; Teen Program (ages thirteen and older), open 9:30 A.M. to 11:00 P.M. "Ultra Nannies" at day-care center.

Children's Activities: Water sports, Sega Dreamcast Center, kids' "nightclub," kids' pool with swim-up soda bar.

Not Included: Departure tax, interisland transfers.

Available for a Fee: Baby-sitting, spa services for adults at nearby Sandals Negril, golf.

BEACHES SANDY BAY

Negril, Jamaica

Negril is on a 7-mile stretch of pure white sand on the west end of Jamaica, about an hour and a half from Montego Bay. The beach is far less formal than other tourist spots in Jamaica, with clothes-optional bathing at some hotels (although not at this resort), which is quite rare in non-French Caribbean islands.

Formerly the Beaches Inn, Beaches Sandy Bay has undergone complete renovations and extensive upgrades. Now one of the Beaches group's smallest properties, it offers extra personal attention that the mega all-inclusives simply can't provide. Because the resort is for couples and families, this attitude of taking care of its guests has great appeal to the honeymooners and young families who make up a big part of the resort's clientele.

The way Beaches Sandy Bay is organized, couples are free to pursue privacy when they want it, romance when they feel it, excitement when they need it, and pampering anytime, day or night. Beaches Sandy Bay is the "in" spot for vacation value.

The focus of this facility is the beach and all that it entails. There are few finer expanses of sand in the Caribbean and enough variety along its shoreline to amuse any and all who walk its perimeter. The resort operates a PADI five-star dive center and offers snorkeling and diving right off the beach. If you have been thinking about taking up scuba diving, this is definitely a place to launch your underwater pursuits. Not only is equipment top-notch—a con-

cern of Americans who come to smaller countries—but staff members also are well-seasoned divers and teachers.

All of the staff here is exceptionally well trained and helpful. With their good humor and high spirits, the employees make this resort hum. Everyone smiles, and everything possible is done to ensure that your worries—and diet—are left at home.

The resort's three restaurants offer varied cuisine: The Sundowner offers new world cuisine with an island flair; La Vista Sul Mare has an Italian menu; and Bayside is buffet style. You'll also find a sports bar, a disco, and a beach bar. The large and centrally located pool and Jacuzzi are just steps from the bar, which suits guests who want to quench their thirsts while sunbathing. Sailing, tennis, volleyball, and snorkeling are ongoing activities from dawn until dusk. There are also baby-sitters, a pool, a playground, and a Sega Center featuring the latest video games for kids. The resort has a modern and well-equipped gym, which also offers some spa services, including various kinds of massages.

All rooms at Beaches Sandy Bay have a view of the Caribbean, and some have in-room Jacuzzis. Suites and villas are available with up to two bedrooms; they are especially well suited for children. Among activities for children is the nearby Anancy Family Fun and Nature Park, which has lake boating, minigolf, go-karts, a fishing pond, nature trail, video arcade, and historical exhibitions.

Beaches Sandy Bay

P.O. Box 44
Norman Manley Boulevard
Negril, Jamaica, West Indies
Phone: 888–BEACHES or 876–957–1500
E-mail: info@beaches.com
Web site: www.beaches.com

Group/Getaway: Families

Accommodations: The 120 rooms and suites cover seven categories rated according to size and location. The simplest are Deluxe rooms with one king bed and a pull-out sofa or two double beds. Premium and Luxury rooms have the same amenities, but more space. Fourteen one-bedroom suites have an oversized living area and refrigerator or kitchenette. Some beachfront suites have two bedrooms with a living-dining area and kitchenette. The Honeymoon Suite comes with a Jacuzzi and spacious living area. Suites and Luxury rooms are oceanfront and have a balcony or patio.

Points of Distinction: Beaches Sandy Bay is located on Negril's world-renowned Seven-Mile Beach. It has a lush, tropical setting with 1,000 feet of white sand.

Open: Year-round.

Minimum Stay: Three nights.

Rates: Based on double occupancy, room rates begin at $215 per person per night; one-bedroom suites begin at $270 per person per night. Children two and under are free; ages three to fifteen are $70 per night.

Frequently Asked Question: *Do I need to bring my own diving gear?* All guests on the all-inclusive package are offered snorkeling gear, tanks, and weight belts for unlimited snorkeling and offshore diving. For guests on the certified divers' all-inclusive package, the shop can provide you with all your diving gear except for wet suits.

Don't Forget to Bring: Any athletic clothing or shoes for sports, sunscreen—especially for the kids.

Favorite Side Trip: Negril, just 3 miles away, for shopping.

Nearest Airport: Sangster International Airport, about an hour and a half from the resort.

ALL-INCLUSIVE SERVICES AND ACTIVITIES

Food and Beverages: All meals and snacks, alcoholic and nonalcoholic beverages, welcome cocktail, afternoon tea.

Outdoor Activities: Tennis, croquet, volleyball.

Water Sports: Swimming, snorkeling, scuba diving, windsurfing, watercycling, sailing, kayaking, paddleboat rides.

Facilities: Two pools, heated whirlpool, gym, pool table, meeting facilities.

Entertainment: Nightly.

Other: Weddings; golf at Sandals Golf and Country Club in Ocho Rios (transportation not included); tips and gratuities; airport transfers.

Children's Services: Children's program for kids ages three and over, nursery.

Children's Activities: Outdoor activities, arts and crafts.

Not Included: Transfers to Beaches Negril and Sandals Negril (adults only) and use of facilities there.

Available for a Fee: Baby-sitting, beauty salon, laundry and dry-cleaning services; spa treatments for adults at Sandals Negril.

COUPLES NEGRIL

Negril, Jamaica

For couples who want to rekindle the flame, for couples who need a getaway from harried lifestyles, for couples getting married or honeymooning, for couples who need to heal—Couples Negril is a good antidote. No demands, no children as reminders of those left behind. Just romantics with the same goal of tuning in to one another.

Couples Negril, a $36 million resort that opened in 1998, resides on eighteen acres with 1,000 linear feet of white-sand beach in western Jamaica. As guests arrive, the panoramic view of the sea, sand, and sky offers its greetings.

Although somewhat commercial from its decade of development, Negril is quaintly bohemian in its casualness. Couples tied that concept together with rich Caribbean colors and Jamaican art to create "Negril Chic" decor—and chic it is. There are 216 spacious guest rooms and suites located in nine low-rise buildings that reflect a seductive charm.

With all the competition for tourists along Negril's beach, resorts must have superb facilities to remain afloat. Couples' restaurants are upscale, with carefully selected multicultural menus. Orioles, indoors with a panoramic view of the sea, serves gourmet international cuisine for dinner only; Cassava Terrace has alfresco dining for breakfast and lunch; and Calico Jack grills on the terrace by day and serves Mediterranean cuisine in the evening.

There are four bars, including an inviting swim-up pool and beach bar where you must indulge yourself in at least one piña colada. By night, there is easy listening to live jazz played by the pool. Beach parties, outdoor buffets, and theme parties are continuously held throughout the week.

For daytime activity there is a full-service water sports center, a golf course nearby with no greens fees (a real plus for enthusiasts), tennis courts, a Cybex fitness center, and ongoing arts and craft classes. We recommend that part of your time be spent exploring Negril Beach. Don't miss Rick's Cafe, set on a cliff overlooking the azure sea, with a view of divers plummeting from 50-foot cliffs.

If it is time to pop the question and tie the knot, a full-time wedding coordinator can arrange all wedding details, including, of course, the honeymoon.

Couples Negril

P.O. Box 91
Norman Manley Boulevard
Hanover, Negril, Jamaica, West Indies
Phone: 800–COUPLES or 876–957–5960
Web site: www.couples.com

Group/Getaway: Couples

Accommodations: There are nine low-rise buildings that include 216 rooms, each with a bay or garden view. All rooms are air-conditioned and have balconies. The eighteen luxury suites include Deluxe Garden View, Ocean View, and Beachfront. Rooms are "Negril Chic," with chartreuse duvet covers, olive green silk drapes, and bright red chairs on beautiful blue tile floors; all have private balconies or patios.

Points of Distinction: Couples' location on 1,000 feet of spectacular beach allows for extensive water sports activities, including diving or snorkeling on Negril's famous nearby reef.

Open: Year-round.

Minimum Stay: Three nights.

Rates: Based on double occupancy, from $485 to $735 per couple, per night, depending on view.

Frequently Asked Question: *What type of cuisine is served at the restaurants?* Chef Sham, who has received many awards, including the International Award of Excellence, takes his work very seriously, planning multi-cultural menus for each of the five restaurants.

Don't Forget to Bring: Sunscreen and scuba regulator for diving.

Favorite Side Trip: Rick's Cafe, a well-known establishment set on a 50-foot cliff overlooking the ocean where locals dive.

Nearest Airport: Sangster International Airport, a one-hour-and-fifteen-minute drive from the resort.

ALL-INCLUSIVE SERVICES AND ACTIVITIES

Food and Beverages: All meals and snacks, alcoholic and nonalcoholic beverages, twenty-four-hour room service.

Outdoor Activities: Tennis, volleyball, golf.

Water Sports: Swimming, windsurfing, sailing, snorkeling, kayaking, scuba diving, canoeing, water aerobics.

Facilities: Freshwater pool, two Jacuzzis, floating tanning decks, four lighted tennis courts, fitness center with Cybex equipment.

Entertainment: Live jazz, beach parties, outdoor buffets, theme parties.

Other: Taxes and gratuities, glass-bottom boat rides, sunset catamaran cruises, airport transfers.

Available for a Fee: Beauty salon and spa services.

COUPLES SWEPT AWAY RESORT

Negril, Jamaica

Couples Swept Away is obviously for twosomes only, which is not a unique concept to Jamaica or the entire world of all-inclusive resorts. What distinguishes Couples Swept Away is its fantastic ability to help its guests enjoy the highlights of Negril's 7-mile beach with some of the best fitness and sports activities in the world. Couples Swept Away's twenty-acre site of picturesque villas and suites tends to attract the active, athletic, energetic, and health-conscious.

Jamaicans know how to have fun, and this comfortable and relatively private place on a busy beach offers team sports, individual sports, and any number of other ways to burn a calorie or two. Individual training programs are designed for interested guests after they have received fitness evaluations by the resort's certified instructors at the beginning of their visit. Sports classes and activities begin at 7:00 A.M., and doors stay open until 11:00 P.M.

In between sessions, nutrition and rehabilitation are an important part of the process as well. Couples Swept Away serves food around the clock at four different restaurants on the grounds, including Feathers, which has been voted one of the best restaurants in the Caribbean. There's a fruit and veggie bar for those who take their good habits on vacation.

An on-site spa (services are extra) is available for body wraps, scrubs, mineral baths, massages, facials, waxing, pedicures, and manicures. There is even an aromatherapist, who mixes custom potions to meet the needs of each visitor.

We were particularly impressed with the fact that no building on the grounds is taller than the royal palms that are planted throughout the property. The transition between elevated suites and the open grounds is subtle and becoming. To its credit, Couples Swept Away has managed to stay natural and avoid the sometimes plastic, institutional feel of many resort communities.

With so much emphasis on its extraordinary ten-acre spa and fitness complex, it is important to note that Couples Swept Away also has one of the best golf and waterfront programs in the Caribbean. Unlimited golf is complimentary and only ten minutes from the grounds. At the beach, the diving instructors are skilled and friendly. Snorkeling, sailing, and waterskiing are all part of the price and should not be missed.

Couples Swept Away Resort

P.O. Box 77
Norman Manley Boulevard
Negril, Jamaica, West Indies
Phone: 800–268–7537 or 876–957–4061
E-mail: info@couples.com
Web site: www.couples.com

Group/Getaway: Couples, Spa & Wellness

Accommodations: There are 134 secluded and intimate Verandah Suites located in twenty-six villas spread over twenty acres of tropical gardens.

Points of Distinction: The lush grounds are exceptionally beautiful and private. The Olympic-size pool may be the only one of its kind in the country, and the fitness facilities are second to none. Weddings are complimentary and include minister's fee, marriage license, flowers for the bride and groom, a wedding cake, and champagne. For details and documentation requirements, contact the resort's wedding coordinator.

Open: Year-round.

Minimum Stay: Three nights.

Rates: Based on double occupancy, rates begin at $485 to $640 per couple, per night, with a 50 percent surcharge for singles.

Frequently Asked Questions: *How do I get to Couples Swept Away?* You are transferred from Sangster International Airport to the resort (a ninety-minute drive) in resort vans at no additional cost. *Is tipping accepted?* No, it is included in the rates and is not allowed at any time. *What type of guest is Couples Swept Away best suited for?* Energetic couples. The activities here are designed for men and women, with most of them oriented toward sports, health, and fitness.

Don't Forget to Bring: Plenty of sunscreen, tennis gear, golf clubs, and shoes to walk Negril's 7 continuous miles of beach.

Favorite Side Trip: A mile down the beach is a "clothing-optional" stretch of sand.

Nearest Airport: Sangster International Airport in Montego Bay, an hour and a half from the resort.

ALL-INCLUSIVE SERVICES AND ACTIVITIES

Food and Beverages: All food and drinks (alcoholic and nonalcoholic), room service.

Outdoor Activities: Basketball, squash, tennis, racquetball, golf, beach volleyball.

Water sports: Swimming, snorkeling, kayaking, sailing, windsurfing, waterskiing, scuba diving, aquacise, glass-bottom boat tours, wake- and kneeboarding.

Facilities: Lap pool, basketball court, weight gym and fitness center, racquetball court, jogging track, steam rooms, saunas, whirlpools, pool tables, game room, three restaurants, fruit and veggie bar.

Entertainment: Manager's cocktail party, beach party, sunset party cruise, piano lounge, cabaret shows, nightly live music, dancing, weekly honeymoon party, satellite television room.

Other: Taxes, gratuities, and airport transfers; yoga, body sculpting, and high/low-impact aerobics; two-hour massages.

Available for a Fee: Spa and salon; motorbikes to explore Negril and nearby villages and national parks.

GRAND LIDO NEGRIL

Negril, Jamaica

Terry MacMillan, author of best-selling books and movies, was inspired to write the screenplay *How Stella Got Her Groove Back* at Super-Club's Grand Lido Negril. If you haven't seen the movie and are contemplating visiting this resort, rent it. Grand Lido Negril is a fine Caribbean resort on any terms, and a top-notch all-inclusive. Grand Lido Negril has received the coveted award for Best Resort in Latin America and the Caribbean by *Condé Nast Traveler*'s Readers Choice Awards, as well as an AAA Four Diamond rating.

Tucked away in the protected Bloody Bay on the western coast of Jamaica, the resort is on a 2-mile stretch of the world-famous Seven-Mile Beach on twenty-two acres of manicured grounds. Couples, singles, and families with children age sixteen and older enjoy 208 mostly beachfront suites.

A state-of-the-art fitness center, spa, tennis with lessons and tournaments, golf, water sports, video theater with a big screen, and reggae and salsa dance classes can fill in when you've had your fill of the beach. Scuba certification is available, as is one clothing-optional beach.

There is no need to leave the property for dinner. Grand Lido views food as a serious issue. The Gran Terrazza, La Pasta, and the Cafe Lido offer a variety of choices from Italian to continental cuisine. A nice touch is afternoon tea in the marble foyer. At least once, treat yourself to white-glove gourmet dining at Piacere.

Nightlife here is plentiful and good. The Amici Piano Lounge starts at 6:00 P.M., Atlantis Disco at 10:30 P.M.; nightly live entertainment and theme parties at Gran Terrazza are highlights. There is a whopping total of eight bars.

Among the impressive assets of Grand Lido is the M/Y *Zein,* a luxury power yacht that was once a wedding gift to Princess Grace and Prince Rainier from Aristotle Onassis. The resort uses it to take its guests on romantic daily sunset cruises, cocktail gatherings, and even complimentary weddings.

Regarding weddings: If you do not have the time, patience, or inclination to plan an "at-home" wedding and want to couple it seamlessly with a honeymoon, Grand Lido Negril has an impressive offering. Given a minimum three weeks' notice, at no cost, the hotel will arrange the entire event, including the wedding cake, champagne, flowers, marriage license, and a nondenominational ceremony with witnesses, leaving you with little to do but enjoy it.

Grand Lido Negril

P.O. Box 88
Negril, Westmoreland, Jamaica, West Indies
Phone: 800–GO–SUPER or 876–957–5010
Web site: www.superclubs.com

Group/Getaway: Couples, Sports & Fitness

Accommodations: There are 208 spacious suites, which include air-conditioning and ceiling fans, satellite television, AM/FM cassette entertainment systems, direct-dial telephones, coffee and tea, hair dryer, iron and ironing board, in-room safe, and laundry and dry-cleaning service. A junior suite has a large bedroom with king-size bed or two twin beds, a sunken living room, and small balcony or patio overlooking gardens or the au naturel beach. A one-bedroom beachfront suite includes a dining room, extra loveseat, complete entertainment console, and a minibar replenished daily.

Points of Distinction: As a flagship of the SuperClubs group, Grand Lido Negril set a high standard of excellence that has obviously been upheld, given all its awards.

Open: Year-round.

Minimum Stay: Three nights.

Rates: Based on double occupancy, rates begin at $460 to $925 per person, per night, with a $100 supplement per person December 26 to January 3. Children under age sixteen are not allowed.

Frequently Asked Questions: *If we prefer not to eat the same type of food every night, do we have options?* There are five different types of restaurants to choose from that include Piacere, an elegant French restaurant that requires a jacket but no tie; the open-air Gran Terrazza for extravagant breakfasts and lunch buffets; La Pasta, which serves Italian specialties; Cafe Lido, which specializes in continental dishes; and The Outdoor Grill. *Are there any medical facilities?* There is a registered nurse with regular office hours on premises. A medical emergency doctor is on call twenty-four hours a day. (There will be a charge if the doctor is called.)

Don't Forget to Bring: A romantic surprise for your partner.

Favorite Side Trips: Black River Safari for a nature tour; Dunn's River Tour to climb the waterfalls.

Nearest Airport: Sangster International Airport, Montego Bay, one and a half hours from the resort.

ALL-INCLUSIVE SERVICES AND ACTIVITIES

Food and Beverages: All meals and snacks, alcoholic and nonalcoholic beverages, twenty-four-hour room service.

Outdoor Activities: Tennis, croquet, including lessons (reserve times upon arrival), bicycle tours, beach volleyball, shuffleboard, volleyball, table tennis.

Water Sports: Kayaking, snorkeling, waterskiing, swimming, sailing, wind surfing, underwater vision boat rides, scuba diving.

Facilities: Two freshwater pools, Jacuzzi, state-of-the-art fitness center (includes movie room), nude beach, eight bars.

Entertainment: Piano lounge, disco, theme parties, lunchtime jazz, nightly live entertainment.

Other: Manicure and pedicure, glass-bottom boat rides, scuba and snorkeling instruction, airport transfers, taxes, gratuities.

Available for a Fee: Tours, massages ($1.00 per minute), facials, medical services.

HEDONISM II

Negril, Jamaica

Advice to anyone considering a Hedonism II vacation: Go single, or at least claim to be single. Sure, 30 percent of the visitors to this resort are couples, but the action tends to involve those who are unattached.

Just about any activity at Negril's 7-mile beach is designed to push young men and women together. With four bars and an endless list of beach parties and theme parties throughout the week, even the meekest and mildest among us can't screw this up.

The pool bar opens at 10:00 A.M. (who wakes up that early?), and the Hurricanes Disco Bar is open until 5:00 A.M. If you like the flying trapeze acts in the circus show, you can take lessons at Hedonism II's own Flying Trapeze and Trampoline Clinic. There are toga parties and pajama parties, body painting competitions, and the Hedonism II Beach Side Bash. You can croon at the cabaret on Oldies Night or belt out a karaoke tune on any night.

During a stay at Hedonism II, those who can't dance will learn to dance, those who can't sing will learn to sing, and those who can't move will learn moves they never knew they had.

Find someone cuddly enough to spend the rest of your life with and Hedonism II throws in a free wedding, with flowers, champagne, music, a wedding cake, a marriage certificate, and a nondenominational marriage officer. Upon request, you'll even get a complimentary best man, maid of honor, and witnesses.

However, understand that local laws regarding marriage are stringent. You have to stay in Jamaica at least fifteen days before a ceremony can be performed. If two weeks is too agonizing a time to wait, the requirement can be reduced to three days with a special waiver (about as difficult to get as a slice of pizza and a pair of sunglasses).

In this small but surprisingly popular niche of all-inclusives for singles, Hedonism II has managed to make its guests feel as if they are pushing the envelope of acceptable behavior—but safely. This kind of controlled chaos is challenging to create week after week, but Hedonism II has been doing it better than anyone else for years.

Hedonism II

P.O. Box 25
Negril, Jamaica, West Indies
Phone: 800–423–4095 or 876–927–5200
Web site: www.superclubs.com

Group/Getaway: Singles

Accommodations: Rooms and suites face the ocean, nude beach, or gardens. Rooms are separated by views and type of beach, all have tile floors, air-conditioning, private shower and bath, and mirrored ceilings above the bed. Rooms have either two twin beds or one king-size bed and are on a "shared" basis; clients travelling alone share with guest of the same sex or opt to pay a single supplement.

Points of Distinction: There is a nude beach. Dirty dancing is common, but this sort of daring behavior is tempered by good humor. If a guest books fourteen nights any time during the year, he or she will be rewarded with a three-night complimentary stay.

Open: Year-round.

Minimum Stay: Three nights.

Rates: Based on double occupancy, $350 to $495 per person, per night, with a $75 per person supplement December 26 to January 3, and a $150 single supplement throughout the year.

Frequently Asked Questions: *Are there a nude-only beach and pool?* Yes; these areas are separate, and clothing is mandatory in all other areas of the resort. *What types of dining are available?* All meals are served buffet style. There is also a pasta restaurant for casual evening dining, and a bar and cafe are located on the beach. *Are tours of the island available?* The tour desk offers a variety of tours at additional cost.

Don't Forget to Bring: Your favorite beer mug.

Favorite Side Trip: An all-time favorite is a tour to Dunn's River Falls (approximately $53 per person). Another is Rick's Cafe for watching the sunset.

Nearest Airport: Sangster International Airport, a two-and-a-half-hour drive from the resort.

ALL-INCLUSIVE SERVICES AND ACTIVITIES

Food and Beverages: All meals, alcoholic and nonalcoholic beverages, snacks, afternoon tea.

Outdoor Activities: Bicycling, beach volleyball, tennis, basketball, badminton, shuffleboard, table tennis.

Water Sports: Waterskiing, windsurfing, kayaking, sailing, scuba diving, snorkeling.

Facilities: Tennis courts, swimming pool, squash courts, fitness center.

Entertainment: Disco, live music, cabaret, karaoke, beach parties, toga parties, pajama parties, theme parties, body painting competitions.

Other: Scuba lessons, reggae and merengue dance classes, glass-bottom boats, nude Jacuzzi, circus workshop with trapeze and trampoline, mixology classes, airport transfers.

Available for a Fee: Motorized watercraft at nearby marinas, golf ($55 greens fee; $50 cart fee), gambling at nearby casino.

SANDALS NEGRIL BEACH RESORT AND SPA

Negril, Jamaica

On the "un-busy" western tip of Jamaica, Sandals remains relatively private and secluded, allowing visitors the time and space to relax with only an occasional hassle from local beach strollers asking if you'd like to get your hair braided or buy shells or maybe even marijuana. Although the government and the resort owners along the many miles of Negril Beach have decreased the volume of pestering that once was common here, local entrepreneurs are still present in a minor way. We don't advocate buying illegal substances—Jamaica jails are no place for tourists—but do enjoy this extraordinary beach, especially when you have a resort as organized as Sandals to return to. The sand is powdery white, the surf is tap-water clear, and the sea is as blue as a blueberry Slush Puppy. The forest that climbs down from the low ridge Jamaican mountains is vibrantly green; it runs rampant through the Sandals property and breaks only upon reaching the beach.

Sandals resorts are famous (in many cases infamous) for honing the science of pampering couples. Sandals Negril provides a level of indulgence that mixes relaxation with action, well suited to the younger crowds who tend to frequent it.

The spa is extensive, featuring a fully equipped fitness center and a huge variety of massages and body therapies available at an additional cost.

Although relaxation and bodywork are positives to enjoying a Sandals vacation, relaxation isn't only derived from sunbathing on the private offshore island. If you are someone who relaxes by expending energy as easily as conserving it, the resort offers a variety of impressive land and water activities. Scuba and snorkeling are the best means of freeing the soul while exploring the underwater depths of the Caribbean. Windsurfing gets you onto open waters. Sailing is just as accessible, and there are many other modes of watercraft available, including kayaks, canoes, and paddleboats.

Playing on the theme that friendly competition is sound vacation fun, Sandals is forever organizing team events, including lawn chess, where in the warm, sun-drenched air, Sandals guests match wits while physically lifting their pieces with two hands and walking off each move. Along with volleyball, basketball, and Ping-Pong, there are racquetball, squash, and tennis. Croquet, shuffleboard, and billiards can also be played, not to mention golf at Sandals' own eighteen-hole, par seventy-one course in Ocho Rios, about three hours away (greens fees included; transportation extra).

Throughout the Caribbean, Sandals devotes much effort to offering diverse and well-cooked meals to its guests, and Sandals Negril is no exception. There are four restaurants on the grounds, serving Asian, Caribbean, French, European, and American low-fat cooking. We particularly enjoyed "The 4C's," which stands for Coconut Cove Calorie Counter.

Karaoke sing-alongs run all night long, and sometimes the disco remains open until sunrise. There is a weekly beach party, as well as several different theme nights.

Sandals originated the now-common Hurricane Guarantee, which stipulates that while the possibility of a hurricane striking a Sandals is remote, the company is prepared to offer a free replacement vacation, including airfare, to anyone whose trip is interrupted by this natural disaster.

Sandals Negril Beach Resort and Spa

P.O. Box 12
Negril, Jamaica, West Indies
Phone: 800–SANDALS or 876–957–5216
Web site: www.sandals.com

Group/Getaway: Couples, Spa & Wellness

Accommodations: There are 223 rooms and suites that include air-conditioning, king-size bed, hair dryer, telephone, private bath and shower, in-room safe, clock radio, coffee-maker, and satellite television. Beachfront Honeymoon Suites and One-Bedroom Loft Suites include a mahogany four-poster bed, full bath, fully stocked wet bar, terry robes, and daily *New York Times* via fax.

Points of Distinction: Sandals Negril offers 7 miles of beach, white sands, calm water, and fabulous sunsets.

Open: Year-round.

Minimum Stay: Two nights.

Rates: Based on double occupancy, per person rates for one night begin at $285 for Deluxe Rooms and $370 for a Honeymoon Beachfront One-Bedroom Loft Suite.

Frequently Asked Questions: *Is there a dinner dress code?* Proper attire is required at dinner seating; this does not include jacket and tie, however. No beachwear, tank tops, or bare feet. Dress shorts are permitted, except at The Sundowner, where long pants and shirts with collars are required. *Are there golf courses in the vicinity?* There are golf courses in Montego Bay, approximately one and a half hours from the resort (greens fees are not included). Guests can enjoy complimentary greens fees at Sandals Golf and Country Club in Ocho Rios. Transportation costs $150 for four people by car, or $75 per person for round-trip airfare. Caddies are mandatory, although not included in the fee. Negril Hill Golf Course is about fifteen minutes from the property.

Don't Forget to Bring: Bathing suit, sunglasses, and sunscreen.

Favorite Side Trips: Dunn's River Falls in Ocho Rios; rafting trips; shopping for crafts in Negril; Bobbie Cay; a ten-minute swim to a public island for sunbathing; Negril's Hi-Lite tour.

Nearest Airports: Negril Airport, five minutes away, offers flights from Montego Bay via Air Jamaica Express. Sangster International Airport in Montego Bay is one and a half hours from the resort.

ALL-INCLUSIVE SERVICES AND ACTIVITIES

Food and Beverages: All meals and snacks, alcoholic and nonalcoholic beverages.

Outdoor Activities: Tennis, volleyball, racquetball, squash, golf, basketball, outdoor chess, croquet, shuffleboard, horseshoes.

Water Sports: Canoeing, kayaking, snorkeling, scuba diving, waterskiing, aqua cycling, paddleboating, windsurfing, sailing catamarans.

Facilities: Three freshwater pools, two whirlpools, spa, fitness center, saunas, steam rooms, lighted tennis courts, private offshore island.

Entertainment: Live entertainment nightly, jazz band, bingo, fashion shows, karaoke, piano bar, theme nights, weekly beach barbecue party.

Other: "Stay at One, Play at Six" program; shuttle service to Beaches Negril and Beaches Inn; weddings; taxes, gratuities, and transportation from the airport; aerobics; glass-bottom boat rides; billiards; twenty-four-hour butler service.

Available for a Fee: Tours and excursions, spa services, dry-cleaning service, laundry, money exchange bureau, special services (such as appropriate van transport from airport) for guests with disabilities, body shop, baby-sitting.

BEACHES GRANDE SPORT RESORT AND SPA

Ocho Rios, Jamaica

Away from Montego Bay, along Jamaica's North Coast, is the village of Ocho Rios, a popular cruise ship stopover and home to Beaches Grande Sport Resort and Spa, formerly the Ciboney Resort, one of Jamaica's premier all-inclusive resorts. After Beaches acquired the resort, it was closed for several months to complete the first phase of a $10 million, multiyear refurbishment. Beaches Grande Sport Resort and Spa reopened in December 2000 as an adults-only, ultra all-inclusive luxury resort that welcomes families (with children over the age of sixteen), singles, groups, and couples.

Beaches combines the best elements of a Caribbean vacation. A wide range of water sports is offered. There is a comprehensive schedule of aerobics, yoga, Pilates, kickboxing, step aerobics, and bodysculpting classes offered in the air-conditioned aerobics studio. Guests can also work out in comfort in the state-of-the-art fitness center, where a personal trainer is available.

Other on-land adventures include mountain-biking, tennis, volleyball, basketball, squash, croquet, and badminton. There are miles of jogging trails, a rock climbing wall, a trampoline, billiards, and four tennis courts (both clay and Har-Tru). All resort guests also have complimentary access (including greens fees and round-trip transfers) to the nearby eighteen-hole, par seventy-one course at Sandals Golf and Country Club.

Guests can enjoy a spectacular array of European spa services at an additional cost, including a choice of ten invigorating facials, five hydrotherapies, seven revitalizing body wraps, and five luxury massages. (Don't pass up the "Moon & Stars" massage performed at dark on the beach.) The Signature Spa features beautiful new treatment rooms, top-of-the-line hydrotherapy equipment, and a serene meditation room with a soothing waterfall. A separate manicure and pedicure area and hair salon complete the full range of services available to guests.

Beaches Grande Sport guests can stay in one of 285 luxurious rooms and in some of the most opulent suites in the Caribbean. Suite Concierge Service offers suite-level guests personalized attention, including VIP check-in, priority dinner reservations, spacious suites, a fully stocked minibar, daily delivery of the *New York Times* via fax, and other special in-room amenities like plush bathrobes.

Guests can savor gourmet cuisine at four world-class restaurants or enjoy a variety of snacks offered throughout the day at the main pool grill. A fresh fruit juice bar serves traditional fresh-squeezed juices and other beverages made with fruit indigenous to the Caribbean. The calorie counter program has been carefully designed to help health-conscious guests maintain healthy eating habits while enjoying all the culinary options.

At night the resort offers a wide variety of entertainment. Enjoy music and dancing every night and karaoke three nights a week at Nicole's Disco; the Manor Bar has entertainment nightly.

Beaches Grande Sport's meeting facilities include a ballroom and a pavilion area that can accommodate up to 400 guests theater style or 250 guests banquet style. The resort's two boardrooms are ideal for smaller meetings or groups. The resort also offers groups complimentary excursions to the breathtaking Dunn's River Falls.

Beaches Grande Sport Resort and Spa

Main Street
P.O. Box 728
St. Ann, Jamaica, West Indies
Phone: 888–BEACHES or 876–974–1027
E-mail: info@beaches.com
Web site: www.beaches.com

Group/Getaway: Couples, Spa & Wellness

Accommodations: Beaches Grande Sport has 285 suites and villas peacefully nestled on fifty acres of tropical gardens overlooking the crystal-clear Caribbean Sea. All rooms have a ceiling fan, fourteen-channel cable television, direct-dial telephone, clock radio, hair dryer, and full bath. Villas have semiprivate plunge pools, spacious living rooms, a kitchen, and bar.

Points of Distinction: Beaches Grande Sport offers twenty-four-hour butler service in its villas.

Open: Year-round.

Minimum Stay: Three nights.

Rates: Based on double occupancy, rates are $225 to $615 per person, per night; singles add a supplement of $100 per night. Extra person rate is $80.

Frequently Asked Questions: *Should I make my spa reservations when I arrive at the resort?* It's best to make reservations to ensure that you receive the scheduled times you want. *Are children permitted?* Only children sixteen and older.

Don't Forget to Bring: Casual clothing for day wear but casual elegance for evenings.

Favorite Side Trips: Dunn's River Falls; Blue Mountain Coffee Plantation tour.

Nearest Airport: Sangster International Airport in Montego Bay is one and a half hours away.

ALL-INCLUSIVE SERVICES AND ACTIVITIES

Food and Beverages: All meals, snacks, and beverages, including wine and liquor.

Outdoor Activities: Tennis, golf (including transfers and greens fees), jogging, croquet, lawn chess.

Water Sports: Windsurfing, sailing, kayaking, swimming.

Facilities: Gym, twenty whirlpools, six tennis courts, squash court, private beach club, jogging trail, walking course, ninety-one swimming pools, library, game room, juice bar, meditation center, group meeting facilities.

Entertainment: Nightly dancing and entertainment, nightclub, piano bar cabaret, theme parties.

Other: Round-trip airport transfers, hotel baggage handling, glass-bottom boat rides, aerobics, taxes, tips and gratuities.

Not Included: Jamaican departure tax.

Available for a Fee: Spa treatments, taxis, airplane transfers, premium beverages, scuba diving certification, land and sea tours.

COUPLES OCHO RIOS

Ocho Rios, Jamaica

Couples Ocho Rios is actually the birthplace of the all-inclusive resort for couples only. As the proud founder of the "made for two" concept (as the name suggests), the resort stays on top of this niche by maintaining the right environment for romance and privacy at a fair price. In the process, Couples Ocho Rios goes head-to-head with Sandals as they compete to outdo each other. In Ocho Rios, Couples now offers excursions off the resort at no extra cost. The resort also maintains a horse barn and equestrian center, also at no extra cost. But the main idea here is to create options that allow all couples, regardless of their interests, to reacquaint, relax, and play.

An Art Deco theme runs throughout the resort, beginning with its approach, where an elaborate fountain and lush gardens lead into an open-air lobby offering an expansive view of the sea. The 212 guest rooms and one-bedroom luxury suites (no room for visitors) face the wide beach and ultra-blue Caribbean. Views from the balconies are breathtaking.

Activities begin as early as 7:00 A.M. Couples can be as active, yet as romantic, as they choose. At the Watersports Center there are daily lessons in scuba and sailing. Or you can enter a golf tournament or tennis match to win prizes. You can even master jumping fences on Thoroughbreds.

One particularly romantic sojourn is to boat over to Tower Isle, the resort's private island, swim up to the bar, have lunch with your favorite person, and enjoy the privacy of the beach. If you're not up for snorkeling or scuba diving, you can take the glass-bottom reef tour or a sunset catamaran cruise, explore Ocho Rios, ride the famous Dunn's Falls, or tour a Sugar Plantation—all at no additional cost.

The dining experience at Couples is varied and well done. All meals are served in six award-winning restaurants with a "no reservations" policy. On the dining room side, the options include Le Gourmet for fine French cuisine, The Verandah for international and Caribbean fare, Bayside for Italian alfresco, Calabash for local Jamaican, The Patio for casual buffets, and The Beach Grill. Couples wants its guests to be spontaneous. The theory is that many options but no appointments enhance romance and relaxation. From dining to sports, everything is done on a "do it when you feel like it" basis.

As a segue into the evening's entertainment, there are five bars on-site that offer everything from soft music to hard reggae. Beach parties and an outdoor international buffet are also regular occurrences at Couples.

Maintaining the theme of a romantic getaway, Couples will organize not only honeymoons but also weddings with great care and attention. If you stay a minimum of six nights, they'll arrange it all—another all-inclusive perk.

Couples Ocho Rios

P.O. Box 330
St. Mary
Ocho Rios, Jamaica, West Indies
Phone: 800–268–7537 or 876–975–4271
Web site: www.couples.com

Group/Getaway: Couples, Sports & Fitness

Accommodations: There are 212 rooms with balconies or patios overlooking the ocean and the gardens. One-bedroom luxury suites and villas have Jacuzzis or plunge pools, wet bars stocked with premium liquor, champagne, and hors d'oeuvres. All rooms have air-conditioning and CD players.

Points of Distinction: Weddings are complimentary for guests staying six or more nights and include a two-tiered cake, sparkling wine, bouquet, boutonniere, and massages. (Marriage license, photographer, and videotape are available for an additional fee.)

Open: Year-round.

Minimum Stay: Three nights.

Rates: Based on double occupancy, one-bedroom ocean- and mountain-view villa suites range from $440 to $750 per couple, per night.

Frequently Asked Question: *Do you need to make reservations for dinner at any of the restaurants?* There is a "no reservations" policy at all restaurants. The Beach Grill is open all day for snacks, and the open-air Patio serves elaborate breakfast and luncheon specials.

Don't Forget to Bring: Golf clubs, tennis rackets, diving gear, and regulator.

Favorite Side Trips: Catamaran sunset cruise, glass-bottom boat reef trip, Dunn's River Falls.

Nearest Airport: Sangster International Airport, a two-hour drive from the resort.

ALL-INCLUSIVE SERVICES AND FACILITIES

Food and Beverages: All meals, nonalcoholic and alcoholic beverages, snacks, afternoon tea, continental breakfast in bed (room service).

Outdoor Activities: Tennis, bicycling, volleyball, horseback riding, golf, squash, croquet, shuffleboard.

Water Sports: Swimming, windsurfing, sailing Sunfish and Hobie Cats, waterskiing, snorkeling, scuba diving, canoeing, kayaking, water aerobics, surfing.

Facilities: Freshwater pool, Jacuzzi, private island for au naturel sunbathers only, floating tanning decks, fitness center, five tennis courts, indoor squash courts, equestrian center and stables, duty-free shop, game room, Ping-Pong.

Entertainment: Piano bar, nightclub, cocktail lounge, reggae bands.

Other: Instruction for sports activities (available daily), reggae dance classes, arts and crafts, airport transfers, gratuities, taxes, service charges.

Available for a Fee: Massage and beauty salon services.

ROYAL PLANTATION SPA & GOLF RESORT

Ocho Rios, Jamaica

The philosophy at Sandals since 9/11 has been to invest, invest, and reinvest. Employee development and facility improvement were first on the list. Nowhere have we seen the fruits of these labors more clearly than at Royal Plantation Spa & Golf Resort—the brightest new star in the Sandals constellation. Opened in 2001, this intimate, 77-bedroom resort is truly elegant. Every room is a suite, and every suite sits on the side of a dramatic rise that offers a superb view of the ocean. Although there are neighboring properties, the geography hides them, offering privacy, beauty, and serenity.

Every so often, we've encountered resorts that have great feng shui, a sense of balance and harmony among all elements—where architecture and design complement the natural surroundings. At Royal Plantation Spa & Golf Resort it has all come together beautifully, and you realize it the minute you enter the grounds and view the striking blend of mahogany, rosewood, and marble that adorns each building.

We enjoyed the sense of privacy that the beautifully landscaped grounds afford and the kind of romantic appeal that the place holds for couples who want to be together without lots of noise and distraction. Having been to other Sandals resorts in Jamaica, we recognize that the staff at Royal Plantation has been meticulously trained to complement the understated, casually elegant manner of this resort. They are friendly but never forward, watchful but never intrusive. Because every guest is considered a VIP, room service is always available—on the beach, in your suite, or anywhere else we can think of.

But as with all Sandals, there is no lack of things to do here. Two attractive beach areas provide all of the water activities you'd expect at an ultra all-inclusive. There is nightly entertainment, as well as a bar that could easily be part of a fine London hotel.

Two other features of the resort stand out. Dining here is gourmet, highlighted by a French restaurant and European chef, Hugo Hirn, who many claim is the most creative culinary master in the Caribbean. After two dinners that featured an incredibly tasty mix of Jamaican spices mixed with French specialties of meats, fowl, and European wines, we can't say enough about the kitchen of this very classy place. White-gloved waiters go out of their way to please. A second special feature is the outstanding spa, which offers a wide and interesting array of holistic body treatments. Jamaica has one of the most demanding training and licensing programs for massage therapists in the world; cruise lines work hard to recruit Jamaican masseuses, and now we know why. We enjoyed moonlit massages on the beach—a couples option—listening to the waves lap the shore as the graceful hands of the spa staff made the night exquisitely relaxing.

One of the advantages of being in Ocho Rios is that Sandals maintains other resorts only minutes away. If you want to visit swim-up bars or enjoy an up-tempo disco night, the staff at Royal Plantation Spa & Golf Resort will arrange private transportation to Sandals Ocho Rios or Grand Sport. We liked that, too, especially knowing we could return to our private veranda at will to enjoy a quiet nightcap and watch moonlight illuminate the soft water below.

Royal Plantation Spa & Golf Resort

P.O. Box 2
Main Street
Ocho Rios, Jamaica, West Indies
Phone: 800–726–3257 or 876–974–5601
E-mail: mmachado@brp.sandals.com
Web site: www.royalplantation.com

Group/Getaway: Singles, Couples, Spa & Wellness

Accommodations: There are a total of 80 suites in six different categories. All suites include VCR, air-conditioning, CD player, fans, AM/FM clock radio, iron, ironing board, satellite television with movie channels, hair dryer, plush robes, coffeemaker, in-room bar, amenity kit, daily *New York Times* via fax, electronic in-room safe, telephone, dataport, full bath, whirlpool bath (some suites), twenty-four-hour room service, balcony or patio with ocean view.

Points of Distinction: Georgian-style architecture and signature beach butler service.

Open: Year-round.

Minimum Stay: None.

Rates: Based on double occupancy, rates begin at $425 per person, per night ($545 for singles).

Frequently Asked Question: *What's the nightlife like?* There is nightly entertainment—jazz trio, Caribbean steel band, dancing with the resident band, fire dancer, crab racing, cultural shows, and weekly beach party.

Don't Forget to Bring: A jacket, dress pants, and collar shirts for dining in the elegant French restaurant.

Favorite Side Trip: Dunn's River Falls, the world-renowned waterfalls, included.

Nearest Airports: Ninety minutes by car from Sangster International Airport in Montego Bay and fifteen minutes from Boscobel Aerodrome.

ALL-INCLUSIVE SERVICES AND ACTIVITIES

Food and Beverages: All meals, alcoholic and nonalcoholic beverages, snacks, twenty-four-hour room service for all suites.

Outdoor Activities: Tennis, golf, chess on the ocean.

Water Sports: Aqua tricycles, glass-bottom boat rides, windsurfing, sailboating, Hobie Waves, snorkeling, canoeing, scuba diving. Resort dive course for beginners is offered. Surcharge for night dives, PADI Certification, and Open Dive Referral courses.

Facilities: Meeting facilities, game room, two tennis courts, freshwater swimming pool, two outdoor whirlpool baths, sauna and steam rooms, fully equipped fitness center, including cardiovascular machines and weight equipment.

Entertainment: Piano bar, billiards, cards, board games, DVDs, and videos.

Other: Complimentary transfer and exchange privileges to all Beaches and Sandals resorts in the Ocho Rios area (Sandals Dunn's River, Sandals Ocho Rios, and Grande Sport Villa Golf Resort and Spa by Beaches), except Beaches Boscobel. Golf—championship eighteen-hole Sandals Golf & Country Club with complimentary green fees. Round-trip transfers, airport transfers, taxes and gratuities.

Available at a Fee: Tours and excursions, car rentals, laundry, dry-cleaning services, beauty salon services, spa services, telephone, fax, and Internet.

SANS SOUCI RESORT & SPA

Ocho Rios, Jamaica

Folks flying to Jamaica's Ocho Rios for a Sans Souci vacation look very different from those flying home after a week of pampering. Buried among seaside jungle foliage, Sans Souci sits in the farthest reaches of a hidden blue-water cove. The entire resort provides high levels of comfort within the guest rooms and hedonistic indulgences throughout the property. Many of the rooms have their own whirlpools, and there are a slew of outdoor Jacuzzis. Pools, whirlpools, mineral pools, and pool bars dot the Sans Souci landscape, as if the bath-warm waters of the Caribbean weren't enough. Even Charlie, the resort's own ninety-seven-year-old turtle, who is turns out is a she, has her own clear-water pool. She looks good for her age, as will anyone passing the daylight hours at Charlie's Spa.

Views from Charlie's Spa are calming enough. More calming, however, are the spa's massages, facials, and body scrubs. Pedicures and manicures are given as well, and, on top of it all, a soothing treatment of reflexology draws out the last vestiges of stress the world has heaped upon you—a world made more distant by San Souci's extravagance.

Wandering musicians stroll throughout the resort, both day and night. A saxophone might sing from the shaded cover of palm trees. A violinist could stand inconspicuously on an open hillside overlooking the sea, while a guitarist's strum might complement the tickling of water against the white-sand beach.

At night the beach becomes an island carnival, with Arawak performances and various theme parties. Among them are the Caribbean Carnival Barbecue and a torch-lit Beach Fiesta. There is the Grand Gala Buffet, and, for late night, there's the midnight Beachside Bonfire.

For food and drink, guests choose from among four bars, a beachside grill, and three full-service restaurants. And do not doubt the quality of meals at Sans Souci. Food is prepared by a team of chefs, with each chef coming from a different continent, guaranteeing variety and good flavor. After a decade of SuperClubs' management, the San Souci is now independently operated. But you will find familiar faces as the management and staff were invited to stay on.

Sans Souci Resort & Spa
White River
P.O. Box 103
St. Mary
Ocho Rios, Jamaica, West Indies
Phone: 866–55–SOUCI or 876–994–1353
   (direct)
Web site: www.tradewindtours.com

Group/Getaway: Couples, Spa & Wellness

Accommodations: There are 146 luxurious suites, eight penthouses, and eight veranda rooms. All are air-conditioned and are equipped with television, AM/FM radio, direct-dial telephone, hair dryer, iron and ironing board, in-room safe, private terrace, refrigerator stocked with sodas, beer, water and juice, and coffee and tea service. All suites also include twenty-four-hour room service, and laundry and dry-cleaning service.

Points of Distinction: If you stay four nights or more, six spa treatments are included in your package. Here you can enjoy the rare therapeutic mineral pools or soak in the mineral water Jacuzzi or natural mineral water grotto after a relaxing body scrub, body massage, facial, or reflexology from a certified therapist. Legend has it that if you soak in the grotto with your loved one, and if your love is true, it will last forever.

Open: Year-round.

Minimum Stay: Three nights.

Rates: Based on double occupancy, rates are from $420 to $885 per person, per night. The single supplement is $200 per night.

Frequently Asked Questions: *Is Jamaica dangerous?* Like any country with high unemployment, there are places a visitor should not explore, especially at night. But if you use common sense, most places in Jamaica are safe to visit. It is customary for some people on the street to try to sell you anything you desire. But if you are approached, do not be afraid—it's a national tradition. *How long are the complimentary spa treatments?* All treatments last twenty to twenty-five minutes. You are welcome to

schedule a one-hour paid treatment or pay additional for half-hour treatments.

Don't Forget to Bring: A hat, sunscreen, and an appetite.

Favorite Side Trip: Dunn's River Falls is on every tourist's destination wish list, but it is spectacular and worth seeing and climbing.

Nearest Airport: Sangster International Airport, Montego Bay, is a two-hour drive from the resort.

ALL-INCLUSIVE SERVICES AND ACTIVITIES

Food and Beverages: All meals, alcoholic and nonalcoholic beverages, snacks, afternoon tea, twenty-four-hour room service.

Outdoor Activities: Tennis, golf, basketball, volleyball, shuffleboard, bocce, bicycling.

Water Sports: Swimming, snorkeling, waterskiing, sailing, windsurfing, kayaking, glass-bottom boat rides.

Facilities: Pool with mineral water, fitness center, library, television lounge, game room.

Entertainment: Nightly karaoke, themed gala parties.

Other: Spa treatments, including massage, body scrub, reflexology, manicure, and pedicure; taxes and gratuities; transportation to and from the airport.

BREEZES RUNAWAY BAY

Runaway Bay, Jamaica

For many couples, the choice is between beach and golf. There are those who golf and don't want to "do" the beach, and those who prefer lying on the sand and aren't thrilled about teeing off. Breezes Runaway Bay solves this dilemma by offering couples one of the finest expanses of sand on Jamaica, adjoining one of the best golf courses in the Caribbean.

Breezes, with its pools, Jacuzzis, and gardens, runs lengthwise between white-sand beach and the resort's own greens and fairways. No stretch of the eighteen-hole PGA course is more than 200 yards from the blue surf of Runaway Bay, along Jamaica's North Shore. But there is much more here than golf and beach. As easy as it is to relax at Breezes, it is just as easy to join in the fun.

Breezes offers a huge variety of activities that you can do on your own or with instruction. Runaway Bay is well suited for windsurfing, sailing, and snorkeling. On land, bicycles are available to tour a bit of the island, and, for those who enjoy nature, the low mountain range that runs behind the resort is laced with narrow pathways that weave their way through thick tropical forest. Virtually every day there are staff-organized pickup games of basketball, soccer, volleyball, and, believe it or not, cricket where cricket is played best.

Of the many sports offered here, two that are taken the most seriously are golf and tennis. There are ongoing schools for each, with resident pros who utilize video-assisted clinics. Four tennis courts allow competitions during the day and at night under the lights. A total of twenty-eight hours of golf instruction is available each week in a lecture room, on a ten-bay golf range, large practice green, sand trap, and chipping area. And golf school instruction doesn't cost extra. The PGA-approved golf course is home to the Heineken World Cup Western Hemisphere Golf Tournament and the Jamaican Open, which also speaks to its quality. So strict is Breezes about the all-inclusive concept that tipping is not permitted on any quarters of the resort, including the golf course, which is something of a boon to duffers.

In spite of these bonus all-inclusive opportunities, Breezes is moderately priced, seeking the value-conscious traveler. The resort has targeted honeymooners, offering weddings absolutely free, including the minister, marriage license, a wedding cake, champagne, flowers, and music—even a best man and maid of honor.

Even though there is an au naturel beach and Jacuzzi at the resort, we didn't find it to be a place only for the young and restless. Couples well into their fifties were present and enjoying themselves as much as the younger crowd, especially when the steel bands started playing. Throughout the week, there are toga parties, pajama parties, and many types of beach parties. There are four bars on-site, including a swim-up pool bar, and there is a nightclub that closes when the last person leaves.

We noted that Breezes has a "Sunshine" guarantee: For every day that the sun doesn't show its face, you receive a voucher for a free day, good for a year at any Breezes property around the world. With eight sister hotels in Jamaica, the Bahamas, and Brazil, you might even pray for rain.

Breezes Runaway Bay
P.O. Box 58
Runaway Bay, Jamaica
Phone: 877–GO–SUPER or 876–973–2436
E-mail: info@superclubs.com
Web site: www.superclubs.com

Group/Getaway: Couples, Sports & Fitness

Accommodations: There are 238 air-conditioned rooms and suites, including Superior, Deluxe, Premium, and Luxury Rooms, and Ocean View Suites, all surrounded by twenty lush, green acres. All rooms have a king-size bed or two twin beds, love seat or armchair, and marble bathrooms.

Points of Distinction: Breezes Runaway Bay has an excellent golf program with an eighteen-hole PGA golf course adjacent to the hotel, a golf school complete with pro instructors, a lecture room with video equipment, and a ten-bay golf range, large practice green, sand trap, and chipping area.

Open: Year-round.

Minimum Stay: Two nights.

Rates: Based on double occupancy, $187 to $303 per person, per night.

Frequently Asked Question: *Do I need to bring my own golf equipment?* It's a good idea to bring your own, but you can rent clubs for $14. There are no greens fees.

Don't Forget to Bring: Appropriate athletic clothing and shoes for sports or plenty of sunscreen if you plan to visit the au naturel beach.

Favorite Side Trip: Shopping in Montego Bay, 40 miles away.

Nearest Airport: Sangster International Airport is approximately an hour and twenty minutes from the resort.

ALL-INCLUSIVE SERVICES AND ACTIVITIES

Food and Beverages: All meals, alcoholic and nonalcoholic beverages, snacks. Room service for continental breakfast only.

Outdoor Activities: Tennis, golf, beach soccer and volleyball, cricket, bicycle touring, walking.

Water Sports: Scuba, snorkeling, windsurfing, waterskiing, sailing, kayaking, swimming, pool volleyball.

Facilities: Four lighted tennis courts, eighteen-hole PGA golf course, putting green, two freshwater pools, fitness center, three Jacuzzis, four bars.

Entertainment: Theme parties, nightclub, toga parties, beach parties, pajama parties.

Other: Taxes, gratuities, and airport transfers; golf and tennis schools with resident pros.

Available for a Fee: Departure tax ($21 per person), golf cart ($35), and caddie services ($12).

FRANKLYN D. RESORT

Runaway Bay, Jamaica

The Franklyn D. Resort (FDR) has been an innovator of the family all-inclusive experience since the concept was born more than a decade ago. For families with young children hoping to visit a resort that virtually guarantees kids' happiness while giving adults a much needed break, this Jamaican getaway is a top choice.

When families first arrive at Jamaica's Montego Bay, the FDR shuttle bus takes them on the hour-and-a-half drive to the resort on Runaway Bay. Upon arrival at the resort, each family is introduced to its own highly trained and loving Vacation Nanny. These women adore kids, have been screened for their great energy and patience, and are readily available to meet almost every need. Should parents want time alone to go shopping, scuba diving, or participate in other activities, the Vacation Nanny will care for the children by taking them to the playground, by the poolside to play games, or on a stroll around the property. She will also provide additional assistance to parents by bathing, dressing, and feeding infants at meal times. She has been trained to respect your privacy by being on hand only when needed.

There are no standard rooms at the Franklyn D. Resort, but rather seventy-six one-, two-, or three-bedroom suites, fully self-contained with kitchens, patios or terraces, and in-house satellite television. The homelike atmosphere allows guests to vacation in a more private setting similar to an elegant Jamaican house. Because children under sixteen stay, eat, and play free, we think this resort is a great value.

While parents plan a full range of tropical activities, from scuba, sailing, and tennis to sampling Bloody Marys, kids stay busy at a fully supervised mini club featuring activities for all ages. Highlights include a kiddie's disco, outdoor arts and crafts center, and a mini arcade. A specially designed program for teenagers is also offered and includes time at FDR's state-of-the-art Computer Learning Center. A unique feature of the center is the integration of a Cyber Cafe, where guests can surf the Internet (with supervision) in a relaxed and cool environment.

Too often, where there is a kids' program there is mediocre food. FDR breaks the mold with a nice mix of Jamaican, international, and Italian fare, served in all three of the property's restaurants. At the Piano Bar the ocean view offers a quiet place to relax with a choice of top-shelf liquor and soft piano music. And with a resort full of super nannies, you can actually slow down and enjoy it.

Franklyn D. Resort

P.O. Box 201
Runaway Bay, St. Ann, Jamaica, West Indies
Phone: 888–FDR–KIDS or 876–973–4591
E-mail: fdrinfo@fdrholidays.com
Web site: www.fdrholidays.com

Group/Getaway: Families

Accommodations: There are seventy-six one-, two-, and three-bedroom suites, each with its own kitchen, patio or terrace, and in-house satellite television.

Points of Distinction: The Vacation Nanny makes your family feel at home by taking on maid and baby-sitting duties, even rinsing wet swimsuits, making sandwiches, and supervising your children all day. If parents want to stay up late, baby-sitting services are available for a small charge. The Cyber Cafe allows the opportunity to "keep in touch" through the Internet.

Open: Year-round.

Minimum Stay: None.

Rates: Based on seven-nights, double occupancy, rates begin at $2,100. Children under sixteen years play, stay, and eat for free. Single supplement $50 to $100, depending on season.

Frequently Asked Question: *Do we eat meals with our children?* By all means, it is your choice. If you desire some adults-only meals during your vacation, the Vacation Nanny will be there to accompany the children.

Don't Forget to Bring: Strong, waterproof sunscreen for kids.

Favorite Side Trip: Dunn's River Falls is approximately an hour and a half from FDR. The cool, clear water cascades down the limestone cliffs that rise from the ocean. Climbing the falls is a challenge, and the slide down is a thrill to visitors.

Nearest Airport: Sangster International Airport, in Montego Bay, is an hour and ten minutes from the resort.

ALL-INCLUSIVE SERVICES AND ACTIVITIES

Food and Beverages: All meals, snacks, afternoon tea, nonalcoholic beverages, beer and bar drinks.

Outdoor Activities: Tennis, bicycling.

Water Sports: Scuba diving, windsurfing, kayaking, snorkeling, sailing, swimming.

Facilities: Gym, swimming pool.

Entertainment: Disco, karaoke, floor shows, magicians.

Other: Taxes, gratuities, and airport transfers; Vacation Nanny; glass-bottom boat rides.

Children's Services: The Kid's Center includes three clubs: Explorers (ages three to five), Adventurers (ages six to eleven), and Teens (ages twelve and up).

Children's Activities: Outdoor activities, water sports, arts and crafts, French lessons, Nintendo games, kiddies' disco, Super Boy and Miss FDR contests, limbo party, magic show, donkey rides.

Available for a Fee: Special excursions arranged for teens.

GRAND LIDO BRACO

Trelawny, Jamaica

A little seaside village with cobble-stone streets, a town hall on the square, street vendors, artisans, and sparkling azure waves lapping the shore might describe an old-world scene, maybe along the Mediterranean, or even early New England. It is actually part of a new development at all-inclusives: creating villages of authentic character on their grounds. This one belongs to Grand Lido Braco, a member of the SuperClubs chain that has been in the forefront of the all-inclusive movement on Jamaica—the island where it all got started in the Caribbean.

About an hour east of Montego Bay's Sangster International Airport is one of the finest beaches on Jamaica's North Coast. At the town of Trelawny, SuperClubs constructed a village reminiscent of old Jamaica, with streets of real cobblestone and gingerbread architecture intended to capture the spirit of life in Jamaica—ironically, before SuperClubs and Sandals were created. Its brochures state that it is so real that visitors don't have to leave the grounds to shop, experience Jamaica, or understand Jamaica's past. Well, not quite. Even as the Caribbean's most spectacular island, Jamaica still has its full share of poverty, crime, and unemployment—aspects, naturally, that resort owners would like to protect their guests from knowing. Some argue that the fast-growing "village" concept is too Disneyesque for a Caribbean island. If this were Braco's only asset, we would not include it in this book, but Braco actually offers excellent programs on and off its beach and provides a level of comfort and service that is outstanding.

Among these assets is free golf at the resort's own nine-hole private course and free entrance to Super-Clubs' eighteen-hole championship course 25 miles away (transportation is provided). Braco's spa gives complimentary manicures and pedicures. Its restaurants offer a broad and excellent range of dining, from Piacere, a gourmet dining facility, to Victoria Market for alfresco continental cuisine. We also applaud Nanny's Jerk Pit, which features authentic Jamaican cuisine, and MunaHana, which specializes in Japanese food. If you want more variety, you can also eat at the Italian Pasta Bar.

Braco knows how to entertain people, and the nightlife here is electrifying. The old-fashioned lampposts on the streets are illuminated, Caribbean music pulsates through the village, the Piano Bar hums, and famous Jamaican entertainers perform. Every night there is a good show with lots of dancing—great for couples with high energy.

As for the village, although it's not authentic, we must compliment management for bringing in Jamaican artisans to run the operation. Streets have shops and galleries featuring woodcarvers, artists, and a coconut hat maker, as well as sugar cane, fruit, peanut, and coconut vendors. We also noted that the Town Hall is not just included for aesthetics. It is used for meetings, private dinners, entertainment, and even weddings. And every Friday night there is a street parade that gives people a chance to laugh and dance together, as they used to in the villages of Jamaica some years ago.

Grand Lido Braco

Rio Bueno PO, Trelawny, Jamaica, West Indies
Phone: 800–GO–SUPER or 876–954–0000
  (direct)
E-mail: info@superclubs.com
Web site: www.superclubs.com

Group/Getaway: Couples

Accommodations: There are 232 rooms and suites, including Garden View, Ocean View, Beachfront, and Ocean Front one-bedroom suites. Each suite has a king-size bed and a spacious living area, private bath, and patio or balcony.

Points of Distinction: Grand Lido Braco is a re-created nineteenth-century Jamaican village, complete with Caribbean gingerbread architecture and a town square.

Open: Year-round.

Minimum Stay: Three nights.

Rates: Based on double occupancy, per person rates per night range from $375 for a Garden View Room to $745 for an Au Naturel One-Bedroom Ocean Front Suite during the winter season.

Frequently Asked Question: *Is the golf course challenging?* Guests have full access to the nine-hole executive course on property. However, for golfers who want something a bit more challenging, there is the PGA rated golf course at SuperClubs' private eighteen-hole golf course at Runaway Bay, only twenty-five minutes away. Greens fees, transportation, and professional instruction are all included.

Don't Forget to Bring: The three "S"s—sunglasses, sunscreen, and sandals.

Favorite Side Trip: Montego Bay.

Nearest Airport: Sangster International Airport, an hour from the resort.

ALL-INCLUSIVE SERVICES AND ACTIVITIES

Food and Beverages: All meals, snacks, afternoon tea, alcoholic and nonalcoholic beverages, twenty-four-hour room service.

Outdoor Activities: Golf, tennis, soccer, bicycling, volleyball, hiking.

Water Sports: Scuba diving, snorkeling, waterskiing, windsurfing, swimming, fishing, Sunfish sailing, kayaking.

Facilities: Two swimming pools, hiking trails, golf course, fitness center, pond for fishing, game room, library, Jacuzzis, conference rooms. Nearby: Eighteen-hole golf course at Runaway Bay.

Entertainment: Nightly disco, piano bar.

Other: Taxes, gratuities, and airport transfers; weddings and renewal of vows; sports instruction; billiards; manicure and pedicure; art and reggae classes.

Available for a Fee: International PADI certification.

THE BODY HOLIDAY AT LESPORT

Castries, St. Lucia

St. Lucia is a terrific island blessed with friendly people and much beauty. Now you can concentrate on inner beauty as well. The LeSport resort had such a massive makeover in 2001 that it has emerged with even a new name, The Body Holiday at LeSport.

The focus is on rejuvenation that combines pampering and activity aimed at giving the visitor lifelong insights. The purpose is to purge the demons of stress from the busy people the resort attracts.

It begins when the visitor books a vacation. One of the program specialists will contact the visitor to help plan the program from the extensive menu of land and water sports, fitness classes, and spa treatments at Oasis, a facility modeled architecturally after the Alhambra Palace. But rather than overlooking the Spanish city of Grenada, the resort overlooks the Caribbean from the northern tip of St. Lucia in the Lesser Antilles. The sun rises on one side, warms the shallow surf throughout the day, and then sinks in a blaze of color beneath the water horizon, visible from the balconies and beaches of LeSport.

The environment at LeSport is extremely peaceful. Throughout the grounds, stone-bottom pools center lushly manicured courtyards. Delicately sculpted statues rise from lily ponds.

Whether it's fun and festivity that relieves your stress, or expenditure of energy through weights or aerobics, or even if it's pure, uninterrupted relaxation—you can pick your elixirs here.

Members of LeSport's staff struck us as unusually committed to creating an integrated program for each client, tailored to meet his or her needs and interests. Using the resort's Oasis spa, they might recommend thalassotherapy treatments, which are several phases of seawater soaks, algae bubble baths, jet showers, and seaweed nutrient wraps. The mind drifts while the process continues. Or they might add a soft loofah rub of oils and salts. With natural products from Europe, LeSport visitors receive treatments of aromatherapy, reflexology, hair care, and a Swiss needle shower. Massages include Swiss and Thai techniques. Classes in t'ai chi, yoga, meditation, and stress management are options as well. In the process of enjoying these treatments, it's not hard to understand why stress disappears.

LeSport life cannot become full until your plate is empty. The food at LeSport was inspired by Michel Guerard, the French chef who made cuisine légère an art form. Epicureans will appreciate its freshness and creativity. Tables are laden with fresh fruits, salads, and superb delicacies from the sea. And the wine list is outstanding for a Caribbean resort.

After dinner, entertainment starts at the Terrace Bar, where local artists put on a spectacular show every night. If you wish to end the day on a more low-key note, the Piano Bar stays open until the last guest goes to bed—it's a company policy.

The Body Holiday at LeSport

Cariblue Beach
P.O. Box 437
Castries, St. Lucia
Phone: 800–544–2883 or 758–450–8551
E-mail: tropichol@aol.com
Web site: www.thebodyholiday.com

Group/Getaway: Couples, Spa & Wellness

Accommodations: There are 154 guest rooms and two suites with partial ocean views and oceanfront available. Rooms are decorated in soothing pastels, with white wicker furniture and a private terrace with views of the bay and the crescent beach below. Cotton robes, a hair dryer, a scarlet hibiscus blossom, and a marble-tiled bathroom with a basket of toiletries are included in each room.

Points of Distinction: There is an extensive spa and relaxation facility that offers a series of baths and treatments designed to rejuvenate the body, including thalassotherapy, a prescribed restorative treatment for fatigue.

Open: Year-round.

Minimum Stay: None.

Rates: Based on double occupancy, from $230 to $498 per person, per night, to $578 on holidays; single supplement is $90. Garden rooms for singles are $236 to $366 per night, $446 on holidays. Minimum age is twelve from July through October, sixteen the remainder of the year.

Frequently Asked Question: *What spa services are included in the all-inclusive price?* Hydromassage, reflexology, aromatherapy, seaweed nutrient wraps, salt loofah rubs, body massage, facials, hair care, Swiss needle shower, relaxation temple, saunas, and hot and cold plunge pools are all included.

Don't Forget to Bring: Casual clothing and spa wear, appropriate athletic shoes, lots of sunscreen.

Favorite Side Trips: Excursions to neighboring islands and Friday night visits to a nearby fishing village for a street "fete," arranged by the resort staff.

Nearest Airports: Vigie Airport, twenty minutes from the resort, and Hewanorra International Airport, ninety minutes away.

ALL-INCLUSIVE SERVICES AND ACTIVITIES

Food and Beverages: All meals, snacks, afternoon tea, wine and liquor, room service (with twenty-four-hour notice).

Outdoor Activities: Archery, golf, fencing, bicycle touring, tennis, volleyball.

Water Sports: Swimming, snorkeling, windsurfing, sailing, kayaking, waterskiing, scuba diving.

Facilities: Oasis health spa, three pools, gym.

Entertainment: Nightly.

Other: Selected spa services, golf greens fees and transfers to nearby nine-hole course, golf school, fitness and relaxation classes, gratuities, taxes.

Available for a Fee: Beauty treatments, hiking up the Pitons, overnights on St. Lucia's highest mountain.

JALOUSIE HILTON RESORT AND SPA

Soufriere, St. Lucia

The dormant volcanic peaks, Gros and Petit Pitons, stand guard over Jalousie Bay as if to protect the Jalousie Hilton Resort and Spa. It deserves safekeeping. Graced with fruits and flowering bushes, its verdant surroundings are a tropical El Dorado. Native fruit trees of mango, banana, papaya, coconut, and starfruit line the open areas of the resort. The sweet smells of hibiscus, jasmine, bougainvillea, and oleander suffuse the area as tiny hummingbirds crowd into boughs.

The underpinning of Jalousie's success has been its ability to create a world of activity, entertainment, and dining that is of such high standards, guests have little desire to leave the beautiful grounds to go elsewhere. To entertain children—and please their parents—Jalousie has created The Learning Center for kids from five to seventeen years of age. It is a terrific program that teaches about the natural environment of the island, including volcanoes, marine biology, and the rainforest. Mini drama productions and a host of other creative activities make up the balance of the day.

For adults, the Jalousie Hilton's claim to fame is its spa and great scuba and snorkeling opportunities. The spa has an extensive and enticing assortment of rejuvenating treatments using natural ingredients from St. Lucia's rainforest. The world-class dive center has an experienced dive team that can teach beginners or inspire experienced divers. Because St. Lucia is blessed with an abundance of shallow-water reefs, the dive sites have vibrant coral and tropical fish.

A bonus at Jalousie that attests to the depth of its exclusive offerings is its unique, executive golf course, where each hole has been modeled after a world-famous golf green. It is a fun course, made more difficult by surroundings that are spectacular. It's simply not easy to keep your eye on the ball when the backdrop is a tropical forest next to a half-mile-high, sleepy volcano just across the Caribbean Sea. For tennis lovers, adults and children, there is also a complimentary one-day tennis clinic on four outdoor Laykold courts.

The accommodations at Jalousie complement its activities. Winner of the 1997 British Airways Environmental Award, the resort's colonial structure is maintained on 325 acres with great sensitivity to the eco-culture of the area. The four restaurants on the grounds—the Verandah Restaurant, Bayside Bar and Grill, Pier Restaurant, and the Plantation Restaurant—are equal to the superior elegance of the resort's sixty-five villas, thirty-five villa suites, and twelve Sugar Mill Rooms.

This special getaway is romantic, which has made it very popular with honeymooners. Jalousie's wedding packages bring many couples to the resort to tie the knot or renew their vows. In order to reserve all-inclusive rates for any package, you must call the resort's toll-free or direct number.

Jalousie Hilton Resort and Spa
P.O. Box 251
Bay Street
Soufriere, St. Lucia
Phone: 800–774–1500 (Hilton reservations),
    888–744–5256, or 758–456–8000
E-mail: rdomingues@jalousie-hilton.com
Web site: www.jalousie-hilton.com

Group/Getaway: Families, Spa & Wellness

Accommodations: There are sixty-five Villas, thirty-five Villa Suites, and twelve Sugar Mill Rooms tucked into the hills around the bay and surrounded by tropical flowers, giant ferns, and palms. All have spectacular sea and mountain views and include high ceilings, cool tile, and verandas, and some have private plunge pools.

Point of Distinction: Once a thriving sugar plantation, Jalousie is nestled between the famous Piton Mountains in a fertile tropical valley.

Open: Year-round.

Minimum Stay: None.

Packages: The wedding package includes all wedding and legal arrangements, champagne, a three-tier wedding cake, candlelit dinner for two, and even a $250 first wedding anniversary certificate for a return visit.

Rates: Based on double occupancy, room rates are from $184 to $408 per night. The meal-all-inclusive plan is a supplemental $160 per person, per day. Children up to age twelve are 50 percent off.

Frequently Asked Questions: *Does Jalousie provide tennis lessons for individuals as well as groups?* Enjoy private or group lessons on one of four outdoor Laykold courts, three of them lit for night play. St. Lucia's top-ranked professional, Vernon Lewis, is on staff. *What is nearby recreation?* Horseback riding.

Don't Forget to Bring: Tennis rackets, golf clubs, bathing suit cover-ups, spa wear, and casual elegant clothing for dining.

Favorite Side Trips: Sulphur springs and mineral baths in the village of Soufriere, ten minutes from the resort; rain forest; botanical gardens; Chiseul craft market.

Nearest Airport: Hewanorra International Airport is forty-five minutes from the resort.

ALL-INCLUSIVE SERVICES AND ACTIVITIES

Food and Beverages: All meals, snacks, afternoon tea, nonalcoholic beverages, house-brand liquor, twenty-four-hour room service.

Outdoor Activities: Tennis, squash, racquetball, basketball, hiking, golf.

Water Sports: Swimming, snorkeling, scuba diving, waterskiing, Jet Skiing, sailing, deep-sea fishing.

Facilities: Fitness center, spa, swimming pool, four Laykold tennis courts, dive center, putting green, beach.

Entertainment: Disco Center with pool tables, bar, and dancing.

Children's Services: The Learning Center for children ages five to seventeen.

Children's Activities: Arts and crafts, participatory drama productions, storytelling, video games, lessons about the natural environment, dance class.

Not Included: Tips, service charges, taxes.

Available for a Fee: Ironing and laundry services, spa treatments.

RENDEZVOUS

Castries, St. Lucia

Appropriately named, Rendezvous was designed and is run with romance in mind. In a lush, seven-acre tropical garden along 2-mile Malabar Beach, this resort is an oasis exclusively for couples—no singles, no children—an idyllic 100-room property that is sensuous, sophisticated, and private.

It began with a mission statement when Craig Barnard, Rendezvous's owner, hatched the idea of converting a twenty-room, family-run hotel into one of the first all-inclusive resorts in the Caribbean. Where others saw a simple hotel on a fabulous and uncrowded beach, he saw a place that "Adam and Eve would relish, where love and romance are exalted and couples can celebrate and invigorate their love in a very special garden by the sea." Clearly this man had a strong vision!

For more than a decade, the resort operated as part of the Couples all-inclusive chain; it was renamed "Rendezvous" in 1993 by its parent company, SunSwept Resorts. Along with the name change have come major renovations that give the resort a competitive edge among top all-inclusive resorts in the Caribbean. Rooms and suites are elegant with nice homey touches such as four-poster beds, marble floors, and private terraces or balconies nestled in lush tropical gardens or facing the gentle and richly blue sea. Every room was given a fresh look with a $5 million renovation program in late 2002.

Even at a romantic all-inclusive, couples can't live on love alone, so diversions were created—restaurants, a full and well-run sports center, lots of water sports, and great access to shopping and touring. The food at Rendezvous is especially good, particularly at the upscale Trysting Place restaurant, where a healthy nouveau cuisine is served. The resort also allows for creative romantic interludes, so you can just as easily skip off to a romantic picnic at a secluded location to match your mood and whims. Three bars offer good cheer, including the Piano Bar, which stays open until the last couple goes to bed. The staff at Rendezvous is very attuned to the private needs of its guests and has mastered that fine line between being appropriately attentive and intrusive.

The resort has a "learn a sport" program with unlimited instruction in virtually every activity offered. Among the choices are archery, weekly golf clinic, waterskiing, kayaking, sailing, and volleyball. The resort also offers bicycle tours, as well as shopping excursions to Castries, the island's capital, with duty-free shopping at Pointe Seraphine.

One of Rendezvous's more successful ventures has been to develop a program for couples wishing to tie the knot. The resort handles all the details, including the marriage license and coordination of the wedding dinner—at no cost to the couple who stays six nights and provides one week's notice.

Rendezvous
Malabar Beach
P.O. Box 190
Castries, St. Lucia
Phone: 800–544–2883 or 758–452–4211
E-mail: tropichol@aol.com
Web site: www.theromanticholiday.com

Group/Getaway: Couples

Accommodations: One hundred rooms that include Verandah Suites, Seaside Lanai, Beach Cottage, Luxury Oceanfront Rooms, Seaside Junior Suites, and Luxury Oceanfront Suites. All rooms have balconies, air-conditioning, and four-poster king-size beds.

Point of Distinction: Rendezvous is strictly a couples-only resort. The setting is very romantic, with gardens full of exotic vegetation and flowers. The complimentary weddings are popular here.

Open: Year-round.

Minimum Stay: None.

Packages: Wedding Package.

Rates: Begin at $183 per person, per night for standard rooms and $300 for a luxury ocean-front suite.

Frequently Asked Question: *What wedding arrangements are included at Rendezvous?* Complimentary weddings can be arranged for guests staying six nights, with a minimum one-week notice. Rendezvous will arrange details, including marriage license, registrar and legal fees, services of a wedding coordinator and witnesses, decorated wedding arch and table, a special dinner for the wedding party, and breakfast in bed the next morning. Available for an extra charge are bridal bouquets, groom's boutonniere, tiara, live music, wedding cake, and still or video photographic services.

Don't Forget to Bring: Appropriate footwear for sport and workouts, swimwear cover-ups, and casual elegance for evening wear, or a wedding dress!

Favorite Side Trips: Castries, the capital of St. Lucia, and duty-free shopping at Pointe Seraphine.

Nearest Airports: George Charles Airport, a five-minute drive from the resort; and Hewannora International Airport, a one-hour-and-fifteen-minute drive away.

ALL-INCLUSIVE SERVICES AND ACTIVITIES

Food and Beverages: All meals and alcoholic and nonalcoholic beverages; dining exchange with Cariblue restaurant at The Body Holiday at LeSport.

Outdoor Activities: Tennis, volleyball, bicycling, archery, golf.

Water Sports: Swimming, windsurfing, diving, kayaking, pool volleyball, waterskiing, sailing.

Entertainment: Piano bar.

Facilities: Sauna, lighted tennis courts, swimming pools, whirlpools, fitness center.

Other: Flowers and champagne for honeymooners, catamaran cruises, Pigeon Point land tours, weekly golf clinic, taxes, gratuities, airport transfer.

Available for a Fee: Overseas calls, laundry service, golf, tours to neighboring islands, Pavilion Spa treatments.

ST. JAMES CLUB

Gros Islet, St. Lucia

St. James Club, the former Wynd- ham Morgan Bay Resort, is nestled in twenty-two acres of lush tropical landscaping, bordered by the palm- fringed white-sand beach of Choc Bay on the island of St. Lucia. Clearly this property has gained much from its location. St. Lucia is a safe place where family life is honored. Volcanic, it has dramatic vistas, including one peak that is not dangerous but still smolders on occasion. Choc Bay is a calm body of water ideal for families, even though St. James is a decidedly romantic place.

Is it possible to mix honeymooners with kids? Many of the larger all-inclusive chains say no, but at St. James, it seems to work very well. Part of the reason is the open lay- out of the grounds, which gives visitors a chance to spread out on the property's beachfront. Children also enjoy Kids Klub, a well-supervised, high-energy program that makes kids smile all day and then fall over at night from joyous exhaustion.

We liked St. James Club's ambience. There are more and less luxurious resorts listed in this book, but few that make its visitors feel as comfortable. The staff is more than friendly, displaying a kind of interest in their guests that is genuinely moving. The property somehow matches the tropical settings perfectly, allowing everyone to get down to the busi- ness of vacationing with as little confusion as possible.

The resort has 240 rooms with private terraces or balconies that mostly face the deep blue hues of the Caribbean. The trade winds blow gently across them as the abundant bird popula- tion sings to the guests. The resort faces west, so sunsets are spectacular, and St. James Club's designers had them in mind when they constructed the property's bars and dining rooms. It's very easy to raise the temperature of passion after a day or two of sunsets. In fact, the resort organizes weddings, and we were not surprised to learn that the resort averages one ceremony per week in the hotel.

St. James Club's activities are extensive, including recreational activities such as waterskiing, deep-sea fishing, scuba diving, snorkeling, horseback riding, windsurfing, and kayaking. Scuba packages are also available as well as mountain climbing in the famed and dramatic Pitons (peaks), which lie just downwind of the resort. The popular Kids Klub program offers super- vised indoor and outdoor activities for chil- dren ages five to twelve, including games, sand castle building, tie-dye, and a weekly "Pirates Night," when the kids enjoy a bon- fire dinner on the beach.

St. James Club

P.O. Box 2167, Choc Bay
Gros Islet, St. Lucia
Phone: 800–345–0356 or 758–450–2511
Web site: www.eliteislandresorts.com

Group/Getaway: Couples, Families

Accommodations: There are two suites and 238 air-conditioned guest rooms with balconies or terraces. Superior Rooms have ocean views, Deluxe have oceanfront views, and Standard have garden views. All include coffeemaker, hair dryer, and cable television; converter/adapters are available on request.

Points of Distinction: With its volcanic mountains, St. Lucia offers one of the most spectacular landscapes in the Caribbean. Besides the gorgeous general surroundings, the hotel sits on a calm body of water, manageable for young swimmers, making this a family-friendly, as well as romantic, resort.

Open: Year-round.

Minimum Stay: None.

Packages: St. James Club is part of the Elite Island Resorts group and now offers many packages, including some that allow visits to other Elite Island resorts.

Rates: Based on double occupancy, rates begin at $295 to $450 per night per person; children are $55 to $75 additional per day.

Frequently Asked Question: *What is this area of St. Lucia like?* The island of St. Lucia is a mix of small fishing villages, secluded coves, banana plantations, and jungle. The most dramatic scenery is the twin volcanic peaks of the Pitons, which rise sharply from the shoreline to form distinctive landmarks.

Don't Forget to Bring: Hiking shoes—there are many walking opportunities on the island.

Favorite Side Trips: Drive into a dormant volcano nearby, tour the Great House, or visit the lush tropical rainforest.

Nearest Airports: Vigie Airport, fifteen minutes from the resort, or Hewanorra International Airport, which is one hour away.

ALL-INCLUSIVE SERVICES AND ACTIVITIES

Food and Beverages: All meals, snacks, afternoon tea, wine, liquor, and premium bar drinks.

Outdoor Activities: Tennis, badminton, archery, croquet, table tennis, beach volleyball.

Water Sports: Swimming, sailing, waterskiing, windsurfing, snorkeling, kayaking.

Facilities: Four tennis courts, fitness center, steam room, sauna, Jacuzzi, gift shop, drugstore.

Entertainment: Caribbean fire dancing, limbo, live entertainment, and music.

Other: Scuba lessons in pool, pedal boats, banana boat rides, airport transfers, gratuities.

Children's Services: Kids Klub for children ages five to twelve.

Children's Activities: Outdoor activities, water sports, arts and crafts, games, "Pirates Night."

Available for a Fee: Tours to the tropical rain forest, a volcano, and a banana plantation; horseback riding; deep-sea fishing; golf at St. Lucia Golf Country Club (an eighteen-hole course) or Cap Estate, a championship golf course.

BEACHES TURKS AND CAICOS RESORT AND SPA

Providenciales, Turks and Caicos Islands

Club Med invented the all-inclusive concept, but Jamaica-based Sandals made it a household word. It started in Jamaica with couples-only resorts, then fanned out to other islands, introducing the "Beaches" concept for families seeking all-inclusive vacations. The latest innovations include high-end, all-inclusive spas and, in 1997, Sandals opened Beaches Turks and Caicos Resort and Spa as a spa getaway for families, singles, and couples—an ultra all-inclusive that was designed to leave no one out.

An hour and a half from Miami by jet, this resort sits on a 12-mile crescent of beach on the undeveloped Turks and Caicos Islands. South of the Bahamas, the Turks, as divers affectionately call them, have one of the longest coral reefs in the world and 230 miles of white, sandy beaches on eight lightly populated islands. Having been to Sandals resorts for couples and a Beaches resort in Jamaica for families, we wondered if combining clientele would work. It does.

Children stay busy in any of six separate, age-based programs, staffed by enthusiastic child-care workers. Toddlers participate in Cubs, a program that involves kids in water sports and beach activities as well as movies, games, crafts, and field trips. Beaches entertains teens in many of the same ways, and also operates a teen's nightclub with karaoke.

The options for adults are at least as varied as those for children. Because cruise ships haven't discovered Turks and Caicos, its reefs are pristine. If you can pull yourself away from sun-bathing and snorkeling, you'll find a state-of-the-art fitness center with Cybex equipment, water aerobics, hot and cold plunge pools, free weights, and step machines. Just around the corner is another superb asset—a European health spa with more body therapies than the Turks has islands. Spa services are available for an additional charge.

The Sandals formula for success has always included a strong element of gastronomy, figuring that if guests eat well, they'll feel even better. At Beaches Turks and Caicos Resort and Spa there are nine gourmet restaurants featuring innovative cuisine that spans the globe. Choices include Japanese, Southwestern, seafood, French haute cuisine, church-dinner Americana, Italian, and a Parisian cafe. You can dine indoors, outdoors, under the stars, or overlooking the beach.

As a bonus, Sandals has introduced the Sandals and Beaches Blue Chip Ultra Hurricane Guarantee. In the unlikely event of a hurricane hitting any of the Sandals or Beaches properties, the company will offer a free replacement vacation, including round-trip airfare, to be taken at any Sandals or Beaches resort of your choice. We hope no one has to use it, but it is a typically clever Sandals idea that adds extra value to this all-inclusive property.

Beaches Turks and Caicos Resort and Spa

P.O. Box 186
Lower Bight Road
Providenciales, Turks and Caicos Islands, British
    West Indies
Phone: 888–BEACHES or 649–946–8000
E-mail: info@beaches.com
Web site: www.beaches.com

Group/Getaway: Families, Spa & Wellness

Accommodations: There are 453 rooms and twelve categories of elegant accommodations to choose from. All rooms offer tasteful furnishings and private balconies or patios with garden or ocean views, plus air-conditioning, two double beds or a king, a ceiling fan, private bath, and satellite television. The Presidential Villa Suite includes VIP check-in, *New York Times* faxes daily, Roman bath, and views of ocean or garden.

Points of Distinction: Beaches Suite Concierge Service provides suite guests with privileged treatment and deluxe amenities, including VIP check-ins, plush robes, daily *New York Times*, faxes, private cocktail parties, tour arrangements, and restaurant reservations.

Open: Year-round.

Minimum Stay: Three nights.

Rates: Based on double occupancy, from $330 per person, per night for a Deluxe Room. Presidential one-bedroom Villa Suites start at $500 per person, per night. Single supplement is $110. Ask about holiday surcharges ($50 to $90 per night). Children ages two to fifteen, $70 per child per night; under age two stay free.

Frequently Asked Question: *Will my husband and I still be able to relax if we bring our children?* Beaches attempts to ensure that every member of the family enjoys the vacation, regardless of age. There are separate programs for infants, kids, and teens designed with fun activities and attractions. The resort also offers "Ultra Nannies," who specialize in handling kids with "kid" gloves.

Don't Forget to Bring: Golf clubs.

Favorite Side Trips: The world's only conch farm; Iguana Island; scuba diving excursions.

Nearest Airport: Providenciales Airport, a twelve-minute drive.

ALL-INCLUSIVE SERVI[CES] AND ACTIVITIES

Food and Beverages: All meals and snacks, nonalcoholic beverages, wine, and liquor.

Outdoor Activities: Beach volleyball, tennis, shuffleboard, croquet, basketball, lawn chess.

Water Sports: Scuba diving, snorkeling, windsurfing, kayaking, sailing, swimming, aqua cycling.

Facilities: Six pools (including one for scuba certification), lighted tennis courts, fitness center, sauna, three Jacuzzis, meeting facilities, outdoor amphitheater.

Entertainment: Cocktail parties, theme nights, talent night, nightly shows with live entertainment.

Other: Guided dives, billiards, weddings, round-trip airport transfers, taxes, tips, gratuities, service charges.

Children's Services: Nursery for infants, kids' club for four age levels, Teen's Club, water park, game room.

Children's Activities: Outdoor activities, water sports (including scuba diving for ages twelve and older), tennis clinics, Sega Dreamcast Center, teens' "nightclub" with karaoke (open 8:00 to 11:00 P.M.).

Available for a Fee: European-style spa that features Swedish massage, aromatherapy, reflexology, facial treatments, body wraps, body scrubs, hydrotherapy, pedicures, manicures; laundry and dry-cleaning services; deep-sea fishing; golf; parasailing; scooter rentals; hair braiding; private baby-sitting; Ultra Nanny Service.

WYNDHAM SUGAR BAY RESORT AND SPA

St. Thomas, Virgin Islands

St. Thomas, the main island of the Virgin Islands chain, has had an ongoing public relations crisis for two decades. With a reputation for high crime and drug traffic, it was often portrayed on American television as the Caribbean's most dangerous island. Then came hurricanes. But all is not what it once was. In truth, St. Thomas is no longer dangerous to tourists and has had a major face-lift since it was throttled by the hurricanes of 1997. A mountainous island with lovely beaches and unquestionably the best shopping in the Caribbean, St. Thomas has extensive air service, which makes it well suited for families. Given these considerations, we were not surprised to discover that Wyndham Hotels has established an outstanding, family-oriented resort here.

Wyndham Sugar Bay Resort and Spa is a 300-room property that is exceptionally beautiful. It sits high above the water, offering breathtaking views from most of its rooms and suites. In another part of the property is a unique lagoon and swimming complex made up of three interconnecting freshwater pools with a waterfall, suspended bridge, hot tub, and romantic grotto. Because of the newness of this property, its physical plant is very impressive. There is a high-tech fitness center, as well as spa, restaurants and an entertainment complex. Created for active vacationers, the resort also has a golf package that includes the use of the Mahogany Run Golf Course, the island's eighteen-hole championship links. Wyndham also maintains the island's top tennis complex, with a 220-person gallery around center court and four lighted courts. A dive shop will arrange for scuba outings around St. Thomas and St. John.

For parents traveling with children, the resort offers a popular Kids Klub program that includes supervised indoor and outdoor functions for children ages five to twelve. Nature hikes, twice-weekly bonfires with marshmallows and hot dogs, and hermit crab hunts are also regularly offered. Twice a day kids even get to feed iguanas.

We found ourselves amid many couples and families at Wyndham Sugar Bay who were on the go. Beyond tennis, there were pick-up basketball games, water sports, and every kind of aerobics.

Guests can also venture into the heart of St. Thomas to indulge in serious shopping at the quaint shops of Charlotte Amalie and the Red Hook shopping district. And there is always the beach, where a raised flag on your beach chair indicates you want something cold to drink.

Dining and entertainment options at the property are quite extensive, which is a good thing because Charlotte Amalie—even vastly improved—is safer by day than by night. After dining in either the Manor House Dining Room or the Mangrove Cafe, you can retire to the Turtle Rock Sports Bar or the Ocean Club, an Art Deco nightclub featuring live entertainment and dancing. Baby-sitters are always available. Movies at the resort's amphitheater, which has features twice daily, are appealing for families who want to enjoy the evening together.

The newest addition to Wyndham Sugar Bay is Journeys Spa, which offers an array of pampering treatments and Golden Door products. The ultimate Journeys Spa experience may be an oceanside massage, the sure route to utter bliss.

Wyndham Sugar Bay Resort and Spa

6500 Estate Smith Bay
St. Thomas, Virgin Islands 00802
Phone: 800–WYNDHAM or 340–777–7100
Web site: www.wyndham.com

Group/Getaway: Families

Accommodations: There are 300 air-conditioned rooms, each with private balcony, two double beds or one king, private bath, hair dryer, dressing area, refrigerator, coffeemaker, ceiling fan, color satellite television, and direct-dial telephone and voice mail. Superior rooms have a hillside, tennis, or pool view, Deluxe rooms have a partial ocean view, and Luxury rooms have a full ocean view. Three rooms are disabled-accessible.

Points of Distinction: Three interconnecting freshwater swimming pools with suspension bridge and romantic grotto are very appealing, as is Magens Bay, rated as one of the world's three most beautiful beaches.

Open: Year-round.

Minimum Stay: None.

Packages: Three-day dive packages begin at $505. Night dives are also available at an additional cost. Rates for the five-night Dive Package for two begin at $1,670.

Rates: Based on double occupancy, from $235 per person, per night for a Superior Room to $250 for a Luxury Ocean-View Room. Single rates are $265 to $400 per night; children ages three to twelve $60, ages twelve to eighteen $110, and under three are free.

Frequently Asked Question: *How's the diving?* There are many good diving sites to choose from, including local favorites like Joe's Jam, where you will see some of the best coral formations around and a coral-encrusted anchor that dates back to the 1800s. There's also Packet Rock shipwreck, a great place to look for artifacts, and Buck Island cove to see a shipwreck, coral formations, and a reef.

Don't Forget to Bring: Diving equipment, golf clubs, and extra credit cards for shopping.

Favorite Side Trips: Short boat ride to St. John, one of the most natural and beautiful isles of the region. Downtown shopping at the quaint shops of Charlotte Amalie.

Nearest Airport: Cyril E. King International Airport, about fifteen minutes from the resort.

ALL-INCLUSIVE SERVICES AND ACTIVITIES

Food and Beverages: All meals and snacks, noalcoholic beverages, house-brand liquor.

Outdoor Activities: Day and night tennis, beach volleyball, basketball.

Water Sports: Windsurfing, sailing, swimming, scuba diving and snorkeling clinics.

Facilities: Five lighted tennis courts, basketball courts, three freshwater swimming pools, snorkelling equipment, fitness center, Jacuzzi.

Entertainment: Nightly.

Other: Room taxes, gratuities, airport transfers, and valet parking; shuttle bus to tennis center, water park, and parking areas; concierge desk.

Children's Services: Kids Klub for children ages four to twelve.

Available for a Fee: Night diving, dive equipment, parasailing, Jet Skis, motorized chairs, tennis instruction, boat rentals, laundry, baby-sitting services, spa treatments.

AFRICA

SAMBURU SERENA SAFARI LODGE

Nairobi, Kenya

Seven hours by car, directly north of Nairobi, is Kenya's semiarid Northern Province and the vast reservation of one of Africa's most active and prominent tribes: the Samburu. The people herd cows across the plains, spear always in hand and red blanket wrapped around their thin and erect shoulders. With hair dyed red and bodies bedecked with beads, they form dramatic shapes on a horizon that reflects some of the most beautiful plains on Earth.

Across the land is an ancient trace of mountains that have become smoothed hills undulating as far as the eye can see. A blue-flushed Somali ostrich dawdles among a small herd of zebra; impalas and lesser kudus dart through the brush; sometimes elephants, lions, cheetahs, and leopards are observed. Directly in the middle of this reserve is Samburu Serena Safari Lodge, created as a base for safari-goers to explore the open animal kingdom that surrounds it.

The lodge is a series of thatched-roof cabins made of exotic African woods that echo the architectural style of the Samburu people. Rooms are spacious and cooled by breezes off the meandering Uaso Nyiro River that flows through the encampment. The guest rooms are spacious, with private verandas that expose uninterrupted vistas of the languid river and the wildlife it attracts.

Although the lodge is rustic, it is by no means primitive. Overlooking the outdoor swimming pool, the open-air dining room serves guests sumptuous international menus, buffets, and barbecues alongside authentic African dishes. Kenya has superb farmland, so vegetables, fruits, and beef are abundant and delicious. Samburu artifacts and a wonderful set of murals depicting the landscape of the reserve enhance the decor of the dining and lounge areas.

First choice of transportation for the game drives is a seven-person all-terrain vehicle. For a loftier view, try a ride on the back of a camel, perhaps, followed by a welcome champagne breakfast guaranteed to take your mind off your sore spots.

Safari drives in the Samburu National Park are almost mystical at times because of the clarity of light and the vast scale made possible by the openness of the plain. The Samburu people are kind and quiet. The cumulative effect of landscape and culture separates this part of Africa from all others and makes the Samburu Serena Safari Lodge an extraordinary all-inclusive experience.

Samburu Serena Safari Lodge
Williamson House, Fourth Floor
4th Ngong Avenue
P.O. Box 48690, 00100
Nairobi, Kenya
Phone: 011–254–2–710511
E-mail: mktg@serena.co.ke
Web site: www.serenahotels.com

Group/Getaway: Couples, Adventure

Accommodations: There are sixty-two guest rooms with private verandas to enjoy uninterrupted vistas of the river and the wildlife that it attracts, as well as the many crocodiles that make the waters their home. Inspired by the indigenous Samburu tribe, the cabins are artistically decorated with native materials.

Point of Distinction: The landscape here is home to a variety of rare game, and it is also inhabited by hundreds of different bird species. Reflecting the architecture of the native Samburu people, the lodge blends into its natural environment by making full use of native materials.

Rates: Six-night safari packages start at $1,970 per person, based on double occupancy. A single supplement is $250. Children under twelve not advisable.

Open: Year-round.

Minimum Stay: Two nights.

Frequently Asked Question: *How many people can be accommodated on a safari drive?* The lodge has three all-terrain vehicles that can each seat seven people. Camel safaris are also available for experiencing the plains, the desert palms, and the winding Uaso Nyiro River with its abundant wildlife.

Don't Forget to Bring: Binoculars, a camera, hiking boots, warm clothing for occasional cool evenings, hat, and sunscreen.

Favorite Side Trip: Crocodile Point, where you can enjoy a champagne breakfast after an early morning game drive.

Nearest Airport: Nairobi Airport, a seven-hour drive by car, or a one-hour flight from Nairobi to Samburu Serena Airstrip.

ALL-INCLUSIVE SERVICES AND ACTIVITIES

Food and Beverages: All meals, nonalcoholic beverages, champagne breakfast, afternoon tea. Lunch boxes, fruit, flowers, and celebration cakes upon request. Early supper available for children upon request.

Outdoor Activities: Game drives, guided nature and bird walks.

Water Sports: Swimming.

Facilities: Swimming pool.

Entertainment: Daily traditional tribal dances, lectures on Samburu culture.

Other: Park entrance fees, telephone, fax, radio, binoculars, hair dryer, nurse on call twenty-four hours, medevac to hospital from nearby airstrip.

Available for a Fee: Baby-sitting, additional alcoholic beverages, daily laundry and pressing service.

SWEETWATERS TENTED CAMP

Nairobi, Kenya

Sweetwaters Tented Camp and Ol Pejeta Ranch House offer visitors to Africa a very different kind of safari experience. Because the Sweetwaters game reserve is a 24,000-acre private ranch, it has all of the game associated with Kenya's national game parks, but none of the restrictions on viewing it. At Sweetwaters, guests have the opportunity to experience walking safaris, night game drives (when most kills occur), and picnics that are organized in the middle of the grassy plains.

Typically, Kenyan driving safaris in national parks occur in enclosed pop-top vans. When game is viewed by one, others soon arrive, initiating a kind of photo frenzy that takes something away from the sense of experiencing the naturalness of these spectacular animals. At Sweetwaters, the managers want their guests to see, feel, and know the bush intimately but safely. Located in savanna grasslands among whistling thorn shrubs and acacia trees, Sweetwaters built a small village of thirty luxuriously appointed and spacious *en suite* (includes private bath) tents in the magnificent plains, approaching the snow-capped peaks of Mount Kenya.

We must pause here to emphasize the extraordinary beauty of this vast, sweeping landscape. This part of Kenya—just three hours by car from Nairobi—has a greatness of scale that casts an odd spell over those who get to know it. You might see a Masai warrior standing with a spear against the horizon or a lioness tearing into an impala that she has killed for her cubs.

The facilities within the camp include a swimming pool and an original farmhouse with dining room, bar, and reception. Each tent overlooks a vast watering hole where game appears in large numbers from late day until dusk. During the day, visitors can choose to go on game drives in four-wheel-drive vehicles, walking safaris escorted by a knowledgeable ranger, bird walks, or even camel safaris. Children of all ages are allowed on the drives, as long as they remain quiet.

The most dramatic events at Sweetwaters are the night game drives, which are not allowed in most African game parks. After dinner, a driver and guide take guests into the plains to bring them eye to eye with zebras, giraffes, gazelles, or even the big cats during and after a kill. Many of the predators of the plains are nocturnal, making the night a cacophony of sights and sounds. We found these drives unforgettably exciting.

For young children or less intrepid adults, Sweetwaters has an observation post (complete with cocktail bar) overlooking the floodlit watering hole, where the animals can be quietly observed during the course of the evening.

Near the tented encampment on the ranch is a special complex of buildings once owned by the billionaire Adnan Khashoggi. Called the Ol Pejeta Ranch House, it houses twelve people who participate in a special all-inclusive program that includes all alcoholic beverages, unlimited day or night game drives, camel rides, and a variety of activities at the famed Mt. Kenya Safari Club, including golf and horseback riding.

Meals at all Sweetwaters facilities are wonderfully prepared and tasty, served by a very hospitable and courteous Kenyan staff. Always smiling and helpful, their warmth contributes a great deal to the experience of the safari.

Sweetwaters Tented Camp

The Norfolk Hotel
P.O. Box 58581, 00200
Nairobi, Kenya
Phone: 800–845–3692 or
011–254–2–216940
E-mail: walden@comcast.com
Web site: www.lonrhohotels.com

Group/Getaway: Families, Adventure

Accommodations: There are thirty en suite tents, each with its own veranda, facing a large watering hole and snow-capped Mount Kenya. Five have double beds, twenty-one have twin beds, and four have three beds. Nearby is Ol Pejeta Ranch House with two guest rooms, a master suite, and a cottage with two guest rooms. The Ranch House has its own swimming pools, lounges, and dining rooms.

Points of Distinction: Sweetwaters Tented Camp offers visitors an exclusive experience away from the large numbers of safari vehicles and people found in more traveled game parks in Kenya. Since Sweetwaters is a private game reserve, many activities are available that are not permitted in Kenyan National Parks, including walking, night game drives, and dining outside of camps and lodges. The camp's watering hole looks completely accessible from the camp, but between it and the camp there is actually a moat and an electric fence for the protection of the guests.

Open: Year-round.

Minimum Stay: Two or three nights recommended.

Packages: "Out of Africa" wedding packages start at $500. Call for details.

Rates: Based on double occupancy, tent rates are $185 to $320 for two people, per night. Single occupancy tents are $95 to $245. Children up to age two are free, from two through sixteen are 25 percent of room rate. Ol Pejeta Ranch all-inclusive rates are $500 to $525 per night for two people sharing a room and $325 to $335 for a single.

Frequently Asked Question: *How far is Sweetwaters Tented Camp from Nairobi?* A three- to four-hour scenic drive.

Don't Forget to Bring: A camera and binoculars, and lightweight casual safari wear for the daytime, sweater or light jacket for chilly evenings. Be sure to bring swimwear, and trousers and shoes for camelback riding. For sun protection, bring a broad-rimmed hat, sunglasses, a high-factor sunscreen, long-sleeved shirts, and trousers.

Favorite Side Trip: To Sweetwaters Chimpanzee Sanctuary in Nanyuki, a fifteen-minute drive away. It is home to more than twenty-five chimps, most of them orphaned or abused, which are cared for before being released to live on their own.

Nearest Airport: Nanyuki airstrip, about a one-hour drive from Sweetwaters.

ALL-INCLUSIVE SERVICES AND ACTIVITIES

Food and Beverages: All meals, tea and coffee, afternoon tea, bush luncheons and dinners, safari sundowner drinks.

Outdoor Activities: Walking safaris, camel safaris, game drives in four-wheel-drive vehicles, bird walks.

Water sports: Swimming.

Facilities: Swimming pool.

Other: Taxes, gratuities.

Children's Services: Although there is no special children's program, Sweetwaters is a "family-friendly" camp. Baby-sitting services are available, as is nanny accommodation. Depending on the number of children resident in camp, group activities such as treasure hunts can be organized. Special children's menu (served early in the Rhino Dining Room).

Not Included: Airport transfers from Nairobi, game reserve fees.

Available for a Fee: Alcoholic and non-alcoholic beverages, game drives, daily activities package.

MALAMALA GAME RESERVE
Kwazulu Natal, South Africa

Inside the thatched-roof bungalows of MalaMala's main camp, guests enjoy all the luxury of any five-star resort. There are two bathrooms with heated towel racks in every guest room. A current edition of the *New York Times* is faxed to each room daily.

But in contrast to these luxurious environs, just outside the thin bungalow walls roam some of Africa's fiercest wildlife. Lions, leopards, jackals, and hyenas compete for game; hippos and wide-horned buffalo wallow in pools of the Sand River, while giraffes and impalas graze in the surrounding grasslands. Elephant and rhino sightings are also extremely common.

It is this combination of surreal comfort inside and the intrigue of the MalaMala wildlife outside that draws people to this private South African resort and game reserve. To view these species up close, photo safaris are conducted in open four-wheel-drive vehicles by teams of naturalists and local Shangaan trackers. Each of the resort's rangers is intimately familiar with the bush of the MalaMala Game Reserve.

MalaMala boasts that 76 percent of the people it takes on safari become members of the "Big Five Club," meaning most of their guests will spot the reserve's most admired species—lion, leopard, elephant, rhinoceros, and buffalo.

Safaris are conducted mainly in the early morning and just before sundown. With the sun ghostlike and beet red on the African horizon, these are the two times of day when the animals are most active and the park most serene and beautiful. After dark, spotlight safaris extend the intrigue, giving guests the opportunity to view predators on the hunt.

MalaMala is organized like a small country, where fantasies, such as drinking a fine wine to accompany an ostrich burger or staring down a lion, are realized. From the niche of African safari camps that occupy a small corner of the all-inclusive market, this particular resort is remarkable for its outstanding service and fantastic game venue, which is almost as close as your pillow.

MalaMala Game Reserve
Private Bag X284
Hillcrest, Kwazulu Natal
3650 South Africa
Phone: 011–27–31–765–2900
E-mail: reservations@malamala.com
Web site: www.malamala.com

Group/Getaway: Couples, Adventure

Accommodations: There are twenty-five luxurious air-conditioned guest rooms housed in thatched-roof huts with exterior verandas overlooking the Sand River. Insect-proof screens are on all windows and sliding doors. Rooms include rattan furnishings, bathrooms with electric shaver plugs, international direct-dial telephones, and twenty-four-hour electricity, air-conditioning, and/or heating. One room is fully wheelchair-accessible.

Points of Distinction: An extraordinary effort is made to bring visitors into the African bush while providing them with comfort and luxury.

Open: Year-round.

Minimum Stay: Seven-day stays recommended, but no minimum stay.

Rates: Based on double occupancy, prices per person, per day are $500. Single accommodation, add 50 percent. Children under twelve years of age sharing a room with adults will be accommodated at 50 percent of the quoted rate per day. Age restrictions may apply. Not recommended for children under twelve.

Frequently Asked Question: *What is the best time for viewing animals?* Sightings of most species occur on any day of the year at any time of day. During August, ground waters are dry and the Sand River becomes very popular. This is when viewing is easiest, requiring little more than setting up camp near the river's deeper pools.

Seasonal Activities: January and February are birthing periods for many species. March and April are the best months to watch mature animals with their young. This is also an especially good time to watch an actual kill.

Don't Forget to Bring: Antimalaria prophylactics (essential year-round). Comfortable walking shoes, sunhats, sunglasses, sunscreen. A knapsack to carry extra clothing and supplies. (Safaris can keep guests away past sunset, when temperatures are likely to drop.)

Favorite Side Trips: Johannesburg, Victoria Falls in Zimbabwe, and the Okavango Delta in Botswana.

Nearest Airport: Skukuza Airport, in the Kruger National Park, is a forty-five-minute drive away. Connections are made through Johannesburg.

ALL-INCLUSIVE SERVICES AND ACTIVITIES

Food and Beverages: All meals, nonalcoholic beverages, purified water, snacks, afternoon tea.

Outdoor Activities: Game drives, spotlight night game drives, walking tours, and tennis. Nearby: golf.

Water Sports: Swimming in a filtered pool.

Facilities: Swimming pool, the Monkey Club video den and library, wine cellar.

Other: Taxes and gratuities, airport transfers; insect repellent supplied in all bedrooms and vehicles; daily *New York Times* faxed to each bedroom; complimentary laundry services; fax facilities.

Not Included: Arrival and departure taxes, entrance fees into conservation area if arriving by road, transport to and from the reserve.

Available for a Fee: Private game drives, twenty-four-hour room service, liquor, minibar purchases.

SABI SABI PRIVATE GAME RESERVE

Kruger National Park, South Africa

If you have ever dreamed of taking an African safari but were never sure how to do it, Sabi Sabi is a world-class all-inclusive luxury solution. And be sure, no video or photograph of African wildlife can prepare you for the excitement of a herd of elephants marching through the trees around you or a pride of lions feeding beside your cottage, with only a window separating you from the bush. Nothing transmits the sense of awe and wonder you feel when a rhinoceros turns the corner to stare down your entire safari crew. At Sabi Sabi, everything you learned in science class becomes a vivid reality.

Sabi Sabi Game Reserve is the oldest and largest private game reserve in South Africa, located along the southern border of Kruger National Park. It is exceptional not only for its variety of wildlife but also for its large population of big game. Sabi Sabi is midway along the migration routes of some of the world's largest, rarest animals. Elephants move through the reserve in larger numbers than anywhere else on the planet. Lion populations remain strong as well. Also common at the reserve are giraffes, hyenas, leopards, and buffalo.

Awakened predawn by the resort's rangers, Sabi Sabi guests surrender the luxury of their guest rooms for a day of safari adventures. No one lets his or her guard down for a single moment while on the hunt. The first stop in the bush is for breakfast. With the sun rising over a remote section of the reserve, the party overlooks a secluded watering hole to witness a parade of thirsty game.

The day passes quickly as the party moves from point to point throughout the park. When night falls, the safari only gets better. Unaffected by the flash of headlights or flashlight, nocturnal predators track hiding prey. It is during this time that it is most possible to be an actual witness to a predatory kill.

Upon return to the Selati Lodge, the feast begins. A variety of venison dishes are prepared, along with impala steaks and warthog kabobs. Wines from South African vineyards fill every cup while party members discuss the day's sightings.

Sabi Sabi has been leading private safaris for a long time, and no one in Southern Africa does it better.

Throughout the safari adventure, moments occur when all notions of civility and society disappear. There you stand, in a primal environment, experiencing the rawest elements of nature. Entrusting your safari to the expertise of Sabi Sabi is worth the considerable time and expense of traveling halfway around the globe for this all-inclusive adventure.

Sabi Sabi Private Game Reserve

Mailing address: P.O. Box 52665
Saxonwold 2132, South Africa
Phone: 800–524–7979 or
   011–27–11–483–3939
E-mail: res@sabisabi.com
Web site: www.sabisabi.com

Group/Getaway: Couples, Adventure

Accommodations: There are three completely separate luxury lodges: the Bush, Earth, and Selati. Each one has superb cuisine, a filtered swimming pool, and is fully licensed. Selati Lodge has eight twin-bedded, thatched-roof, air-conditioned suites, including Lurenco Marques Honeymoon Suite, beautifully sited on the banks of the Msuthlu River. Bush Lodge has twenty-five twin-bedded, thatched-roof, air-conditioned chalets, one suite with wheelchair access, and five luxury suites set in the heart of the bush overlooking a watering hole. Earth Lodge is the new eco-lodge. Sensitively landscaped into the environment, it is the epitome of bush elegance, style, and luxury. Unprecedented in their opulence and befitting of royalty, the Mandleve and Ivory Presidential suites offer private pools and exclusive personal safaris. There is a health and wellness center as well as an art gallery. The lodges are several miles apart.

Points of Distinction: Sabi Sabi is the only private game reserve on the Sabie River, biologically the richest waterway in South Africa. The Shangaan tracker guides are experts. By keeping in constant radio contact with one another, they give guests the best possible opportunity to see Africa's big game.

Open: Year-round.

Minimum Stay: Three nights recommended.

Packages: Fly-in safari package. Call for details.

Rates: Rates begin at $570 to $1,600 per person, per night, based on double occupancy.

Frequently Asked Question: *What types of animals can we expect to see?* The "Big Five": elephants, rhinos, buffalo, lions, and leopards. You'll also see wild dogs, cheetahs, zebras, and giraffes, all indigenous to this area. And there are also more than 350 bird species.

Don't Forget to Bring: Warm clothes for winter and night safaris, comfortable walking shoes, bathing suit, clothing that won't alarm the animals (mainly natural colors: no red, yellow, or orange), binoculars, and camera. Note: Antimalaria tablets should be taken prior to your visit.

Favorite Side Trip: Blyde River Canyon, a gigantic gorge and one of South Africa's most spectacular sights.

Nearest Airport: Johannesburg International Airport. There are daily scheduled flights from Johannesburg and Durban to Nelspruit. Sabi Sabi is a two-hour scenic drive from Nelspruit. Fly-in safari packages and helicopter transfers are available on request.

ALL-INCLUSIVE ACTIVITIES AND SERVICES

Food and Beverages: Three meals, tea and coffee, sundowner drinks (during evening Land Rover safaris), house beers and wines, snacks.

Outdoor Activities: Safaris in open Land Rovers, environmental-awareness walking safaris.

Water Sports: Swimming.

Facilities: Swimming pool at each lodge, curio shop.

Other: Services of rangers and Shangaan trackers, transfers to and from Skukuza Airport in the Kruger National Park, room taxes.

Not Included: Tips, Sabie Sand Wildtuin entrance fees into the national parks, airport taxes, special helicopter transfers from airport.

Available for a Fee: Additional beverages, bar service, curio shop purchases.

ASIA

BANYAN TREE MALDIVES

Vabbinfaru, Maldives

The Maldives are difficult to find on a map. They are a ghostlike trail of atolls southwest of Sri Lanka, stretched across the Indian Ocean. Satellite photos show the span of more than 2,000 islands to resemble a parade of jellyfish. Among all those islands is Vabbinfaru, home of the Banyan Tree Maldives.

Upon arrival at Malé (pronounced ma-LAY) International Airport, Banyan Tree guests ride to the resort not by taxi, not by shuttle bus, but by speedboat.

We figured this must be Atlantis. The Maldive Archipelago is a land of water—water so warm it is unfelt to the touch, so clear it is unseen to the eye. Boats floating in a lagoon seem to hang in midair, their shadows flat to the shallow, sandy bottom. Afternoon dips feel like baths. Snorkeling brings to mind those dreams you've had of flying. Islands rise no higher than 6 feet above the waterline, which makes them appear to be floating across the sea.

Banyan Tree Maldives is not an occupant of an island—the entire island is the resort. It is small enough that a walk around its beach brings you to the same place you left just fifteen minutes earlier. The distance between the sunrise side of the island and the sunset side is the length of three football fields.

Guests stay in distinctive round units with thatched conical roofs inspired by chambered nautilus shells. Units are set directly on the beach against a treeline of coconut palms. Room decor is appropriately tropical, with wicker furniture and louvered windows and doors to let in the Maldivian sea breeze. Each hut occupies its own private portion of beach and lagoon.

There are many activities available to Banyan Tree visitors. Most revolve around water. Fishing, sailing, and windsurfing are options, as are canoeing and kayaking, but snorkeling is the reason most guests seek this resort. Because the Maldives sit on aged coral reefs, the diver's world is a remarkable, rainbow-colored underworld of fish, flora, and fauna. To reach the nearest coral, you merely walk out your front door, cross the sparkly white beach, and wade through the swimming-pool lagoon. There, where the water deepens slightly, lies the sea world's jungle gym that is nothing short of incredible.

In the water or on the shore, Banyan Tree's ocean seclusion has a calming effect on one's mind and is naturally romantic. Banyan Tree's honeymoon package offers champagne and special dining to newlyweds.

Banyan Tree Maldives
Vabbinfaru Island, North Malé Atoll
Republic of Maldives
Phone: 800–525–4800 or 011–960–443–147
E-mail: maldives@banyantree.com
Web site: www.banyantree.com

Group/Getaway: Couples, Spa & Wellness

Accommodations: There are forty-eight elegant villas with the option of beachfront or garden settings. Each villa has an open terrace and private landscaped garden, recessed sitting area, four-poster king-size bed, step-down shower, hot and cold freshwater shower, fully stocked minibar, in-villa safe, bathrobes, and IDD (international direct dial).

Point of Distinction: The resort is known for eco-friendly programs. Guests may participate in some of them, including helping to plant coral fragments onto the reef as part of the award-winning barnacle and lotus reef regeneration project. Or you might help clean the reef of nasty, harmful creatures, such as Crown-of-Thorns starfish and coral-eating snails.

Open: Year-round.

Minimum Stay: Three nights between December 22 and January 10; no minimum the rest of the year.

Rates: Based on double occupancy, nightly rates for two range from $555 for Garden View Villas to $1,500 for a Presidente Villa.

Frequently Asked Question: *What is the weather like?* The Maldives have two main seasons: The wetter monsoon season is from May to November, when temperatures are between 75 and 85 degrees and there are occasional showers. From December to April is the drier and hotter season, when temperatures are between 80 and 90 degrees.

Don't Forget to Bring: A bathing suit and sandals: you'll live in them and won't require much else.

Favorite Side Trips: The two islands that are near Vabbinfaru, Baros and Ihuru. Boats are available to rent so you can visit these islands.

Nearest Airport: Malé Airport, a twenty-minute speedboat ride from the resort.

ALL-INCLUSIVE SERVICES AND ACTIVITIES

Food and Beverages: All meals, coffee, and tea.

Outdoor Activities: Volleyball.

Water Sports: Snorkeling, fishing, water-skiing, windsurfing, kayaking, canoeing, scuba diving.

Facilities: PADI dive center, spa.

Other: Massage and beauty treatments, private sandbank dining.

Not Included: Airport transfers, taxes, and gratuities.

Available for a Fee: Alcoholic beverages, other nonalcoholic beverages, boat rental for trips to other islands.

TIGER TOPS JUNGLE LODGE
Kathmandu, Nepal

In the shadow of the Himalayan Mountains, Tiger Tops Jungle Lodge offers nothing less wondrous than a hearty game of elephant polo. Beyond sport, visitors travel around Tiger Tops in large bamboo baskets attached to the backs of elephants.

Tiger Tops Jungle Lodge is a "tree top hotel" built appropriately from local materials and decorated in the style used by local Tharu tribes. The managers of Tiger Tops are pioneers of environmentally sensitive resorts who go well out of their way to enhance the environs of the Royal Chitwan National Park, where Tiger Tops is located. One of Asia's richest and most spectacular wildlife sanctuaries, Chitwan is situated 75 air miles southwest of Kathmandu yet seems centuries away in its remoteness.

Safaris into the Chitwan jungle are conducted from the backs of docile pachyderms. Wandering the elephant grass that rises higher than the elephants themselves, your chances of spotting a family of endangered one-horned rhinos are good. Many species of deer also hide in the marsh grass to avoid their enormous and stealthy predators, among them leopards and Royal Bengal tigers. From riverbanks, gavial crocodiles can be seen searching the water for fish. The marsh mugger is there as well. As its ominous name suggests, the marsh mugger is a crocodile that seeks prey as large as humans by stealthily waiting in swamps to "mug" them. Swimming among the crocodiles are

perhaps the oddest of all creatures living in this exotic world: the gangetic dolphins. These fascinating animals swim the rivers around Tiger Tops, far from any sea or ocean.

Another exciting option is to travel to Tiger Tops via a three-day raft trip on the Seti or Trisuli River with Tiger Tops' own river-running company called Himalayan River Exploration. It provides a thrilling introduction to white water followed by two days of floating through the scenic gorges and middle hills dropping onto the Terai Plains.

For those who prefer to travel over land, Tiger Tops is accessible from Kathmandu by road, a pleasant five- to six-hour drive through the Himalayan foothills into the Chitwan Valley.

Whether they have come by car or raft, most guests arrive with a keen appetite—a condition that Tiger Tops satisfies well. In a dining room overlooking the vast grasslands, meals are served alfresco. There are simple but tasty Nepalese lunches, and three-course Western-style dinners. A fully stocked bar is open until the last guest retires to bed.

And, yes, elephant polo is a very popular sport, with four beasts per side and jockeys thwacking a little white ball with extra-long clubs. If you return often enough, they'll even let you partake. (The annual elephant polo world championship takes place every December.)

Tiger Tops Jungle Lodge

Tiger Tops Mountain Travel International
P.O. Box 242
Dhapasi
Kathmandu, Nepal
Phone: 011–977–1–436–1500
E-mail: info@tigermountain.com
Web site: www.tigermountain.com

Group/Getaway: Couples, Adventure

Accommodations: Two lodges, one with twelve rooms and another with eight; five bungalows are located away from the lodge. The lodge is built from local materials and decorated in the style of the Tharus. All rooms have attached bathrooms. Tiger Tops Tented Camp is just 3 miles from the lodge. The camp includes twelve safari tents with twin beds and attached baths.

Points of Distinction: The lodge is built with local materials and is completely solar powered. The sal and bamboo trees are the main timber used. Showers are gravity fed and manually operated. Food is cooked on an open hearth in traditional style.

Open: September through June (tented camp September through April).

Minimum Stay: Two nights recommended.

Rates: Based on double or triple occupancy year-round, beginning at $350 per person, per night; single supplement $150 per night. At the tent camp rates begin at $200 per person, based on double occupancy.

Frequently Asked Questions: *How difficult is it to get there?* Meghauli airstrip, where the elephant polo is played in December, is a twenty-five-minute flight from Kathmandu. Then there is a forty-minute escorted drive to the lodge (two and a half hours by elephant). By car, it takes five to six hours from Kathmandu. *What is the proper attire for the lodge?* Attire at the lodge is casual. Comfortable, jungle-colored clothing (beige, brown, khaki, and green) is most appropriate. A bathing suit is handy during the summer months. Warm clothes are recommended for winter months for use in the mornings and evenings. A windbreaker is useful, since the mornings can be quite breezy.

Don't Forget to Bring: Hats, sunglasses, and sunscreen are recommended—and these should be of the kind you will not mind getting wet. Hiking boots are ideal. Binoculars add greatly to your enjoyment of bird and wildlife viewing. Neutral-colored clothing is recommended for a visit to the jungle. Light clothing is needed for daytime and a sweater and warm jacket for evenings from November to March. Don't forget the insect repellent.

Favorite Side Trips: Pokhara Lodge (a five-hour drive), located at the base of the Annapurna Range and the tenth-highest peak in the world; a one-hour flight to Kathmandu to take a mountain flight to see Mt. Everest; a two-day raft trip down the Trisuli River.

Nearest Airport: The most direct route is to take the daily thirty-minute trip from Kathmandu on a Yeti Airlines Twin Otter. The flight lands guests at Meghauli airstrip in the Chitwan Valley.

ALL-INCLUSIVE SERVICES AND ACTIVITIES

Food and Beverages: All meals and afternoon tea.

Outdoor Activities: Watching tigers in the jungle, exploring trails with naturalist guide, elephant safaris.

Water Sports: Swimming.

Other: Airport transfers from Meghauli.

Not Included: Taxes, park fees, gratuities.

Available for a Fee: Nonalcoholic beverages (including bottled water), alcoholic beverages, snacks, soda.

CHIVA-SOM INTERNATIONAL HEALTH RESORT

Hua Hin, Thailand

Chiva-Som is a charming resort on seven acres of peaceful white beach on the Gulf of Thailand. Known as one of the world's leading health resorts, Chiva-Som has the rare ability to combine a luxury tropical vacation with some Eastern approaches to wellness. This combination sets this elegant Thai establishment apart from all other resorts.

The elegant but casual pavilions of Chiva-Som are surrounded by lush gardens and cascading waterfalls. From seaside rooms, there are mesmerizing views of the ocean—fine spots from which to witness a fabled Thai sunrise each day.

The philosophy at Chiva-Som, which is Thai for "Haven of Life," is that a healthy body, mind, and spirit lead to personal fulfillment. With an international staff of doctors, nurses, dieticians, chefs, and personal trainers, guests customize their stays to do anything and everything they wish to improve their well-being. The program starts within an hour of your arrival, when you will have a short physical exam followed by the creation of a personalized activity and treatment plan based on your individual needs and interests. The eclectic assortment of fitness and leisure activities ranges from mountain biking to yoga, body sculpting, many water sports, and the infamous and delectable Thai massage. With only fifty-seven guest pavilions and a four-to-one staff-to-guest ratio, it's hard to go wrong at Chiva-Som.

Among the many elements of this resort that impressed us is its blending of sophisticated technology with Buddhist values of finding balance in all things. At the heart of Chiva-Som is the ultramodern spa that has been created to provide a pleasing spatial sense that complements the harmonious ambience of the resort. Separate heat treatment facilities for male and female guests feature conveniently appointed changing rooms, saunas, steam rooms, Jacuzzis, cool plunge pools, and relaxation lounges overlooking landscaped courtyards. The resort advocates a rejuvenation and antiaging therapy developed by an internationally renowned German doctor (Dr. Claus Martin), yet places equal value on making the mind still through meditation and relaxation. But this resort is not merely for health fanatics or vacationers on a quest for truth; Chiva-Som has much appeal to the traveler in Asia who wants to do little else but relax on powdery sand beaches and occasionally snorkel the resort's fabulous reefs.

What is it like? Your day might commence with an energizing power walk on the beach or a stretch in the open pavilion overlooking the sea. A balmy breeze blows, and the air is redolent with the perfume of scented flowers. You bathe in a huge, open-air marble pool. Next to you stands a tall, ice-cold glass of juice, freshly squeezed from locally grown oranges. The gymnasium and bathing pavilion are supervised by qualified instructors, and service is impeccable. Throughout the day, various exercise sessions are provided in the air-conditioned dance studios. And the beach always awaits and is never far away.

Ranked No. 1 in the Best Overseas Spa category by *Condé Nast Traveler,* Chiva-Som aims to send you home with a healthy approach to life to use forever after. As an added incentive, you can go home and brag that you lived next to a king for a week; the king's royal summer palace has been standing next door for centuries.

Chiva-Som International Health Resort

73/4 Petchkasem Road
Hua Hin, Prachualo Khirikham 77110,
    Thailand
Phone: 800–525–4800 or
    011–66–32–536–536
E-mail: reserv@chivasom.com
Web site: www.chivasom.net

Group/Getaway: Couples, Spa & Wellness

Accommodations: There are fifty-seven units, oceanview rooms or pavilions, inspired by traditional Thai architecture, surrounded by tropical gardens, lakes, and waterfalls. Guest rooms with spacious terraces overlook the Gulf of Thailand. All rooms feature private baths.

Points of Distinction: Chiva-Som unites Thai and Western elements of philosophy, health, and exercise to achieve a harmonious atmosphere. Having fun and taking the positive approach to wellness are emphasized.

Open: Year-round.

Minimum Stay: None.

Packages: Please inquire.

Rates: Based on a seven-night stay, double occupancy rates range from $5,050 to $6,800 for two people.

Frequently Asked Questions: *Is there a structured schedule for all guests?* There are numerous activities and services, and you are invited to participate in as many or as few as you wish. *For whom is the resort best suited?* Adults who are interested in a rejuvenating, healthy, holiday experience. Children under sixteen are not permitted at Chiva-Som.

Don't Forget to Bring: Plenty of comfortable exercise clothes and proper sports shoes.

Favorite Side Trips: Bangkok is a three-hour drive. The king's summer palace is nearby, as well as the Pala'u Waterfall and the Floating Market.

Nearest Airports: Hua Hin Airport is 1 mile away; Don Muang is 144 miles away (a two-hour drive).

ALL-INCLUSIVE SERVICES AND ACTIVITIES

Food and Beverages: All meals and non-alcoholic beverages.

Outdoor Activities: Mountain biking, beach power walking.

Water Sports: Swimming, sailing, windsurfing.

Facilities: Bathing pavilion with exercise pool, plunge pool, and Jacuzzi; steam room; fitness center; sauna.

Other: Seven-day special packages include medical consultation; daily massage; loofah scrub and spa bath; Oriental foot massage; floatation chamber; traditional Thai, Swedish, and massage therapies; body definition and sculpting class; strength training; personal training; and yoga, t'ai chi, and meditation.

Not Included: Taxes, gratuities, and service charges.

Available for a Fee: Alcoholic beverages; spa services, including massage therapies (traditional Thai, Swedish, shiatsu, aromatherapy, back and shoulder, reflexology, G5 vibro), body wrap, body polish and hydrotherapy, Thai Body Glow; golf; tennis; horseback riding. Packages may include these services.

THE PACIFIC

BEDARRA ISLAND RESORT

Queensland, Australia

There are seven notable resorts on or just off the northeastern coast of Australia along the Great Barrier Reef that belong to the P&O Australian Resorts Group. For couples visiting that part of the world who want any kind of relief from the demands of travel, Bedarra Island Resort stands out as a major respite, chock-full of beauty and romance.

Bedarra Island is a rainforest haven for a maximum of fifteen couples, and let there be no mistake about it, it is as exclusive as it is expensive. But in the context of value, if you have the money to spend, Bedarra will bring you more tranquillity, service, fine food and wine, and customized fun than most places on Earth.

The perimeter of the island is probably less than 5 miles around, but the island's fine interspersion of beaches and rainforest is the domain of only the few couples who visit the island and the 100 or so staff members who see to it that each guest's whims are met. Privacy comes easily, as does motoring to a beach you can call your own for a day, where refreshments might include lobster, top Australian wines, Swiss chocolate, or any other requests you make to the waiting team of chefs. Or your perfect day might be spent fishing, snorkeling, playing tennis on grass courts, sailing, or taking excursions to nearby islands. We like the fact that another P&O resort, Dunk Island, is just a few minutes away and offers activities such as golf, horseback riding, squash, and even tandem skydiving to Bedarra Island guests (additional fees apply).

A few important points about the island involve its geology. Most of Bedarra is interspersed with the kind of sugar-white sand beaches that only coral reefs can become— soft and healing in some peculiar, alluring way. But because the rest of the island was formed millions of years ago by volcanic action, Bedarra has evolved into a hilly rainforest. There are fascinating walks led daily by staff experts that introduce visiting couples to the special qualities of the rainforest, especially its medicinal powers and the primordial beauty of its lush landscape. In fact, every couple at Bedarra has its own private treetop villa that peeks out from the rainforest onto the beaches and azure waters that are only a minute away. This sense of Robinson Crusoe privacy is one of the resort's most distinguishing features.

The main lodge has a wonderful dining area that offers exquisite meals. Crayfish, mudcrabs, and baby barramundi are market selected and flown in daily. If it's not fresh, it's not on the menu, which changes daily. The liquor, wine, and imported beer selection is also quite amazing, and it's offered twenty-four hours a day. A sculpted and unobtrusive pool adjoins the dining area and bar, as does a library and lounge with an extensive video selection.

The philosophy at Bedarra Island Resort is to treat the island as your own home, to come and go as you please. We're not surprised that the resort's guest registry includes return trips by visitors from all corners of the world.

Bedarra Island Resort
P.O. Box 268
Mission Beach
Queensland, Australia
Phone: 800–225–9849 or
    011–61–7–4068–8233
E–mail: poresorts@aol.com
Web site: www.poresorts.com/bedarra

Group/Getaway: Couples

Accommodations: There are fifteen private, freestanding luxury villas (double-story or split-level) and two cliff-top pavilions surrounded by lush rainforest. Four split-level villas feature a living area and a bedroom that includes a king-size bed overlooking the ocean and neighboring islands. A premium villa and another upgraded villa known as the Point offer spectacular views. The nine two-story villas are uniquely designed, with an upstairs lounge, double balconies, and lower-level bedrooms and bathrooms. These villas are located close to the beachfront and the central resort facilities.

Points of Distinction: Bedarrra is completely private and uniquely pristine, offering the riches of the rainforest with the very best of the Great Barrier Reef.

Open: Year-round.

Minimum Stay: None.

Rates: Based on double occupancy, $950 to $1,450 (Australian dollars; approximately $589 to $899 U.S.) per person, per night. Book seven nights, pay only for six.

Frequently Asked Question: *Are there modern amenities?* Each room has a king-size bed, air-conditioning, ceiling fans, television, VCR, and CD stereo system, as well as a refrigerator, complimentary minibar, hair dryer, robes, and a hammock. Telephone service is available around the clock.

Don't Forget to Bring: Casual clothing for daytime, and smart casual for after 6:00 P.M.; camera, sunscreen, and appropriate footwear for island walks.

Favorite Side Trip: Nearby Dunk Island, a fifteen-minute ride by jetty, is mostly a national park and is known as one of Australia's most beautiful rainforest islands. Guests from Bedarra Island Resort can enjoy additional activities here such as a six-hole golf course, squash courts, horseback riding through the rainforest or on the beach, spa treatments, and tandem skydiving, all for additional fees.

Nearest Airport: Cairns International Airport, then a scenic forty-five-minute flight to Dunk Island and a fifteen-minute jetty ride to the island.

ALL-INCLUSIVE SERVICES AND ACTIVITIES

Food and Beverages: All meals, twenty-four-hour wine and liquor, all nonalcoholic beverages, beach picnics.

Outdoor Activities: Tennis, rainforest walks.

Water Sports: Fishing, catamaran sailing, sailboarding, waterskiing, motorboats.

Facilities: Video library of recent releases and classics, saltwater swimming pool, spa, fitness room.

Other: Private charters for romance and also for game fishing. There are no taxes or tipping in Australia.

Children's Services: No children under sixteen years are allowed.

Not Included: Transfers to Dunk Island, snorkeling.

Available for a Fee: Scheduled snorkeling and scuba diving trips to the Great Barrier Reef; private reef fishing and sailing charters; therapeutic massage on the beach.

LIZARD ISLAND RESORT

Queensland, Australia

Northern Australia's Great Barrier Reef is indeed a conjurer's name, a sparkling, watery magnet for those seeking one of the world's most spectacular aquatic wonders. The region's islands are considered some of the crown jewels of the Pacific. Lizard Island, the northernmost, is a household name in Australia that is associated with a haven for luxury-lovers.

Flying halfway around the world to reach this hideaway—crossing the international date line after ten hours and then spending ten more going from Sydney to Cairns, then to the northeastern coast of Queensland, and finally taking an hour's flight to Lizard Island—is not for everyone. Still, the list of those who should consider this sojourn is not short.

Couples who seek an ultimate if expensive romantic experience will not be disappointed. Neither will adventurers craving water sports nonpareil. For divers and snorkelers, the outer reef's "Cod Hole" is considered one of the world's best reef sites. Game fishing in this region is crowned by the annual Qantas Black Marlin Classic in October, attracting worldwide competition. And plain old beach and palm-tree lovers who love to windsurf or kayak can attain vacation nirvana here. For full-fledged bird-watchers, Lizard Island is another kind of treat, hosting exotic birds like sooty oyster-catchers and red-footed boobies. Declared a national park in 1939, Lizard Island also has a museum-sponsored research center. In truth, the fact that there's not much on Lizard Island besides nature is the lure.

The resort's forty-two luxuriously rustic rooms, suites, and villas do little to interfere with nature on this pristine isle, with its twenty-four prized and remote beaches. In spite of its modern amenities, each room has ceiling fans and private balconies, con-

sistent with the unadorned ambience of the place. Although they are very private, none of these chambers is far from the expansive swimming pool, lounge area, tennis court, and restaurant. Sunset Point Villas particularly impressed us with their sail-covered decks with ocean views, timber decor, and spacious, open floor plans.

The staff of Lizard Island is exceptional, offering a magical combination of unobtrusive and attentive service that encourages guests to take the management's advice to treat the island as their own. To visitors, it seems as if life is quickly reduced to powdery white beaches, multiblue waters, a big azure sky, and a lush rainforest.

When it is time to dine, the theme of Lizard Island's restaurant is "Cuisine Moderne," a luxurious way to create and present South Sea island foods. The esteemed kitchen of Lizard Island offers exceptional meals of freshly caught seafood, tender cuts of local meat, island garden produce, and tropical fruit throughout the day, all served with smiling, friendly pride.

Before leaving Lizard Island, virtually every guest asks about the genesis of the resort's name. The explanation that every staff member has memorized is that in 1770, the first European to explore the island was none other than the infamous Captain Cook. While taking a break from pirating and marauding, he stopped at this beautiful island to get a better idea of how to pass through the reef. As he climbed the highest hill, he was greeted by yard-long, albeit friendly, monitor lizards, which inspired him to name the island after them. Some two centuries later, little has changed—and up-close and personal encounters with the friendly reptiles are still possible today.

Lizard Island Resort
PMB 40
Cairns
Queensland, Australia
Phone: 800–225–9849 or
    011–61–7–4060–3999
E-mail: poresorts@aol.com
Web site: www.poresorts.com/lizard

Group/Getaway: Couples, Adventure

Accommodations: There are forty-two private rooms, all with a balcony, king-size or twin beds, air-conditioning, ceiling fans, refrigerator, CD player, telephone, Internet access, and bathrobes. The magnificently designed Sunset Point Villas overlook Anchor Bay and Sunset Beach. Anchor Bay Rooms, located on the beach, feature private balconies set among native gardens.

Points of Distinction: Lizard Island is the step-off point for the world-famous Cod Hole dive site.

Open: Year-round.

Minimum Stay: None, but seven nights are recommended.

Rates: Based on double occupancy, $740 to $1,450 (Australian dollars; approximately $459 to $899 U.S.) per person, per night; $440 Australian (approximately $273 U.S.) per night for additional adult or child age ten to fourteen years. Book seven nights, pay only for six.

Frequently Asked Question: *Is there telephone service if I need to call home?* The resort has a modern satellite phone and Internet access, available to guests day and night.

Don't Forget to Bring: Underwater camera equipment for spectacular photos.

Favorite Side Trip: A hike to Cook's Look, the highest point on the island.

Nearest Airport: From Cairns Airport, it is a stunning one-hour flight to Lizard Island. Regularly scheduled connecting flights via Cairns are offered by Qantas and Ansett; charter flights are available.

ALL-INCLUSIVE SERVICES AND ACTIVITIES

Food and Beverages: All meals and snacks, nonalcoholic beverages, picnics, afternoon tea, room service.

Outdoor Activities: Tennis, hiking, bocce.

Water Sports: Swimming, windsurfing, waterskiing, sailing catamarans, kayaking, snorkeling, fishing, paddle-skiing, outboard dinghies, sailboats.

Facilities: Lighted tennis courts, freshwater swimming pool, gym.

Other: Gratuities, glass-bottom boat trips, basic fishing gear.

Children's Services: No children under age ten allowed.

Not Included: Airport transfers.

Available for a Fee: Wine and liquor; laundry service; diving instruction; pavilion spa treatments; research station tour; scuba diving; expeditions arranged through but not sponsored by the resort, such as special boat charters, reef trips, and game-fishing charters.

TURTLE ISLAND

Fiji

If Americans are willing to venture as far as the South Sea Islands to pursue gently swaying palms, uninhabited beaches, and clear blue water—in essence, many of the things that make the best Caribbean and Hawaii destinations so attractive—their destination has to be good . . . very, very good. Fiji's Turtle Island resort is precisely that. It was named one of the top ten resorts in the Australia–New Zealand–South Pacific region by **Condé Nast Traveler** readers. But "resort" is definitely not the word to describe this 500-acre private island. An exclusive "ecological and cultural preserve," open to only fourteen visiting couples at a time, is a much more accurate description.

In 1972 owner and former cable television guru Richard Evanson discovered the island while on his way to Australia. Although Evanson was a brilliant businessman, his private life was in shambles, and so was the little island that had been ravaged by farming and erosion. He bought it, and Turtle Island (named for its once-inspiring turtle population) became his project and life cause. The island changed him, and he changed the island, developing it into an award-winning model of what eco-tourism is all about. His personal dream from the beginning was to preserve and strengthen the island's native flora and fauna and the traditional way of life of the local inhabitants.

The resort practices eco-tourism, using solar water heating and locally grown organic produce. Evanson has also been a pioneer in helping to preserve the culture of the Fiji people.

Expect to learn much about their traditions, history, and beliefs and to take part in ceremonies and rituals. It is unique and often so special that you become sorry that all of life cannot be part of this ongoing endeavor, whether while relaxing on one of the secluded beaches, hiking the tropical woods and grassy highlands, strolling the mangrove boardwalk, or diving among the coral reefs. Add to this mix exceptional food, accommodations, and service, and a chance to meet people who are attracted to the same things that prompted you to venture here.

Not surprisingly, the fourteen cottage suites or **bures**—each with a view of the spectacular Blue Lagoon made famous by the Brooke Shields movie of the same name—are built in the traditional Fijian manner. Vegetables are grown organically in ever-present gardens and included in the gourmet South Pacific cuisine.

When you step out of the seaplane that ferries you to Turtle Island (it's part of the package), don't be surprised to find departing guests and staff literally in tears at separating. We thought it was a bit much until it was our turn to leave this version of paradise, and we found our eyes welling. It really is that special, even with its caveats: It is quite expensive, and it is limited to mixed-gender couples who owner Richard Evanson insists must be neither loud nor boorish. But know that this same owner is a big-hearted man who cares deeply about the people of the region. Each year he turns the entire island into a hospital for two weeks to host a bevy of international eye doctors who offer free surgery and care to area natives in need of special attention (eye problems are more common in this part of the world). In the balance, Turtle Island may not be for everyone, but if it calls to you, you may want to spend the rest of your days in Fiji.

Turtle Island

Yasawa Islands
Fiji, South Islands
Phone: 877–288–7853 or 360–256–4347
E-mail: usa@turtlefiji.com
Web site: www.turtlefiji.com

Group/Getaway: Couples

Accommodations: Bungalows are built in the unique Fijian style and include wood floors, four-poster king-size bed, large indoor jetted spa tubs, and veranda with a queen-size daybed. These bures have every luxury you could expect (including indoor jetted spa-tub) and are located on the famous Blue Lagoon. The two-room bures come equipped with towels, bathrobes, hair dryers, Bose CD stereo systems, full wet bar, and icemaker.

Points of Distinction: The island is reserved for only fourteen couples at a time; perfectly orchestrated so each couple can enjoy any one of the two or three private beaches during their stay, including "Paddy's Beach," named after a character in *The Blue Lagoon*, which was filmed on Turtle Island. Upon arrival, guests are asked to set their clocks one hour ahead. This "Turtle Time" was established when Brooke Shields was filming because she did not like early morning wake-up calls, and Turtle Island owner Richard Evanson never changed the clocks back.

Open: Year-round.

Minimum Stay: Six nights.

Rates: Nightly rates begin at $1,646 per couple. In addition, guests are offered free international airfare for two with a minimum seven-night stay.

Frequently Asked Questions: *Are children allowed on the island?* Children are welcomed with their families twice a year: from late December to mid-January and the first two weeks in July. (Private Fijian nannies are provided.) The rest of the year the island is restricted to couples only. *How many pieces of luggage are allowed on the plane?* The seaplane strictly permits thirty-three pounds of luggage per person. You will need little. Dress is casual on the island, and there is daily laundry service available at no charge. *Can I bring my own equipment for fly-fishing and scuba diving?* Yes, bring whatever you like, just remember the weight limit on luggage. If you do not have equipment, you're not to

worry—Turtle Island has plenty for you to use. *How should I dress?* Most guests dress in casual attire. Shorts, T-shirts, light pants, jeans, and shorts are acceptable. Shoes are rarely worn from the time you arrive until the time you depart, although you may want to bring sandals or water socks and some comfortable walking/hiking shoes.

Don't Forget to Bring: Long sleeves for occasional chilly evenings, and plenty of sunscreen.

Favorite Side Trips: Boat trips to neighboring islands to meet villagers (travelers voted Fijians the "friendliest people in the world"), partake in the ancient Kava ceremony, or visit the mission and listen to the children's choir.

Nearest Airport: Nadi International Airport, a thirty-minute seaplane ride to the shore of the resort via Turtle Island Airways.

ALL-INCLUSIVE SERVICES AND ACTIVITIES

Food and Beverages: All meals, room service, private picnics, wine and liquor, champagne sunrise breakfasts, private dinners.

Outdoor Activities: Horseback riding, mountain biking, hiking.

Water Sports: Sailing, swimming, windsurfing, kayaking, snorkeling, scuba diving, deep-sea and fly-fishing.

Other: Sunset cruises; snorkeling fins, masks, and snorkels; scuba equipment; hammocks; trips to neighboring islands; airport transfers; daily laundry service.

Not Included: 10 percent Fijian government tax.

Available for a Fee: A Lomi Lomi massage (Hawaiian full-body massage with two trained massage therapists working rhythmically), commemorative DVD filmed by the island's own professional videographer featuring you and your companion enjoying the paradise of Turtle Island.

VATULELE ISLAND RESORT

Vatulele, Fiji

Fiji consists of more than 300 islands spread over half a million square miles of ocean in the heart of the South Pacific. With its tropical weather and unpolluted waters, it offers more all-inclusive resorts than any country outside of the Caribbean. Among these is Vatulele Island Resort, named No. 1 for best value in Fiji by *Travel & Leisure* magazine and Best Boutique Resort 1999 by Fiji Tourism. The development of Vatulele (pronounced *vah-too-lay-lay*) as a five-star tropical escape was the vision of Emmy-award–winning Australian television producer Henry Crawford and his creative partner, Martin Livingston, a fifth-generation Fijian. Their efforts have resulted in Vatulele on one of the southern islands of the Fijian chain, where the climate is drier and the beaches are broad and spectacular.

It took Crawford and Martin two years to find the ideal South Seas location, and several more to create a site amid the natural beauty where weary travellers could escape the pressures of faster lives to enjoy all that the resort has to offer.

Vatulele's calling card is relaxation and romance, and they come easily at this getaway, where a primarily Fijian staff is among the friendliest and kindest in the world. In addition to celebrity guests (actress Kate Winslet has vacationed here), many couples honeymoon at the resort. Each month a few weddings are held on-site, which the resort organizes with great appeal and efficiency.

Among Vatulele's host of other exceptional qualities for Westerners flying ten hours from Los Angeles to take a South Seas vacation, its most famous attribute is its remarkable scuba diving opportunities. There may be no better place to take your first plunge into the exhilarating world beneath the sea than at this all-inclusive resort. The quality of the scuba diving sites at Vatulele has been one of the South Pacific's well-kept secrets for many years; it is the region's only luxury resort that has earned a Golden Palm award for its dive facility and resident instructors. Vatulele offers a variety of courses for all abilities, from the beginner to the globe-trotting thrill seeker. There is a terrific resort course to get guests started, followed by open-water certification and various specialty courses.

The cross-section of diving possibilities includes soft coral, hard coral, and pelagics, with underwater visibility ranging from above average to excellent; there are few currents. The island is surrounded by deep water with large drop-offs offering twenty-two dive sites within fifteen minutes' travel.

Another popular activity that brings Vatulele to the fore is sport-fishing. The ocean around the island abounds with sport fish, including giant tuna, wahoo, and mahi-mahi; much of the catch is sent fresh to the resort's dining room each night.

Vatulele Island Resort

P.O. Box 9936
Nadi Airport
Fiji, South Islands
Phone: 800–828–9146 or 011–679–550–300
E-mail: res@vatulele.com
Web site: www.vatulele.com

Group/Getaway: Couples

Accommodations: There are eighteen villas, or bures, set in a natural jungle surrounding, which allows for plenty of privacy. Each bedroom has a king-size bed and dressing area with twelve glass doors that open onto a terrace. The two-level Point is set apart from the others in a spectacular location.

Points of Distinction: Vatulele is the only five-star island resort in Fiji with a PADI-certified dive facility and resident instructors.

Open: Year-round.

Minimum Stay: Four nights; however, five are recommended, and six or seven are average.

Rates: Based on double occupancy, per night rates begin at $1,238 per couple ($2,250 for the Point), $660 for singles. Charge for an additional adult sharing the bure is $330; children twelve to sixteen years (maximum two children sharing with two adults) $88 per night. Honeymoon special: Book seven nights or more and receive three additional nights free.

Frequently Asked Question: *Are guests an international mix?* Half the guests are American, with the remainder divided between Australians, New Zealanders, and Europeans.

Don't Forget to Bring: Casual clothing (dress on the island is informal), rubber-soled shoes, a sweater for cool evenings during winter, which is June through August.

Favorite Side Trip: Snorkeling to enjoy the outstanding coral reefs, much different from the Caribbean variety.

Nearest Airport: Nadi International Airport, a twenty-five-minute flight on light aircraft from the resort.

ALL-INCLUSIVE SERVICES AND ACTIVITIES

Food and Beverages: All meals, nonalcoholic beverages, wine, French champagne, and liquor, room service, snacks, afternoon tea.

Outdoor Activities: Tennis.

Water Sports: Kayaking, windsurfing, snorkeling, sailing.

Other: Excursions to villages and other islands, taxes.

Children's Services: Children under twelve are not allowed.

Not Included: Airport transfer. Although tipping is not required, some guests might choose to contribute to a staff Christmas fund; however, it is not mandatory.

Available for a Fee: Private massage, scuba diving, sportfishing.

THE WAKAYA CLUB

Suva, Fiji

The Wakaya Club is a resort of 200 acres on a tiny island four hours by plane from the nearest continent. Much of its property is oceanfront jungle with its own lagoon and lengthy stretch of secluded beach. Only eighteen guests share the acreage, ensuring an adults-only, crowd-free vacation with world-class accommodations and outstanding personal service in a truly glorious setting.

The grounds are typical of a tropical South Pacific Island. Palm trees rise high above the resort, with flowering bushes and smaller trees growing in the shade beneath. The lagoon is perfect for a swim or snorkel, but a warm-water pool is on-site as well. Beaches remain empty throughout most of the day, allowing for a quiet walk or a private moment. Groomed walking paths bring guests through the darker portions of the forest, where horses, deer, and pigs still roam free. On an island completely surrounded by coral reef, guests of Wakaya have available the best snorkel and scuba sites in the world. Lali drums sound the call for dinner, when the resort's four chefs (that's four chefs for eighteen guests!) pres-

ent the finest seafood caught in local waters, along with Wakaya-raised venison and vegetables grown in the resort's own organic gardens. Meals are served inside a dining room pavilion with tribal-carved beams overhead, or outside on the rambling deck overlooking the lagoon. Wines selected from France and Australia accompany every meal.

For diversion many guests use the lagoon for sailing and windsurfing while others seek only the sun-drenched beach. Croquet is played on a vibrantly green lawn, and tennis is played under the sun or, in the evening, beneath halogen light. A nine-hole golf course is laid out among coconut groves. *Boules,* similar to bocce, is played in an open, sand-floored bure, witnessed by symbolic statues of shrunken heads.

It isn't long before the feeling of being so distant goes away. That feeling is quickly replaced by one of connection and belonging. You won't feel homesick while at Wakaya, yet you will feel homesick for Wakaya when you finally do leave this unique island.

The Wakaya Club

P.O. Box 15424
Old Town Road
Suva, Fiji, South Islands
Phone: 800–828–3454 or 011–679–448–128
E-mail: info@wakaya.com
Web site: www.wakaya.com

Group/Getaway: Couples

Accommodations: Guests stay in bures, traditional Fijian thatched cottages set in a grove of palms and native foliage. Constructed mostly of wood and bamboo, each 1,500-square-foot bure has a fully stocked wet bar and ceiling fans; some have air-conditioning. Bathrooms feature an oversized tub, separate shower, three sinks, and a bidet. Vale O House (House in the Clouds) is a three-bedroom estate with its own swimming pool featuring a remote-controlled waterfall, Jacuzzi, tennis court, personal kitchen and laundry staff, and on-call driver.

Point of Distinction: The resort is used often by people with recognizable faces and names. Here, with so few people on the island, they can be themselves and enjoy their time.

Open: Year-round.

Minimum Stay: Five nights.

Rates: Based on double occupancy, rates per couple per night begin at $1,475. The Governors Bure begins at $1,875. Rates for Vale O House are $3,500 to $6,500, depending on the number of occupants.

Frequently Asked Questions: *When swimming, snorkeling, or diving, what is the danger from sharks?* Very slight. Although sharks are prevalent in this part of the world, the giant fish remains mainly outside the reef (Wakaya and most other islands in the region are within reef barriers). Even outside the reef, sharks know their regular prey and do not normally pursue humans. *Is the weather much different from season to season?* A temperature comparison between January and July shows only a six-degree difference. Seasons are felt more by the fish that tend to visit the reef in stronger numbers from October to February.

Don't Forget to Bring: A personal journal; you will find the time and clarity of mind to do the writing you've always wanted to do. It might be a good opportunity also to write some old friends you haven't seen in a while.

Favorite Side Trip: What is so special about Wakaya is its isolation. A side trip would be to explore the backside of the island or ride a glass-bottom boat over the top of the reef.

Nearest Airport: Nandi International Airport, a one-hour flight by seaplane from the resort.

ALL-INCLUSIVE SERVICES AND ACTIVITIES

Food and Beverages: All meals, nonalcoholic beverages, room service, snacks, afternoon tea, wine and liquor.

Outdoor Activities: Golf, croquet, tennis, boules.

Water Sports: Snorkeling, scuba diving, swimming, sailing, windsurfing.

Facilities: Billiards and pool room, fitness center with aerobic equipment and free weights, video area, warm-water pool.

Other: Glass-bottom boat tours, massage, taxes and gratuities. Additional tips may be left as a community donation.

Available for a Fee: Deep-sea fishing.

YASAWA ISLAND RESORT

Yasawa Island, Fiji

Visiting the Yasawa Island for the first time, it's easy to think you have arrived in heaven a la Gaugin. Visitors are seduced by the gorgeous mountains, beaches, and lagoons of this cluster of sixteen volcanic islands, and nowhere more so than at Yasawa Island Resort.

Located 35 miles northwest of Viti Levu, Fiji's "Big Island," the luxurious resort actively courts romance-minded visitors by featuring privacy, lushness, top-notch cuisine, and a superb wine list. The weather here is almost predictably pleasant (the climate is semiarid), and you can count on living your life outdoors in your bathing suit or *sulu* (cotton wraparound). The island has eleven remarkable beaches, including one of the most spectacular beaches we have ever seen. This long expanse of deep sand is broken by a teapotlike rock outcrop, which also separates two villages.

The out-of-the-way retreat is located on a 13-mile-long, narrow and mountainous island. Sixteen individual bures ("boo-rays"; the word means both bungalow and sanctuary) create a small, villagelike cluster along the waterfront's wide sandy beach. A central bure used for dining and dancing faces a large pool, itself surrounded by handsome umbrellas and comfy deck chairs.

Some of the world's best swimming, snorkeling, diving, windsurfing, and fishing spots are near the beachfront or a quick boat ride away. While you are here you may want to sign on for a PADI diving course. Tennis, croquet, and bus trips to the villages are some other popular activities. Local guides will take you on bush walks, including one that will give you 360-degree views of the island and the surrounding ocean.

The individual bures are nestled between a lushly planted greensward and a beautiful sandy beach. If you choose one of the ten one-bedroom deluxe bures, for instance, you will enjoy a spacious split-level bungalow divided into living room and bedroom, as well as your own hammock in a separate thatched beach hut. Fragrant frangipani and hibiscus scent your indoor and outdoor play spaces.

Up until 1987, this island was considered off-limits to land-based tourism. In 1996 Yasawa Island Resort's owners, Aussies Denise and Garth Downey, first saw the resort, originally named Yasawa Island Lodge. They were struck by the wonderful mix of location, culture, and geography that distinguished it from all of the other island groupings among Fiji's 300 islands.

The Downeys were hooked! They decided two things: one, to get married there, and two, to buy the resort. Theirs is a warm and personal approach to the guests, the resort, its grounds, and the people of the island.

While there are group activities, such as special dinners and singing and dance performances, Yasawa has above all an understanding of privacy. Of course you are invited to make plans to eat with the group at a communal dining area—either at the open main building or, if you wish, on the beach. But, if you decide to dine *à deux* at your own bure, or on one of the many nearly deserted beaches or at an offshore island, the well-trained staff instinctively knows how to serve you best. Think fantasy—think **Blue Lagoon**—and it will happen.

Whether you come to Yasawa Island Resort to celebrate your wedding or honeymoon or to have quality time with someone special, you'll discover great dining, sunning, snorkeling, diving at private beaches, thoughtful service, and a feeling that you have sampled another culture, all in one luxurious setting.

Yasawa Island Resort
P.O. Box 10128
Nadi Airport
Fiji, South Islands
Phone: 877–828–3864 or
    011–61–3–679–672–2266
E-mail: yasawa@connect.com.fi
Web site: www.yasawaislandresort.com

Group/Getaway: Couples

Accommodations: Each of the sixteen bures lining Yasawa's sandy beach is decorated elegantly in the Fijian style and features king-size bed, private hammock, air-conditioning, ceiling fan, bath with double shower, double vanity, walk-in wardrobe, sundeck, living room, telephone, refrigerator, and radio with CD player. The honeymoon bure is a split-level style and features a 1,000-square-foot deck.

Points of Distinction: The Downeys' wine collection is considered by some to be the best in Fiji. The barrier beaches and extensive coral growths make diving and snorkeling spectacular.

Open: Year-round.

Minimum Stay: None.

Rates: Based on double occupancy, $820 to $1,275 for two people, per night for a secluded beachfront bure.

Frequently Asked Questions: *For whom is the resort best suited?* Couples and honeymooners who seek a vacation filled with activities, from hiking up the mountain to adventuring through the rainforests. Yasawa offers the simplicity of relaxing on one of the many private beaches or having a romantic picnic alone. Children under age twelve are welcome only during January; children age twelve and older are welcome anytime. *Are wedding ceremonies performed on the island?* Yasawa can plan a traditional Fijian wedding with a local minister, traditional outfits for the bride and groom, and a thirty-voice choir. *How is the fishing?* Fantastic—don't miss the chance to spend a day on the high-speed game boat, a Black Watch 30.

Don't Forget to Bring: Casual lightweight clothing, sunscreen, a hat, and books by your favorite "beach authors."

Favorite Side Trips: The caves are breathtaking, and the Blue Lagoon is better than you imagined. Treks through the bush make you feel as if you are the last of the great explorers. The private beaches are great for romantic picnics.

Nearest Airport: Nadi Airport on Viti Levu is a thirty-minute seaplane flight to the resort. Luggage restrictions apply.

ALL-INCLUSIVE SERVICES AND ACTIVITIES

Food and Beverages: All meals and snacks, nonalcoholic beverages, afternoon tea, room service.

Outdoor Activities: Bush walks, tennis, croquet, caving.

Water Sports: Windsurfing, catamaran sailing, hand-line fishing, swimming, snorkeling.

Facilities: Horizon pool, library.

Entertainment: Singing and dance performances.

Other: Parlor games; boat or bus trips to eleven private beaches; visits to villages to see shell markets and traditional dances and ceremonies, taxes. Gratuities are not customary in Fiji; however, guests are welcome to leave a monetary contribution to a local school or church.

Not Included: Air transfers from Nadi ($350 per person, round-trip).

Available for a Fee: PADI dive course, game fishing, wedding arrangements, wine and liquor, massage and facials.

HUKA LODGE

Taupo, New Zealand

In the 1920s a young Irishman named Alan Pye was exploring New Zealand's North Island when he was overcome by the startling beauty of a convergence of streams that formed a lake with the most beautiful, crystal-clear water he had ever seen. He later learned from frontier trappers that it was called Lake Taupo and was known for its abundance of rainbow trout. Pye built a home a few yards from the largest river that fed the lake, calling it Huka Lodge. Sixty years later, Huka Lodge was discovered by the current owner, Alex Van Heeren, who converted it into a property that might be the most remote luxury all-inclusive in the world. But its seclusion has not affected its popularity. In the last decades it has been a much appreciated hideaway of Robin Williams and Kate Winslet; Queen Elizabeth II has visited the lodge four times.

Huka Lodge, which received *Condé Nast Traveler*'s 2003 Gold List highest rating for Australia and New Zealand, has twenty guest suites that overlook the snow-capped peaks in the distance. From the lodge's Great Room, you can enjoy a roaring fire while taking in an unbelievably panoramic view. With its history of fishing and hunting, the lodge has trophy rooms that now function as meeting places for predinner cocktails, and downstairs, a sophisticated and elegant wine cellar doubles as a dining room. But the real prize that awaits Huka guests at the end of the day is an extraordinarily sumptuous meal.

A trio of mountains surrounds the lodge to the south, and vast pine forests border it to the north. Lake Taupo rests just a short walk from the Huka Lodge, and the famous Huka Falls pour clear water into the lake from a few hundred yards upstream. In these environs, Huka Lodge serves outdoor enthusiasts who come to enjoy hiking, biking, kayaking, and, most of all, fishing. The crystal lake still claims some of the most sought-after rainbow and brown trout in the world. The lodge's experienced guides seem to take great joy in helping guests successfully pursue them. And no expense is spared. Boats and even Jet Skis get you to hard-to-reach coves and hiding spots along the lake. Or you can take a helicopter or a four-wheel-drive vehicle to secluded and magnificent fishing along the area's twenty-three streams and rivers. Although Huka Lodge is a fisherman's retreat, the lake is large enough to accommodate many interests. You can picnic in your own bay, water ski, swim, or investigate Maori rock carvings.

Sunset on Lake Taupo is magnificent and best admired from an area known as the Western Bays. The managers of the resort often set up barbecues on the beach facing west. It is a fitting conclusion to a day of high adventure. Soon stars appear in great abundance. It is a sight, among many, that visitors never forget.

Huka Lodge
Huka Falls Road
P.O. Box 95
Taupo, New Zealand
Phone: 011–64–7–378–5791
E-mail: reservations@hukalodge.co.nz
Web site: www.hukalodge.com

Group/Getaway: Couples, Adventure

Accommodations: There are twenty guest suites, set privately in the bush. All have underfloor heating, a spacious bedroom, separate dressing room, minibar, private bath, and outdoor terraces. The glass-ceiling bathrooms afford a view up into the towering trees and feature a sunken bath, separate shower, and double sinks. Huka Cottage has three double suites.

Point of Distinction: The famous Huka Falls are just 240 feet upstream from the lodge.

Open: Year-round.

Minimum Stay: None.

Rates: Based on double occupancy, $745 to $1,300 (New Zealand dollars; approximately $450 to $720 U.S.) per person, per night; singles, $1,120 to $1,950 New Zealand (approximately $620 to $1,080 U.S.) per night.

Frequently Asked Question: *What is the dress requirement?* Smart, casual dress for dinner. Ties and jackets are not required.

Favorite Side Trips: A relaxing cruise on the *African Queen*, a historic 62-foot riverboat, or a more adventurous excursion on the Huka jet to visit the Aratiatia Dam and Huka Falls.

Nearest Airport: Taupo Airport is fifteen minutes from the lodge.

ALL-INCLUSIVE SERVICES AND ACTIVITIES

Food and Beverages: Full breakfast, evening cocktails, and a five-course dinner.

Outdoor Activities: Activities are not included in the cost.

Facilities: Jacuzzi, airline desk, game room, gift shop, indoor pool, business services, wine-tasting room, tennis court, 20-meter indoor lap pool, sauna, steam room.

Other: Airport transfers.

Not Included: Gratuities, 12.5 percent GST.

Available for a Fee: Fishing, hunting, waterskiing, horseback riding, alpine skiing, bungee jumping, tandem skydiving, sailing, golf at a nearby course, massages, wilderness escapes, limousine tours, wine, lunch (which can be purchased at the lodge or at one of many cafes in Taupo— a ten-minute drive from the lodge).

CLUB MED BORA BORA

Vaitape, Bora Bora

Activities at Club Med Bora Bora are similar to those of other Club Meds and resorts found elsewhere. However, given the extraordinary natural beauty of this secluded French Polynesian island resort's surroundings, these same activities seem more impressive. Indeed, it is hard to find words to describe the magic that emanates from the island of Bora Bora. Seen from the air, the view has been compared to that of a tiny emerald in a setting of turquoise, encircled by a sheltering necklace of sparkling pearls. We concur.

Sailing is done over waters that can barely be seen. Windsurfers and waterskiers skim these same waters as if magically floating over the sand and coral that lie 20 feet below. From place to place, the water changes color, ranging from the palest turquoise to the deepest blues. Mountain bikers pedal the bright green hillsides of a currently dormant volcano on an island that doesn't have an airstrip because it lacks even a slight stretch of flat ground. And if the above-water beauty weren't enough, the island is completely surrounded by a wide band of coral reef, making snorkeling and scuba an almost religious experience. Visitors to the resort spend much of their time beneath the surface of the water.

The Club Med village occupies the inner rim of a protected lagoon with a thick tropical forest growing tightly around its edges. Newly renovated, the resort features modern, hard-roof bungalows, each with its own ocean-view balcony. All told, the resort accommodates 150 couples or singles.

The resort features tennis and a fitness center, dining in the main lodge, and nightly entertainment. But it is activities of a marine nature that distinguish this place from Caribbean or Mediterranean resorts. Bora Bora is virtually unchanged since its original formation from a volcano. The same is true for its coral reefs, considered to be some of the most spectacular in the world. Nearly every water sport is enjoyed at Club Med, but most famous is its snorkeling. The lagoon's countless species of tropical fish and brilliant coral gardens are a visual treat of the first order. Kayaking, sailing, and swimming are not only very popular here but also seem to be a privilege to undertake in such incredible surroundings.

Almost as superior as the water in Bora Bora are the island's beaches. Sunbathing at this Club Med is luxurious and pursued in European style. Locals and tourists alike take a casual approach to wearing bathing attire. Although children are allowed, the resort is geared toward couples and honeymooners.

Club Med does an excellent job of offering unusual excursions, although at an extra cost. Highlights include an extensive viewing of coral from a glass-bottom boat, shark and stingray feeding, scuba diving, and safari mountain excursions in four-wheel-drive vehicles.

We appreciated the fact that Bora Bora is only 20 miles around. When we felt like leaving the Club Med village, we could explore the island's entire coastline on foot or bicycle, a bonus in a place that James Michener called "the most beautiful island in the world."

Club Med Bora Bora

B.P. 34 Anau
Vaitape, Bora Bora
French Polynesia
Phone: 800–CLUB–MED or
    011–689–604–604
Web site: www.clubmed.com

Group/Getaway: Couples, Adventure

Accommodations: There are 150 spacious rooms, each with air-conditioning or ceiling fan, personal safe, mini refrigerator, international telephone, terrace or balcony, and television.

Points of Distinction: Club Med Bora Bora has some of the most beautiful spots for snorkeling and diving in the world.

Open: Year-round.

Minimum Stay: None.

Rates: Based on double occupancy, from $1,190 to $1,540 (for land cost only) per person for seven nights; singles add an additional $250 to total cost. Rates for children ages two to fifteen are $336 to $770.

Frequently Asked Question: *Where is the resort located?* Club Med Bora Bora is on Bora Bora, the smallest of the Polynesian islands in the South Pacific. The village is set on the south coast in the Bay of Faaopore.

Don't Forget to Bring: Sandals, which are standard footwear, and appropriate clothes and shoes for sports.

Favorite Side Trips: Shark feeding while snorkeling, helicopter tours, parasailing, lagoon cruises, trekking through tropical forest.

Nearest Airport: Bora Bora Airport, a ten-minute bus ride from the resort. Transfers come from Faaa Airport near Papeete on Tahiti, a forty-five-minute flight to Bora Bora.

ALL-INCLUSIVE SERVICES AND ACTIVITIES

Food and Beverages: All meals, snacks, afternoon tea, picnics; alcoholic and non-alcoholic beverages throughout the day, a new Club Med policy.

Outdoor Activities: Tennis, volleyball, basketball, archery.

Water Sports: Windsurfing, sailing, snorkeling, kayaking, canoeing.

Facilities: Glass-bottom boats, catamarans, tennis courts.

Entertainment: Karaoke, dancing, gymnastics.

Other: Step and stretch, aerobics, pirogue rides, guided sailing and rowing trips. Airport transfers included only if you book air reservations through Club Med.

Not Included: Club Med membership fee, $55 for each adult and $25 for each child. Unless Club Med books your flight, you are responsible for airport transfers to the hotel ($20 per person) and flights from Faaa Airport on Papeete to Bora Bora.

Available for a Fee: Scuba diving. For an extra cost, the resort's Excursion Program offers Jeep safaris, island tours, shark feedings, aqua safaris, sunset cruises, helicopter tours, deep-sea fishing, horseback riding, waterskiing, and parasailing.

100 BEST ALL-INCLUSIVE RESORTS OF THE WORLD

Resort	Region	Location	Adventure
NORTH AMERICA			
The Balsams Grand Resort Hotel	The Northeast	New Hampshire	✔
Blackberry Farm	The South	Tennessee	
Cal-a-Vie	The West Coast and Hawaii	California	
Canyon Ranch in the Berkshires	The Northeast	Massachusetts	
The Cloister Hotel	The South	Georgia	
Club Med Sandpiper	The South	Florida	
The Golden Door	The West Coast and Hawaii	California	
The Grand Hotel	The Midwest	Michigan	✔
The Greenhouse	The Southwest	Texas	
Hilton Head Health Institute	The South	South Carolina	
Hotel Hana-Maui at Hana Ranch	The West Coast and Hawaii	Hawaii	
Hotel Sierra Nuevo Vallarta	Mexico	Nuevo Vallarta	
Kona Village Resort	The West Coast and Hawaii	Hawaii	✔
The Kripalu Center for Yoga and Health	The Northeast	Massachusetts	
Laramie River Ranch	Rocky Mountain	Colorado	✔
The Lodge and Spa at Cordillera	Rocky Mountain	Colorado	✔
The Lost Creek Ranch	Rocky Mountain	Wyoming	✔
Meliá Cozumel	Mexico	Cozumel	
Miraval Life in Balance Spa and Resort	The Southwest	Arizona	
Mountain Trek	Canada	British Columbia	✔
Occidental Allegro Cozumel	Mexico	Cozumel	
Occidental Royal Hideaway Playacar	Mexico	Playa del Carmen	
Old Glendevy Ranch	Rocky Mountain	Colorado	✔
The Point	The Northeast	New York	✔
Presidente Inter-Continental Ixtapa	Mexico	Ixtapa	
Presidente Inter-Continental Los Cabos	Mexico	Los Cabos	
Presidente Inter-Continental Puerto Vallarta	Mexico	Puerto Vallarta	
Rancho de los Caballeros	The Southwest	Arizona	✔
Rancho La Puerta	Mexico	Baja California	✔
Rawah Ranch	Rocky Mountain	Colorado	✔
Red Mountain Resort and Spa	Rocky Mountain	Utah	✔
Reef Club Cozumel	Mexico	Cozumel	

Couples/Romance	Diving/Snorkeling	Dude Ranch	Families	Sportfishing	Gambling	Golf	Horseback Riding	Kids' Program	Safari	Singles	Downhill Skiing	Cross-Country Skiing	Spa/Wellness	Tennis	Sports/Fitness	Weddings	Other
✔			✔			✔		✔		✔	✔			✔	✔		
✔				✔			✔						✔	✔	✔	✔	Cuisine
✔						✔				✔			✔	✔	✔		Cuisine
✔										✔		✔	✔	✔	✔		Cuisine
✔			✔			✔	✔	✔					✔	✔	✔		
			✔			✔		✔						✔	✔		
✔										✔			✔	✔	✔		Cuisine, holistic
			✔			✔	✔	✔						✔			Historic hotel
										✔			✔		✔		Women only
						✔				✔			✔	✔	✔		Weight loss
✔	✔		✔			✔	✔						✔	✔		✔	
✔	✔		✔				✔	✔		✔				✔	✔		
✔	✔		✔	✔			✔	✔						✔	✔		
✔										✔			✔		✔		
✔		✔	✔	✔			✔	✔		✔							Overnight pack trips
✔							✔			✔	✔	✔	✔	✔	✔		Cuisine
✔		✔	✔			✔	✔			✔			✔	✔	✔		Cuisine
✔	✔		✔				✔	✔		✔				✔	✔	✔	
✔						✔	✔			✔			✔		✔		Fasting programs
✔										✔			✔		✔		
✔	✔		✔			✔		✔						✔	✔	✔	
✔	✔			✔		✔	✔							✔	✔	✔	Cuisine
✔		✔	✔	✔			✔			✔							Hunting
✔				✔		✔	✔				✔	✔	✔				Cuisine
✔	✔		✔	✔		✔		✔		✔				✔	✔		
✔	✔		✔	✔		✔		✔		✔				✔	✔		
✔	✔		✔			✔		✔		✔				✔	✔	✔	Desert horticulture
✔		✔	✔				✔	✔		✔				✔			
✔										✔			✔	✔	✔		Cuisine
✔		✔	✔	✔			✔			✔							Cuisine
			✔			✔	✔							✔	✔		✔
✔	✔		✔			✔	✔			✔				✔	✔	✔	

Resort	Region	Location	Adventure
Topnotch	The Northeast	Vermont	
Triple Creek Ranch	Rocky Mountain	Montana	✔
The Tyler Place	The Northeast	Vermont	
Vista Verde	Rocky Mountain	Colorado	✔
Wilderness Trails Ranch	Rocky Mountain	Colorado	✔
Yes Bay Lodge	The West Coast and Hawaii	Alaska	✔

THE CARIBBEAN AND THE BAHAMAS

Resort	Region	Location	Adventure
Almond Beach Club and Spa	Caribbean	Barbados	
Almond Beach Village	Caribbean	Barbados	
Beaches Grande Sport Resort and Spa	Caribbean	Jamaica	
Beaches Negril	Caribbean	Jamaica	
Beaches Sandy Bay	Caribbean	Jamaica	
Beaches Turks and Caicos Resort and Spa	Caribbean	Turks and Caicos	
Biras Creek	Caribbean	British Virgin Islands	
Bitter End Yacht Club	Caribbean	British Virgin Islands	✔
Breezes Bahamas	Caribbean	Bahamas	
Breezes Runaway Bay	Caribbean	Jamaica	
Club Med Columbus Isle	Caribbean	Bahamas	✔
Club Med Paradise Island	Caribbean	Bahamas	
Club Rockley	Caribbean	Barbados	
Couples Negril	Caribbean	Jamaica	
Couples Ocho Rios	Caribbean	Jamaica	
Couples Swept Away Resort	Caribbean	Jamaica	
Curtain Bluff Resort	Caribbean	Antigua	
Divi Aruba Mega Beach Resort	Caribbean	Aruba	
Franklyn D. Resort	Caribbean	Jamaica	
Galley Bay	Caribbean	Antigua	
Grand Lido Braco	Caribbean	Jamaica	
Grand Lido Negril	Caribbean	Jamaica	
Half Moon Golf, Tennis, and Beach Club	Caribbean	Jamaica	
Hamaca Coral by Hilton Beach Hotel and Casino	Caribbean	Dominican Republic	✔
Harmony Club	Caribbean	Bermuda	
Hedonism II	Caribbean	Jamaica	
Jalousie Hilton Resort and Spa	Caribbean	St. Lucia	
Jumby Bay	Caribbean	Antigua	

Couples/Romance	Diving/Snorkeling	Dude Ranch	Families	Sportfishing	Gambling	Golf	Horseback Riding	Kids' Program	Safari	Singles	Downhill Skiing	Cross-Country Skiing	Spa/Wellness	Tennis	Sports/Fitness	Weddings	Other
✔			✔			✔	✔	✔		✔	✔	✔	✔	✔	✔		
✔		✔		✔			✔				✔	✔		✔			
✔			✔	✔				✔						✔	✔		
✔		✔	✔	✔			✔	✔			✔	✔					Cattle drives
✔		✔	✔	✔			✔	✔		✔						✔	Salmon fishing
✔			✔	✔						✔							
✔	✔					✔								✔	✔	✔	Dine-around program
✔	✔					✔								✔	✔	✔	Dine-around program
✔	✔					✔							✔	✔	✔		Cuisine
	✔	✔						✔						✔	✔		Sega game center
	✔		✔		✔			✔						✔	✔		
	✔		✔			✔		✔					✔	✔	✔	✔	Cuisine
✔	✔			✔										✔	✔	✔	Cuisine
✔	✔		✔	✔						✔				✔			Sailing programs
✔	✔				✔	✔				✔				✔	✔	✔	
✔	✔					✔				✔				✔	✔		Cuisine
✔	✔			✔						✔				✔	✔		
✔	✔		✔		✔			✔		✔				✔	✔		
	✔		✔	✔		✔		✔						✔	✔		
✔	✔					✔							✔	✔	✔	✔	
✔	✔					✔	✔						✔	✔	✔	✔	
✔	✔					✔							✔	✔	✔		
✔	✔			✔										✔	✔		Fine wines
	✔	✔			✔	✔		✔						✔	✔		
	✔	✔						✔						✔			
✔	✔			✔		✔								✔			Cuisine
✔	✔					✔								✔	✔	✔	
✔	✔													✔	✔	✔	
✔	✔		✔	✔		✔	✔	✔						✔			Cuisine
	✔		✔		✔	✔		✔						✔	✔		Cigar factory visits
✔	✔		✔	✔		✔								✔			
	✔				✔					✔				✔		✔	Au naturel
✔	✔		✔	✔		✔				✔			✔	✔	✔	✔	
✔	✔		✔	✔	✔	✔	✔						✔	✔	✔	✔	

Resort	Region	Location	Adventure
LaSource	Caribbean	Grenada	
LeSport	Caribbean	St. Lucia	
Necker Island	Caribbean	British Virgin Islands	
Occidental Club on the Green	Caribbean	Dominican Republic	
Occidental Grand Pineapple Beach	Caribbean	Antigua	
Paradisus Punta Cana	Caribbean	Dominican Republic	
Peter Island Resort	Caribbean	British Virgin Islands	
Radisson Cable Beach and Golf Resort	Caribbean	Bahamas	
Rendezvous	Caribbean	St. Lucia	
Royal Plantation Spa & Golf Resort	Caribbean	Jamaica	
St. James Club	Caribbean	St. Lucia	
St. James's Club	Caribbean	Antigua	
Sandals Montego Bay	Caribbean	Jamaica	
Sandals Negril Beach Resort and Spa	Caribbean	Jamaica	
Sandals Royal Bahamian Resort and Spa	Caribbean	Bahamas	
Sans Souci Resort & Spa	Caribbean	Jamaica	
Spanish Bay Reef Resort	Caribbean	Cayman Islands	
Wyndham Rose Hall Golf Resort and Country Club	Caribbean	Jamaica	
Wyndham Sugar Bay Resort and Spa	Caribbean	U.S. Virgin Islands	

AFRICA, ASIA, AND THE PACIFIC

Resort	Region	Location	Adventure
Banyan Tree Maldives	Asia	Maldives	✔
Bedarra Island	The Pacific	Australia	
Chiva-Som International Health Resort	Asia	Thailand	
Club Med Bora Bora	The Pacific	Society Islands	✔
Huka Lodge	The Pacific	New Zealand	✔
Lizard Island Resort	The Pacific	Australia	
MalaMala Game Reserve	Africa	South Africa	✔
Sabi Sabi Private Game Reserve	Africa	South Africa	✔
Samburu Serena Safari Lodge	Africa	Kenya	✔
Sweetwaters Tented Camp	Africa	Kenya	✔
Tiger Tops Jungle Lodge	Asia	Nepal	✔
Turtle Island	The Pacific	Fiji	
Vatulele Island Resort	The Pacific	Fiji	
The Wakaya Club	The Pacific	Fiji	
Yasawa Island Resort	The Pacific	Fiji	

Couples/Romance	Diving/Snorkeling	Dude Ranch	Families	Sportfishing	Gambling	Golf	Horseback Riding	Kids' Program	Safari	Singles	Downhill Skiing	Cross-Country Skiing	Spa/Wellness	Tennis	Sports/Fitness	Weddings	Other
✔	✔					✔				✔			✔		✔		
✔	✔					✔							✔	✔	✔		Cuisine
✔	✔	✔												✔	✔		Private island
✔	✔			✔		✔	✔							✔	✔		Cigar aficionados
✔	✔			✔	✔					✔				✔	✔		
✔	✔		✔	✔			✔	✔						✔	✔	✔	
✔	✔			✔		✔								✔		✔	
✔	✔		✔		✔	✔		✔						✔	✔	✔	
✔	✔					✔							✔	✔	✔		
✔	✔					✔							✔	✔	✔		Cuisine
✔	✔		✔	✔			✔	✔						✔	✔	✔	
✔	✔		✔	✔	✔	✔		✔					✔	✔	✔		
✔	✔													✔		✔	Boating
✔	✔												✔	✔	✔	✔	
✔	✔				✔								✔	✔	✔	✔	Cuisine
✔	✔					✔							✔	✔	✔		
✔	✔		✔	✔						✔							
✔	✔		✔		✔	✔		✔		✔				✔	✔		
	✔			✔			✔		✔	✔				✔	✔		
✔	✔			✔									✔		✔		
✔	✔			✔		✔	✔							✔	✔		Cuisine
✔										✔			✔	✔	✔		
✔	✔		✔	✔						✔				✔			
✔				✔		✔				✔							Cuisine
✔	✔			✔									✔	✔	✔		
✔						✔			✔								
✔									✔								
✔									✔								
✔			✔						✔							✔	
✔									✔								
✔	✔			✔			✔								✔	✔	
✔	✔			✔						✔					✔	✔	
✔	✔			✔		✔								✔	✔		
✔	✔			✔										✔	✔	✔	

Resorts of the World That Offer All-Inclusive Packages

NORTH AMERICA

UNITED STATES

Alaska

	Telephone	Web site	Special Features
Annie Mae Lodge	800-478-2346	www.anniemae.com	Whale watching, fishing
Camp Denali & North Face Lodge	907-683-2290	www.campdenali.com	Wilderness guides, hiking, boating, viewing Mt. McKinley
Denali Wilderness Lodge	800-541-9779	www.denaliwild.com	Fly-in adventure lodge
Glacier Bay Country Inn & Whalesong Lodge	800-628-0912	www.glacierbayalaska.com	Wildlife observation
Gustavus Inn	800-649-5220	www.gustavusinn.com	Wildlife observation
Kantishna Roadhouse	800-942-7420	www.seedenali.com	Hiking, fishing, viewing Mt. McKinley
Kenai Backcountry Lodge	800-334-8730	www.alaskawildland.com/lodges	Accessible by boat, wildlife safaris
Prince William Sound Lodge	907-248-0909	www.alaska.net/~pwslodge/	Beachcombing, sportfishing
Salmon Falls Resort	800-247-9059	www.salmonfallsresort.net	Fishing
Stephan Lake Lodge	907-696-2163	www.alaskaone.com/stephanlake	Fishing, hunting
Waterfall Resort	800-544-5125	www.waterfallresort.com	Fishing, wildlife tours

Arizona

	Telephone	Web site	Special Features
Arizona Biltmore	800-950-0086	www.arizonabiltmore.com	Spa, luxury
The Boulders Resort & Golden Door Spa	800-553-1717	www.wyndham.com/hotels/PHXTB	Spa, golf
Canyon Ranch Health Resort	800-742-9000	www.canyonranch.com	Spa, fitness
Grapevine Canyon Ranch	800-245-9202	www.gcranch.com	Horseback riding
Marriott's Camelback Inn Resort	800-242-2635	www.camelbackinn.com	Spa, luxury, golf
Merv Griffin's Wickenburg Inn Dude Ranch & Tennis Club	900-659-7000	www.phoenix-az-hotels.com/ merv-griffins-wickenburg-inn.htm	Horseback riding, wildlife, tennis, children's program
Phantom Ranch	888-297-2757	www.grandcanyonlodges.com	Horseback riding, hiking
Ranch de la Osa	800-872-6240	www.guestranches.com/ranchdelaosa	Horseback riding, hiking, biking
Saguaro Lake Ranch Resort	602-984-2194	www.duderanches.com/Arizona.htm	Fishing, water sports
Scottsdale Resort and Conference Center	800-528-0293	www.scottsdale-resort.com	Tennis, golf, gym
Tanque Verde Guest Ranch	800-234-3833	www.tvgr.com	Horseback riding, gym, tennis, children's program

	Telephone	Web site	Special Features
California			
The Ashram	818–222–6900	www.ashram.com	Fitness, beauty, spa, yoga
Bacara Resort	877–422–4245	www.bacararesort.com	Luxury resort, spa, golf
Bernardus Lodge	888–648–9463	www.bernardus.com	Wine country, spa treatments, gourmet cuisine
Claremont Resort and Spa	800–551–7266	www.claremontspa.com	Historic hotel, huge spa
Esalen Institute	831–667–3000	www.esalen.org	Spa, spectacular setting
Fairmont Sonoma Mission Inn & Spa	707–938–9000	www.sonomamissioninn.com	Romantic getaway, spa
La Costa Resort and Spa	800–854–5000	www.lacosta.com	Spa, golf, fitness, family, kids
L'Auberge Del Mar Resort & Spa	800–553–1336	www.aubergedelmar.com	Spa, tennis, golf
The Lodge at Skylonda	866–282–3743	www.aubergeresorts.com/html/ldgsky.htm	Fitness, spa
Meadowood	800–458–8080	www.meadowood.com	Spa, croquet, opera on the grass
The Oaks at Ojai	800–753–6257	www.oaksspa.com	Spa, golf, fitness, yoga
Osmosis Enzyme Bath and Massage	707–823–8231	www.osmosis.com	Unique Japanese spa
The Palms at Palm Springs	800–753–7256	www.palmsspa.com	Spa, yoga, golf, fitness
Post Ranch Inn	800–527–2200	www.postranchinn.com	Spa, 30 unique units on 98 acres
Colorado			
Cheyenne Mt. Conference Resort	800–428–8886	www.cheyennemountain.com	Business travel, water sports, golf, tennis
Drowsy Water Ranch	800–845–2292	www.dude-ranch.com/drowsy.water.html	Yoga, spa, New Age
Lane Guest Ranch	303–747–2493	www.ranchweb.com/laneranch/	Horseback riding, teen/kids program
Latigo Ranch	800–227–9655	www.latigotrails.com	Horseback riding, children's program
Lost Valley Ranch	303–647–2311	www.ranchweb.com/lost/	Family, horseback riding, hiking, fishing
The Nature Place	719–748–3475	www.thenatureplace.net	Natural history programs
The Peaks Resort & Spa	970–728–6800	www.wyndham.com/hotels/TEXTP/main.wnt	Spa, luxury, downhill and cross-country skiing
Tall Timber Resort	970–259–4813	www.talltimberresort.com	Golf, tennis, sports
Tumbling River Ranch	800–654–8770	www.tumblingriver.com	Horseback riding, children's program, activities
Wilderness Trails Ranch	800–527–2624	www.wildernesstrails.com	Horseback riding, water sports, children's program
Wind River Ranch	800–523–4212	www.windriverranch.com	Horseback riding, hiking

217

	Telephone	Web site	Special Features
Florida			
Dodgertown Sports and Conference Center	866-656-4900	www.verobeach.com/DodgertownSportsAndConferenceCenter/	Tennis, golf, gym
The Disney Institute	321-939-4600	www.disneyinstitute.com	Spa, fitness, sports
Eden Roc Resort & Spa	800-327-8337	www.edenrocresort.com	Spa, exercise, sports
The Regency House	800-454-0003	www.regencyhealthspa.com	Spa, luxury, golf
Safety Harbor Resort & Spa	800-458-5409	www.safetyharborspa.com	Spa, fitness, tennis
The Wyndham Palace Resort & Spa	866-833-9330	www.wyndham.com/hotels/MCOPY/main.wnt	Spa, fitness
Georgia			
Chateau Elan	800-233-9463	www.chateauelanatlanta.com	Spa, luxury, golf
Greyfield Inn (Cumberland Island)	904-261-6408	www.greyfieldinn.com	Hiking, biking
The Lodge on Little St. Simons Island	888-733-5774	www.littlestsimonsisland.com	Guides, hiking, biking
Hawaii			
Four Seasons Hualalai	800-819-5053	www.fourseasons.com/hualalai	Big Island, luxury, top-rated spa, Jack Nicklaus golf course, cultural center
Four Seasons Wailea	800-819-5053	www.fourseasons.com/maui	Maui, understated luxury, spa with Hawaiian treatments, Spago restaurant
Grand Wailea Resort	800-888-6100	www.grandwailea.com	Maui, Spa Grande, extensive grounds
Lodge at Koele and Manele Bay Hotel	800-321-4666	www.islandoflanai.com	Lanai, top-rated golf courses, luxury ocean-side and up-country hotels
Mauna Lani Resort	800-323-7500	www.maunalani.com	Big Island, elegant spa, culinary programs
Princeville Resort	800-826-4400	www.princeville.com	Kauai, awesome location, spa
Idaho			
Teton Ridge Ranch	208-456-2650	www.tetonridge.com	Luxury, cross-country skiing, horseback riding, hiking
Illinois			
The Heartland Spa	800-545-4853	www.heartlandspa.com	Spa, sports
Maine			
Attean Lake Lodge	207-668-3792	www.atteanlodge.com	Fishing, boating

	Telephone	Web site	Special Features
Quisisana Lodge	207-925-3500	www.quisisanaresort.com	Music lovers, concerts by staff
Migis Lodge	207-655-4524	www.migis.com	Water sports, fishing
Northern Pines Health Resort	207-655-7624	www.maine.com/norpines/	Spa, cross-country skiing, fitness
Maryland			
The Tides Inn	800-843-3746	www.the-tides.com	Boating, golf, yachting
Minnesota			
Birdwing Spa	320-693-6064	www.birdwingspa.com	Spa, fitness, cross-country skiing
Grandview Lodge	800-432-3788	www.grandviewlodge.com	Golf, boating
Gunflint Lodge	800-328-3325	www.gunflint.com	Gym, hiking, cross-country skiing, fishing
Nelson's Resort	800-433-0743	www.nelsonsresort.com	Family resort
Missouri			
The Elms	800-843-3567	www.elmsresort.com	Spa, fitness
Tan-Tar-A Resort Golf Club and Spa	800-826-8272	www.tan-tar-a.com	Golf, children's program
Montana			
Averill's Flathead Lake Lodge & Dude Ranch	406-837-4391	www.averills.com	Tennis, water sports, boating, scuba, horseback riding
Beartooth Ranch & JLX Outfitters	406-328-6194	—	Horseback riding, fishing, wilderness
Lake Upsata Guest Ranch	800-594-7687	www.upsata.com	Boating, white-water rafting, children's program, hiking, wildlife tour
Lone Mountain Ranch	800-514-4644	www.lonemountainranch.com	Horseback riding, children's program, activities, skiing
Mt. Sky Guest Ranch	800-548-3392	www.mtnsky.com	Tennis, horseback riding, fishing, hiking, children's programs
New Hampshire			
Twin Lake Village	603-526-6460	www.twinlakevillage.com	Golf, children's program, boating
New Mexico			
The Lodge at Chama	505-756-2133	www.lodgeatchama.com	Hunting, spa
Vista Clara Ranch	505-466-4772	www.vistaclara.com	Spa, Native American treatments, fitness program
New Jersey			
The Spa at Bally's Park Place Casino Hotel	609-340-2000	www.parkplace.com/ballys/atlanticcity/	Spa, casino

	Telephone	Web site	Special Features
New York			
Athenaeum Hotel	800-821-1881	www.athenaeum-hotel.com	Golf, tennis, fishing, marina
Homowack Resort Hotel	800-243-4567	www.seva.net/stay/resorts.html	Ice rink, bowling, golf, shooting, tennis
Gold Mt. Chalet Resort	800-395-5200	www.goldmtnresort.com	Gym, tennis, cross-country skiing, fishing
Granit Hotel & Country Club	800-431-7681	www.roundthebend.com/catskill/catshot1.html	Golf, tennis, boating
Gurney's Inn Resort Spa and Conference Center	631-668-2345	www.gurneys-inn.com	Spa, fitness
Harrison Conference Center at Glen Cove	516-671-6400	www.harrisonglencove.com	Fitness, tennis
The Inn at Lake Joseph	845-791-9506	www.lakejoseph.com	Sports, wildlife
Jeronimo's Resort	800-888-4683	www.jeronimo.com	Tennis, golf, fishing
Kutsher's Country Club	800-431-1273	www.tennisresortsonline.com/tr	Golf, tennis
Mohonk Mt. House	800-772-6646	www.mohonk.com	Golf, tennis, hiking, children's program
Nevele Grande Resort and Country Club	800-647-6000	www.nevele.com	Golf, skiing, tennis
New Age Health Spa	800-682-4348	www.newagehealthspa.com	Spa, golf, yoga, cross-country skiing
Scott's Oquaga Lake House	607-467-3094	www.scottsfamilyresort.com	Golf, tennis, water sports
Troutbeck Inn	800-978-7688	www.troutbeck.com	Cross-country skiing, tennis
Vatra Mt. Valley Health Resort	888-486-8376	www.huntermtn.com/l-vatra.htm	Spa, weight management, exercise
Villa Roma Resort and Conference Center	800-533-6767	www.villaroma.com	Golf, tennis, sports, nightclub
North Carolina			
High Hampton Inn & Country Club	800-334-2551	www.highhamptoninn.com	Children's program
Westglow Spa	800-562-0807	www.westglow.com	Spa, yoga, fitness
Ohio			
The Kerr House	419-832-1733	www.thekerrhouse.com	Spa, luxury, golf
Pennsylvania			
ACE Center	800-523-3000	—	Golf, tennis
Cliff Park Inn & Golf Course	800-225-6535	www.cliffparkinn.com	Golf, fitness
Deerfield Spa	800-852-4494	www.deerfieldspa.com	Spa, yoga, t'ai chi
Glendorn	800-843-8568	www.glendorn.com	Shooting and fly-fishing instruction, tennis

	Telephone	Web site	Special Features
Skytop Lodge	800–617–2389	www.skytop.com	Golf, tennis, fishing, hiking
Rhode Island			
Weekapaug Inn	401–322–0301	www.weekapauginn.com	Water sports, sailing
Tennessee			
Tennessee Fitness Spa	800–235–8365	www.tfspa.com	Spa, weight training, fitness
Texas			
Dixie Dude Ranch	800–375–9255	www.dixieduderanch.com	Horseback riding, fishing
Four Seasons Resort & Club	800–819–5053	www.fourseasons.com/dallas	Spa, golf, spa, gym
Flying L Guest Ranch	800–292–5134	www.flyingl.com	Golf, horseback riding, sports
Lake Austin Spa Resort	800–847–5637	www.lakeaustin.com	Spa, outdoors programs, cooking and nutrition classes
Mayan Dude Ranch	830–796–3312	www.mayanranch.com	Horseback riding, tennis, fishing
Utah			
Alta Peruvian Lodge	800–453–8488	www.altaperuvian.com	Gym, tennis, hiking, fishing
Utah Trails Resort	800–871–6811	www.utahtrailsresort.com	Wilderness survival, ATVs, tipi lodging
Zion Ponderosa Ranch Resort	800–293–5444	www.zionponderosa.com	ATVs
Vermont			
Basin Harbor Club	800–622–4000	www.basinharbor.com	Children's program, boats, historic hotel
Green Mountain at Fox Run	800–448–8106	www.fitwoman.com	Spa, boating, skiing, women's retreat
New Life Fitness Vacations	800–228–4676	www.newlifehikingspa.com	Exercise, stress management
Twin Farms	800–894–6326	www.twinfarms.com	Hiking, skiing, biking, fishing
The Woodstock Inn	800–448–7900	www.woodstockinn.com	Golf, skiing, fitness
Washington			
Hidden Valley Guest Ranch	800–526–9269	www.hvranch.com	Riding, hiking
Salish Lodge and Spa	800–272–5474	www.salishlodge.com	Spa, fitness, kayaking, mountain biking
West Virginia			
The Greenbrier	800–624–6070	www.greenbrier.com	Spa, cross-country skiing, golf

	Telephone	Web site	Special Features
Wisconsin			
Abbey Resort and Fontana Spa	800-558-2405	www.theabbeyresort.com	Spa, fitness
The American Club	800-344-2838	www.destinationkohler.com	Golf, spa, cuisine
Canoe Bay Resort	715-924-4594	www.canoebay.com	Luxury inn, canoeing, hiking cuisine
Grand Geneva Resort and Spa	800-558-3417	www.grandgeneva.com	Golf, spa, skiing
Wyoming			
CM Dude & Stock Ranch	800-455-0721	www.cmranch.com	Horseback riding, fishing
Double Bar J Guest Ranch	307-455-2681	www.guestranches.com/doublebarj/index_old.htm	Horseback riding, fishing
Double Diamond X Ranch	800-833-RANCH	www.ddxranch.com	Horseback riding, fishing
Heart Six Guest Ranch	888-543-2477	www.heartsix.com	Horseback riding, fishing, hunting, children's program
Lazy L & B Ranch	800-453-9488	www.lazylb.com	Horseback riding, fishing
Moose Head Ranch	307-733-3141	www.wyomingdra.com/moosehead	Horseback riding, fishing
Paradise Guest Ranch	307-684-7876	www.paradiseranch.com	Horseback riding
R Lazy S Ranch	307-733-2655	www.rlazys.com	Horseback riding, fishing, white-water rafting, children's program
Rimrock Dude Ranch	800-208-7468	www.rimrockranch.com	Horseback riding, wilderness, fishing, hunting, rodeo
Triangle X Ranch	307-733-2183	www.trianglex.com	Horseback riding, fishing, hunting
CANADA			
Alberta			
Fairmont Chateau Lake Louise	403-522-3511	www.chateaulakelouise.com	Luxury hotel, Willow Stream spa, skiing, hiking, spectacular setting
WillowStream Spa at the Fairmont Banff Springs Hotel	403-762-2211	www.banffsprings.com	Spa, luxury, downhill and cross-country skiing, fitness
British Columbia			
Flying U Guest Ranch	250-456-7717	www.flyingu.com	Working cattle ranch, airstrip, boating
The Hills Health & Guest Ranch	250-791-5225	www.thehillshealthranch.com	Golf, yoga, spa, horseback riding, biking
King Pacific Lodge	888-592-5464	www.kingpacificlodge.com	Fly-in lodge, fishing, kayaking, wildlife observation
King Salmon Resort	800-663-7090	www.kingsalmonresort.com	Fly-in salmon fishing resort, wildlife viewing

	Telephone	Web site	Special Features
Sundance Guest Ranch	250-453-2422	www.sundance-ranch.com	Horseback riding, children's lounge
Thunderbird Lodge	800-732-2801	www.thunderbirdlodge.com	Fishing, seaplane, boating
The Wickaninnish Inn	800-333-4604	www.wickinn.com	Ancient Cedars Spa, winter storm-watch stays and hikes
Northwest Territories			
Bathurst Inlet Lodge	867-873-2595	www.bathurstinletlodge.com	Extremely secluded, scenic
Frontier Fishing Lodge	877-465-6843	www.frontierfishing.ab.ca	Fishing
High Arctic Lodge	800-661-3880	www.higharctic.com	Fishing
Kasba Lake Lodge	800-663-8641	http://kasba.com	Fishing, boats, guides
Petersons Prelude Lake Lodge	867-920-4654	www.yahoo.com/p/hotel/359865	Fishing, cross-country skiing
Ontario			
Arowhon Pines Resort	705-633-5661	www.arowhonpines.ca	Sports, sailing
The Briars	800-465-2376	www.ontariosfinestinns.com/inn_briars.html	Tennis, golf, children's program
Fern Resort	800-567-3376	www.fernresort.com	Children's program, water sports, cross-country skiing
Hockley Valley Resort	519-942-0754	www.hockley.com	Skiing, water sports
The Inn at Manitou	800-571-8818	www.manitou-online.com	Tennis, spa, fitness, boating
Killarney Mountain Lodge	800-461-1117	www.muskieontario.com	Fishing, hunting, hiking, water sports
Lake Obabika Lodge	705-561-8409	www.obabika.com	Fishing, nature
Quebec			
Auberge du Parc	800-463-0890	www.aubergeduparc.com	Spa, golf
Saskatchewan			
Sportsman's Lodge	800-668-4558	www.sportsmanslodgecanada.com	Seaplane access only, fishing
MEXICO Int Tel: +501			
Acapulco			
Club Bananas Tropical	74-84-22-80	www.acapulco.hotelguide.net/data/h100009.htm	Activities
Las Brisas Acapulco	800-396-1885	www.acapulco-hotels-online.com	Luxury casitas, hillside location
Majestic	74-83-227-13	www.accommodations-source.com/hotels/ACA_acapulco/hotel_majestic.html	Disco, beach club

	Telephone	Web site	Special Features
Parador del Sol	800-297-0144	www.acapulco.the-hotels.com/parador-del-sol.htm	Mini golf, health clubs, dance club
Akumal			
Club Akumal Caribe	800-351-1622	www.locogringo.com/akumal/clubakumal.htm	Beach with reef, diving
Baja			
Palms De Cortez Hotel	800-368-4334	www.bajaresorts.com	Water sports, scuba, tennis, fishing
Rancho Buena Vista	800-258-8200	www.ranchobuenavista.com	Water sports, tennis
Cabo San Lucas			
Hotel Palmilla Resort	800-637-2226	www.palmillaresort.com	Famous Jack Nicklaus-designed 27-hole golf course
Las Ventanas al Paraiso	888-525-0485	www.lasventanas.com	Spa, stunning architecture, luxury
Villa Las Conchas	604-514-9070	www.villa-lasconchas.com	Spa, snorkeling, parasailing
Cancun			
Adventura Spa Palace	800-635-1836	www.palaceresorts.com	Adults only, spa
Beach Palace Hotel	800-695-8284	www.promocaribe.com	Children's program
Blue Bay Club & Marina	800-BLUE-BAY	www.cancun.com/hotels/bluebay/club.stm	Mexican Colonial-style, children's program
Blue Bay Village	800-BLUE-BAY	www.cancun.com/hotels/bluebay/village.stm	Adults only
Cancun Marina Club Hotel	800-221-5333	www.cancun-hotels.net/cancunhotels/marina_club/	Water sports
Carrousel Cancun—A Golden Tulip Hotel	800-555-8842	www.yucatanres.com/pclubCarouselCancun.htm	Live shows, theme parties
Club Med Cancun	888-932-2582	www.clubmed.com	Land and water sports, marina
Costa Real Hotel & Suites	800-543-7556	www.real.com.mx/costareal.asp	Children's program
Crown Paradise Club	800-601-5312	www.hotels-cancun.com/crown-paradise/	Family
Hotel Sierra Cancun	800-448-5028	www.hotels-cancun.com/sierra-cancun/	Tennis, water sports
Hotel Suites Sunset Cancun	998-883-0856	www.cancun.hotelguide.net	Luxury, honeymoon, aerobics
Howard Johnson Hotel Kokai Cancun	800-654-2000	www.hotelkokai.com	—
Jack Tar Village Cancun	800-360-1818	www.cancun-travelnet.com/jacktarvillagecancun.htm	Scuba lessons, marina, adults
Moon Palace	800-360-1818	www.cancun-travelnet.com/moonpalace.htm	Snorkling, kids' club, Mayan ruins
Occidental Caribbean Village Cancun	800-858-2258	www.occidentalhotels.com	Children's program
Omni Cancun Hotel & Villas	800-THE-OMNI	www.omnihotels.com	Diving, fishing, golf, beauty salon, shopping arcade

	Telephone	Web site	Special Features
Royal Solaris Caribe	800-388-9779	www.cancunblast.com/hotels/royalsolariscaribe.html	Marina, disco
Sunset Lagoon Hotel & Marina	800-221-5333	www.cancun.lodgingguide.net	Marina, own beach
Sun Palace	800-346-8225	www.expertszmexico.com	Water sports, tennis, gym, scuba
Tucan Cun Beach	998-891-5900	www.tucancunbeach.com	Water sports center, golf
Yalmakan Cancun Hotel & Marina	800-654-5543	www.yalmakan.com	Water sports, tennis
Copper Canyon			
Cabanas Divisadero Barrancas	14-15-11-99	www.coppercanyonhotels.com.mx	Canyon trips
Copper Canyon Sierra Lodge	800-776-3942	www.coppercanyonlodges.com	Canyon tours, hiking
Cozumel			
Club Cozumel Caribe	800-327-2254	www.clubcozumelcaribe.com	Nautilus gym, kids' club, starlight cruises, boating, fishing
Crown Princess Cozumel	800-266-9446	—	Gym, disco, children's program
Diamond Resort Cozumel	800-628-2216	—	Dive, honeymoon
El Cozumeleno Beach	800-437-3923	—	Families
Galapago Inn	800-847-5708	—	Dive resort, scuba
Cuernavaca			
Hosteria las Quintas	800-990-1888	www.hlasquintas.com	Spa, fitness, water sports, boating
Guadalajara			
Rancho Rio Caliente	650-615-9543	www.riocaliente.com	Spa, yoga, hiking, spa cuisine
Huatulco			
Crown Pacific Huatulco	888-279-9161	—	Water sports, children's program
Royal Maeva Resort	909-471-8208	www.tropicalsands.com/Resorts/Maeva/maevagroup.htm	Children's club, scuba, water sports, gym
Ixtapa/Zihuatanejo			
Club Med Ixtapa	800-CLUB-MED	www.clubmed.com	Children's program, horseback riding, fishing, water sports
Hotel Spa Ixtapan	800-638-7950	www.hotelixtapan.com	Tennis, golf, horseback riding, water sports
Ixtapa Hotel & Spa	714-30304	—	Spa, golf, boating
La Casa Que Canta	800-525-4800	www.slh.com/casaquecanta/	Exquisite cliff-side hotel, private pool suites, golf

	Telephone	Web site	Special Features
Manzanillo			
Club Maeva Hotel & Resort	800-GOMAEVA	www.pacificmexico.com/resorts/clubmaeva.html	Water sports, children's program
Hotel Sierra Manzanillo	800-448-5028	www.lodging4less.com/manzanillo-hotels.php	Water sports, tennis
Las Hadas Golf Resort & Marina	341-331-0101	www.lashadasbrisasmanzanillo.com	Golf, boating, unusual architecture
Los Angeles Locos Hotel	800-483-7986	www.sunresortslosangeleslocos.com	Water sports, tennis, tours
Playa De Oro Manzanillo	800-882-8215	www.pacificmexico.com/resorts/manzanillo.html	Tennis, beach club
Mazatlan			
Sea Garden	866-270-2847	www.anyhotelanywhere.com/findhotel3.cmf/198507	Tennis, golf
Sierra Nuevo Vallarta	800-448-5028	www.pacificmexico.com/resorts/sierranuevo.html	Disco, water sports, scuba, children's program
Nuevo Vallarta			
Diamond Resort Nuevo Vallarta	800-858-2258	www.mexicohotels.com/worl5000.html	Water sports, children's program, tennis, scuba
Four Seasons Punta Mita	800-819-5053	www.fourseasons.com/puntamita	Spa, Jack Nicklaus golf course, cultural programs
Grand Velas Suites & Spa Resort	877-398-2784	www.grandvelas.com	Water sports, golf, spa
Occidental Grande Nuevo Vallarta	866-270-2847	www.occidentalhotels.com	Wind surfing, sailing, kayaking
Playa Del Carmen			
El Dorado Resort & Spa	800-727-7388 (Infinity Resorts)	www.eldorado-resort.com/doradoresort/	Adults only, spa and health club
Occidental Caribbean Village Playacar Golf & Beach Club	800-858-2258	www.locogringo.com/playa/caribbeanvillage.html	Water sports, golf, boating, children's program
Robinson Club Tulum	800-CLUB-770	www.playaguide.com/resorts/robinson.html	Land and water sports, children's program
Puerto Vallarta			
Costa Azul	800-365-7613	www.costaazul.com	Water sports, mountain biking, eco-adventures
Crown Paradise Puerto Vallarta	888-300-6394	www.hotels-puerto-vallarta.com/crown-paradise/	Adults only
Meliá Puerto Vallarta	800-33-MELIA	www.solmelia.com	Pool, scuba diving lessons; golf nearby
Qualton Club & Spa	800-446-2727	www.qualton.com	Spa, exercise
Vista Club Playa de Oro	866-270-2847	www.vallartaonline.com/accommodations/hotels/vistaclub/default.asp	Water sports, tennis

CENTRAL AND SOUTH AMERICA

	Telephone	Web Site	Special Features
CENTRAL AMERICA			
Belize	**Int Tel: +501**		
Duplooy's Hotel and Jungle Cottages	800–882–2636	www.tourtech.net/bel_cayo_duplooy.html	Jungle bungalows; canoeing; overlooks river and jungle
El Pescador Hotel	800–242–2017	www.elpescadorpg.com	Sportfishing resort
Lamanai Outpost Lodge	888–733–7864	www.lamanai.com	Overlooks Lamanai Mayan Ruins; river safari
Lighthouse Reef Resort	800–423–3114	www.lighthousereefresort.com	Scuba diving
Maruba Jungle Resort & Spa	322–2199	www.maruba-spa.com	Spa, safari, adventure tours
Maya Mountain Lodge	824–2164	www.mayamountain.com	Canoeing to Mayan Medicine Trail
Paradise Inn	888–875–9453	www.travel-belize.com/crooktre.htm	Located in Crooked Tree Wildlife Sanctuary
Rum Point Inn	888–747–1381	www.rumpoint.com	Boating, fishing, scuba diving
St. George Caye Lodge	800–678–6871	www.gooddiving.com	Scuba diving
Costa Rica	**Int Tel: +506**		
Barcelo Playa Tambor Beach Resort	800–858–0606	www.travelsite.com.cr/playa-tambor.htm	Fishing, water sports
Hotel El Establo Monteverde	645–7070	www.monteverdeinfo.com/establo	Hiking in cloud forest, Quaker-owned
Lapa Rios Rainforest Ecolodge	735–5130	www.laparios.com	Luxury in the jungle, birding, jungle walks
Ocotal Beach Resort	258–6363	www.ocotalresort.com	Scuba diving, sport fishing
Volcano Lodge	645–7070	www.arenal.net/hotel/volcano-lodge.htm	Watch Arenal volcano erupt
El Salvador	**Int Tel: +503**		
Tesoro Beach & Country Club	34–902–180–743	www.interhotel.com/el_salvador/en/hoteles.93245.html	Tennis, golf, marina
Honduras	**Int Tel: +504**		
Anthony's Key Resort	800–227–3483	www.anthonyskey.com	Scuba diving
Bahia Resort	45–42–12	www.bayislandsonline.com	Water sports, dive resort
Fantasy Island Beach Resort Dive & Marina	888–636–3655	www.fantasyislandresort.com/us/	Scuba, private island, water sports
Lost Paradise Inn	445–13–06	www.lost-paradise.com	Water sports, scuba
Posada del Sol	800–642–3483	www.posadadelsol.com	Gym, marina, dive center

	Telephone	Web Site	Special Features
Panama	**Int Tel: +507**		
Contadora Resort & Casino (Contadora Island)	800–207–6900	www.hotelbook.com/static/welcome_28231.html	Water sports, deep-sea fishing
Tropic Star Lodge	800–682–3424	www.tropicstar.com	Fishing
SOUTH AMERICA			
Brazil	**Int Tel: +55**		
Ariau Jungle Lodge	877–566–8454	www.kontiki.org/brazil/ariau.htm	Touring jungle
Club Med Itaparica	800–CLUB-MED	www.clubmed.com	Island resort, sports, children's program
Club Med Rio das Pedras	800–CLUB-MED	www.clubmed.com	Water sports, children's club
Chile	**Int Tel: +56**		
Cumilahue Fishing Lodge	63-4810-15	www.travel.yahoo.com/p/hotel/327073	Fishing
Explora Atacoma Lodge	800–811–8829	www.chile-tours.com/explora.htm	Luxury desert resort, stunning architecture, spa
Hotel Salto Chico	61-229–081	www.ventistar.com/explora.html	Land exploration, children's program, skiing
Portillo Hotel	800–811–8829	www.chile-hotels.com/portillo.htm	Skiing resort
Valle Nevado Ski Resort	800–811–8829	www.chile-hotels.com/vallenev.htm	Skiing
Colombia	**Int Tel: +57**		
Decameron Cartagena	655–1055	www.decameron.com/Cartagena.asp	Fishing, children's program
Decameron Royal Aquarium	866-321–8747	www.travellastminute.ca/LMT-Panama&SanAndres.html	Sailing, horseback riding, hiking
Guyana	**Int Tel: +592**		
Emerald Tower	22–72011–14	www.towerhotelguyana.com/emeraldtower.htm	Nature resort, rainforest
The Gazebo	22–66306	www.turq.com/guyana/stay.html	Water sports, jungle tours
Shanklands Rain Forest Resort	22–51586	www.turq.com/guyana/stay.html	Rain forest, nature, water sports
Timberhead Eco-Resort	22–54483	www.turq.com/guyana/stay.html	Jungle, wildlife
Peru	**Int Tel: +51**		
Amazon Camp	94-23–3931	www.interhotel.com/peru/en/hoteles/109709.html	Wildlife, rainforest
Amazon Lodge	221–3341	www.peru-hotels.com/iquimaz.htm	Jungle, canoeing
Explorama Inn	94-25–2530	www.s-h-systems.uk/peru/iquitos48028.html	City hotel, jump-off point for jungle exploring

	Telephone	Web Site	Special Features
Explorama Inn Explornapo	94-25-2530	www.travel-peru.net/canopy_walkway_iquitos.htm	Jungle, hiking
Hotel Monasterio	888-723-0699	www.davidtours.com/monasterio.html	Historic Cuzco hotel
Hotel Ruinas Machu Picchu	510-420-1550	www.inca1.com/peru.htm	Hotel at edge of ruin, newly renovated
Venezuela	**Int Tel: +58**		
Dunes Resort (Allegro)	800-645-1179	www.fortmeyers.com/turks/allegro_venezuela_dunes.html	Water sports; golf available
Flamingo Beach Resort	295-261-1131	www.ecotourismonline.com/margarita/accommodation.asp	Water sports, children's program
Laguna Mar	800-858-2258	www.latintravel.com/academy/hotels.cfm?country=venezuela	Lighted tennis courts, basketball, volleyball, casino
Margarita International Resort	95-61-1667	www.casinocity.com/ve/islademargarita/venebarak/	Tennis, gym, casino

CARIBBEAN ISLANDS AND THE BAHAMAS

	Telephone	Web Site	Special Features
Antigua and Barbuda			
K-Club	268-460-0304	www.caribbean.wheretostay.com/property/049.html	Water sports
Rex Blue Heron	800-255-5859	www.rexcaribbean.com/Resorts/Antigua/RexBlueHeron/rex.blue.heron.antigua.html	Water sports and entertainment
Rex Halcyon Cove	800-777-7739	www.caribbeanpalms.com/resorts/rexantigua.html	Water skiing, horseback riding
Royal Antiguan	800-345-0356	www.eliteislands.com	Beach and tennis resort, children's program
Sandals Antigua	800-SANDALS	www.sandals.com	Sports, boat sailing
Sunset Cove Resort	268-462-3762	www.caribbeanhighlights.com/sunset/	Boating, fishing
Aruba			
Americana Aruba Beach Resort & Casino	297-8-24500	www.casinochecker.com/real_casinos/world/aruba/	Casino, children's program
Aruba Grand	800-345-2782	www.arubagrand.com	Casino, diving
Aruba Marriott Resort & Stellaris Casino	800-223-6388	www.marriott.com/epp/?Marshacode=AUAAR	Casino, children's program
Bushiri All-Inclusive Beach Resort	954-562-3814	www.tropicalresort.com/bushiriaruba.htm	Honeymoon, children's program
Holiday Inn Aruba Beach Resort & Casino	297-58-63600	www.holidayinn.aruba.ichotelsgroup.com	Theme nights, fitness center
La Cabana All Suite Beach Resort	800-835-7193	www.lacabana.com	Water sports, casino/showroom

	Telephone	Web Site	Special Features
Occidental Grand Aruba	800-858-2258	www.occidentalhotels.com	Swimming, kayaking
Renaissance Aruba Beach Resort & Casino	800-421-8188	www.arubarenaissance.com/travel/carib/aruba	Full water sports facilities, children's program, casino
Tamarijn Aruba Beach Resort	800-426-5445	www.ehi.com/travel	Tennis, water sports
Wyndham Aruba Beach Resort & Casino	800-WYNDHAM	www.wyndham.com/hotels/AUAPB/main.wnt	Casino, water sports
Bahamas			
Atlantis Paradise Island	888-528-7155	www.atlantis.com	Huge resort in four wings, walk-through aquarium, water sports
Club Viva Fortuna	242-373-4000	www2.vivaresorts.com/vf/	Wedding packages, dive club
Lucayan Beach Resort & Casino	242-373-7777	www.interhotel.com/bahamas/en/hoteles/23608.html	Must be at least 16 years old; water sports
Nassau Beach Hotel	242-327-7711	www.nassaubeachhotel.com	Six tennis courts
Peace & Plenty Beach Inn	800-525-2210	www.peaceandplenty.com	World-class bonefishing, three small resorts
Pt. Lucaya Resort and Yacht Club	800-LUCAYA-1	www.portlucayaresort.com	Marina, children's program
Sheraton Grand	800-782-9488	www.sheratongrand.com	Snorkeling
Barbados			
Coconut Court Beach Hotel	246-427-1655	www.coconut-court.com	Children's program, water sports packages
Crystal Cove Hotel	877-364-1100	www.islandinns.com/ob.html	Tennis, golf, windsurfing
Island Inn Hotel	800-448-0011	www.bajan.com/barbados/hotels/islandin/islandin/htm	Scuba lessons, cruises
Mango Bay Club	800-223-9815	www.mangobaybarbados.com	Water sports, water skiing, snorkeling, scuba, boating
Oasis Hotel	800-223-9815	www.barbados.org/hotels/oasis	Catamaran sailing, scuba lessons
Sandy Lane	246-444-2000	www.sandylane.com	Ultra elegant, golf, spa, tennis, children's program
Turtle Beach Hotel	246-428-7131	www.hotelsdeluxe.com/turtlebeach/	Golf, fishing, horseback riding
Welcome Inn Beach Hotel	800-223-6810	www.funbarbados.com/Lodgings/welcomeinn.cfm	Indoor/water activities, children's program
Bermuda			
Ariel Sands	800-468-6610	www.arielsands.com	Luxury cottages, spa, snorkeling pool, tennis
Cambridge Beaches	800-468-7300	www.cambridgebeaches.com	Antique-filled cottages, world-class spa, marina
Grotto Bay Beach	800-330-8272	www.grottobaybeach.com	Snorkeling, boating, diving
Bonaire			
Harbour Village Beach Resort	800-424-0004	www.harbourvillage.com	Spa, luxury, snorkeling, hiking and biking

	Telephone	Web Site	Special Features
British Virgin Islands			
Guana	800-223-1108	www.guana.com	Private island, secluded beaches, hiking
Mango Bay	800-621-1270	www.caribbeans.com/2bvi/3mango/3mango.htm	Hiking, snorkeling
Cayman Islands			
Pirates Point Resort	345-948-1010	www.piratespointresort.com	Diving, water sports, sailing
Southern Cross Club	800-899-2582	www.southerncrossclub.com	World-class diving, fishing
Treasure Island Resort	345-949-7777	http://cayman.wheretostay.com	Tennis, scuba diving
Curacao			
Habitat Curacao	5999-864-8800	www.habitatdiveresorts.com	Diving, spa, mountain biking
Dominican Republic			
Allegro's Caribbean Village Luperon	809-571-8180	www.dominican.republic.hotelguide.net/data/h100005.htm	Children's program, archery
Amhsa Camino Del Sol	809-571-0894	www.amhsamarina.com	Horseback riding, tennis, volleyball
Amhsa Casa Marina Bay	809-538-0020	www.amhsamarina.com	Kid's Club, volleyball, tennis, water sports
Amhsa Casa Marina Beach	809-571-3690	www.amhsamarina.com	Tennis, water sports
Amhsa Casa Marina Reef	809-571-3535	www.amhsamarina.com	Boating, water sports, evening entertainment
Amhsa Grand Paradise Bavaro	809-221-2121	www.amhsamarina.com	Kid's Club, horseback riding, volleyball, spa
Amhsa Paradise Beach Club & Casino	809-320-3663	www.amhsamarina.com	Bicycles, tennis, horseback riding
Amhsa Paraiso Del Sol	809-571-0894	www.amhsamarina.com	Badminton, horseback riding, evening entertainment
Bayside Hill Resort & Beach Club	800-322-2388	—	Nine-hole golf, fitness
Casa de Campo	800-877-3643	www.caribinfo.com/hotels/dominican_republic.html	Golf, horseback riding, polo
Club Med Punta Cana	800-258-2633	www.clubmed.com	Sports, water sports, non-motorized sports
Coral Costa Caribe	800-338-4962	www.resortvacationstogo.com	Casino, pro tennis lessons, kid's program, water sports
Coral Marien Beach Hotel & Spa	800-330-8272	www.changes.com/resorts/coral-marien/	Kid's club, water park, scuba diving, golf
Gran Ventana Beach Resort	809-412-2525	www.abstravel.com/tours/gran_ventana_beach_resort.shtml	Live music, water sports, snorkeling
Iberostar Bavaro Resort	800-330-8272	www.changes.com/resorts/iberostar-bavaro/	Casino, discoteque, water sports
Iberostar Costa Dorada	800-330-8272	www.conquestvacations.com/IBCD.html	Water sports, windsurfing, tennis

	Telephone	Web Site	Special Features
Iberostar Hacienda Dominicus	800–538–7461	www.changes.com/resorts/iberostar-hacienda-dominicus/	Snorkeling, spa, billiards, children's program
Interclubs Fun Royale	809–320–4811	www.caribinfo.com/hotels/dominican_republic.html	Archery, children's program, golf
Interclubs Fun Tropicale	809–320–4811	www.caribinfo.com/hotels/dominican_republic.html	Archery, children's program, water sports
Meliá Caribe Tropical	800–33–MELIA	www.solmelia.com	Tennis, pool, non-motorized sports, kids club, tram ride
Occidental Allegro Flamenco Punta Cana	800–858–2258	www.occidentalhotels.com.	Deep-sea fishing, water sports
Occidental Allegro Grand Flamenco Puerto Plata	800–858–2258	www.occidentalhotels.com	Robert Trent Jones golf course, water sports
Occidental Allegro Jack Tar Puerto Plata	800–858–2258	www.occidentalhotels.com	Golf, casino, games
Occidental Allegro Playa Grande	800–858–2258	www.occidentalhotels.com	Water sports, Robert Trent Jones golf course
Occidental Allegro Punta Cana	800–858–2258	www.occidentalhotels.com	Water sports, snorkeling, fitness
Playa Naco Golf & Tennis Resort	800–322–2388	www.caribinfo.com/hotels/dominican_republic.html	Windsurfing, horseback riding, children's program
Puerto Plata Beach Resort and Casino	809–586–4243	www.america-hotels-travel.net	Windsurfing, casino/disco
Puerto Plata Village	809–320–5113	www.dominican.republic.hotelguide.net	Golf course, children's program
Riu Bachata Puerto Plata	800–742–6081	www.hotels4travellers.com	Water sports, dancing lessons, nightly entertainment
Riu Mambo	800–742–6081	www.hotels4travellers.com	Nightly entertainment, vegetarian menu
Riu Merengue	800–742–6081	www.hotels4travellers.com	Water sports, children's program
Rumba Heavens	800–742–6081	www.hotels4travellers.com	Golf, scuba diving
Sea Horse Ranch	809–635–0991	www.sea-horse-ranch.com	Luxury villas, horseback riding, tennis
Talanquera Country & Beach Resort	809–526–1510	www.thedominicanrepublic.net	Beach, boat rides, disco, cave tours, horseback riding
Victoria Resort Hotel	809–320–1200	www.dominican.republic.express-hotel-guide.com	Live music, water sports
Grenada			
Coyaba Beach Resort	473–444–4129	www.coyaba.com	Swim-up bar, tennis
Rex Grenadian	800–255–5859	www.rexcaribbean.com	Windsurfing
Spice Island Beach Resort	473–444–4259	www.grenadaexplorer.com/spice/index.htm	Honeymoon, private pool and whirlpool suites
Guadeloupe			
Club Med Caravelle	800–258–2633	www.clubmed.com	Sports, yoga, tennis
Jamaica			
Bay Vista Village	876–995–3071	www.beautiful-jamaica.com/HOTELS4.htm	Tennis, fitness

	Telephone	Web Site	Special Features
Boscobel Beach	888–703–2582	www.allinclusivevacationresorts.com/1115.html	Children's center
Breezes Montego Bay	877–GO–SUPER	www.superclubs.com	Disco, all water sports
Coral Seas Beach Resort	877–552–8299	www.visitnegril.com/coral-seas.html	River safari, scuba, children's program
Coral Seas Cliff Resort	877–552–8299	www.visitnegril.com/coral-seas.html	On the cliffs
Coral Seas Garden Resort	877–552–8299	www.visitnegril.com/coral-seas.html	Bird sanctuary, Royal Palm reserve, river safari
Club Ambiance	800–822–3274	www.clubambiance.com	Adults only; PADI 5-star diving school
Club Caribbean	800–426–5445	www.clubcaribbean.com	Families
Eaton Hall Hotel	800–926–6836	www.worldwidevacations.com/caribb/jamaica/jam134.htm	Small, intimate, relaxed
The Enchanted Garden	809–554–2008	www.caribbean.wheretostay.com/property/424.html	Spa, gym, tennis
Fern Hill Club	876–993–7374	www.portantoniojamaica.com/contact.htm	Tennis, honeymoon, cave rafting
Holiday Inn Sunspree Resort	800–465–4329	www.holiday-inn.com	Complete children's program, disco
Jack Tar Village Montego Bay	800–999–9182	www.caribbean.wheretostay.com/property/426.html	PADI 5-star dive facility
Negril Inn	876–957–4209	www.caribbean.wheretostay.com/property/629.html	Sports, water sports
Point Village	877–764–6852	www.pointvillage.com	Children's center
Renaissance Jamaica Grande Resort	800–932–2198	www.marriott.com	Honeymoon/wedding, children's program, casino
Round Hill Hotel and Villas	800–972–2159	www.roundhilljamaica.com	Rafting, plantation tours
Sandals Inn	800–SANDALS	www.sandals.com	Budget
Sandals Ocho Rios Resort	800–SANDALS	www.sandals.com	Water sports, tennis, basketball, fitness center, golf
Sandals Royal Caribbean	800–SANDALS	www.sandals.com	Golf, boat sailing, plantation style
Shaw Park Beach Hotel	888–254–0637	www.clickcitytravel.com/findhotelb.cfm/_10215544	Disco nightclub, health club
Starfish Ocho Rios Resort	800–818–2964	www.caribbeanvisitorcenter.com/listhotels.aspx	Kids' program
Starfish Trelawny Beach Hotel	800–569–5436	www.starfishresorts.com	Children's program, water sports
Martinique			
Club Med Buccaneers Creek	800–258–2633	www.clubmed.com	Nightlife, tennis
Puerto Rico			
Radisson Ambassador Plaza Hotel and Casino	800–468–8512	www.radisson.com	Swimming, snorkeling
The Westin Rio Mar Beach	888–627–8556	www.westinriomar.com	Children's activities, fitness, spa

	Telephone	Web Site	Special Features
Wyndham El Conquistador Resort & Country Club	800-468-5228	www.wyndham.com	Championship golf course
Wyndham El San Juan Hotel and Casino	877-999-3223	www.wyndham.com	Casino, children's program
St. Barts			
Le Jardins de Gustavia	888-349-7800	www.paradiselodging.com	Shell Beach, quiet spot
La Residence Villas	800-621-1270	www.caribbeans.com/2stbarts/2stbarts/htm	Sweeping views, seven swimming pools
Sereno Beach Hotel	800-621-1270	www.caribbeans.com/2stbarts/2stbarts/htm	Hobie cats sailing, scuba diving, fitness center
St. Barths Beach Hotel	800-621-1270	www.caribbeans.com/2stbarts/2stbarts/htm	French atmosphere, windsurfing school, tennis
St. Kitts and Nevis			
The Golden Lemon Villas & Spa	869-465-7260	www.goldenlemon.com	17th-century Great House, lap pool, snorkeling, scuba
Jack Tar Village Royal St. Kitts Beach Resort & Casino	866-235-9330	www.allinclusiveresorthotels.com/all-inclusive/jack-tar-village-st-kitt.htm	Children's program, casino
Ottley's Plantation Inn	800-772-3039	www.ottleys.com	Gardens, 18th-century sugar plantation
St. Lucia			
Anse Chastanet Resort	800-223-1108	www.ansechastanet.com	Unique rooms, spectacular setting, honeymoons
Club St. Lucia	800-777-1250	www.splashresorts.com/club_home.html	Family, bungalow style
East Winds Inn	758-452-8212	www.eastwinds.com	Surrounded by coral reef, snorkeling, honeymoon
Ladera Resort	800-223-9868	www.ladera-stlucia.com	Spectacular hillside setting, open-air accommodations
Rex Papillon	800-255-5859	www.rexcaribbean.com	Water sports activities, children's program
Rex St. Lucian	800-255-5859	www.rexcaribbean.com	Scuba diving
Royal St. Lucian	800-255-5859	www.rexcaribbean.com	Sailing, spa
Sandals Halcyon St. Lucia	800-SANDALS	www.sandals.com	Tropical gardens, seven bars
Sandals St. Lucia Golf & Spa Resort	800-SANDALS	www.sandals.com	Water sports, tennis, basketball, fitness center, entertainment
Stonefield Estate Villa Resort	758-459-7037	www.stonefieldvillas.com	Spectacular view, scuba diving, rainforest tours
Ti Kaye Village Resort	758-456-8101	www.tikaye.com	French creole cottages, snorkeling, secluded beach
Windjammer Landing Beach Resort	800-613-7193	www.windjammer-landing.com	Lighted tennis courts, body treatment center

	Telephone	Web Site	Special Features
St. Martin/Maarten			
Great Bay Beach Hotel & Casino	599-542-2446	www.greatbayhotel.com	Sailing, sunset cruise
Hotel L'Esplanade Caraibes	877-364-1100	www.islandinns.com/40.html	Honeymoon, deep-sea fishing, diving
Le Flamboyant Hotel & Resort	800-221-5333	www.west-indies-online.com/Le-Flamboyant/default.html	Honeymoon, diving, water sports
Privilege Resort & Spa	800-874-8541	www.privilege-spa.com	Spa, luxury, sports
St. Vincent and The Grenadines			
Petit Byahaut	809-457-7008	www.outahere.com/petitbyahaut	Cave snorkeling, water sports, rain forest
Young Island Resort	800-223-1108	www.youngisland.com	Private island, four private yachts
Tortola			
Prospect Reef Resort	800-356-8937	www.prospectreef.com	Diving, fitness center
Trinidad and Tobago			
Chaconia Hotel	868-628-0941	www.chaconiahotel.com	Newly renovated, shopping, golf, surfing nearby
Rex Turtle Beach	800-255-5889	www.rexcaribbean.com	Snorkeling
Turks and Caicos			
Club Med Turkoise	800-258-2633	www.clubmed.com	All sports; no children allowed
Meridian Club	866-746-3229	www.meridianclub.com	Fishing, snorkeling
Windmills Plantation	800-822-7715	www.windmillsplantation.com	Swimming, secluded beach
U.S. Virgin Islands			
Bolongo Bay Beach Club and Villas	340-775-1800	www.bolongobay.com	Sports bar, parasailing
Chenay Bay Beach Resort	800-548-4457	www.chenaybay.com	Tropical sports, wedding, honeymoon
Marriott Frenchman's Reef	800-223-6388	www.marriottfrenchmansreef.com	Scuba diving, health club, spa
Hibiscus Beach Hotel	800-442-0121	www.st-croix.com/hibiscus/	Casual, snorkeling

EUROPE

	Int Tel: +376		
Andorra			
Hotel Roc Blanc	871-400	www.andorrahotels.com	Spa, health

	Telephone	Web Site	Special Features
Austria	**Int Tel: +43**		
Grand Park Hotel Bad Hofgastein	6432–63560	www.spas.about.com/cs/austriaresort/index.htm	Beach, water sports, tennis
Josefinenhof Hotel Park	4242-3003–0	www.josefinenhof.at	Spa
Zuerserhof Hotel	5583-2513–0	www.zuerserhof.at	Winter resort, gym, tennis, golf
Croatia	**Int Tel: +385**		
Pakostane	800-258-2633	www.clubmed.com	Children's club, tennis, sailing
England	**Int Tel: +44**		
Champneys at Tring (Hertfordshire)	1442 291 111	www.champneys.com	Extensive grounds, health spa, gym sports
Grayshott Hall Health Fitness Retreat (Surrey)	1428 602 000	www.grayshott-hall.co.uk	Spa, exercise, Alfred Tennyson's home
Henlow Grange Health Farm (Bedfordshire)	6281 1111	www.spafinder.com	Fitness classes, spa, manor house
Hoar Cross Hall Health Resort (Straffordshire)	1283 575 671	www.hoarcross.co.uk	Spa, exercise, Jacobean manor
Inglewood Health Farm (Berkshire)	1488 682–022	www.inglewoodhealth.co.uk	Spa, tennis, gym, nutrition consultant
France	**Int Tel: +33**		
Hotel Le Bellecote	4-79–08-10–19	www.lebellecote.com	Skiing, gym
Carlina Hotel	4-79–08-00–30	www.lodgingfrance.com/Courchevel/Carlina/	Skiing, gym
Club Med Chamonix	800-258-2633	www.clubmed.com	Skiing, children club, fitness
Club Med Opio	800-258-2633	www.clubmed.com	Tennis, golf, spa, children's program, circus school
Club Med Tignes Val Claret	800-258-2633	www.clubmed.com	Skiing, children's program
Hotel le Chastillon	4-93-23-26–00	www.isolahotelreservations.com/fr/	Skiing
Hotel Miramar	5-5941–3001	www.touradour.com/towns/biarritz/miramar/ fr/hotel_miramar_biarritz.htm	Spa, activities
Hotel Thalazur Antibes	888–783–1342	www.cmtravelonline.com/thalazur.htm	Spa, fitness room
Les Ducs de Savoie Hotel	4-79–08-03–00	www.lesducsdesavoie.com	Skiing, gym
Les Sherpas Hotel	4-79–08-02–55	www.hotel-les-sherpas.com/gb/partenaire.htm	Skiing
Mont Chalusset Hotel	4-73–86-00–17	www.hotel-montchalusset.com	Casino, thermal springs
Riva Bella Normandie Hotel	2-31–96-4040	www.spafinder.com	Spa
Sofitel Dietetique	2-97-50–20-00	www.spaworldtravel/com/france	Spa, gym, tennis

	Telephone	Web Site	Special Features
Germany	**Int Tel: +49**		
Brenner's Park Hotel	72-21-9000	www.brenners-park.com	Spa, gym
Hotel Schloss Hugenpoet	2054-1204-0	www.travel-hotels-germany.com/nordrheim-westfalen-hotels/bochum-hotels-3.htm	1695 castle with moat; tennis
Schlosshotel Buhlerhohe	7226-550	www.lhw.com	Spa, skiing, golf, tennis
Greece	**Int Tel: +30**		
Club Med Corfou Ipsos	800-258-2633	www.clubmed.com	No bath or electricity; tennis, water sports
Club Med Gregolimano	800-258-2633	www.clubmed.com	Waterskiing, wakeboard
Club Med Kos (Kos Island)	800-258-2633	www.clubmed.com	Sports, water sports, children's club
Club Med Mare Nostrum	800-258-2633	www.clubmed.com	Beginner's lessons for water sports, thalassotherapy
Hydra Beach Hotel & Bungalows (Peloponnesus)	27540-41206	http://travel-yahoo.com/p/hotel/327542	Water sports, tennis
Kydon Hotel (Crete Island)	2821-52280	www.kydon-hotel.com	Nearby water sports; golf and tennis
Mediterranean Hotel (Cehalonia Island)	671-28760	—	Water sports, nightclub
Ireland	**Int Tel: +353**		
Nuremore Hotel	800-869-4330	www.hotel-ireland.com/hotels/ecoastmid/monaghan/nuremore-hotel/	Golf, tennis, gym, fishing, deep-sea fishing
Italy	**Int Tel: +39**		
Abruzzo Marina Hotel (Teramo)	85-930-397	www.abruzzo2000.com/abruzzo/hotel/teramo	Scuba, water sports, fishing
Arizona Hotel (Forli)	541-644-422	http://interhotel.com/italy/en/hoteles/42705.html	Water sports
Cala Di Volpe Hotel	789-976-111	www.luxurycollection.com/caladivolpe	Putting green, tennis, harbor
Club Med Caprera (Sardinia)	800-258-2633	www.clubmed.com	Largest sailing school, tennis, children's club
Club Med Cefalu (Sicily)	800-258-2633	www.clubmed.com	Adults only; sailing, kayaking summer only
Club Med Donoratico	800-258-2633	www.clubmed.com	Tennis, sailing, circus school, children's club
Club Med Kamarina (Sicily)	800-258-2633	www.clubmed.com	Tennis, children's club, circus school
Club Med Metaponto	800-258-2633	www.clubmed.com	Tennis, children and baby's club, circus school; open May to September
Club Med Otranto	800-258-2633	www.clubmed.com	Golf, snorkeling, sailing (summer); adults only
Colibri Hotel (Savona)	19-69-26-81	www.mototurista.it/citta.php/cittaA41.php	Family hotel, marina

	Telephone	Web Site	Special Features
Columbia Hotel	49-866-9606	www.venice.hotelguide.net/hl1sc.htm	Spa
Hotel Elma Park	81-994-122	www.hotelelma.it	Water sports, gym, tennis, children's program
Hotel Europa Palace (Capri)	81-837-3800	www.made-in-italy.com/travel/spas/capri/capri.htm	Spa, gym, water sports
Hotel Terme Continental	49-793-522	www.venice.lodgingguide.net/venice-lodging-continental-terme-hotel-100016.htm	Spa, gym, tennis, miniature golf
Gallia Palace Hotel	564-922-022	www.tuscany.net/galliapalace/index.htm	Golf, tennis, water sports
Grand Hotel Astoria (Gorizia)	431-835-50	www.vacans.it/grado-hotels	Gym, spa, children's program
Grand Hotel Diplomat (Rimini)	541-962-200	www.itahotels.com/cattolica/diplomat.htm	Gym, tennis, children's program
Grand Hotel Don Juan (Teramo)	85-800-8341	http://duialca.com/donjuan/	Gym, tennis, marina
Grand Hotel Porro (Parma)	524-578-221	www.hotelbenessere.it	Spa, gym, jogging track
Grand Hotel San Michele (Cosenza)	982-910-12	www.esperia.it/smichele_ing.htm	Gym, golf, tennis
Grand Hotel Trieste & Victoria	49-866-9101	www.golftoursandtravel.com/grandhoteltriestevictoria.htm	Spa, gym, tennis
Grotta Giusti Terme (Tuscany)	572-90771	www.grottogiustispa.com/flash.html	Spa, exercise
Hotel Bristol Buja	498-669-390	www.thermalia.co.uk/html/hotels/italy_bristol.html	Spa
Hotel Pitrizza (Sardinia)	789-30-111	www.italy-online-travel.com/hotels/Hotel-Pitrizza-Sardinia.html	Club style
Hotel Regina Isabella & Royal Sporting	81-994-322	www.reginaisabella.it	Spa, tennis
Hotel Smeraldo Terme	49-866-9555	www.hotelbenessere.it	Spa, tennis
Hotel Terme di Saturnia (Tuscany)	564-600-800	www.termedisaturnia.com	Spa, tennis, gym
Hotel Terme Metropole	49-8619-100	www.emmeti.it/welcome/veneto/abano/alberghi/metropole/	Tennis, miniature golf, spa
Il Pellicano Hotel	564-85-8111	www.jpmoser.com/ilpellicano.html	Tennis, beach club, water sports
International Hotel Bertha	49-891-1700	www.bertha.it	Gym, tennis
Pila Club Valtur	877-582-2284	www.clubvaltur.com	Skiing
Ritz Hotel Terme	49-866-9990	http://hotel-albanoterme-italy.com/reservations.htm	Spa, gym, tennis
Romazzino Hotel	789-977-111	www.ehi.com/travel/ehi/italy/sardinia-hotels-romazzino-hotel.htm	Water sports, tennis
Sestriere Club Valtur	877-582-2284	www.clubvaltur.com	Skiing
Spa'Deus di Christina Newburgh, Health and Fitness Resort (Tuscany)	578-632-32	www.spadeus.it	Spa, gym

	Telephone	Web Site	Special Features
Norway	**Int Tel: +47**		
Beito Mt. Hotel (Beitostoelen)	61-34-10-50	www.hotlink.com/Europe/norway.htm	Sports hotel, skiing, tennis, gym
Bjerke Gard (Lillehammer)	61 252 933	www.lillehammerturist.no	Farm-house inn, near skiing, open-air Maihaugen Museum
Comfort Hotel Bakerie (Trondheim)	877-997-5400	www.bestlodging.worldres.com/script/node.asp?n=2375	Skiing, golf, bicycling
Comfort Hotel Saga (Tromso)	877-997-5400	www.bestlodging.worldres.com/script/node/asp?n=2375	Horseback riding, skiing, fishing
Dr. Holms Hotel (Geilo)	32-09-06-22	www.ski-holidays.com	Hiking, tours
Gala Mt. Resort (Galaa)	61-29-81-09	www.travel.yahoo.com/p/hotel/347910	Gym, fishing, skiing
Quality Hotel Oppdal (Oppdal)	7240 0700	www.noreg.as/hotel/info/90	Skiing, muskox safaris, river rafting
Radisson SAS Beitostoelen Resort	877-678-9330	www.radisson.com	Boating, skiing, snowmobiling, horseback riding
Portugal	**Int Tel: +351**		
Club Med Da Balaia	800-258-2663	www.clubmed.com	Fitness; open March to November
Slovakia	**Int Tel: +421**		
Hotel Tri Studnicky (Tatra Mts.)	44-547-8000	www.tatry.net/jasna/tristudnicky	Hiking, mountain panorama
Spain	**Int Tel: +34**		
Club Med Ibiza	800-258-2663	www.clubmed.com	Summer only; children's club, tennis, fitness
Hotel Don Miguel Marbella	392-666-400	www.marbella-hoteles.com	Two golf courses, tennis, water sports
Hotel Incosol & Spa (Marbella)	952-666-400	www.marbella-hoteles.com/incosol_spa_hotel_marbella.html	Spa, water sports, cross-country skiing, golf
Hotel Termes Montbrio	977-814-000	www.spafinder.com	Spa, golf, tennis
S'Algar Hotel (Minorca)	971-15-17-00	http://travel.yahoo.com/p/hotel/384224	Tennis, miniature golf, playground
Sweden	**Int Tel: +46**		
Quality Hotel and Spa Selma Lagerlof (Sunne)	565-16600	www.travel.yahoo.com/p/hotel/352590	Spa, golf, tennis, hiking skiing
Switzerland	**Int Tel: +41**		
Club Med Pontresina	800-258-2663	www.clubmed.com	Cross-country skiing, children's program
Club Med Saint Moritz–Roi Soleil	800-258-2663	www.clubmed.com	Skiing, fitness center
Club Med Valbella	800-258-2663	www.clubmed.com	Winter only; skiing, children's program
Club Med Wengen Palace	800-258-2663	www.clubmed.com	Winter only; skiing

	Telephone	Web Site	Special Features
Hotel Crans Ambassador	27–485–4848	www.crans-ambassador.ch	Spa, gym, skiing, tennis, golf
Le Mirador (Lake Geneva)	21–925–1111	www.mirador.ch/corps-e.htm	Spa, fitness, water sports, skiing, tennis, golf
Turkey	**Int Tel: +90**		
Club Kardia (Izmir)	232–722–1111	www.travel.yahoo.com/p/hotel/361359	Gym, water sports, fishing, children's program
Club Med Foca	800–258–2633	www.clubmed.com	Water sports, children's club, tennis
Club Med Kemer	800–258–2633	www.clubmed.com	Water sports, tennis
Club Med Palmiye	800–258–2633	www.clubmed.com	Children's program, land and water sports
Dedeman Palandoken Ski Center	442–316–2414	www.travel.yahoo.com/p/hotel/393525	Skiing, kids club
Klassis Resort Hotel & Spa (Istanbul)	212–727–4050	www.premierespasoftheworld.com/spas.html	Spa, fine setting

ASIA AND THE PACIFIC

ASIA

India	**Int Tel: +91**		
Bangaram Island Resort	484–668221	www.bangaram.hotels.india-tours.com	Water sports, fishing, hut lodgings
Hotel Lake Palace (Udaipur)	4869–2023	www.rajasthan-tours.com/hotels/udaipur/lake.html	Safari, romantic
Quality Inn Corbett Jungle Resort	11–2571–9400	www.tourmyindia.com/jungleresorts/quality.html	Wildlife resort, safari
Tiger Tops Corbett Lodge (Not affiliated w/Tiger Tops Corp.)	11–2571–9400	www.indiatourpackages.com/corbett-national-park.html	National park, safari
Welcomgroup Bay Island (Port Blair)	11–2371–4747	www.ehotelsindia.com/welcomgroup_andaman.htm	Overlooks sea; games and sports
Windamere Hotel (Darjeeling)	11–2371–4747	www.travel.yahoo.com/p/hotel/394910	Private gardens, hiking
Indonesia	**Int Tel: +62**		
Amandaru (Bali)	361–975333	www.amanresorts.com	Luxury, spa, gym, pavilion suites
Amanwana Resort (Moyo Island)	371–22223	www.amanresorts.com	Luxury, wildlife, water sports, boating
Club Med Bali	800–258–2633	www.clubmed.com	Sports complex, water sports, fishing, boating
Japan	**Int Tel: +81**		
Club Med Sahoro	800–258–2633	www.clubmed.com	Ski hotel, sports center, children's program

	Telephone	Web Site	Special Features
Malaysia	**Int Tel: +60**		
Club Med Cherating Beach	800–258–2633	www.clubmed.com	Water sports, children's program
Maldives	**Int Tel: +960**		
Biyadoo Island Resort	447171	www.maldives-travel.org/hotels_it/malbiy.htm	Water sports, scuba, boating, fishing
Club Med Kani	800–258–2633	www.clubmed.com	Water sports, boat trips, spa
Ellaidoo Tourist Resort	450586	www.travel.yahoo.com/p/hotel/327106	Water sports
Embudu Village (Male Island)	444776	www.ourmaldives.com/resorts/embudu	Water sports, disco, sports, diving
Four Seasons Resort Maldives	800–819–5053	www.fourseasons.com/maldives/	Water sports, yoga, sports
Fun Island Resort	444558	www.mal-dives.com/funisland/	Scuba, water sports
Hilton Maldives Rangali Island	450629	www.hilton.com	Spa, diving, gym, yacht
Hudhuveli Beach Resort	443982	www.travel.yahoo.com/p/hotel/385940	Water sports, scuba, uninhabited island other than resort
Kanifinolhu Resort	322451	www.asamaldives.com/kanifinolhu.html	Water sports
Lhohifushi Tourist Resort	441909	www.s-h-systems.co.uk/maldives/north-male-atoll	Water sports, scuba
Makunudu Island	446464	www.makunudu.com	Scuba, water sports
Meeru Island Resort	443157	www.meeru.com	Water sports, scuba, boating
Nika Hotel	450516	www.interhotel.com/maldives/en/hoteles/46645.htm	Scuba, water sports, fishing
Paradise Island	440011	www.villahotels.com/paradise	Water sports, live entertainment
Taj Exotica Resort & Spa (Emboodhu Finolhu Island)	333737	www.bonvoyage-maldives.com/html/taj_exotica_resort__spa.html	Lagoon villas, water sports
Villivaru Island Resort	447070	www.innermaldives.com/resorts/villivaru.html	Fishing, scuba, water sports
Nepal	**Int Tel: +977**		
Gaida Wildlife Camp	1–434520	www.visitnepal.com/gaida/index.htm	Elephant rides, safari
Machan Wildlife Resort	1–225001	www.nepalinformation.com/machan/machan.htm	Safari, wildlife
Sri Lanka	**Int Tel: +94**		
Club Palm Garden Hotel	34–76115	www.asiatours.net/srilanka/hotels/club_palm_garden.html	Water sports, boating, tennis, miniature golf

	Telephone	Web Site	Special Features
Thailand	**Int Tel: +66**		
Amanpuri (Phuket)	76 324 333	www.amanresorts.com	Spa, luxury pavilions, cruises, swimming
THE PACIFIC			
Australia	**Int Tel: +61**		
Great Barrier Reef			
Bedarra Bay Resort	7-4068-8233	www.dive-au.com.au/island_resorts/bedarrai.html	No children under 16; water sports
Club Med Lindeman Isle	800-258-2633	www.clubmed.com	National park, mini club for kids, fishing and water sports
Flag Whitsunday Waters Resort	7-4954-9666	www.choice1.com/whitsunday_waters_resort.htm?CID=4193	Spa, children's activities, miniature golf, tennis
Green Island Resort	7-4031-3300	www.barrier-reef-holidays.com/reefgreenisland.htm	Reef tours, scuba, water sports, small luxury hotel
Haggerstone Island Guest House	7-3876-4644	www.great-barrier-reef.com/haggerstone/	Snorkeling, diving, fishing, coral reefs, shipwrecks
Hayman Island Resort	800-330-8820	www.hayman.com.au/	Peerless resort, luxury, snorkeling, scuba
Heron Island Resort	800-225-9849	www.poresorts.com.au/heron/default.htm	Scuba, fishing, wildlife, surfing
Hinchinbrook Island Resort	7-4066-8270	www.hinchinbrookresort.com.au/	Tree houses and cabins, solitude
Lady Elliot Island Resort	7-3536-3644	www.ladyelliot.com.au/	Scuba, reef walking, whale watching
Orpheus Island Resort	7-4777-7377	www.orpheusisland-australia.com/	No children under 15; scuba, spa
South Molle Island Resort	7-4946-9433	www.aussiedirections.com.au/Qldtrav/southmole.html	Golf, children's activities, tennis, gym, weddings, spa treatments
New South Wales			
Hunter River Retreat	2-4930-1114	www.hunterriverretreat.com	Vineyard, horseback riding, grass tennis courts
Kims Beach Hideaway	800-525-4800, 2-4332-1566	www.lh.com/kims/	Water sports, spa
Millamolong Station	2-73-67-5341	www.inthesaddle.com/aumi.htm	Sheep station, tennis, horseback, polo
Northern Territory			
El Questro Homestead	8-9169-1777	www.elquestro.com.au	Fishing, heli-fishing, hiking, cattle station
Ooraminna Bush Camp	8-8953-0170	www.cbl.com.au/ooraminna	Bushwalking, horseback riding, active cattle ranch

	Telephone	Web Site	Special Features
Queensland			
Binna Burra Mt. Lodge	7-5533-3622	www.binnaburralodge.com.au/	Hiking, bush walks, adventure, children's programs
Bloomfield Rain Forest Lodge	0-4035-9166	www.bloomfieldlodge.com.au/homeaus.htm	Tropical rain forest, water sports, tours
Daintree Eco Lodge & Spa	7-4098-6100, 800-794-9767	www.daintree-ecolodge.com.au	Rain forest, river cruises, spa, biking
O'Reilly's Rainforest Guesthouse	7-5544-0644	www.oreillys.com.au	Adjacent to national park with rain forest, waterfalls, hiking, vineyard
Pajinka Wilderness Lodge Cabins	8-9486-7880	www.australianhotel.net/hotels/1347/page2.html	Fishing, wildlife, Aboriginal culture
Planet Downs	7-3265-5022	www.bloxsom.aust.com/planetdowns/	Horseback riding, Aboriginal culture
Thala Beach Lodge	7-4098-5700	www.thalabeach.com.au	Rain forest, Great Barrier Reef access
Tasmania			
London Lakes Lodge	3-6289-1159	www.wildernessaustralia.com.au/properties/t_london_lakes.htm	World-championship fly-fishing, natural wildlife habitat
Victoria			
The Mansion Hotel Werribee Park	3-9731-4000	www.slh.com/australia/werribee/hotel_werman.html	Fitness center, spa, golf
Mt. Buffalo Resort	3-5755-1500	www.mtbuffalo.com/index.htm	Skiing, water sports, horseback riding, rock climbing, national park
Trackers Mt. Lodge	3-5758-3346	www.fallscreek.com.au/accom/trackers_mountain_lodge.asp	Skiing, spa
Fiji Islands	Int Tel: +679		
Beachcomber Island Resort	661-500	www.fijiresorts.com/beachcomber-island-resort/	Water sports, boating, miniature golf
Cousteau Fiji Islands Resort	800-246-3454	www.fijiresort.com	Snorkeling, diving, children welcome, ecology friendly
Matangi Island Resort	888-628-2644, 725-227-FIJI	www.matangiisland.com	Yacht trips, honeymoon, tree house, water sports; private island
Moody's Namena	8813-764	www.moodysnamenafiji.com	Private island; scuba, fishing, boating; children over 16 only
Namale Resort	850-400	www.namalefiji.com	Plantation, land and water sports, scuba, spa
Nukubati Island	800-525-4800, 881-3901	www.nukubati.com	Private island; water sports, fishing, boating, scuba, land safari, tennis

	Telephone	Web Site	Special Features
New Caledonia	**Int Tel: +687**		
Hotel Ibis Noumea	800–221–4542, 26–20–55	www.hideawayholidays.com.au/nou_SYD_ibis.htm	Scuba, water sports
Kuendu Beach Resort	24–30–00	www.hideawayholidays.com.au/nou_kuendu.htm	Water sports, riding
L'Escapade Resort	28–53–20	http://perso.wanadoo.fr/caledonie/Guide/selogere.htm	Water sports, small island
Novotel Malabou Beach Resort	47–60–60	www.dawsons.com.au/Accommodations/PacificRegion/NewCaledonia/	Water sports
Novotel Surf Noumea	800–221–4542, 28–66–88	www.hideawayholidays.com.au/nou_SYD_novotel.htm	Walk to beach; gym, casino
New Zealand	**Int Tel: +64**		
Blanket Bay	3–442–9442	www.blanketbay.com	Backcountry fly-fishing
Brooklands Country Estate	7–825–4756	www.brooklands.net.nz/	Mountain biking, tennis, pool, spelunking
Grasmere Lodge	3–318–8407	www.grasmere.co.nz/	Tennis, fishing, skiing, cattle ranch, clay-pigeon shooting
Lake Brunner Lodge	3–738–0163	www.lakebrunner.com/	Fishing, boating
Lake Rotoroa Lodge	800–525–4800, 3–523–9121	www.slh.com	Water sports, skiing, hunting, fishing, boating, wine tours
Lake Taupo Lodge	800–525–4800, 7–378–7386	www.laketaupolodge.co.nz	Skiing, fishing, tennis, golf
Lilybank Lodge	800–525–4800, 3–6806–535	www.lilybank.co.nz/mirror.html	Horseback riding, climbing
Lodge at Paratiho Farms	3–528–2100	www.paratiho.co.nz/	Private luxury suites on a working sheep ranch
Matakauri Lodge	3–441–1008	www.matakauri.co.nz	Fishing, mountain sports
Okiato Lodge (Bay of Islands)	9–403–7948	www.okiato.co.nz	Luxury, fishing, sailing, scuba, hunting, cuisine
Solitaire Lodge (Rotorua)	800–525–4800, 7–362–8208	www.solitairelodge.co.nz	Fishing, water sports, boating, bush walks, cultural activities
Tongariro Lodge (Rotorua)	7–386–7946	www.tongarirolodge.co.nz	Fishing, tennis, thermal springs, private chalets, gourmet cuisine
Wharekauhau Lodge (Palliser Bay)	800–525–4800, 6–307–7581	www.wharekauhau.co.nz	Farm, tennis, horseback riding, fitness
Whare Kea Lodge (Wanaka)	3–443–1400	www.wharekealodge.co.nz	Adventure sports, skiing

	Telephone	Web Site	Special Features
Papua New Guinea	Int Tel: +675		
Ambua Lodge (Southern Highlands)	542–1438	www.babs.com.au/ambua	Mountains, nature-friendly
Karawari Lodge (Western Highlands)	542–1438	www.pngtours.com/lodges.html	River/jungle resort, riverboat
French Polynesia	Int Tel: +689		
Bora Bora Lagoon Resort	60-40-00	www.visit-tahiti.com/borabora/borabora-lagoon-resort.html	Over-water bungalows, secluded location, snorkeling
Hotel Bora Bora	60-44-60	www.amanresorts.com/	Luxury bungalows, diving, cruising
Moana Beachcomber Parkroyal	60-4900	www.tahiti.org/en/besthotels.html	View tropical fish in lagoon from bungalow villas built on stilts
Tetiaroa Village	82-63-3	www.travel.yahoo.com/p/hotel/395156	Fishing, bird sanctuary, water sports

AFRICA AND THE MIDDLE EAST

AFRICA

	Telephone	Web Site	Special Features
Botswana	Int Tel: +267		
Chobe Chilwero	800–801–8722	www.akhotelsandresorts.com/aksafarilodges/botswana.php	Luxury safari camp; no children under 12
Chobe Game Lodge	650–340	www.botswana.co.za/chobe-game-lodge-botswana.html	Game lodge; no children under 16
Khwai River Lodge	2721-424–1037	www.botswana.co.za/khwai-river-lodge-botswana.html	Safari
Mashatu Game Reserve	84–5321	www.mashatu.com	Safari, game drive
San–Ta–Wani Safari Lodge	26–0351	http://interhotel.com/botswana/en/hoteles/23209.html	Safari
Savuti South Camp	66–0302	www.hotel.chobe-national-park-botswana.travelmall.com	Safari, eight guests only
Kenya	Int Tel: +254		
The Aberdare Country Club	866-733–4263	www.classicsafaris.com/camps%20&%20lodges/aberdareclub.htm	Golf, sports
Amboseli Serena Safari Lodge	302–2620	www.serenahotels.com	Safari

	Telephone	Web Site	Special Features
The Ark Lodge	171–55620	http://interhotel.com/kenya/en/hoteles/105922.html	Game viewing; no children under 7
Blue Safari Club (Manda Island)	121–33470	www.bluesafariclub.com	Water sports, activities
Buffalo Springs Tented Lodge	165–2259	www.vastray.com/buffalo.htm	Game and bird watching
Delamere Camp	20–331191	http://travel.yahoo.com/p/hotel/333552	Safari
Diani Reef Grand Hotel (Mombasa)	10–2723	http://travel.yahoo.com/p/hotel/394806	Sports
Giraffe Manor (Nairobi)	2–89–078	www.giraffemanor.com	Manor house, Rothschild giraffe center
Keekorok Game Lodge (Masai Mara)	2–336–807	www.kenya-travels.com/kenyasafaris/keekoroklodge.htm	Safari, activities
Kilaguni Lodge (Tsavo NP)	—	http://travel.yahoo.com/p/hotel/341758	Safari
Lake Baringo Club (Masai Mara)	2–540–780	www.blockhotelske.com/properties/baringo1.htm	Bird watching
Lake Bogoria Hotel	37–40225	www.bogoriasparesort.com/	Pool heated by volcanic rock, game viewing
Lake Nakuru Hotel	37–85446	www.kenyaonetours.com/camps/camps.htm?Lake_Nakuru_Lodge	Safari, game viewing
Lake Naivasha Country Club	800–223–6486	www.kenyaonetours.com/camps/camps.htm?Lake_Navaisha_Country_Club	Boating, bird watching
Lake Turkana Lodge	20–760–226	http://travel.yahoo.com/p/hotel/392518	Boating, deep-sea fishing
Main Governor's Camp (Masai Mara)	2–331871	www.southerncrosssafaris.com/kenya/governorscamps.htm	Safari
Mara Serena Safari Lodge (Masai Mara)	305–2059	www.serenahotels.com	Safari
Marsabit Lodge	2–33–020	http://travel.yahoo.com/p/hotel/486638	Game viewing, safari; next to volcano
Meru Mulika Lodge	20–200000	http://travel.yahoo.com/p/hotel/368617	Safari
Mount Kenya Safari Club (Sweetwaters)	2–216940	www.africanholiday.com/lodges/safari_club.htm	Golf, safari, tennis, horseback riding, fishing
Naro Moro River Lodge	27–626–22	http://travel.yahoo.com/p/hotel/343257	Safari, activities
Ngulia Safari Lodge (Tsavo)	147–30091	http://ngulialodge.kenya-safari.co.ke/	Safari
Olkurruk Mara Lodge	2–336–838	www.vastray.com/olkurruk.htm	Safari
Outspan Hotel (Mt. Kenya)	800–223–6486	www.kenyaonetours.com/camps/	Safari
Safariland Club (Hell's Gate NP)	31–21047	http://travel.yahoo.com/p/hotel/351966	Tennis, water sports, horseback riding, boating
Salt Lick Hilton Safari Lodge (Tsavo NP)	888–733–4263	http://travel.yahoo.com/p/hotel/325636	Safari; children over 5 only
Sarova Lion Hill Hotel	37–850235	www.sarovahotels.com/LionHill/LionHill.htm	Tours, safari, Lake Nakuru
Sarova Mara Camp	050–22386	www.sarovahotels.com/Mara/MaraHome.htm	Safari, dancing and entertainment

	Telephone	Web Site	Special Features
Sarova Shaba Lodge	164–30638	www.sarovahotels.com/Shaba/ShabaHome.htm	Safari
Taita Hills Hilton Safari Lodge (Tsavo NP)	888–733–4263	www.classicsafaris.com/camps%20&%20lodges/taitahills.htm	Sports, private sanctuary
Trade Winds Hotel (Mombasa)	10–2621	http://travel.yahoo.com/p/hotel/343345	Near game reserve, on beach, water sports
Treetops Hotel (Aberdares NP)	866–865–3692	http://kenya.com/treetops.html	Safari
Tropical African Dream Village (Malindi)	123–20442	www.planhotel.ch/kenya/klocation.html	Beach resort
Two Fishes Hotel (Mombasa)	127–2101	http://interhotel.com/kenya/en/hoteles/45404.html	Fishing, boats, sports
Voi Safari Lodge (Tsavo NP)	20–336–858	http://travel.yahoo.com/p/hotel/396345	Safari
Mauritius Island	**Int Tel: +230**		
Club Med La Pointe aux Canonniers	800–258–2663	www.clubmed.com	Sports, boating, fishing
Island Sports Club Hotel	683–5353	www.beachhotelsmauritius.com/islandsportsclub/	Water sports, fishing, boating
Morocco	**Int Tel: +212**		
Agadir Club Valtur	877–582–2284	www.clubvaltur.com	Sports, water activities
Club Med Village (Agadir)	800–258–2663	www.clubmed.com	Sports
Club Med Village (Marrakech)	800–258–2663	www.clubmed.com	Sports; children over 6
Club Med Village (Ouarzazate)	800–258–2663	www.clubmed.com	Sports, fishing, boating
Club Med Yasmina	800–258–2663	www.clubmed.com	Beach, sports, horseback riding
La Gazelle d'Or	8–85–20–39	http://interhotel.com/morocco/en/hoteles/107765.html	Sports, parklike setting
Mozambique	**Int Tel: +258**		
Zongoene Lodge	224–2000	www.zongoene.com	Birding, fly-fishing, scuba diving, snorkeling
Senegal	**Int Tel: +221**		
Bird Island Lodge	3–233–22	—	Sports, scuba diving
Club Med Cap Skirring	800–258–2663	www.clubmed.com	Beach, sports, activities, golf
Club Med Les Almadies	800–258–2663	www.clubmed.com	Ocean resort, sports, fishing, boating, gym
Hobbe Hotel	96–11–70	http://interhotel.com/senegal/en/hoteles/110994.html	Boating
Seychelles	**Int Tel: +248**		
Banyan Tree Seychelles	383–500	www.banyantree.com	Villas, spectacular beach

	Telephone	Web Site	Special Features
South Africa	**Int Tel: +27**		
Alphen Hotel (Cape Town)	410-21-79-5011	www.cape-hotels.com	No children under 10; declared a National Monument
Blue Marlin Hotel (Scottburgh)	39-978-3361	www.bluemarlin.co.za	Overlooking ocean; children's program
Cathedral Peak Hotel (Drakensberg)	36-488-1888	www.cathedralpeak.co.za	Mountain resort, multiple activities and sports, children's program
High Rustenburg Hydro Resort (Stellenbosch)	21-883-8600	http://travel.yahoo.com/p/hotel/361949	Health spa
Londolozi Game Reserve	11-803-8421	www.londolozi.com/	Camps, luxury, safari, Relais & Chateaux
Long Lee Manor (Shamwari Game Reserve)	203-1111	www.shamwari.com/longlee.asp	Manor house, safari
Motswari Private Game Lodge	11-463-1990	www.africa.co.za/ttmotswari.html	Safari
Ngala Game Reserve (Kruger NP)	11-809-4300	www.wheretostay.co.za/ngala	Safari
Phinda Forest Lodge (Hluhluwe)	11-809-4300	www.safarinow.com/go/PhindaForestLodge/	Sand forest, safari
Phinda Private Game Reserve (Hluhluwe)	11-809-4300	www.slh.com/south-africa/hluhluwe/hotel-estsou.html	Luxury safari; Small Luxury Hotels of the World; scuba
Shamwari Lodge	42-203-1111	www.shamwari.com/lodges.asp	Safari, choice of several lodges
Singita Game Reserve (Nelspruit)	11-234-0990	www.singita.com	Safari, Relais & Chateaux
Ulusaba Game Reserve (Skukuza)	13735-5460	www.ulusaba.com	Safari
Tanzania	**Int Tel: +255**		
Lake Manyara Serena Lodge	57-4058	www.serenahotels.com	Safari
Ngorogoro Serena Safari Lodge	57-4058	www.serenahotels.com	Safari, overlooking crater
Tunisia	**Int Tel: +216**		
Abou Nawas Sunrise Club	73-427144	http://travel.yahoo.com/p/hotel/338391	Sports
Club Med Djerba La Douce	800-258-2582	www.clubmed.com	Replicating typical Tunisian town; land and water sports
Club Med Djerba La Nomadi	800-258-2582	www.clubmed.com	Straw hut village; boating and sports
Club Med Hammamet	800-258-2582	www.clubmed.com	Moorish style; children age 2 and older
Les Oasis Hotel (Tozeur)	6-450-522	http://interhotel.com/tunisia/en/hoteles/114013.html	Business center
Les Orangers Hotel (Hammamet)	2-280-144	www.tunisia-orangers.com	Water sports, children's program
Sahara Beach Hotel (Monastir)	3-461-088	http://travel.yahoo.com/p/hotel/384502	Land and water sports
Zambia	**Int Tel: +260**		
Chichele Lodge	62-45062	http://travel.yahoo.com/p/hotel/394856	Safari

	Telephone	Web Site	Special Features
Lilayi Lodge	1–279022	www.lilayi.com	Safari, activities
Mfuwe Lodge	1–754926	www.mfuwe.com	Safari
Musungwa Safari Lodge	32–63035	http://travel.yahoo.com/p/hotel/341818	Safari, sports, gym, fishing, boating
Zimbabwe	**Int Tel: +263**		
Fothergill Island Safari Camp	703–633	www.zimbabwe-explorer.co.zw/html/Kariba/lodges/fothergill.htm	Safari, fishing, boating
Matetsi Game Lodges	888–882–3742	www.ccafrica.com/destinations/zimbabwe/default.asp	Children over 12; safari
Pamuzinda Safari Lodge	628–44215	http://travel.yahoo.com/p/hotel/392552	Children over 12; safari
THE MIDDLE EAST			
Egypt	**Int Tel: +20**		
Four Seasons Sharm El Sheikh (Sinai)	800–819–5053	www.fourseasons.com/vacations/sharmelsheikh/index.htm	Villas, spa, Red Sea diving
Tourist Village Magawish (Harghada)	65–442620	www.touregypt.net/h144.htm	Boat rides, water and land sports
Israel	**Int Tel: +972**		
Ein Gedi Resort Hotel	—	www.inisrael.com/eingedi/index.html	Spa, Dead Sea mud and bathing

ABOUT THE AUTHORS

Travel experts Jay Paris and Carmi Zona-Paris first became interested in all-inclusive vacations when they had the opportunity to visit and write about these popular get-aways as co-founders of *Outbound Traveler* magazine (1994 to 1998).

Photojournalist Jay Paris is a former senior editor of *Ohio Magazine*. His photographs and features have appeared in *Time* magazine, *Yankee*, *Reader's Digest*, the *Boston Globe Sunday Magazine*, and *A Day in the Life of Rural America* (Silver Image Publishing, 1988). Carmi Zona-Paris has contributed to a variety of publications, including *Yankee*. She has worked in television and radio and is a former advertising and public relations professional.

Jay and Carmi are avid travelers and the co-authors of *A Study of Culture and Heritage in Europe: A Manual for Travel Counselors* (Institute for Certified Travel Agents, 1999) and *Walking Nova Scotia: A Walking Guide* (Walking Magazine, 1992). Other joint projects include founding "The Travel Page," a syndicated feature section that appeared in sixteen New England newspapers; hosting a Boston-based radio travel show; and publishing travel guides for a variety of international clients.

In 1999 Jay and Carmi established an Internet-based school curriculum to help students broaden their awareness of the world through international video conferencing and virtual travel. For the past few years they have expanded these efforts to work with at-risk children here and abroad.

ABOUT THE EDITOR

Third edition editor-writer Carol Fowler is a freelance journalist and former *Contra Costa Times* travel editor. A member of the Society of American Travel Writers, she places travel stories in newspapers across the country and is the author of *Insiders' Guide to Berkeley and the East Bay* (Globe Pequot Press).